Communication Skills for Engineers and Scientists

Second Edition

SANGEETA SHARMA
Professor
Department of Humanities and Social Science
Birla Institute of Technology and Science, Pilani

BINOD MISHRA
Professor
Department of Humanities and Social Science
Indian Institute of Technology Roorkee

PHI Learning Private Limited

Delhi-110092
2026

*In fond memory of **Shri Asoke K. Ghosh** (October 1942 – February 2024), Founder Chairman and Managing Director of PHI Learning, whose vision endlessly inspires.*

The Legacy Continues. . . .

Published by Pushpita Ghosh, PHI Learning Private Limited, Rimjhim House, 111, Patparganj Industrial Estate, Delhi-110092 and Printed by Syndicate Binders, A-20, Hosiery Complex, Noida, Phase-II Extension, Noida-201305 (N.C.R. Delhi).

₹795.00

COMMUNICATION SKILLS FOR ENGINEERS AND SCIENTISTS, Second Edition
Sangeeta Sharma and Binod Mishra

ISBN-978-81-19364-11-4 (Print Book)
ISBN-978-81-19364-10-7 (e-Book)

The export rights of the book are vested solely with the publisher.

To

all our students
who feel
communication skills
are as important as
any other core skills
either in engineering
management, law or
other lucrative professions

Contents

Foreword

In today's world of information technology and global competition, expressing oneself effectively is inevitably crucial. The present-day workplaces invest huge amount of effort and money in orienting their employees in all the four areas of communication skills—writing, speaking, reading, and listening. Educational institute, in addition to emphasizing the core disciplines, take extra initiative to hone the communication skills of their students for the job market.

This book addresses various areas of communication and provides numerous examples bordering on Indian situations. The interested readers, including both students and industry professionals, would find the book functional because of its interactive approach, clarity of expression, and suitable exercises in almost all the chapters.

The authors, both teachers in two reputed institutes, have utilized their classroom experiences in making the book stand out among the books available in the market. I hope that their industrious efforts will meet the needs of both the industry and the academia. I congratulate the authors on their efforts and commend the book to the readers.

(L.K. Maheshwari)
Vice-Chancellor, BITS Pilani
Rajasthan

Preface

The lapses of the past have always been the harbinger of the present and the future. The book in your hand is also the realization of overcoming the past lapses in order to cope up with the challenges of future. In this regard it is pertinent to express our gratitude and acknowledgement for the encouragement provided to us by many individuals in our venture.

We are deeply indebted to Prof. V. Ramgopal Rao, the Vice Chancellor BITS Pilani, Prof. Sudhir Kumar Barai, the Director BITS Pilani and Prof. K.K. Pant, the Director of IIT Roorkee for their unstinted support and encouragement to language and communication teachers. Their exhortations have proved quite instrumental in the publication of the second edition of the book.

We also express our appreciation to Prof. Krishna Mohan, Former Professor and Group Leader, Languages Group, BITS Pilani for inspiring and guiding us from time-to-time. Moreover, our sincere thanks are also due to our department colleagues both at BITS Pilani and at IIT Roorkee for their genuine suggestions periodically.

We shall be failing in our duties if we forget to express our appreciation to our family members for their cooperation as without their support, this book would not have been possible. Their generosity has worked like life-force in this endeavour.

We are grateful to our research scholars of BITS Pilani, namely Pooja Chatterjee, Manish Shivhare, Salman Riyas, Asita. A and scholars of IIT Roorkee namely, Subin Daniel, Rangnath Thakur, Rajbir Samal, G. Thiyagraj, Sampda Swaraj, Wasim Raza, Ghulam Rabani, Priyanka Singh, Pragya Dev, Sangjukta Roy, Shohib Bashir and Ashish Murmu who patiently proofread the chapters and also provided their inputs in developing/adding a chapter on Technology. We are especially thankful to Anuj Vashishtha for providing illustrations for each chapter in the new edition. Their feedback and cooperation have really been indispensable in bringing out the second edition of this book. We also wish to thank the publisher, PHI Learning Pvt. Ltd.

for its careful and speedy processing of the book. Finally, we thank God for raising our dampened spirits and guiding us through the myriad trials and tribulations that we underwent.

Sangeeta Sharma
Binod Mishra

Preface to the First Edition

In the fast changing and competitive world of today, the ability to communicate effectively is perceived as *sine qua non* for the undergraduate or postgraduate students of all disciplines. However, it becomes more imperative for the professionals who are dealing with technical forms of communication. The core competence of professionals is judged on the basis of their élan and expertise with regard to writing and speaking skills. With the proliferation of English medium institutions over the years, our pupils seem to be more at ease in using English as a medium of spoken communication. In the recent past, new channels of communication, e.g. SMS, e-mail, have emerged and the form in which language is used in these channels is having a profound influence on students' writing skills, especially when drafting documents. Moreover, in the modern media, such as advertisements, celluloid, we often find that English language is used in a contorted form. If the students use this form of English language when communicating as used in these media, it will be a reflection of their casual attitude.

This book aims at equipping the young undergraduates of science and engineering with good communication skills and preparing them for a golden future. Today more importance is given to the way the contents are presented. A professional's communicative ability is judged on his or her preparedness and promptness in drafting technical documents, such as business letters, technical reports and memo. This text tries to prepare the readers in meeting the challenges of the professional world and aims at helping them in being able to successfully communicate their evaluation, analysis, conclusions, recommendation, and take corrective measures through verbal and non-verbal presentation of ideas.

The book is divided into two parts. In Part A, Chapter 1 we have explained the meaning of technical writing. Often, communication within a team rebounds because of numerous factors. In Chapter 2, on Communication Breakdown, we discuss various reasons for the breakdown of communication and how one can overcome them. The reasons for such a breakdown may be at the source, between people and in organizational levels. Since there cannot be a singular way of overcoming these barriers, in Chapters 2 and 3 we have expatiated on various stages of communication breakdown and their remedial measures. In Chapters 4 and 5, we have provided several forms of business writing keeping into consideration the technicalities that differentiate technical writing from general writing. Reports, letters, memos, and other technical documents differ over other forms of writing in terms of form, layout, principle and language. Suitable words and phrases, sentence construction, proper paragraph length, cohesion and readability are the elements that lend accuracy and spontaneity to technical business writing. In Chapter 6 these have been elaborated. We have given examples of diverse forms of business correspondence and technical documents to lend authenticity. As technical reports have become so important in today's professional world, in Chapter 7 this topic has also been dealt with exhaustively. In Chapter 8, apart from the guidelines, importance, structure and types of reports, we have presented numerous sample reports to make the book student-friendly. In Chapter 9, advertising, another form of communication, is explained.

Students need to be exposed to the professional settings. Presentation skills are the prime requirements of a modern-day professional. One has to clarify, convince and cooperate in order to ensure organizational effectiveness. The success of a presentation depends on how effectively it is written. Chapter 10 in Part B covers this aspect. In Chapters 11, 12, 13 and 14 we have dwelled on Communicating without Words, Interviews, Speeches, and Negotiation Skills that will orient young professionals with the verbal and non-verbal skills. In Chapter 11, we have given an in-depth analysis of different elements of non-verbal communication, such as Kinesics, Proxemics, Chronemics, Paralanguage and Haptics. A distinguishing feature of the text is the emphasis on real-life situations which will help students in the future. Today, professionals have to work not in isolation but in groups. Care has been taken to familiarize the students with how to work in teams. In Chapter 15, Group Communication rooted in team culture has been elaborated on keeping into consideration the requirements of collective and individual efforts. We have discussed separately in Chapter 16 the frequently mis-spelt words so as to acquaint the readers with the most frequently used words in their professional lives.

We have written the text after realizing the Indian classroom situations and market conditions. Interactions with students who faced the rigours of recruiters during their campus placements provided us with ample instances that helped us in writing the book. We have tried to bridge the gap between the recruiters' expectations and the students' aspirations. Every effort has been made to make the book application oriented. With this end in view, we have provided chapter-end exercises based on the contents of the text.

We are indebted to Prof. S. Venkateswaran, the former Vice-chancellor and the present Advisor of BITS Pilani for his valuable suggestions. We are grateful to Prof. L.K. Maheshwari, Vice-chancellor of BITS Pilani and Prof. S.C. Saxena, Director of IIT Roorkee for their unstinted support to language teachers.

We express our appreciation to Prof. Krishna Mohan, Former Professor and Group Leader, Languages Group, BITS Pilani for inspiring and guiding us from time to time. Moreover, we are indebted to late Dr. Meera Banerjee whose association with us will always keep our memory refreshing. We express our sincere thanks to our colleagues at BITS, Pilani—Prof. Meenakshi Raman, Dr. Sanjay Kumar, Dr. Pushp Lata, Dr. Geetha B, Dr. Gajendra S. Chauhan, Dr. Sanjeev Kr. Choudhary, Dr. Devika, Ms. Sushila Rathore, Mr. Virendra Singh Nirban, Dr. Appa Swami, Ms. Ruchika Sharma, Ms. Poonam Vyas and Ms. Shweta Shree. Special thanks to Ms. Monica Sharma and Dr. Usha Manjunath for providing illustrations and sample report respectively. We are also grateful to Prof. Pashupati Jha, Prof. Renu Rastogi, Dr. Rashmi Gaur, Dr. Nagendra Kumar, Dr. R. Khushu Lahiri and Dr. Smita Jha of IIT Roorkee for their timely suggestions. We would like to thank Murtaza Ali Hussainy for providing appropriate illustrations for the text.

We express our appreciation to our family members for their cooperation as without their encouragement this book would not have been possible. Their generosity has worked like life-force in this endeavour.

We are grateful to our students whose feedback served as a great stimulus for writing this book. We also wish to thank the publishers, PHI Learning Pvt. Ltd. for their careful and speedy processing of the book. Finally, we thank God for raising our dampened spirits and guiding us through the myriad trials and tribulations that we underwent.

Sangeeta Sharma
Binod Mishra

Part A

1

Technical Report Writing: An Overview

Technical writing aims to get work done, to change people by changing the way they do things.

—M. JIMMIE KILLINGSWORTH & MICHAEL K. GILBERTSON

We live in a technical world today. Our home and our office, marketplace or playground, a short travel or a long journey—all depend on technicalities. A slight lapse may lead to serious consequences. Whether it is the gas tragedy of Bhopal, major train accidents across the country, mine accident at Gazlitand, Dhanbad or various unfortunate incidents—all were results of human failure. The failure in most of the cases was because of our lack of ability to express the technicalities in clear language. Since we live in a dynamic world, the ways and methods of expression keep on changing at a rapid pace. Success in today's world is commensurate with the familiarity of using technical gadgets in the most efficient manner. Organizations throughout the world are busy conducting studies on various topics with the help of effective means of communication. A modern-day professional, apart from working for his organization, collects information, gathers data, compares, analyses them, and prepares reports to understand the lapses that have occurred in the company and tries to find solutions to overcome them. Reports have become *a sine qua non* both for professionals and for organizations to maintain their equilibrium and élan in the business world. The task, then, of the modern-day executive is to prepare reports from time to time. The objective of the reports is to help an executive understand and evaluate a problem so that he can take immediate actions to rectify and rationalize it.

Writing report is an important skill in the modern-day world. All of us have to carry out some kind of business dealing, in addition to our personal tasks. A good report in a business world includes the ability to understand a problem and then suggest solutions for it. All these are related to our ability to present things effectively. We, as human beings, need to communicate effectively to carry out our basic business requirements. A professional comes in touch with variety of people having different needs. Not all of them have the same ability to understand our ideas and thoughts. Hence, the need arises to communicate in a language that is understandable to all.

The aim of this text is to acquaint the readers with the requisite communication skills needed in the present-day world. There is an attempt to encourage the readers to communicate effectively at all stages and in all situations. The examples cited in the book have been taken from our day-to-day lives to give the readers an aura of pleasantness and a familiarity with the noises and silences, which we as human beings experience while communicating.

TECHNICAL WRITING

Speaking and writing are integral parts of our day-to-day communication. Before going into detail about technical writing and speaking, we should know what 'communication' is. It is the expression of our ideas or emotions. But this definition has its limitation since animals too communicate their ideas and emotions by means of gestures which include staring, standing, stamping their feet or making cries. In this book, we are concerned with human communication. We, as human beings, communicate to serve some purpose. A broad definition of communication, then, is the transmission and interchange of facts, ideas, feelings, or courses of action.

If we pause for a while to think about the different ways humans and animals communicate, we will come across some similarities and a few dissimilarities. Table 1.1 shows the difference between human and animal communications.

Table 1.1 Difference between Human and Animal Communications

Human communication	Animal communication
Sounds and words	Sounds only
Creativity	Meaningless cries
Arbitrary	Non-specific
Context-free	Context-bound
Redundancy	No such facility
Dynamic	Fixed
Ever changing	Static
Culture preserving	Not culture specific

Communication can be both oral and written. Since here we are dealing with technical report writing, written communication becomes our main concern. Often one may have a query as to what makes any writing technical.

Is technical writing full of technical jargons? Has it got a technical grammar or construction? Does it deal only with technical matters? Keeping all the fears aside, we can define a technical writing on the ground that it serves a specific purpose. We keep on writing throughout the day. A letter, an e-mail, an article, a story, a poem—all may not be technical. But they become technical if they serve a specific requirement. A letter to a business organization asking for adjustment and a story or a poem with plenty of allusions and allegories (e.g., T.S. Eliot's *The Waste Land*) become technical because of their content, structure and relevance.

A technical writing, then, is a writing desired to meet specific goals. Killingsworth and Gilbertson define it by saying "technical writing aims to get work done, to change people by changing the way they do things".[1]

FEATURES OF TECHNICAL WRITING

Imagine one of your friends wanting to buy a digital camera, writes long letters to several shops in Mumbai, placing an order for one. It takes him two months to get the camera. Do you know what was the reason? He could not place the right order. His letters kept travelling from one digital camera shop to another. Likewise, another friend of yours sent his resume to a reputed firm for a job but failed to get any response. The reason might have been with the resume itself. You will come across many such instances nowadays. For any writing to get immediate attention, there are many factors responsible. A written document has to be clear, concise, well-organized, grammatically correct and effective.

Clarity

People in business organizations are not necessarily men of letters. In organizations, we come across people of different backgrounds. If many are from metropolitan cities, there are also people coming from small towns and hamlets. Moreover, in an organization, workers hail from different strata of society. But all of them want clear information. In the case of either an order, complaint or adjustment being made clearly specifying the right model, the right make-up and the exact tool can make the task easy. Clarity is the *mantra* that works miracles in technical writing. While sending a reminder or making a request for clearing outstanding dues, the references of previous letters make things more vivid for both the parties. Clarity saves time and checks further confusion or controversy.

Conciseness

Today, we hear everybody saying, "I am very busy". Nobody seems to have the time to spare for you. And it is true of people all over the world. People have to write several letters and respond to innumerable queries both at

[1]Killingsworth, M. Jimmie and Michael K. Gilbertson. *Signs, Genres and Communities in Technical Communication Amityville,* NY: Baywood, 1992, p. 232.

home and at the office. Especially in business circles, time management becomes difficult. Everyone wants and to the point messages. People neither always have the time nor do they want to stress themselves to unearth messages that are longer and contain abstruse expressions. Moreover, they are not always calm and relaxed. In such conditions, no one has the tolerance and patience to decipher long documents. The tendency to write long sentences and pack them with trite expressions at times can cost an individual heavily. Long sentence constructions not only tire the reader's mind, but also reveal the ineptness of the sender. Sometimes the sender also confuse the reader by sending elaborate messages. A technical writer needs to be concise. One needs to be very specific to be concise. Most of us have heard the saying "brevity is the soul of wit", be concise to be wise.

Organization

The organization of any business document lies in the pattern you choose to weave your sentences and the force you impart to them. Organization means sequencing your message in a way that facilitates the readers. It may also mean the structure you follow when writing the document. A technical writing, hence, should be properly structured. A poorly ordered writing gives a bad impression and fails to attract the reader. While drafting a technical writing—be it a letter, memo or a proposal, all you need to do is to follow the present-day format of writing. Half the importance of your document lies in its organization. A neatly written or typed letter with proper spacing and required font size is a reflection of the writer's personality.

Grammar

A technical writing should have a proper grammatical structure. The role of grammar in making a statement or a premise meaningful can't be ignored. While speaking on a topic, the speaker can control the situation with his verbal ability and style. A lot matters the way a speaker pauses and stresses points at appropriate places. But in writing, these are not possible. Hence, the sender of the message has to ensure the correctness of the statement by means of grammatical structure and, to a great extent, by the use of punctuation marks. A technical writing should be free from errors and poetical experiments (which is usually called poetic license). A grammatically correct document brings a good impression. The omission of punctuation may mar your fortune. Wrong spelling is another detriment to your chances of getting an assignment. It reflects your background and at times your culture.

Effectiveness

A technical writing should be *effective*. Effectiveness depends on the use of language and also the target audience. When writing a report, one should keep in mind the three W's. Why is it written? For Whom is it written? And When should it be written? A technical writer should understand the purpose, the person and the period. If one knows the right time, the right work and the right person, the purpose will be met. Apart from these, the efficacy of a technical writing also depends on the use of the language in a specific situation. Use of harsh words in a complaint letter or sugar-coated words while writing the final collection letter is not advisable.

Read the following incident to understand how many wise people sacrifice effectiveness at times.

> Last Saturday there was a meeting to discuss the introduction of some new courses. The boss asked his fellow employees to give their views. One of the employees raised his hand enthusiastically and spoke nearly for five minutes. But at the end of his suggestion, the members present started looking at each other, wondering what was said. Read what the ardent employee had argued:
>
> What happens these days is that all of us want to pursue all courses without any interest. As a result, what happens is we pursue nothing. No course is as important as any course since it costs them nothing in expressing their interest. What is mandatory today is that one should introduce and offer all courses and reject no course at all. Because what I feel is that all courses are pretty easy and in my opinion what happens is that all courses without a jaundiced view should be offered and no courses should be made compulsory and every other course be made optional. In my opinion, it is the student who should be asked about the introduction of new course. Finally, I would emphasize that no course should be introduced as an experiment. Hope I have communicated my views well; haven't I?

Now ask yourself. Did the employee express himself well? Perhaps your answer will be no. Let us discuss what his deficiencies were. Many of you will agree that he wanted to say something. But his sentences were too long. Several words used were mere repetitions. There was no connection between his message and its meaning. He didn't care for his audience. As a result, communication failed. Communication doesn't mean only expressing your ideas. It also matters how you communicate. Thus, communication is a *process*.

COMMUNICATION: NATURE AND PROCESS

Communication is derived from the Latin word *communicatus* which means "to impart" or share. It can be understood as making some information common. It is giving or exchanging of information, signals or messages by means of talking, gestures or writing. *American College Dictionary* defines communication as "the imparting or interchange of thoughts, opinions, or information by speech, writing or signs".

Today is the world of communication. We are surrounded with all sorts of gadgets that help us in communicating. To send urgent information to someone, all you need to do is to give that individual a call or send him/her an e-mail. When a mishap or accident occurs in an organization, you hear a siren. The very nature of the sound either alarms or cautions you. The doorbell of your house, the early morning siren of a factory, the terrifying sound of an ambulance, the rotating red light on the vehicles of important officials are all messages, however different their natures may be. When you have a message to deliver, you decide the channel and also think about the capability or accessibility of the receiver. Thus, forms of we find that there are something very common. The sender has an idea, which he wants to communicate to the receiver with the help of some channel. The receiver's background helps the sender to decide the channel. The message may be in the form of words or symbols, which both parties are familiar with. The elements of communication are: *sender, message, channel, receiver* and *response.* See Figure 1.1.

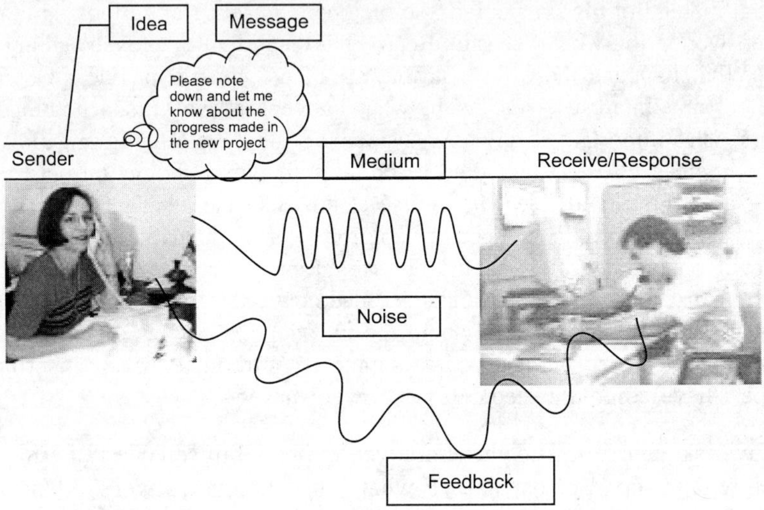

Figure 1.1 Schematic representation of a communication model.

Thus, communication in any form or any medium is an interaction between individuals. This interaction at times may be for resolving a crisis, settling a deal, asking a question, or having a conversation not only for a specific purpose but also for fun. Communication can be defined in a number of ways. Let us look at some definitions of communication.

Communication is social interaction through symbols and message systems. George Gerbner, "On Defining Communication: Still Another View, *Journal of Communication*, **16** (2), 99, June 1966.

Considered as a process, communication can be defined and classified in many ways; as internal or external, verbal or non-verbal, as impressing content or relationships, as being intentional or unintentional and so on.

Larmy L. Barker and Robert J. Keller

Communication is the process involving the transmission and reception of symbols eliciting meaning in the minds of the participants by making common their life experiences.

E John Baird Jr.

Communication is the transfer of information and understanding from one person to another person. It is a way of reaching others with facts, ideas, thoughts and values. It is a bridge of meanings among people so that they can share what they feel and know. By using this bridge a person can cross safely the river of his understanding that sometimes separates people.

Keith Davis in *Human Behaviour at Work*

A close analysis of the above-mentioned definitions results in the following common observations:

1. Communication is the transmission of signals from one person to another.
2. It involves the conscious use of symbols directed towards some goal.
3. Communication involves the perception of commonly understood symbolic stimuli of language.
4. Communication may bring about a change in a person or in an organization if used for a specific purpose.

From these points, we can frame our own definition of communication as:

> "A dynamic process in which man consciously or unconsciously affects the knowledge or experiences of another through the use of words or symbols".

Communication, then, is a process—a two-way process. The various components of communication are sender, receiver, message, channel, response and feedback as shown previously in Figure 1.1.

All of us have ideas which we want to convey to others. Our communication is successful when our ideas are expressed meaningfully and have an effect on others. Communication is a process, and for this process to be complete, you have to understand the various elements/components involved. In any communication there are two, or more than two parties involved. The person who sends his idea is the ***sender*** and the person who receives this idea is called the ***receiver***. The sender selects a medium or channel to send his idea. The receiver decodes the sender's message. The message is considered successful if the receiver sends a response. The response of the receiver gives the sender a clue to understand the effectiveness of the message. This observation by the sender is called feedback. You can understand the nitty-gritty of communication with the help of Figure 1.2 that shows a model given by C.E. Shannon and W. Weaver.

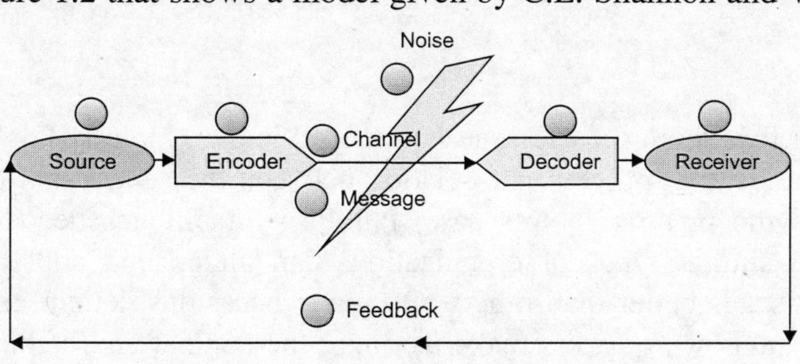

Figure 1.2 Shannon-Weaver model.

Sender

The sender is the first important element of a communication process. He transmits or disseminates information to those he wants to and to those who are in need of it. Much depends on the sender of a message. During hours of crucial importance, the background, attitude and mood of the sender come under scrutiny. A slight lapse on the part of the sender may affect the fortune of a group, community or even of a nation. The sender has to be responsible enough while sending a message lest he should create disharmony or invite unnecessary trouble.

Message

If the sender is the first important element in a communication process, then the message is also equally important. Message is the information that the sender sends. It is an idea, sometimes data, a meaningful utterance or statement issued by the sender. The message may be in the form of words, symbols, gestures, etc. Nowadays, the beep of your cell phone, electronic traffic lights, and icons on your computer are all messages. You will read about such messages in detail in *Chapter 11*. Further communication is not only verbal but it is also non-verbal. When we communicate without words, it is called *non-verbal communication.*

Channel

The medium through which the sender transmits his message or idea is called the *channel*. The selection of channel depends on the sender's mood and receiver's expectation, and also the situational need. You may think of sending a message by using technology, viz. telephone, computer, fax, or sometimes through post. But on many occasions, you may want to have a personal interaction. So, think for a while before you decide the channel through which you will send the message. If you want to send a birthday wish to one of your distant relatives, wishing him through phone, e-mail or SMS will be more effective than sending a greeting card by snail mail. But when you have to offer your condolences to a friend who lost his father, you would certainly want to do it in person. Moreover, when dealing with official responsibilities, written messages appear more effective.

Receiver

The person for whom the message is intended is the *receiver*. For the success of a communication process, the relation between the sender and the receiver comes into the picture. In this case, familiarity facilitates decoding. People working in similar types of organizations can understand and decode each other's messages better than others. On many occasions, letters, mails, phone calls from unknown quarters make us doubt the content and credibility of the message. In official circles, messages sent by official medium are not only liked less but also ignored. This may lead to difficulties too. Like the sender, the receiver also has to be careful while decoding the message and sending the response. Never jump to conclusions in haste, for a hasty response may result in wastage of time and undue problems.

Feedback

When a sender sends a message, he waits for a response. There are times when the sender doesn't receive a response. The sender, in such a situation, starts checking what went wrong. This examination or evaluation of the receiver's response is called feedback that helps the sender to understand the effectiveness of the message. Nowadays, feedback is one of the best measuring scales to bring further improvements and overcome lapses in one's work. Feedback helps in the improvement of not only organizations, but also individuals. Care, however, has to be taken that feedback is not confused with response. While response is the reaction of the receiver, feedback is the analysis of the nature of the response.

COMMUNICATION: SUCCESS OR FAILURE

We have discussed that interaction between two parties with a meaningful purpose and proper medium results in successful communication. But on many occasions two parties communicate, yet there is no response. Think for a while. You speak to your colleague but he shows no reaction. You repeat your message and ask the colleague the reason for not responding. You come to know that he was lost in thoughts or some other anxiety kept his mind occupied. Thus, the success of communication depends on the cooperation between the two parties. At times people grumble that their messages didn't carry any response. You can't say that the process didn't take place. Rather there were certain reasons that either impeded the response or obstructed the receiver from sending one. You come across such situations quite often when your communication breaks down many a time. You will study various reasons for the breakdown of communication, which are also, barriers called communication barrier. Such barriers are discussed in detail in *Chapter 2*.

For instance, what happens when you send a message in Kannada to a person and wait for a response? Only after 15 days do you discover from a friend of yours that the person in question is a Kannada, indeed but he can't speak or write the language as he has been living in England right after his birth. Hence, the reason for the breakdown of communication here is because of a language barrier.

TYPES OF COMMUNICATION

You come across different situations in life. As human beings, you have to communicate with various people and in different environments. Sometimes, you converse with your friends and yet at other times, you communicate with your superiors or subordinates. There are also occasions when you have to address a group, participate in a meeting and deliver a talk to a large gathering. All these occasions necessitate human communication to be of different natures.

Human communication can be divided as illustrated in Figure 1.3.

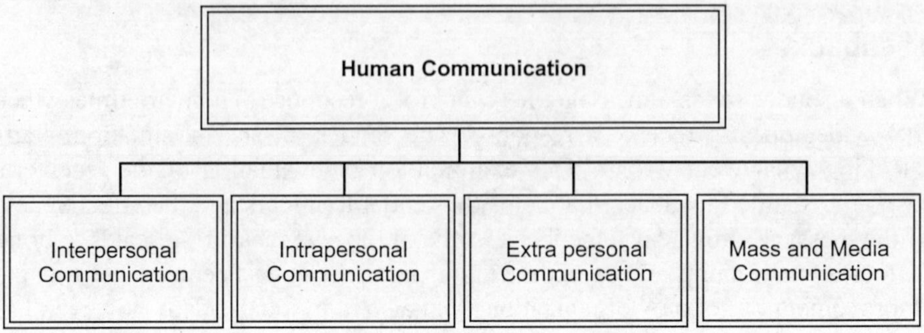

Figure 1.3 Various divisions of human communication.

Interpersonal Communication

This form of communication takes place between two people. When one person communicates with another using words or symbols, it is called interpersonal communication. The success of this form of communication depends on the familiarity of knowledge, background and experience of the individuals involved. People with similar backgrounds, beliefs and experiences communicate better. Their fields of experience often overlap; such a process is called *homophily*. In an environment of better and greater homophily, interpersonal communication becomes meaningful. You often find it interesting to talk with a friend about a book you both have read or a movie you both have seen. John Steward says that interpersonal communication is concerned with what might be called relationship communication since the meanings in interpersonal communication grow to a large extent from the notions we form about others while actively interacting with them. *Examples* of interpersonal communication are conversation, small group meetings, some interviews and letters. (John Steward, "An Interpersonal Approach to the Basic Course", *The Speech Teacher*, **21**, (1) 1972.) See Figure 1.4.

Figure 1.4 Interpersonal communication.

Intrapersonal Communication

There are times when human beings actively communicate with themselves without any visible companion. In this type of communication, a person talks to himself, that is, he talks to his own self. The word 'intra' means within and, thus, intrapersonal communication is talking to one's own self without the involvement of a second person or party. In such a communication, the electrochemical and electro-technical activities of the bodily senses are involved. Eyes become the transmitters of electrochemical impulses, the central nervous system becomes the medium, the brain acts as the receiver, and feedback is produced by the activation of muscles.

Such a communication occurs both in group and in isolation when a person concentrates more on any of the past actions or events. He isolates himself from others, and moves within to interact. We can find a person thumping at the desk or blabbering suddenly without any other individual's participation. Thus, communication can bring a change in a person's self-concept, self-determination and self-motivation. It may help an individual realize his faults and, at other times, infuriate him also. Examples of such communications are soliloquies in dramas and afterthoughts of an individual when he comes out of a meeting on a crucial matter with his boss. See Figure 1.5.

Figure 1.5 Intrapersonal communication.

Extrapersonal Communication

Human beings also communicate with animals, inanimate objects and their surroundings. This is termed as extrapersonal communication. This is most often a communication with less chances of exchange in terms of words between the sender and the receiver. The sender, in such a case, may use words but may receive response in the form of gestures, as in the case, of animals. In the case of inanimate objects, the sender depends solely on his sense perceptions and makes this communication a medium to express his sense of joy sorrow or frustration. See Figure 1.6.

Figure 1.6 Extrapersonal communication.

Mass and Media Communication

There are times when we have to communicate with large groups. In such a communication, the sender uses electrical/mechanical device to send his message. The channel could be newspaper, radio, TV, video, or some other medium. Thus, in this type of communication, though it involves two parties, yet the receiver has less chances to participate actively. The receiver acts as a listener, and the sender too has the limitation of not making a personal rapport with him or her. Feedback and response are difficult to be sought or expected through this medium of communication. See Figure 1.7.

Figure 1.7 Mass and Media communication.

COMMUNICATION FLOW

Communication is called the life blood of an organization. The success of any organization depends on the dissemination of communication. Every organization has its own system of sending and receiving information. You would certainly like to know how communication is managed in a company or an organization.

An organization is a group of individuals of diverse background and responsibilities. Individuals differ in their attitude and their attachment to the company they work for. Organizational commitments enable individuals to seek and hide information according to the requirements of the circumstances. Hence, communication flows in an organization both in formal and in informal ways. Every individual uses both formal and informal means of communication to update himself.

An organization uses formal means of communication to inform, encourage and enrich the employees with the latest developments. But there are certain limits beyond which information is revealed or concealed according to the exigencies of situations. When information and ideas are exchanged within the organization, it is termed *internal communication*. It helps the employees in performing their jobs and also in understanding the aims and objectives of the organization. But when such ideas and information are sent outside the organization, it is called *external communication*. The functions of external communication include responding to queries from outside; persuading customers to buy products, collecting bills, and replying to customer's claims and adjustments.

Internal communication also has formal and informal forms. The formal forms or channels of communication can be categorized into the following:

- Downward Flow
- Upward Flow
- Horizontal Flow

Downward Flow of communication, as the name suggests, moves downwards. When communication from higher authorities is sent to the people at the bottom, it runs downward. Usually, notices, announcements, instructions, orders and reminders come under this category. This mode of communication keeps the employees aware and informed of company procedures and their performance. Caution needs to be exercised while sending downward communication as it may create displeasure and also halt work. A little bit of restraint while disseminating information through downward mode may bring better coordination between the employer and the employee. Depending on an organization's hierarchical structure, the downward flow of communication can come across some obstacles. If communication has to pass through different levels of hierarchy, there are chances of the message getting distorted.

Upward Flow of communication comes from subordinates to their superiors, and junior level employees to their bosses. Communication through this mean aims at helping the bosses perform their tasks efficiently and keeping them informed of the recent developments. Since it is difficult for executives to keep an eye over the progress in all divisions and departments, they seek honest feedback from their immediate subordinates. The present organizational structure of firms aims at ensuring better coordination between employees at all levels. Upward flow of communication process proves its significance only when there exists trust between the boss and his subordinates. Trust and confidence between both the sides can make upward flow of communication an effective tool for the growth of an organization. The medium for upward flow of communication can be phones, e-mails, memos, reports and meetings. The flexible attitudes of employers in a fast changing scenario of today may affect the accurate flow of upward communication. This can be regulated by encouraging more interaction between the employer and the employees.

Horizontal Flow of communication takes place between people of equal status and peer groups. This flow of communication arises when some important decision is to be made. You can find such communication not only among superiors, but also among subordinates. Decisions regarding employment and retrenchment, signing contracts or collaboration, passing new policies, enhancing or curtailing benefits and several group meetings come under horizontal flow of communication. This flow of communication can ensure better decisions provided people are free from biases and individualistic beliefs.

Communication also flows through informal means. The informal network of communication is called *grapevine*. It is less structured and can be between all groups and individuals depending on their relationships. Communication occurs in the form of casual conversations and whispers during official hours and even outside the organization in small gatherings. Considered as rumour mill, grapevine also, at times, provides information difficult to procure through official sources. It is a medium to reveal some very important and secret information before time. Communication of this form is unethical by nature, yet people make use of this medium without spreading the message to everyone.

ETHICAL CONSIDERATIONS

Whether you communicate with individuals or organizations, your concern for the other party becomes important. With the changing working climate and culture, it has become inevitable to care for ethical behaviour. In an open and candid communication atmosphere of today, we have the choice either to be ethical or to be unethical. Ethics means the right conduct by individuals or organizations, and is most important while conducting businesses. You often wonder how to maintain ethical conduct if you have to compete in this crass commercial world. You must understand the kinds of ethical challenges you come across. Imagine you have been appointed to increase the sale of a product that doesn't have a good market. In order to keep your position, you convince customers by making tall and exaggerated claims. Much to the ire of other organizations involved in selling the same kind of product, you criticize their products just to prove yours is better. On another occasion, you are deputed to visit 30 dealers and report about the market conditions. You visit only five dealers and give a false report to your boss or supervisor. Not only this, you discuss a business plan with one of your colleagues and prepare the proposal in your name, including the ideas suggested by him, without giving him credit. All these are violations of ethical codes. You may taste success for some period of time but eventually you will be exposed and then stand helpless.

Overall, you should be responsible and accountable. Organizations respect honesty, integrity, reliability and hence, expectation of high ethical standards has become a must. Companies today aim for long and lasting relationships, which stand on the firm grounds of reliability. As individuals, you should respect ethical standards. The maintenance of individual standard is a reflection of an organization's ethical considerations. Every employee should consider himself as his organization's ambassador and the organization too should have transparent dealings with employees so that a balance is maintained between the ethical standards of the duo.

• EXERCISES •

1. *Communication is a complex process of exchanging information between two parties*. Explain the difference between written communication and oral communication.
2. What are the main features of technical writing?
3. Define communication. Explain each key word with the help of a schematic representation of the communication process.
4. What are the parameters to identify the success or failure of effective communication?
5. Explain the difference between interpersonal and intrapersonal communication.
6. Discuss the flow of communication with appropriate examples.
7. Explain the flow of communication in an organization. Do you consider 'grapevine' a formal network, or an informal one, to gather organizational information? Give reasons in support of your answer.
8. Comment in not more than 50 words on each of the following statements:
   (a) Effectiveness in written communication can be achieved merely by following the rules of grammar and using impressive vocabulary.
   (b) There is no significant difference between written and oral communication.
   (c) A good writer has to plan meticulously before he writes the text of any professional writing.

(d) The success of a piece of writing depends entirely on how the message is conveyed.
(e) The background of receivers plays a vital role in the success of communication.

9. How does feedback influence the communication process?
10. Explain the element of noise in the communication process.
11. What is the role of ethics in communication? Is eavesdropping unethical? If yes, then why?
12. What do you understand by technical communication? Discriminate between technical communication and general purpose communication.
13. What are the disadvantages of *grapevine*?
14. Write whether the following statements are true or false.
    (a) Technical communication is highly structured. _______
    (b) Communication is a strong tool that helps an organization in creating goodwill. _______
    (c) Grapevine is always negative in nature. _______
    (d) Communication depends upon various tangible and intangible elements. _______
    (e) Communication received from signals is a verbal one. _______
    (f) When one man talks to another man, it is called intrapersonal communication. _______
15. Show the differences between the following:
    (a) Feedback and response
    (b) Upward and downward flow of communication
    (c) Written and oral communication
    (d) Animal and human communication
    (e) Ethical and unethical communication

2

Communication Breakdown

> *The single biggest problem in communication is the illusion that it has taken place.*
>
> **—GEORGE BERNARD SHAW**

Even when you become an excellent communicator, you will come across situations where you meant one thing but the receiver of the information understood it as something else. It will not always be the case that you succeed in transmitting the message content in its totality and exactly. You will often find that there are certain things that disrupt the flow of communication. In such a situation, communication suffers a breakdown. Something that interferes with the flow of communication or prevents the smooth passage of a message can be called as **communication breakdown** or **barrier**. See Figure 2.1.

Now, think what could be the reason for this failure in communication? Many a time, you realize it was not the information that you had imparted! You will find yourself saying, “I never said so! I didn’t mean it”, and so on. You realize only later that something had gone wrong in the process of communication. Again, it is only when you critically look at the situation, you can know about the cause of the failure of getting the correct information across. Therefore, to avoid such situations where the meaning of a message gets distorted in the communication process, you have to take the following steps:

1. Identify the cause.
2. Find the solution.
3. Apply the best solution.
4. Follow through.

Figure 2.1 Two individual communicating.

It is not an easy task to adhere to the above-mentioned steps, but with practice you can learn to become a better communicator. *Good communication* doesn't necessarily mean that the listener will accept whatever you say. You might be effective in expressing yourself but people will not necessarily agree with you. However, if you communicate well, they will surely understand you. In the communication process (refer Chapter 1), anything that disturbs the message is called as noise. It is another word for barrier to communication, where the meaning of the message gets distorted. This can exist between two people who are involved in communication, or between two organizations and also within the organization.

Let us classify these breakdowns into three major categories:

1. Breakdown at the source.
2. Breakdown between people/organizations.
3. Breakdown within the organization.

BREAKDOWN AT THE SOURCE

Communication includes several steps to complete the process and can fail miserably if you ignore or skip any of the steps. Unfortunately, many a time, right at the inception stage failure occurs when you are unable to transform your ideas into words. Anything can go wrong when you are formulating the message, including faltering with words when getting into a new situation or being indecisive about the contents.

Faltering with Words

First, you should clearly formulate the ideas in your mind and then put them into words. Sometimes inadequate experience in speaking or writing acts as a hindrance for you in developing effective messages. At times people lack educational qualification or don't have the aptitude to express themselves. They also have limited vocabulary, don't have mastery over grammar, punctuation and style. Therefore, they are frightened of the idea of writing something and showing it to the group. These worries, and lack of knowledge make them ineffective in writing messages. If you have problems, you have solutions as well. It is very important to recognize the problem to find solutions. To improve your writing and speaking skills, you can register for communication courses in your college. Nowadays most colleges have such courses. Also, these days organizations offer many in-house programmes in communication to hone the skills of their employees. Communication and self-help books are an inexpensive alternative. You might join evening classes on language skills, spoken English, etc. to practise your communication skills.

Indecisive about Content

The first hindrance in the communication process is *what to say*. Many of you make the mistake of conveying everything you know about the subject, all at once. The message, which is most important, gets lost in the labyrinth of details. If the message has too much information, it obfuscates the content. The listener is unable to absorb all the ideas presented. When you have to send the message across, you have to decide the sequence of the matter, and what information should you include and what should you leave out. If you fail to provide the receiver the background of the message, you will create confusion. Similarly, if you recommend action first and then follow with explanation, you will excite the receiver for an emotional response that will act as a hindrance to communication.

Unfamiliarity with the Receiver or Situation

You can never create a message if you don't know how it will be used. For example, for a presentation it is necessary to know beforehand the kind of listeners who will come. Similarly, when you write the report, the first step is to analyse the audience. Accordingly, you can decide which topic and sub-topic should be emphasized. You can also decide the length of the report by analysing the audience. You can think of including conclusion and recommendations.

In contrast, lack of familiarity with the audience will act as barriers to communication. You should know about the audience's educational qualification, background, biases, age, status, etc. in order to create messages effectively. If you are writing a report for individuals who are specialist in the same field, you have the liberty to use jargons. But when writing the report for non-technical people, your approach should be entirely different. The tone, context, the language style, all will depend on your relationship with the receiver. If you don't know the audience, your decision will be vague and, while delivering the information, it might lack clarity.

BREAKDOWN BETWEEN PEOPLE

Message is sent to an individual to convey a meaning, but the message by itself has no meaning. The meaning resides in the mind of the sender and the receiver. To understand the meaning of the message, both the interlocutors should share the same concepts in terms of words, gestures, tone of voice and other symbols. If there is disparity on any basis, the chances of distortion of the message increases.

Difference in Perception

The world consists of different kinds of things (living or non-living) and information. The way your mind organizes the myriad sensations into the mind map is a representation of the perception of the reality. Everybody has their own way to perceive the reality but the combination is different. In no case, do two individuals have the same mapping. They will absorb the experiences in a unique and personal way. The pessimist will say, "Ah! the glass is half empty", while the optimist will say, "Oh! the glass is half full". These are different perspectives of the same situation.

Suppose we ask what picture you have in your mind when you hear of the word 'cake'. Some of you associate the word cake with birthdays and celebrations while others might remember getting a cake as a gift on a birthday. There may be some of us who had burnt a cake while baking one, and associate it with the foul burning smell. So our perceptions are associated with the experiences we have gone through.

Since our perceptions are unique, the ideas we wish to express differ from one another. Even when two people experience the same event, their method of describing the situation will differ as they will have different images in their minds. As a sender, we might be giving importance to things which we enjoy or which catches our attention. This is called *selective perception.* As a receiver, we might attach new details to the existing pattern. And that could be the real mis-match to the real communication pattern; as a result, the message gets distorted.

At this juncture, the story that Mahatma Gandhi had narrated is an appropriate example to show how differences in perception exist. The story is about six blind men and an elephant. These blind men were asked to describe an elephant by feeling one. The person positioned near the tail of the elephant felt it and said it was like a snake. The blind man who had felt the leg of the elephant said it was like a pole, the third person, who had the trunk of the elephant in his hand said that it felt like a python and the person who touched the body of the elephant said that it felt like a huge wall. And so, each one of them had a different perception of the elephant. But in a way, all of them were right, because they had those senses from which their conclusions were drawn. But in a real sense, none of them was right, because an elephant doesn't look like a snake or wall, etc. An elephant is an elephant.

Improper Sifting

Sifting through only the information that seems important to the receiver before passing it on further leads to distortion of the message. There are many nodal points from where information has to travel. It can be the secretary taking calls, or student and assistants, to name a few. In some situations, to talk over the telephone you have to cross several barricades of gatekeepers. And on many occasions, the message will be twisted, squirmed, digested and distorted before it reaches the intended receiver. These gatekeepers embellish, add, and truncate the receiver's idea before communicating the same to you. To overcome these barriers, try to get in touch with the receiver through more than one channel of communication. Doing this, you will not only be confirming the authenticity, but also eliminating as many nodal points as possible to remove the chances of distortion. Frame the message as concisely and precisely as possible.

Semantic Gap

When you use words for your message, you communicate many details, such as your community, educational and cultural background. Your language and vocabulary create their own hindrances on your message. For example, a chartered accountant's vocabulary will differ from that of an engineer or a scientist, and this difference in their vocabulary will affect their ability to understand each other and formulate ideas. Besides this, barriers also exist because of the number of meanings associated with some words. For example, the word 'run' has 72 meanings associated with it as a verb and 18 as a noun. Language uses arbitrary symbols to represent reality. The word 'computer' has nothing in it which is the representation of the machine. But, whenever the word 'computer' is uttered, its image comes to our mind. Since language is the arbitrary code, what meaning gets associated in the mind of the individual depends completely on experience and perception.

Even the denotative meaning of a word varies to a great deal. For example, if you say, 'fan' it can mean hand fan, pedestal fan, ceiling fan, table fan or exhaust fan. Though commonly it is agreed that a fan is a device that helps in creating current of air, but the images are different.

There are more chances of variation for the connotative meaning of the words. For example, the word 'pastry' can have several interpretations. It all depends on the experiences you can relate with the object.

Thus, to overcome this semantic barrier, use more concrete and specific words to convey the exact meaning. Avoid unfamiliar and long words as your audience will face difficulty in understanding them. Try to give accurate information, which has fewer chances of distortions. You will read more about the complexities of word in Chapter 6.

Poor Listening

Poor listening is one of the most common reasons for creating hiatus in the communication process. Many a time, there is lack of attention on the listener's part. It is a well-known fact that very few of us have good listening skills. The root cause of this problem is that a speaker can speak up to 120–150 words per minute, which is much less as compared to the listener's ability to listen up to 500–700 words per minute. So there exists a gap between speaking and listening which is called as brain time. During this time, the receiver's mind wanders in different directions and he finds hard to concentrate. There are other factors also for poor listening, which are discussed in Chapter 3. Of course, sometimes the problem lies at the speaker's end as he might put the information in esoteric words which makes the receiver lose interest.

To tackle these problems, verify what has been said by paraphrasing what you have understood. Empathize with the speaker and try to visualize the things from his point of view and don't be in haste to jump to conclusions. Do clarify the meaning by passing non-threatening questions and listening patiently.

Variance in Emotional States

The messages you send will have both content meaning, which will be the subject of the message, and relationship meaning, suggesting the relationship between you and the receiver. The meaning of the message will be distorted miserably when the receiver reacts adversely to any of these meanings.

You often deal with people when they are in different states of mind. In fact, even when you communicate in an infuriating state, the message is neither sent effectively nor received in the proper perspective. In an imbalance state of mind, the person always distorts and twists the message's content. This doesn't mean that you should avoid communicating when you are emotionally charged but only try to be more careful and alert to the message as there are more chances of misunderstanding because of emotionally charged tones.

There may be situations where you may have conflicting emotions about the subject of your message or the audience. Suppose you are writing a proposal to clinch a project that your friend is also aspiring to. When writing the project, you will not be at your best because at the unconscious level you are aware that your friend needs the project more than you. Even though you are a persuasive writer, you might not write an effective proposal.

To come out from this difficult situation, you should be conscious of your own feelings and of others, and try to control them while communicating. Make use of neutral words to avoid arousing negative feelings. Be aware of the situation fully and realize that there is a greater probability for misunderstandings.

Different Backgrounds

Different backgrounds of individuals often act as great barriers to communication. So, they need to be overcome. If the difference in the backgrounds of the interlocutors is wide, smooth communication becomes difficult. The barriers can be in the form of age, gender, economic and social status, health, beauty, popularity, religion, and even the moods to make understanding difficult. If two individuals have similar experiences, it will contribute to better understanding. This is one reason that people from two different states in our country have greater difficulty in communicating because of different backgrounds and cultures.

To overcome this barrier, don't judge others' culture by comparing it with yours. Ethnocentrism should be avoided at all costs. Clarify your background and understand the receiver's sphere of knowledge, background, personality, etc. Don't forget that even the non-verbal codes have different meanings in different regions.

BREAKDOWN IN THE ORGANIZATION

Communication occurs between two parties and, when they are part of the same organization, this communication is more difficult. It is governed by many other factors, rules and regulations of the organization. The message is often profound and controversial. The situation becomes grave because of lack of opportunities for feedback available to the sender and receiver, leaving more reasons to cause misunderstanding.

Inundation of Information

If too less information is bad, too much is not good either. Too much information has an impact on the audience's power of concentrating effectively on the important messages. To cope with such situations, the receiver sometimes ignores an important information, delays in responding to the ones that are not so urgent, answers only part of some of the messages and reacts mechanically to others. Communication gets affected because of such treatment by the receiver. In this technologically competent world, information overload has become a major cause of concern and, therefore, should be dealt with carefully.

To tackle this problem, recognize which information is necessary and which is not. Set your priorities to deal with the information judiciously. Make different compartments to put your documents labelling them as urgent, most urgent and not so urgent. See Figure 2.2.

Abstruse Message

When you are a part of an organization, you formulate your business messages both as an individual and as the member of your organization. Many a time,

Figure 2.2 Information overload.

you adjust your tone and style according to your employer's likings. In fact, there are times when you write applications or business proposals with which you personally disagree. Suppose you are part of a recruitment team. When taking the interview, you find that apart from you no one thinks that a particular candidate is quite suitable for the position. Now it also happens to be your responsibility to send the rejection letter to that particular candidate. You have to communicate the organization's opinion keeping aside your personal feelings which you might find difficult to do with the result that the message is obscure and incomprehensible.

Most of the time, business messages deal with subject matters that are technical or difficult to express. For example, you have to explain the operation of a lathe machine or why profits of Kesoram Industries Ltd. have dropped in the last six months. These topics are dry in content and it is, therefore, often difficult to keep the audience interested in the presentation. To overcome this difficulty, use language that is plain, clear and easy to understand. Be specific and concrete rather than using general and non-specific language. Keep taking constant feedback to know that your message has reached the audience, otherwise paraphrase it.

Innumerable Channels

You often face situations where you have to give attention to a number of messages at a time. For instance, sitting in your office simultaneously, you might be talking over the phone and perusing a report. Then there is a likelihood that both the messages will not get apt attention. Even when writing a message, you might be interrupted for several reasons. Your mobile rings constantly, people intrude, boss sends messages and crises arise. To sum up, your attention is divided in and between so many messages.

To overcome this barrier, avoid dealing with all the messages at the same point of time. Draft your written messages in simple and easy to understand language and deliver it to your readers when they have the time to read. Try to speak to the receiver directly avoiding intermediaries to have clear communication. Keep aside some time in the day for the most important messages to be delivered and received.

DISPARITY IN STATUS

Since in an organization hierarchical structure exists, employees have different professional status. The junior-level employees are often shy and timid in sending messages to the manager and talk only about those things which a manager wants to listen to. Likewise, the senior-level employees will not like to discuss things openly with their subordinates which may, they feel, undermine their authority in the organization. Also, if you are working in one department which looks after a specific job, your attitude and value might differ from the people working in another department in the same organization.

To deal with the barriers because of gulf in status, have an open communication environment. Encourage the employees of all levels to communicate in a transparent environment. Information should never be held back even if it is unpleasant. Have enough courage to pass it on to your superior.

Lack of Trust

The task of building trust amongst employees is a long and arduous one, yet it should be done. It is also rare to find employees of two organizations having cordial relations. This is because of a lack of trust between the two organization's employees as they have no idea as to how supportive and receptive the people of the other organization will be. Even within the same organization as competition grows, people lose trust in each other. They conceal information which is a major cause for communication breakdown.

To overcome trust barriers, you need to be a smart communicator. Don't seclude yourself making someone else a spokesperson. Never hesitate to share key information with colleagues and always include all the relevant people in the decision-making process.

Too Many Transfer Stations

Organizational communication is guided by some regulations, such as, who may communicate with whom and only very few individuals are authorized to make decisions. If your organization has too many formal channels, it will make the communication process very difficult. When your office has all the centralized activities with a high degree of formalization, the horizontal flow of communication will be negatively affected. In the tall hierarchical structure, communication flows through several nodal points and is liable to get distorted. For example, take a look at the following communication situation:

Mr. Ravi says to one of his colleagues: "One of my friends is going to pass away. He had been very close to me and he needs me. I have to pass some time with him. I am unable to go to the office today. If you don't mind, please tell my boss that I won't be going to office in time. If I don't return by afternoon, I'll be on full leave".

Mr. Ravi's colleague to his boss: "Mr. Ravi is going to pass some time with his passing friend. If he doesn't return till afternoon he will be on full leave".

Boss to his clerk: "If there's a phone call for Mr. Ravi, tell him that he is no more today. He has gone to pass away some time with his passing away friend".

The foregoing example shows how the message gets twisted after passing through various channels. Therefore, to overcome this barrier, reduce hierarchical levels by following flat structure. Get communication flow open in all directions; horizontal, vertical, newsletters, memos, open doors policies, etc. to make it effective.

Wrong Choice of Medium

You should choose the right medium to pass on your message. If the wrong medium is opted, then the intended meaning doesn't reach the target audience. You can choose the medium depending on the nature of the message and the receivers at the other end. Value of the medium in the given communication situation is called **media richness** (Bovee:* 1995, 44). It is determined by factors such as:

- The ability to convey a message by taking the help of more than one informational cue.
- The ability to get feedback.
- The ability to develop personal focus.

See Figure 2.3.

*Courtland L. Bovee and John V. Thill, 1995, *Business Communication*, 4th ed., USA: McGraw-Hill.

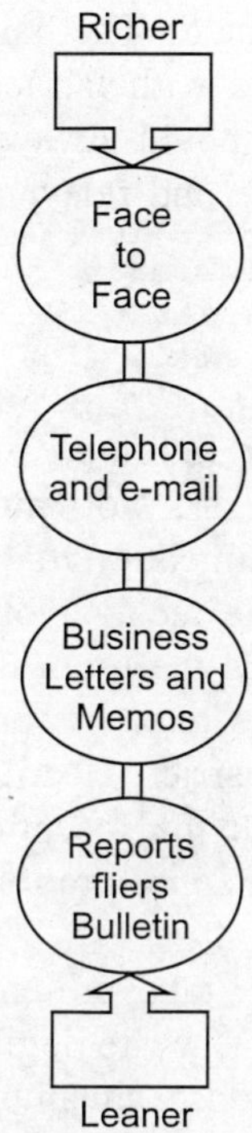

Figure 2.3 Media richness continuum.

Face-to-face is the richest medium of communication as it is personal. The verbal information is in tandem with non-verbal cues. It conveys not only the information, but also the feelings. The speaker gets immediate feedback. Telephone and e-mail message can cull the feedback and with the absence of non-verbal cues, such as facial expression, eye contact and body language, it makes them less rich than face-to-face communication.

Written media can be made personal through addressed mails and letters. But the absence of non-verbal and vocal cues delays the immediate feedback. The leanest media are bulletin, fliers and reports which are very technical and objective. They lack personal focus, non-verbal cues and feedback.

To overcome this media barrier, choose the apposite media for the given message. If you have to transmit non-routine and obfuscating message, choose the rich media. Leaner media should be opted to communicate simple and routine messages. If you have to reprimand someone, don't send fax as then the reaction from the receiver will be awful.

Unethical Communication

In Chapter 1, you have already read about ethical considerations in communication. It is a fact that creating unethical and illegal messages give a bad image to an organization. To be successful, an organization must have an open communication environment. The liaisons within the organization and the outside world can be created with fairness and trust. To avoid unethical communication, your message, should always give the complete information. The message should be adequate and relevant to the situation. Ensure that it is not deceptive at all.

Physical Distractions

Barriers are physical also: poor lighting, extreme climatic conditions, poor acoustic, uncomfortable seats, etc. You might be surprised to know that poor lights affect your communication to a great deal, it may block an otherwise effective message. The receiver of the message may be distracted because of the cacophony outside the room that might be due to unorganized seating arrangements, low chairs, etc. In some cases, even the ill health of the receiver contributes to the barrier. Hearing or visual impairment, pain in the knee, etc. can interfere with the reception of a message. These factors certainly contribute to the lack of concentration and often block communication partially.

To overcome these barriers, take pre-emptive measures. When you are preparing the written document, write legibly in a readable font size. If delivering oral presentation, choose an ambience that is conducive for the audience in reception of the messages. If you are part of the audience, then concentrate fully on the message and ignore distractions.

You must have observed that you should be very careful when creating your messages, both oral and written. Know about the factors responsible in noise formation and try to eliminate them. Above all, facilitate feedback, as that is the most important ingredient for effective communication.

• EXERCISES •

1. What do you understand by barriers? How do they affect the communication process?
2. Discuss the types of barriers that we often come across in interpersonal communication situations.
3. "The effectiveness of an interpersonal communication lies in a good understanding of the differences between the receiver and the sender which otherwise lead to communication breakdown." Analyse the statement in the light of any five interpersonal communication barriers providing suitable examples from your own experiences.
4. "Ignorance of cultural differences often leads to a breakdown in communication."Explain the statement citing two examples.

5. Identify the barriers of communication in the following statements.
   (a) In an aircraft maintenance manual: "Check under carriage locking pin. If bent, replace".
   (The operator examined the pin. It was indeed bent, so he carefully put it back. The aircraft crashed.)
   (b) The patient: "Doctor, I have pain in my neck, in my legs, in my back and I feel weak and sick."
   Doctor (after examination): "You have acute hypochondria".
   Patient: "Doctor I always knew I have some deadly disease!!"
   (c) The doctor was on his usual evening round in the hospital. He went to the patient on bed no. 5 and asked her to move her right leg. The patient started moving it slowly initially and after a while on doctor's request more vigorously. The doctor declared that now the patient was absolutely fit and can be discharged.
   The patient though continued to shiver in high fever.
6. "Sometimes communication fails because of mishearing of a word or a phrase." How can you overcome this barrier?
7. Give examples of communication barriers through transfer stations in the organization. Show how the original message gets distorted by the time it reaches the final recipient.
8. How can you overcome communication barriers? Show some common remedies.

3 Listening

> *Perhaps listening cannot be taught but many of us are convinced that it can be learned.*
>
> —CARL WEAVER

In Chapters 1 and 2, you have seen that communication is a two-way process between the sender and the receiver. The sender may either be a speaker or a writer, having diverse background, experience and knowledge, but the receiver may not be so. The receiver's poor educational background, age and lack of exposure may, at times, mar listening. It may often make you wonder how communication can take place at all without listening. Remember while attending a lecture did you listen to all that your professor was saying in the class. You had been all eyes and ears to the professor, yet when you were asked a question, you suddenly started glancing sideways. It is ironic to talk about listening in a technically advanced world when people are busy either receiving information or answering calls from everywhere and nowhere. Students often are occupied with Walkman, iPods or other gadgets. Are they really listening or simply wasting their time?

As you grow older, you understand the importance of listening. We hear most of the time but listen occasionally. Listening is not as easy as it appears. There have been difficult times often because people have not listened properly. We can't deny that on numerous occasions our attention got diverted even in the most important business meetings, conferences or when attending lectures in our college days. But to give the impression that we were attentive, we kept nodding our heads in agreement though reluctantly or casually. We came to our senses only when caught unaware or had to interpret, answer or explain all that was communicated. These are ample evidences to prove that hearing is not always listening.

HEARING VERSUS LISTENING

In your day-to-day activities, apart from performing various tasks, you also carry out the important task of hearing. Your day starts with gathering information about the world either by switching on the TV or the radio. You come across different pieces of information which you heard but could not remember. Many people watch movies but can't remember most of the dialogue. Yet there are some dialogues which they can recall for a long time. This happens because that particular dialogue/sentence, in addition to being interesting, had touched them. We can say they had listened to that dialogue. When you hear something, you take it casually; but when you listen to something, you do so seriously. Hearing has been called a physiological process whereas listening is a mental one. When you join an organization as a fresher, you listen to every word that your boss, colleagues or subordinates say. But as you grow in years in the organization, you listen more to the words of your boss than anyone else. Moreover, you also develop a tendency that your words too should be listened to.

LISTENING AS A PROCESS

Listening is a process which begins with hearing. Imagine an advocate pleading the case of his client. The man who is being addressed is none other than the judge, though there are others too, who are simply hearing. The fate of the client depends totally on how the judge has heard the argument, interpreted and analysed to give his verdict. The advocate endeavours his best to gather points in his client's favour to make the judge listen. He also works hard to establish a connection between his statements, to make the case appear logical and coherent. Thus, the judge can be said to follow the *process of listening* which comprises hearing, interpreting and then, responding. Any improper step in this process may affect listening and the client's fate. Such listening may be called *perceptive listening*. Raymond S. Ross, in his book *Speech Communication*, quotes Ernest D. Nathan as saying, "Perceptive listening is a conscious cognitive effort involving primarily the sense of hearing reinforced by other senses and leading to understanding. When perceptive listening is inspired by a sincere desire to understand, it becomes more than a sensory process. It is an attitude well expressed 'as a listening spirit'.

MODES OF LISTENING

The three basic modes of listening are *combative*, *attentive* and *reflective*. During combative listening, the listener is more bothered about his own viewpoints than the contents delivered by the speaker. He wastes his energy grabbing the opportunity to barge into the talk and throw upon the points felt at his end. This type of listening is observed when the listener wants to draw attention to his presence. Of course, this reflects immaturity on the part of the listener.

In attentive listening, the listener is patient giving all ears to the speaker. He listens patiently to the speaker and believes each word uttered by him. He neither checks the speaker nor does he mistrust him. The listener lacks independent thinking and gets carried away by what has been said.

In reflective listening, the listener is alert and carefully evaluates each word spoken by the speaker. He pays a lot of attention by paraphrasing and recapitulating what the speaker has said. Simultaneously, he forms his own opinion and reciprocates that in a responsible manner. Amongst these three modes of listening, reflective listening is the most effective one.

ADVANTAGES OF LISTENING

Listening is an important ingredient of learning. You know well how a child starts learning his first language. Before the child learns to write alphabets, he learns sounds and words. This is possible because of listening. The same is true of many people who don't know how to write in a particular language but can speak it as effectively as a native speaker. Linguists also believe that language is not taught but caught. The famous American novelist Ernest Hemingway paid much importance to listening as a tool for learning and had remarked: "I like to listen. I have learned a great deal from listening carefully. Most people never listen". The role of listening in learning a language, thus, can't be ignored. Listening benefits both the speaker and the listener. You come across various communicative situations where listening has its advantages.

Conversation

Possessing the skill of listening can benefit you in a variety of ways. Think of a situation where your friend is talking to you while you are simply nodding to keep him in good humour. You will realize that after some time the conversation has come to an end. Your friend has smelt your lack of interest in the matter and as a goodwill gesture, terminated the talk. Such half-hearted listening, in the long run, may cost you your friendship. Listening helps a great deal in conversation. It strengthens ties and helps relationships to grow. A good conversation is laid on the foundation of listening between the speaker and the receiver. It is a prerequisite to be a good conversationalist. Effective listening ignites conversation to explore new heights and possibilities.

Interviews

Listening plays a key role in interviews. As an interviewee, you have to listen carefully to the questions put by the panel experts. The panellists situate their words in questions so carefully that a slight lapse in listening on your part can cause you to answer a question wrongly. Active listening and listening to every word will keep you focused and to the point. Moreover, your intelligent listening may also help you bring the interviewers to your coveted and secure area where you are more armed. Often, the anchors of TV shows and interviews have an advantage over the interviewees because of their adequate listening abilities. Besides, listening also helps in developing better interviewing skills.

Organizational Activities

You will understand the importance of listening once you have joined an organization. A secretary, while taking notes, must listen carefully lest some significant information is left out. Likewise, executives and their subordinates must ensure effective listening to promote amity and organizational effectiveness. Both in the cases of receiving instructions and making decisions, effective listening plays a crucial role. Employees entrusted with the job of receiving orders over telephones must listen effectively. In addition, they have also to encourage queries from their customers and clients. Giving satisfactory replies to customers' queries depends largely on the listening capability and patience level of the respondent.

Negotiation

In negotiations, listening is rewarding. Effective listening helps in clinching a deal. Moreover, your sharp listening ability can make you extra cautious about the rival group's game plan. It is conscious listening alone that can prompt you to raise your doubts at a particular stage and enable you to agree or disagree with the proposal in question. Moreover, negotiators help in resolving the deadlock between two groups. Certain keywords or phrases, if not listened to carefully can turn the tables. Since an active listener listens not only with ears but also with eyes, he is ready for concessions to achieve a win-win situation during negotiations.

Group Discussion

Effective listening skill establishes the importance of group discussions and meetings. The leader of the group helps maintain unity between the members, and this is possible only through listening. A reticent participant, too, becomes vibrant if he carefully listens to the views of other participants. Effective listening arouses him and gives him momentum. It keeps all other members involved in the discussion, and they, in turn, keep the ball dribbling from one individual to another. Moreover, the panellists also assess the degree of participation and rationality of the candidate's views on the basis of listening. Candidates will be able to react to other participants' viewpoints only through the medium of effective listening. Thus, listening proves to be the measuring scale by which the effectiveness of a group discussion can be assessed.

Meetings

In today's world, where most organizations consider meetings as an important organizational activity, listening acts as a facilitator. Effective listening makes the objectives of the meetings successful and enables every participant to be heard. Since meetings are a good platform to announce new policies, propagate the organization's business and resolve challenges, effective listening becomes mandatory. The leader, through effective listening, infuses new energy in the members and mitigates any misgiving among them. Effective listening between the members and the leader lends a sense of belonging to the entire group. Thus, the importance of listening carries paramount significance in organizational effectiveness.

FACTORS AFFECTING LISTENING

Since listening is a process of filtering the sound and words transferred by the sender to the receiver, it depends on various factors. Effective listening can take place in a conducive atmosphere only. Various factors that affect listening can be categorized as external and internal. See Figure 3.1.

Figure 3.1 Listening atmosphere.

External Factors

Noise

Noise is one of the most common factors responsible for poor listening. Present-day workplaces witness various forms of noise that impede listening. Cell phones, at times, become a liability. At the beginning of every meeting or conference, you may come across announcements such as "switch off your cell phones". People should not be surprised if in the near future this statement is found written on the walls of every building. Many educational institutions have put a blanket ban on the use of cell phones during office hours. Also, speakers often get disturbed and lose link when phones start ringing during presentations. Talking and whispering among the audience are also responsible for creating disturbances both for the speaker and for other listeners.

Another important external factor that contributes to creating noise is the regular flow of traffic. The honks of the traffic, at times, distract our attention. Several times, disturbances on the background during a telephonic talk because of faulty connectivity also mar the effectiveness of listening. Many important instructions issued from the supervisor to the subordinates go unheard because of the presence of noise in the channel.

Venue

The ambience and the place play a significant part in the success of listening. The venue of a meeting, conference or some other important deliberation affects listening to a great extent. A location that doesn't suit the listeners often brings distraction and dissatisfaction. Care must be taken when finalizing the venue and it should be seen that it suits the listeners. A room which is dark and lacks proper ventilation invites trouble both for the speaker and for the listener. Moreover, the seating arrangements and temperature also add to establishing a congenial ambience.

Time

Time is a crucial factor in effective listening. Not all people are ready to listen all the time. In the past, when the telephone was a luxury, people used to be very conscious of the time when one should call the other party. Moreover, they also used to write everything beforehand that they had to convey. This, in turn, resulted in confusing the listeners and they used to get muddle-headed at times because of too much technicality and the message being delivered at a very fast pace. Thus, listening suffered a lot. Even in the present-day world, it has been observed that when ample notice is given before holding a meeting, it prepares people to remain attentive during the meeting. On the other hand, a meeting held at short notice often annoys people. In organizations, meetings after office hours or on holidays often cause inconvenience to the employees and they listen to the dealings only half-heartedly. Top executives in companies often take the caution of meeting people only with appointments so that they can give them a proper hearing. Likewise, in the midst of a meeting asking your boss about your promotion may force him to ignore your query. At times, as a presenter too, you feel that some more time in the organization of the message could have generated serious listening.

Status

The status of the speaker also influences listening. People have a general tendency to listen to only those who have status and respect in the society and in the business circle. A common representative of a company may not influence the listeners as much as a powerful executive of the same organization. The person's status makes people anticipate his rich experience, language and also authenticity/reliability of his words. Many organizations have a policy of sending top-level employees from time to time to bridge the gap between the organization and its clients in the hope of ensuring effective listening of their policies and procedures. The importance of status in the organizational rung is also utilized for damage control at times.

Culture

Culture is yet another external factor that influences or distracts listening. It includes people's way of dressing, mannerisms and value additions. It is human nature to respond positively to things of their liking. People coming from similar cultural backgrounds tend to talk and listen to each other better. You have already read that the better the homophily between the two parties, the better is the communication. Many cultures have certain customs that might appear unusual to people from other cultural backgrounds. When a listener is exposed for the first time to people from other cultures where certain things are inherent in the way they speak, behave and react, listening suffers miserably. For instance, when a Japanese and an American meet, it often creates restlessness because of their different interpretation of the pauses and silence during the conversation. In order to avoid this cultural barrier and for effective listening, one has to be extra-cautious and sensitive.

Internal Factors

Effective listening like any other successful communication, transpires because of the cooperation between the speaker and the listener. A slight deviation from it may result in communication breakdown. There are various internal factors that prompt and procrastinate listening at the same time.

State of mind

All of us know that emotional feelings have an effect on our communication. This is true in the case of listening also. Feelings of anger, envy, frustration and anxiety often disrupt our concentration and block listening. When people are emotionally charged, they often misinterpret words and react unfavourably. In these kinds of states, you develop a sort of disinterest and may be disgusted too towards other activities. As a result, you are unable to concentrate on what is being said. As a speaker, if you are emotionally charged, you will be able to focus less on your topic. This will result in the listeners becoming disinterested.

Ego

Ego is another internal factor that impedes our listening skills. Most often you will find people working at the same hierarchy ignoring each other's ideas and suggestions. This is mainly because of ego. Employees often feel that their colleagues' intention is to blow their own trumpets. Hence, one should ignore their words. Sometimes people pay less heed to the words of their compatriots because of differences of opinion. Even important issues which require active listening often get sidelined because of ego clashes. To listen effectively, one has to be free from ego and biased opinions. People may have differences, but workplaces require all egos to sink in order to achieve the goals set by the organization. A line must be drawn between personal differences and official formalities in the hope that effective listening is the ladder to workplace efficacy.

Prejudgement

You often come across people who have a tendency to judge individuals or messages before having heard them fully. In such a condition, people tend to jump to conclusions on the basis of a particular word or impression and, hence, shirk listening. On other occasions, because of their preconceived notions about some views or people, individuals refuse to listen at all. It is usually seen that both a prejudiced speaker and a prejudiced listener often spoil the entire show. As a listener, one should be patient enough to pay attention to whatever is being said. In case a listener has prior information about a topic, he is benefitted because he can then cross-examine the facts and enjoy ample scope of verification.

Language

Famous speakers often attract listeners' attention by using language in which understanding becomes smooth. Correspondingly, the usage of difficult language distracts listeners. By language, we mean the medium, choice of words and style of expressing the content. Imagine a condition where you deliver a presentation in ornamental English to lower-level employees. You will fail to make them listen. Likewise, if someone speaks in Russian to an Indian, no form of listening will take place. One must remember that effective listening takes place between two parties only when both are exposed to the nuances of a common language. Any attempt to experiment with the new use of a particular word or expression in the same language may also discourage effective listening. Careful speakers often discover in advance their listeners' age, background and linguistic knowledge to ensure effective listening.

MEASURES TO IMPROVE LISTENING

Since listening is an important ingredient of communication, all efforts should be made to utilize it. We find that different kinds of noises engulf us all the time, yet we have to concentrate on listening. The very first requirement for a good listener is to stop talking and concentrate on listening. One has to listen to every word and focus on the context in which a certain word has been used. Moreover, as careful listeners, we should also take into consideration the time factor. When you want people to listen to you, seek advance appointments and allow them the liberty of giving you a time of their convenience. A careful listener, in addition to being open-minded, must provide feedback to the speaker through non-verbal means. You might have experienced that during important meetings and talks, people are seen as busy, holding parallel conversations. Some people are also accustomed to judging the speakers' appearances and not their ideas. As a precautionary measure, such attempts must be thwarted. Organizations spend a large sum of money on calling experts from relevant areas in order that employees are benefitted. Paying little attention to such speakers shows disrespect to time, energy and money both for your organization and yourself. One must remember that listening just for the sake of listening is not listening at all. Rightly it has been said: "hearing is sensation, listening is interpretation".

• EXERCISES •

1. What do you understand by active listening? How is listening different from hearing?
2. Enumerate different modes of listening. Which of them is the best mode?
3. What are the reasons for poor listening? How can you overcome them?
4. "Listening is more important than speaking". Do you agree with the statement? Corroborate the answer with appropriate examples.
5. Many students are not successful in getting the right kind of job because of their poor listening skills. Comment on the above statement.
6. "All hearing is not listening." Explain.
7. How can one become a better listener? Illustrate with proper examples.
8. Read out the passage. Answer the questions given at the end of the paragraph.

   Global consultancy services providers KPMG and Nasscom indicated that the Financial Services industry KPO (knowledge process outsourcing) is poised to be worth £ 5 bn in India by 2010. It is an extremely advantageous position to garner this business, which is often misunderstood. It is not a number game but a mind game, where consultants would play a very strategic role. A couple of years ago, talk of KPO seemed far-fetched, especially as businesses were still struggling to come to terms with what the earlier forms of outsourcing could do for them. These could be in the areas of investment research, IP launching, data analysis, and business research, among others.

Several factors would play a role in attracting this business, including the existing capability of IT services and BPO companies, the comfort zone these companies have built, the push towards global sourcing, and improved remote project management capabilities. There is likely to be a significant shift in the boundaries between outsourceable and non-outsourceable activities and offshoring activities to embrace new locations, and most global banks and insurers are expected to adopt KPO strategies. This could effectively mean that there would be that KPO becoming a more specialized service to a particular vertical or industry. The primary value proposition of KPO is to generate top line while, in the case of BPO, it is largely cost arbitrage.

India's technology companies are looking to Europe and higher-end knowledge businesses to retain the country's position as the world's back-office hub in the face of a sluggish US economy, spiraling costs and competition. KPO services have been seen as periodic service that supports discrete initiatives and are viewed as an integral part of business operations. Upshots include emerging growth opportunities in financial, pharmaceutical and other sectors and a greater emphasis on globalization. Enterprises want the flexibility to respond rapidly to new market opportunities, which is increasingly difficult to deliver using traditional in-house methods. Vendors need to respond to this opportunity by supporting new knowledge requirements with rapid provisioning flexibility.

(a) What is KPO? Are KPO and BPO the same?
(b) What is going to be the worth of KPO by 2010?
(c) What are the factors that attract people to join KPO?
(d) What is the primary value proposition of KPO?

4

Business Letters

Say all you have to say in the fewest possible words or your reader will be sure to skip them, and in the plainest possible words or he will certainly misunderstand them.

—GEORGE ORWELL

Our ability to thrive in today's world is based on our communication skills. As discussed in Chapters 1–3, speaking and writing always have an edge over the other two skills, namely reading and listening. Even when speaking and writing are compared, the latter is more significant because it can be recorded, and, thus, has a permanent value. Despite technical innovations such as the Internet and cell phones, writing still holds its importance because of its reliability and the significance of serving as a record. The success of various search engines lies in the preserving writing from ancient times to the present day.

Writing represents people even in their absence. It is a medium through which people, communities, organizations and nations come to know each other. Many traits of an individual are revealed through a piece of writing. The way one writes reveals one's thought process and background. Moreover, it demonstrates a person's ability to think clearly and logically, in addition to his knowledge of the appropriate use of vocabulary and correct application of language including grammar. Psychologists give much importance even to handwriting and the nuances of sentence formation, for these provide them with adequate clues about the writer's personality.

Writing is an art, and hence, one must invest many years in its inculcation to gain perfection. As in the case of speaking, writing too has various purposes which makes the latter distinct, even unique, because of its structure and style.

Writing in today's business world has become more challenging since it has to address variegated readers with different aims. As professionals, you often write to inform, explain, persuade, motivate, induce, and promote. All these purposes get fulfilled in various forms of writing. This chapter will acquaint you with the nuances of letter writing needed in a business in order to make you a successful professional.

Most organizations today consider the art of business correspondence as a prime factor for success and expansion. Technology has enabled exchanges between employees to be prompt and frequent. Furthermore, the final agreement between any two organizations always culminates in the form of a letter or an MOU (Memorandum of Understanding). It is not surprising, then, that the reputation of an organization often rests on written/printed words. And so, more care and consideration are required while exchanging business letters. One must understand the various expectations involved while drafting a business letter, keeping an eye on the qualities that differentiate it from a general-purpose letter.

BUSINESS LETTERS AND GENERAL-PURPOSE LETTERS

Although both business letters and personal letters have many things in common, the former differs from the latter in relation to the tone, content, length and flow. Business letters follow a neutral tone, but care must be exercised to not hurt the receiver's sentiments. These letters have a formal touch, and the language used is simple, straightforward and focused towards the objective of writing them. Personal letters are free from such restrictions, and with an informal touch, they don't conform to the rigidity of order and coherence. Business and personal letters differ in their approach. Personal letters written carefully and conscientiously can serve as good essays. Letters of great philosophers, writers and leaders preserved in great libraries of the world give a picture of their times and serve as reference books for numerous researches.

REQUIREMENTS OF BUSINESS LETTERS

In whichever profession you might be working/employed at some point, you will have to write and reply to many letters. Undoubtedly, technical assistance provided to people in most organizations lessen their burden to a great extent, yet it fails to control human moods at times. You, as a professional, need to be extra-cautious while drafting letters. As you grow in an organization over the years, your writing plays a crucial role. Based on your letters, many important decisions are made. Some requirements of business letters are helpful in having an edge over general purpose letters. Look at the letter given here, which fails to follow the guidelines of a business letter.

Example I

Dear Manager,

We grew hot and cold when the customers complained about the malfunctioning of the AC supplied by you. We had ordered for high-priced ACs because of their quality.

Yours faithfully
B. Juneja

Example II

Dear Mr. Juneja,

Thank you for your letter dated …. We are grieved to know about your inconvenience.
Kindly send the ACs along with the details of the order. They will be replaced without delay.

Yours faithfully
Vineet Joshi

The first letter shows the shock and anger of the writer, whereas the second one shows consideration. The writer of the first letter makes the complaint more personal and blames the manager. If the first letter had been answered in the same tone, the business relationship would have certainly come to an end.

You can find several lapses in the first letter. The salutation itself reveals the lack of formality and consideration. It also shows the writer's rudeness. Moreover, there is no mention of the order number and the make and the model of the air conditioner. Even though business letters are need-specific and object-oriented, they don't exclude the elements of cordiality and friendliness. One has to keep the suggestions of Sir Ernest Gowers in mind while drafting business letters.

If the person you are replying to is rude, be especially courteous. If he is muddle-headed, be especially lucid. If he is pig-headed, be patient. If he is helpful, be appreciative. If he convicts you of a mistake, acknowledge it freely and with gratitude.

The requirements of effective business correspondence are clarity, courteousness, consideration, conciseness and cordiality.

Clarity

Clarity is the hallmark of any communication. In business transactions, clarity saves you from unnecessary hindrances. For a message to be clear, you have to choose words which are familiar, simple and easy to understand. Many of you, as children, might have had a fancy for using difficult words while writing letters to your friends and close relatives. But if you put yourself in the receiver's shoes, you will understand the kind of inconvenience you had caused. For no one wants to consult a dictionary or a thesaurus while reading a letter. Using unnecessary and difficult words may often tire the reader's mind. Moreover, in today's fast-changing world, no one wants to spend time figuring out the meaning of a letter written in ornamental language that camouflages the real message. Writing clear messages saves the receiver's time and helps in earning goodwill. Clarity also can be ensured by using short sentences and paragraphs. The views of famous English poet and critic, T.S. Eliot, about the economy of words is an eye-opener: "Don't use words too big for the subject. Don't say 'infinitely' when you mean 'very'; otherwise, you'll have no word left when you want to talk about something really infinite".

The following sentences will help you understand how you can make your messages more clear and precise by restructuring them.

Examples

(a) We grew hot and cold when the customers complained about the malfunctioning of the high priced ACs supplied by your firm.
Revised: We have received various complaints from our customers about ACs supplied by your firm. They are not functioning properly. We had ordered for high quality ones.

(b) Will you let me know what I should do to recover my money for the ACs bought at an exorbitant price from one of your distributors notorious for supplying the branded ones? I may kindly be returned the amount incurred on buying your product.
Revised: I shall be glad if the ACs supplied to us are either replaced or the amount refunded. Please let us know about some other reliable brands.

(c) You should know that original documents should not be sent since there is a verification procedure of all records at the time of the interview. We are returning them and anticipate that you will send the duplicate ones.
Revised: Please find enclosed your original certificates. You have to show them at the time of the interview. Send the Xerox copies only now.

Courtesy

A letter, whether personal or business, is a link between two individuals. The human element plays a dominant role while drafting a letter. This human element comes from courtesy. Courtesy shown between two individuals in terms of business leads to a smooth transaction. A business letter is supposed to follow the basic courtesies as regards salutation, tone and language. At times you may have to write unpleasant messages, such as refusing a credit or not agreeing to a customer's request. In such situations too, the tone should be positive and sincere. In India, addressing people by their designation or name (especially if someone is elder or superior to you) is considered discourteous. Addressing someone as 'sir' or 'madam' is considered more courteous than Dear Manager/President/Secretary/Chairman, etc. Here are some examples.

Examples

(a) Have you sent your order for only 25 computers?
Revised: We are glad to receive your order for 25 Pentium IV computers.

(b) We have received your letter of 27th November.
Revised: Thanks for your letter dated 27th November 2022.

(c) You cannot meet the Director. Don't you know that he is out of station?
Revised: Sir, we appreciate your interest in seeking an appointment with our Director. He is out of town for a week; you may contact him on his return.

(d) Will you send me 115 room heaters at the official rate?
Revised: I shall be grateful if you make us available 115 room heaters for our office?

(e) Your firm has been chosen as the best distributor.
Revised: We are extremely delighted to know that your firm has chosen us as the best distributor. .

(f) The Executive committee meeting is postponed.
Revised: We are extremely sorry to announce the postponement of the Executive committee meeting.

(g) You should know that PAN can alone make online tax procedures easy.
Revised: We shall appreciate it if you kindly provide us with your permanent account number. This will speed up the online tax return procedure.

Consideration

If you want to sound courteous in your business letters, you need to be considerate, which comes from being thoughtful about other people's feelings. There is nothing called 100 per cent as regards human behaviour. As we have to face various situations in life, there are bound to be some lapses on our part. But one should maintain one's cool and try to be warm. A courteous word or phrase chosen carefully always helps in winning a lost client and retaining a disgruntled or dissatisfied customer. The best way to show consideration is to keep yourself on the receiving end. Read the expressions given below and see how they can be made more considerate.

Examples

(a) The electric iron we bought at a high price has stopped functioning. Being at a great distance we have been quite crazy as what to do in order to avail the benefits of guarantee. Please send your agent to repair.

Revised: We bought a Philips electric iron last month from your showroom in Kolkata. It has developed some problems. We would appreciate it if you kindly ask the local dealer to undertake the repair.

(b) Your proposal doesn't suit our requirements. There is no other way but to reject it as we have many other better proposals to decide on.
Revised: Thank you for sending your proposal. We are going to discuss all the proposals and shall get back to you shortly.

(c) You have not paid ₹ 25,000 as per our official record. Pay the amount soon.
Revised: Our firm is going to close this year's credit register. We shall appreciate it if the outstanding dues are paid by the end of this month.

(d) Your project is being returned since there are no more funds this year. Send it next year.
Revised: According to our budget allocation for this year, it is difficult to accommodate your project. We will, however, accord top priority to the project in the next financial year.

Conciseness

You often come across letters that are too long. Don't you feel like keeping them aside, especially (if they are handwritten)? The same is true of other individuals too. People tend to get bored with lengthy letters. In an age where people are multi-tasking, they expect business messages to be clear and concise. There are ways to be concise without affecting the meaning. As the saying goes, "Brevity is the soul of wit". Avoid writing long messages using too many phrases and adjectives. You should bear in mind that conciseness can be ensured by eliminating the use of sesquipedalian words and pompous expressions. Remember, small sentences are simple and more effective. Long sentences, because of referents and dangling modifiers, tire the readers. George Orwell in his book *Politics and the English Language* has said: "Say all you have to say in the fewest possible words, or your reader will be sure to skip them; and in the plainest possible words or he will certainly misunderstand them".

Examples

(a) We had bought from your main showroom recently launched highly expensive DVD player which is malfunctioning because of some technical inadequacies.
Revised: We had bought a newly launched DVD from you. It has developed some problems.

(b) Improper verification procedure in the Quality Control Division has brought a sea of complaints from our customers and, hence, needs an investigation without any loss of time.

Revised: We have received several complaints about our quality control division. There is an urgent need to investigate.

(c) You are not the only person to have problem as regards deadlines. You should not ignore the official instructions and should submit your report in no time.

Revised: All of us have time constraints. But one has to submit the report timely as per instructions.

One of the best ways to make your message concise is to select words which are familiar and avoid wordy expressions. Unnecessary repetitions also make the expressions trite. The list given in Table 4.1 can help you change wordy and lengthy expressions into simple and concise ones.

Table 4.1 List of Concise Words in Place of Wordy Expressions

Wordy expressions	Concise
Would like to thank	Thank
Pursuant to earlier notification	As per last notice
We express our inability to	We are unable to
Enclosed herewith	Enclosed
Without any loss of time	Urgent
In no time	Timely
In the event of	If
Due to the fact that	Because
End of the week	Weekend
In the year to come	Next year
The preceding year	Last year
Would like to inform	Inform
Beg to state	State
Wish to draw your attention	Bring to notice
Output	Product
Decipher	Work out
Offer my candidature	Apply
Remuneration	Salary
Clear to the eyes	Visible

Cordiality

Success of any communication depends on cordiality and cooperation between the sender and the receiver. Business letters are no exception to this. As already discussed, business letters should be concise. But one should remember that cordiality is not to be sacrificed because of conciseness. Sometimes when we try to be direct and concise, we tend to become a bit rude. This often occurs when we are in a hurry and use negative expressions. This reveals the writer's opinion about his readers. Negative and lackadaisical attitudes towards the recipient may cost you heavily. You need to develop the habit of saying 'no' without using negative words. Read the following expressions and see how they have been changed to look more cordial.

Examples

(a) We fail to understand what ails the progress of this firm.
Revised: Please inform us of the factors that are affecting the firm's progress.

(b) As you are not a member, we can't entertain your demands.
Revised: As our members are our priority, we regret not being able to entertain your demands.

(c) You have not bothered to send any order.
Revised: We shall be delighted to receive your orders.

(d) Your report doesn't throw light on all the aspects.
Revised: We shall appreciate if you send us a detailed report.

It is advisable to use positive words in place of negatives and generate warmth by using words such as 'we' and 'our' at times.

In addition to keeping in mind the various elements, such as clarity, courtesy, cordiality, conciseness and consideration, while drafting a letter you have to ensure that your letter includes all the essential details. Completeness in a business letter refers to writing the correct address, correct tone, complete grammatical sentences and the exact nature of the order/complaint/adjustment/recommendation, inconvenience, etc. Read the letter given here and you will find how the writer has ignored the norms of a good business letter.

> Dear Sir
>
> After having ordered my consignment, I kept waiting. And you cannot imagine the joy that touched my countenance the day it was delivered to me by the angelic agent of yours. But as luck would have it, all good things must bring some catastrophes.
>
> My happiness soon vanished as I unwrapped the lustrous packet. Before my eyes was a complete disorder, which I had never surmised. Frenzy ran down my bones as I thought of the advance payment that I had sent. It appeared to me the shattering of the faith that had been built over the years. It makes me sit idle and ill at ease about how I can approach you with appeals for compensation, adjustment or reconsideration.
>
> In grief
>
> Yours ever
> Pratul Singh

If you analyse this letter on the basis of the requirements of a business letter, you will find many lapses. The letter, written by an upset customer, suffers from several weaknesses. The writer uses pedantic and flowery language, difficult words and ambiguous expressions. The letter doesn't clearly mention the order, date, make and model of the item ordered for. Moreover, the tone seems to be offending and biased. It doesn't mention the sort of adjustment which the writer seeks. The letter is lopsided and not complete. One can make this letter conform to the requirements of a standard business letter simply by revising it. The revised letter would read like the one given here.

Dear Sir

Thank you for sending us the consignment containing the Nokia cell phone as per our order dated November 25, 2022. We had sent advance payment for the same vide SP 2354, Cheque No. 8875 of UBI, dated October 25, 2022.

We regret to inform you that perhaps by mistake we have been sent Nokia 2610 in place of Nokia N72. We have always availed of your prompt and fair services. Please let us know the procedure for replacement. It will be highly appreciated if you request your nearest dealer in our town to settle the matter.

We look forward to your response.

Thank you

Yours faithfully
Pratul Singh

STRUCTURE AND FORMAT

The effectiveness of a business letter lies not only in the use of the kind of language that makes it cordial, courteous and clear, but also in the form of structure and style followed. Various organizations follow different styles for letters, but the structural elements are more or less the same. As discussed previously, a business letter is an individual's and the organization's link with the outside world. A properly structured business letter reflects one's business etiquette and the reputation of the organization one works for. It is imperative to pay heed to the various parts of the letter. Usually, a standard business letter has 10 parts:

1. Letter Head
2. Date
3. Reference
4. Inside address
5. Subject line
6. Salutation
7. Body
8. Complimentary close
9. Signature
10. Enclosure

These are now briefly discussed.

Letter head

Most business organizations use printed letter heads. As a usual practice, the complete address of the organization is printed at the top centre of the page. Some organizations put them on the right-hand side also. In case there is no such practice of printed letter head, you should write the organization's address in its specified place. The letter head shows the exact location, telephone, fax number and website information such as.

Rajat Steels Company Ltd.
1234, Steel House Complex
Mehsana Road, Mumbai.

Tel No: 022-24538
Fax: 022-245386
http://www.rscl.in

Date

Letters should mention the date on which they are written. Organizations having printed letterheads also specify the place where the date has to be mentioned. Letter heads which don't have this option give the writers the choice to write the date where they wish to. Though many people prefer writing the date on the right-hand side, care ought to be taken that it is written not more than two spaces below the letterhead. Sometimes the date is also written on the left, in accordance with the format that the letter writer follows. The name of the month should come first and then the date and year. You can also start with the date followed by the month and year, separated by a comma.

Reference

In business letters, reference facilitates the writer and also the receiver to understand the context, and to locate the matter fast. The letter usually mentions the year and the previous letter number (if any) in addition to other codes of the organization. Many organizations mention both 'Your Reference' and 'Our Reference'.

REF. NO. T/9/BPVP/2842/2022
Or
Our Reference: HMS/AD/08/252
Your Reference: ICSEic/RG/08/X/17

Inside address

This is usually the address of the person or the firm to whom you are sending the letter. Beginning with the name of the person, it should follow with the organization's address as well. You should be courteous enough to add Shri/ Shrimati, Mr./Mrs./Ms, Dr./Prof. before the names of persons, and Messrs before the name of the firm or organization. It is preferred that the full name of the person being corresponded is written. In case you don't know the name of the person, they should be addressed by designation then.

Examples

(a) Shri Banwari Lal
275, Meerchandani Road
Preetampura-947418.

(b) Prof. Pyarelal Pathak
Department of Aeronautics Engineering
Roopali Engineering College
Manmad-345412.

(c) The Regional Manager
State Bank of Bikaner & Jaipur
Rajnagar, Jaipur-333431.

(d) Messrs. Jacobsons & Co.
Sabjee Mandee, Nayanagar
Patna-800401.

(e) Ms. Malavika Dhameeja
Director (Finance)
Ratlam Steel Company
2526 Sixth Street Charleston
WV-25301.

Subject line

Here, the topic or subject of the letter is written. This prompts the organization in sending the letter to the right person or the office concerned and speeding up the work. The subject line is placed before the salutation in American style and below the salutation in British style. Usually, skip two lines between the subject line and the body. Some organizations also have the practice of writing the subject line in capitals to draw the attention of the readers immediately.

Dear Sir

Subject: Regarding the replacement of damaged cartridges.

Dear Mr. Singhal

SUBJECT: TRANSFER OF MY SAVINGS ACCOUNT.

Salutation

The words by which the writer of the letter addresses or greets the recipient are called salutations. Though depending on the relationship and the frequency of business exchanges between the two, the ideal way to greet the recipient of the business letter is to address him or her by Dear Sir/Madam. However, there is no harm in addressing the recipient by surname, such as Dear Mr. Banerjee, Dear Ms. Katyal, Dear Mrs. Smith. It is often seen that two firms, long in business association, tend to be informal in the course of time, and then the salutation changes from Dear Mr./Mrs./Ms. Arora to Dear Nikhil, My dear Nikhil or Dear Sheetal, etc. However, you should remember that nothing can be more discourteous than greeting a person by his surname without adding Mr./Mrs./Miss, such as Dear Anand/Dear Ahuja, to cite a few. You should use Dear Sirs or Dear Madams while addressing a firm, an organization, a body or an association. The following examples will help you understand further:

(a) Dear Mr. Agarwal
(b) Dear Sir/Madam
(c) Dear Sirs/Madams
(d) Dear Dr. Patel
(e) My dear Akhil
(f) Dear Ms. Sharma

Body

The body of the letter is its heart. It includes the information for which the need to write the letter arises. It is, moreover, an explanation of the problem, inconvenience or order. Since the body of the letter is the most important element, it should be drafted in the most careful and coherent manner keeping in mind the nuances of grammar and tone. The body may be divided into three paragraphs where the first serves as the opening, the second as the explanation, and the third and remaining part as the closing lines. In most cases, the closing lines may express the writer's wish, desire or repetition of the action that the writer wants his readers to take. The body of the letter usually is double-spaced after the subject line or salutation depending on the style one follows.

Complimentary close

It means you are going to end the letter. In a way, it signals a leave-taking. Beginning one line after the body, the first letter of the complimentary close is capitalized. The ideal way to close a business letter is to say, 'Yours faithfully', 'Yours sincerely', etc. However, in changing times when businesses are going global, many other expressions are also being used. Look at the following complimentary closes:

- Sincerely yours
- Truly yours
- Yours cordially
- With best regards
- Yours very truly
- Yours faithfully
- Sincerely

You should remember that a participial ending, such as 'Hoping for a positive response' or 'Looking forward to your reply' is considered obsolete now and, hence, you should refrain from using it. Instead, you should write the complete sentence according to the present-day requirement, such as:

- We hope to get a positive response
- We hope to hear soon from you
- We look forward to your response

Signature

As the word suggests, signature means to write our name as we sign it. It is always written below the complimentary close. After signing, you should write your full name since sometimes it becomes difficult to decipher an individual's name by his signature. In some cases, the designation of the signatory is also written according to the practice of many organizations.

Yours faithfully
Pratul Singh

Yours sincerely
(Pranita Goswami)
Senior Sales Manager

Sometimes, when on behalf of or for an individual some other officer signs, the latter has to write, as in the following example:

Yours faithfully
Bhagwan Das
for Arvind Prakashan, Delhi.

Enclosure

In case you attach any document or testimonials to your letter, then you should list them under this head. If there are many documents of different natures, you should number them. This enables the reader to know about the papers attached and also helps him in verifying them. The general practice is to write 'Enclosures' in an abbreviated form such as 'Encl'.

Encls: 1. Purchase receipt
2. Copy of the order
3. Photocopy of the cheque

FORMAT OF BUSINESS LETTER

All houses are made of bricks, cement, etc. But what makes each house distinct is its layout and format. Likewise, a business letter, in addition to its various requisites, such as structure and style, stands well-crafted by the way it has been formatted. Personal letters more or less have the same format. But business letters have different formats. Once you are in an organization, you should follow the format which is practised there. But at the same time, you should be acquainted with the different formats of writing business letters.

Full Block

Since business organizations consider time as a commodity, they always try to make the best use of it. Many organizations follow the 'full block format' when drafting letters since it takes less time. In a full block format, all parts of the letter start at the left-hand margin. The date, salutation, complimentary close and signature are placed on the left. There is no punctuation followed except in the body of the letter. Double space is observed between the salutation and the subject line, and between the end of the body and the complimentary close.

25 November, 2022.

The Regional Manager
State Bank of Bikaner & Jaipur
Rajnagar, Jaipur-333431

Dear Sir

Subject: Transfer of my Savings Account

I would like to bring to your notice that I have a Savings Bank Account in your bank. Recently I have been transferred from Jaipur to Chandigarh. The details of my account are as follows:

Savings Bank Account No: 534466675, Single operation

I would be highly grateful to you if you could kindly transfer the above policies as early as possible to the nearest branch of Chandigarh.

I look forward to your prompt response.

Yours truly
Vinay Kumar

Encl: 1. Pass book
2. Cheque book

Modified Block

The modified block format is slightly different from the full block format. It is a block because the address, subject line and salutation are aligned with the left- hand margin. The paragraphs in the body are blocked. What makes it a modified block is that date, complimentary close and signature are placed between the right-hand margin and the centre of the page.

To 20 November, 2022

The Dean (Academics)
Netam College of Engineering & Technology
Trivandrum.

Dear Madam

Sub: Confirmation to act as an Expert in the selection committee

Thanks for your invitation to call me as the expert member of the selection committee to recruit lecturers in the Department of Aeronautics Engineering in your college on 11.12.22 at 10:00 A.M. I express my delight to be called and give my consent to be there on the said date. I shall reach Trivandrum in the evening on December 10 by Deccan Airlines.

I shall be delighted if you send someone to the airport to receive me. I don't have much idea about the geography of your town.

With regards,

Yours faithfully
Pyarelal Pathak

27 November, 2022

Prof. Pyarelal Pathak
Department of Aeronautics Engineering
Roopali Engineering College
Manmad-345412.

Dear Prof. Pathak

Subject: Regarding your acceptance to act as an Expert.

Thanks for sending your confirmation to act as an expert. We are glad to know that you have accepted our invitation to act as an expert in the selection committee for recruiting lecturers. Your vast experience in the field of Aeronautical Engineering will help us select the suitable candidates for our institute.

We shall send one of our faculty colleagues to receive you at the airport. The car number will be intimated to you on December 9, 20022.

Thank you again,

Yours faithfully
Preetam Singh
Secretary to Dean (Academics)

Semi-block Format

This format is more or less similar to the modified block style. What makes it different is the use of paragraphs which are indented. In semi-block format, each paragraph begins with an indented line. The date and complimentary close are the same as in the modified block style. The inside address is written on the left-hand margin. Different from full block and modified block styles, this format allows punctuation in salutation and complimentary close. The facility of indented paragraphs interests the readers since it makes reading easier and causes less strain on the eyes.

Rajat Steels Company Ltd.
1234, Steel House Complex
Mehsana Road, Mumbai.

Tel No: 022-24538
Fax: 022-245386
http://www.rscl.in

July 24, 2022

Shri Brijesh Chandra Mathur

Regional Sales Manager
Akansha Steel Company
275, Malleshwari Road
Dharwad-580008

Dear Shri Mathur,

Subject: Regarding the delay in payment.

Your order for 250 steel trunks was sent to your address on June 15, 2022. We have also received information about the safe delivery of the said items. Hope the trunks have been sold by now.

We have received a good number of orders again from other distributors. We would like to know about your requirements too. That would help us send your order in the same lot. We shall also appreciate it if the payment of the previous order is also sent soon. This would facilitate our business transaction timely.

I look forward to your prompt response.

Yours cordially,

Vijendra Sharma
Sales Executive

Simplified Format

Business requirements in the present-day world give preference to ends than to means. As such, with growing times, styles of communication exchange have also undergone certain changes. The simplified format of a letter is an outcome of such a change. This format is used when the writer is not aware of the status and the gender of the receiver. The letter doesn't seem to have a salutation and complimentary close and is addressed quite often to the company and not to any specific individual. The date, complimentary close and signature are spaced on the right-hand margin. To make the letter more specific, the attention line is also written in capital letters.

PARADEEP COLLEGE OF SCIENCE, ARTS & COMMERCE
LEONARD VALLEY, LAKSMANPURI
GANGTOK

Tel No: 03592-256767
Fax: 03592-256767
http://www.pcs.in

July 28, 2022

Regional Tourist Officer
Uttaranchal Tourism
Dehradun

REGARDING EXCURSION

We shall be delighted if you kindly let us know about the tourist places in Uttaranchal and the appropriate time to visit them. Our students are thinking of going on an excursion trip. We would like to send 60 students in a batch. Each batch will have five teachers too.

The details about tourist spots, accommodation and transport facility would allow us to proceed in this regard. We would appreciate it if you also make available the total estimate to help us chalk out the plan.

Ravindra Shetty

In earlier days, many other forms of formats, namely indented and hanging indented, were in use. But with changing times, such formats have become outdated. As technology becomes a guiding force, the letter formats in practice today may become old-fashioned in the future. The introduction and excessive use of emails in business transactions will surely have an impact on business correspondence.

• EXERCISES •

1. What is the importance of writing? How is it different from speaking and reading?
2. Writing letters, especially in business organizations, has undergone a significant change. Comment.
3. State the difference between business and general purpose writing.
4. What are the various purposes of business writing? Give specific examples.

5. Why is letter writing an art? Do you find any difference in writing letters for a specific purpose?
6. In what ways has technology changed the style of letter writing?
7. What are the factors responsible for making your business letter effective?
8. Discuss the various principles of clarity and courtesy in writing business letters.
9. Mention the difference between various formats of business letters.
10. Explain clearly how does language contribute to the success of a business letter?
11. Show your agreement/ disagreement with the following statements:
    (a) An effective business letter should express the writer's thoughts clearly even without conforming to a proper structure.
    (b) When writing a business letter, we should ask about the progress of a particular organization.
    (c) Whatever format you follow, it doesn't make any difference.
    (d) One should end one's complaint letter on a note of dissent.
    (e) Write directly whatever you feel about the experience of dealing with an organization.
    (f) The practice of addressing a firm by name means you are insulting them.
    (g) While writing a business letter, never think about what the receiver feels.
    (h) There is no such rule that the elements of a letter should be followed in its formal order.
    (i) A full block style means all the paragraphs in the body should end in block letters.
    (j) A modified block style means the letter should be written in small caps with no punctuation.
12. Given below are the sentences from some business letters. Revise to make them readable:
    (a) We never expected that you would treat us in such a manner. Was it our fault to continue business relations with such a company of meagre capacity?
    (b) You have not bothered to send 20 cartridges for my order despite the advance payment sent to you via speed post.
    (c) Please explain why you are not making adjustments for the cracks developed in the DVD players bought from your firm last month.
    (d) Our responsibility ends when we have given the goods to the courier. You should know that everything is not in our hands.
    (e) I am confident that you won't find any other candidate better than me as regards my educational qualification and experience and that is the reason you should call me for an immediate interview.

(f) It is very difficult to continue business relations with you. If we get customers like you, our business will come to a halt.
(g) As a member of your constituency, it is my birthright to request for a special grant for your valued members.
(h) Pursuant to your earlier communication, we still feel pressed to satisfy your demand.
(i) As a matter of fact, things go wrong, but that does not mean you keep on dilly-dallying our proposal to adjust the advance payment proffered to you for 20 geysers, 15 of which were either inoperative or outdated.
(j) You should check your mail box before making charges on us. We don't sit idle here.
(k) The books which you have ordered are out of print. As they are 20 years old. One should read new books these days.
(l) The Nokia phone I bought from your local dealer behaves so irrationally that I regret having bought it at such a high price. Why don't you return our money by sending someone to collect it from my house?
(m) Your application can't be entertained as you don't fulfil our required qualifications. Why don't you try next year?
(n) We were really delighted to receive your humble complaint about all that we have done for you all these years. Complaints like this facilitate us to distinguish between the right and the wrong customer.
(o) With reference to your query about the location of our institute, you are advised to see our website. The website contains all the information.
(p) It is not under our control to issue a credit facility to a new customer. We have often been cheated by such people.
(q) As a valued customer, you should know that we have full faith in our quality control division. We are not responsible for the damages that occurred during transportation.
(r) We are glad to offer you the post of Chief Account Officer on the basis of the interview held on November 25, 2021. As you will have to take the responsibility of your office in a short time, we expect you not to refuse our offer.
(s) Please send the quotation for Lenovo computers to our officers who can't work without them.
(t) I am pained to inform you that the Chevrolet Spark car bought from your showroom has not fulfilled the claims made regarding mileage and fuel consumption.

5

Types of Business Letters

The art of art, the glory of expression and the sunshine of the light of letters is simplicity.

—WALT WHITMAN

Business letters, more or less, are guided by the element of formality. The level of formality differs with situations in accordance with the nature of work or objective to be realized. As mentioned in Chapter 4, politeness is the hallmark of most business letters. It is the purpose that necessitates the level of formality and informality of the tone in a business letter. Now you will learn about the types of business letters and also the difference between the tone and the tenor of these letters.

Business letters can be divided into the following categories:

1. Letters of inquiry
2. Letters for ordering goods
3. Credit letter
4. Letters of acknowledgement
5. Sales letter
6. Claim or complaint letter
7. Adjustment letter
8. Collection letter

LETTERS OF INQUIRY AND ORDERING GOODS

In business organizations, you often have to inquire of things and send an order for goods you want for your own use or for the use of the customers.

It is difficult to order goods every now and then. Hence, it is advisable to ask for quotations and then place the orders after making a proper analysis of the details. These days many people order their goods by telephone or by mail. But in order to keep a record of all the sales and purchase, the majority of organizations prefer a written order. You have to be quite careful while drafting a letter for ordering goods. One has to use direct language and give the exact details about the goods ordered lest it should invite any complain.

The letter of inquiry and order, like other business correspondences, too has a beginning, middle or the body followed by a closing. The beginning should, without any ostentation, be straight and direct, mentioning clearly the purpose of the letter, say inquiry or order. The body of the letter should include specific details, such as make, model, number, price, and quantity of goods or items. In addition to a polite closing, the letter of order should also refer to the mode of payment and of transport. The following letters will give the readers an idea of how letters of inquiry and ordering goods should be drafted.

Sample Letter of Inquiry-I

MALVIYA COLLEGE OF SCIENCE & ARTS
MALVIYA NAGAR, VARANASI
www.mcsa.net.in

Tel No: 0542-245556
Fax: 0542-2455567

October 25, 2022

Mr. M. Kartikeyan
Marketing Manager
Multilingual Matters

Dear Sir

We have been using the books of your publishing house for the last six years. Our students find your books reader friendly. Please send us the revised catalogue for the year 2023.

In the coming academic session, we are going to introduce some new courses, viz. Applied Linguistics, Creative Writing, and Translation Studies. Kindly send us the catalogue of the latest titles too. This will help us in ordering copies for our library.

We will appreciate it if you request your distributor or agent in India to respond to us before November 30.

We look forward to your prompt response.

Yours truly

Bishwajeet Niyogi

Assistant Librarian

Sample Letter of Inquiry (Response)-II

MULTILINGUAL MATTERS
Frankfurt Lodge, Clevedon Hall
Victoria Road, England BS 217HH
www.multilingualmatters.com

November 4, 2022

Dear Sir

Thanks for your letter dated October 25, 2022.

We are glad to know your interest in our books. Please find our catalogue for 2022. This covers a selection of our available titles. Some of the titles which are going to be released soon are given below:

1. Language Strategies for Bilingual Families—Suzanne Barron Hauwert
2. Second Language Lexical Process—Ed. Zsolt Lenggyel
3. Creative Writing Studies—Ed. Harper and Jeri Kroll
4. Vocabulary Learning Strategies and Foreign Language Learning—Visnja Pavicie Takak.

We are booking advance orders for these titles. Hope these may be of your interest too. All orders received online carry 20% discount.

We look forward to receiving your order.

Yours faithfully

Madhav Kartikeyan
Marketing Manager

Encl: 2022 Catalogue of Multilingual Matters

CREDIT LETTERS

The words 'credit' and 'collection' are integral parts of business transactions. Business houses buy things on credit and pay according to their privilege. Even big business organizations opt for credit transaction. Thus, a sound business relationship evolves when the two parties understand the advantages of this facility, and don't consider it as a matter of right. To ensure proper business transaction, the dealing between the two parties has to be fair while degree of formality in terms of payment has to be ensured as well.

There is, however, a lot of risk involved in giving credit to a firm, retailer, distributor or even seller. The maintenance of certain formalities finds its importance in giving credit. You have to ascertain the paying capacity of the borrower and also keep into consideration his assets in case he fails to pay. Many organizations also verify the credence of the guarantors as well. It is often reported that either many firms fail to pay credit on time or sometimes some are declared insolvent.

Once in business you often come across letters drafted for accepting the credit or denying credit requests. While drafting a credit request, the writer has to follow certain guidelines. An effective credit letter should clearly mention the type of credit, the items involved when giving a credit and the time by which the credit is to be paid. The person desiring credit should make his request strong by giving the details of his company in addition to providing adequate references.

Sample Letter Asking for Credit

Computer Unique Solutions
415 University Campus
Jodhpur
www.cus.india.in

Tel No. 0291-297678
Fax No. 0291-2976782

December 11, 2022

Mr. Ramse Singha
Chairman, Nirmaan Computers
117, Mahatma Gandhi Road
Jalianwala Marg, Gurgaon, India

Dear Mr Ram

Our firm, Computer Unique Solutions, is interested in opening an account with your establishment. We carry an extensive line of computer hardware and software services in most of the towns of this region. We have received good feedback about our services for the last five years from many reputed institutions.

Kindly provide us with a current catalogue, price list, information regarding your billing procedures and a credit application.

We look forward to receiving this material in the near future.

Sincerely

(Nikita Bhandari)

PA to Managing Director

Sample Letter of Response to a Credit Letter

Nirmaan Computers
117, Mahatma Gandhi Road
Jalianwala Marg, Gurgaon, India

Tel No. 95124-267564
Fax No. 95124-267564

December 20, 2022
Managing Director
Computer Unique Solutions
415 University Campus
Jodhpur

Dear Sir

We are in receipt of your order dated 11.12.2022/UN/COM as detailed in the attached purchase order form. We confirm acceptance of the said order, subject only to the following exceptions:

1. As part of our policy, we require the bank account of financial head of the company.
2. Twenty per cent of the amount credited has to be deposited while opening a credit account with our establishment.
3. In case the agreement is forfeited, the party has to pay an additional 5% as late payment.
4. We expect a minimum of two years' balance sheet of the company we enter into a credit transaction.

On exceptions noted, we shall assume you agree to the same unless objection is received within ten days of receipt of this notice. I hope you would appreciate the transparency in terms of business transactions.

Thank you for your patronage.

Yours sincerely

(Ramse Singha)

While most of the time credit is granted, the chances of refusing credit also can't be eliminated. The letter written in order to grant credit uses direct language, but tact has to be used when refusing one. The letter of acceptance uses a positive tone and is easier than the letter refusing credit. As business organizations consider maintaining relations despite refusing credit at times, the selection of words has to be made quite carefully. If you explain things clearly and honestly, people at the receiving end also understand the difficulty. You have already read the various methods that can be adopted during the time of drafting messages of refusal. Remember, refusing credit doesn't imply losing the client or the customer. Formalities, such as thanking the writer and encouraging him to apply for credit in the future are imperative.

Sample Letter Refusing Credit

JUNEJA TEXTILES
DARI BAZAR, LUDHIANA
www.jtl.org.in

Tel No. 0161-234231
Fax No. 0161-234321

October 18, 2022

Mr. Balvant Singh
Purchase Officer
D.R. Institute of Management Studies
Darbhanga

Dear Sir

We are delighted to see your interest in our newly introduced Sweat shirts '*Warmer*'. We have also received your order for 500 orange coloured sweat shirts with the monogram of your institution. This really is a big order, and we would have been delighted to satisfy your order on a credit basis.

Your credit references and your sound market reputation qualify you for a credit transaction. But because of limited resources and excessive demands, we are sorry for not being able to accept your order. We usually accept orders three months in advance.

We shall be in a position to accept orders for the next year in March. If that suits you, please fill in our order form mentioning the sizes and neck style. We offer a discount of 5% on all advance orders including 20% advance payment for our goods.

We look forward to hear from you soon.

Yours sincerely

(Abhinav Mundra)
Sales Chief

Sales Letter

In the present-day world, writing an effective sales letter is a challenging task. In today's rats' race, goods are being produced and launched every day in the market. For the customers, it is becoming difficult to decide which products to buy and which brands to rely on. It has become common for firms or companies to advertise their products through different media, such as radio, TV, cinema, newspaper, banner and campaign. But these prove very costly, especially for the new business entrants. Moreover, the messages delivered through these media are ephemeral. Furthermore, rural and remote areas cannot be targeted through these media. Reaching people through post is still the most feasible way as it costs less and affects more. People rely more on written words and pay adequate attention to their contents.

Sales letter can prove to be the most effective link between the buyer and the seller. Though the most challenging of all business correspondences, a sales letter makes the reader curious about the product and raises his expectation level. Since this may be the first and only information about the product in many cases, the reader forms his expectation on every written word of the sales letter. The urban customers have various sources of information to verify and compare the item/product launched. But those in the rural areas, who comprise a major chunk of the buyers, give more importance to the printed words. As a result, the sales letter which remains the only proof and assurance for these people should be composed in such a way that there stands little chance of doubt. This makes the writing of a sales letter more challenging.

The main objective of the sales letter, as the name suggests, is to sell. As it is targeted at individual customers, the language used in it is usually persuasive. In the fast-changing and competitive business world, you can't persuade a customer unless you have convinced him. Since the customer, at times, becomes a goodwill messenger of a product also, care is to be taken that his expectation is met.

Writing a sales letter requires some élan, as the writer should see from the perspective of a customer. Sales letter, like other business letters, follow a beginning, middle and closing. However, while drafting a sales letter, you have to use tact to attract, interest, create desire and persuade the customer to act. A sales letter is similar to advertisement and, hence, it too employs the AIDA technique. The AIDA technique when expanded stands for:

- **A**—Attention
- **I**—Interest
- **D**—Desire
- **A**—Action

1. Attention: The opening lines of a sales letter should be captivating enough to grab the attention of the readers. It should have such catchy phrases, statements, sentences, and quotations so as to arouse in the readers the desire to read the entire letter. There may be different ways to attract the attention of the readers. The sentences should be short and simultaneously stimulating.

Making an unusual but striking statement

(a) You know English. But do you speak fluently?
(b) If you feel you are distanced by time and space, read the following.
(c) See what you get when the performance envelope is pushed. (Think note books.)

Questions

(a) Do you want never to retire?
(b) Why do you think owning a car is a dream?
(c) Do you feel disturbed if your child gets obese?
(d) Are you having trouble formatting your documents in a professional manner?

Offers

(a) Buy all eight dictionaries and get 30% off! For exciting offers, visit www.fluencybooks.com.
(b) One GB memory free on every purchase.

Facts

(a) Our course makes you confident, without a teacher and without any classroom coaching.
(b) Big on space, Big on mileage, and Big on savings.
(c) History is not written in books. We create history on blackboards.

Appeals

(a) Give us some space in your house; we will give you more space in the town.
(b) Switch to Tata Indicom and experience the difference.
(c) Get your money anywhere, anytime.

2. Interest: Since the opening lines of the sales letter are to attract the readers, the next thing is to create interest in them. Interest can be created by describing clearly the product or the services you are promoting. You have to explain the benefits or special features of your service. In addition, you can make the letter more specific by making appeals, such as:

(a) They are packed with features that help shorten your business day—like an available 15.4" wide screen display, good for up to 25% more viewable area. But new think pad R 61 note books are also designed to stretch your budget.
(b) The new and updated design comes with exciting features, such as dual-fuel engine, extra-power steering, and pollution control emission. In fact, sprint 900 has an enticing new youthful and sporty look with built- in free MP player.

3. Desire: Once the readers are interested in the product, they will fancy buying it. And this can be strengthened by persuading them to take action. If you point out the benefits to the customer, try your best to motivate them by giving examples. In many cases, providing the readers with brochure or gift coupons will work wonders. Examples are as follows:

(a) Think pad R 61 notebooks are a product of Lenovo, a global company incorporating the former IBM PC division. From the world's best engineers comes the world's best engineered PCs.
(b) Sprint 900 has been manufactured by the world's top engineers who pride on the quality of its engine as compared with the other cars in the market.

4. Action: The purpose of a sales letter finally culminates when it propels the readers to take action. Once you have been able to attract the readers and created in them the desire to buy the product, you should raise in the customer the inclination to visit the nearest shop to take action. You can recapitulate the points stated earlier and persuade them to act. This can be done by providing the readers with a time limit or granting a special concession. Sometimes, supplying the special category form or offer coupons also does the trick. For example:

(a) On the spot admission for board toppers. Rush with your biodata along with filled in proforma.
(b) The camp is being launched for the first time in your city. First 200 people to be registered at 20% less fees.

(c) The offer closes on 10th November 2022.
(d) Online orders sent before this weekend entitled for free subscription of our journal.
(e) To give us a chance to serve you, call us at our tollfree numbers.

Thus, a good sales letter grabs the attention of the readers in the opening paragraph. The next task of the sales letter is to build interest and create a yearning for the product. The writer explains and emphasizes the benefits of the product. As the sales letter progresses towards the closing lines, the readers are motivated to the extent that they are induced to take action. While the closing lines seem to be a recapitulation but they act like a miracle. The end of the letter prepares the readers to buy the product under the impression that the said item would make their life more comfortable. Given here are some sample sales letters.

Sample Sales Letter-I

Sansui Cosmetics
Taparia Marg, Juhu Colony
JAIPUR, (Raj.)
12 July, 2022

Ms Hima Tapekar
256/72, Dogri Colony
Serpentine Street
Noida

Dear Hima

Don't you feel that gradually your skin is not only ageing but also crying? When you get out in the sun, doesn't it howl even louder as it hurts more in the scorching heat? Don't you also hear it saying that it is feeling thirsty? Isn't it lately all the eyes have started ignoring you? I think it is time for you to know the reason for this unpleasant situation.

As our body needs 7–8 glasses of water every day, your skin too requires proper nourishment. Winter Glory has brought out the moisturizer with the fragrance of natural flowers, which makes you feel young again. It helps you regain your youthful vibrancy and also the glow. The fragrance makes you feel as fresh as dew drops. Realize the difference in the attitude of others just in 7 days of its use.

Winter glory is available in three different sizes. The small 2 ml bottle is easy to carry in your bag. The family pack of 1 litre is very economical while the regular pack is just right to be kept on your dressing table. Before your skin dies of thirst, get hold of a pack of Winter Glory and let everyone hold their breath to ask "Who is SHE?"

Yours sincerely

Maneesh Kumar
Sales Manager

Sample Sales Letter-II

Guinnea Motors Inc.
Kapilvastu Marg
Govindpuri, Mumbai-400002
www.guinnea.inc.in

Tel No: 022: 786433
Fax: 022: 786433

October 5, 2022

Mr. Tejash Verma
Executive Engineer
Delhi Metros
New Delhi

Dear Sir

Are you thinking of owning your dream car at an affordable price, then translate your dreams with us? We get your car financed at easy instalments much beyond your imagination with three cheers: Big on space, big on mileage and big on savings.

Our company Guinea Motors Inc. is soon going to launch the new model of Sprint 600 as Sprint 900. The new and updated design comes with exciting features like dual-fuel engine, power steering, pollution control emission. In fact, Sprint 900 has an enticing new youthful and sporty look with built in free MP Player. Sprint 900 has been manufactured by world's top engineers who pride on the quality of its engine as compared with the other cars in the market. The car can accommodate eight people comfortably at a time and also has adequate boot space. The additional features that make you buy our car are free insurance facility and seven years EMI. Free maintenance for three years is ensured at our service stations.

As you are an old client of ours, we would like to extend a gift voucher with attractive gifts on this festive occasion of Diwali. We are happy to offer you fresh models of the car at a cost that is 5 per cent less than our market price on first come, first serve basis.

I hope that you would make a wise choice and buy the new Sprint 900 with its advantageous offer. All you need to do is to give us a call on our toll free number 09775747988.

Thank you

Yours faithfully
Md. Yasin
Chief Sales Manager

In addition to making your sales letter conform to AIDA technique, you must develop the 'you' attitude and use persuasive language. One needs to be careful while making compelling appeals. Remember trying to make people agree by using negative expressions may tire the readers. The relationship between the buyer and the seller is often delicate and needs to be tended affectionately. One should avoid the use of the following expressions:

- You will regret it if you miss this opportunity.
- There can never be such heavy discounts.
- Such opportunities don't come often.

Instead, the ensuing expressions can ensure a positive close of the letter:

- Please avail this opportunity.
- We offer heavy discounts.
- The present scheme is valid till 25th November.

Sample Sales Letter-III

Document Makers
2398 Red Street
Salem, MA 34588

March 10, 2022

Thomas R. Smith
Drivers Co.
3489 Greene Ave.,
Olympia, WA 98502

Dear Mr. Smith

Are you having trouble getting your important documents formatted correctly? If you are like most business owners, then you are having trouble finding the time to economically produce good-looking documents. This is why it is important to have a specialist take care of your most important documents. A specialist's helps you save both time and provides quality to your document.

At Documents Makers, we have the skills and experience to come in and help you make the best possible impression. May we stop by and offer you a FREE estimate of how much it would cost to get your documents looking great? We are proud to say that the documents formatted by our specialists are error free and qualitative.

We offer home services also to our customers having computer and printer facility. The charges in such cases are also reasonable. Since our scheme is limited to only 50 new customers this season, we thought you could be the one to seek our services. If so, give us a call at and set up and appointment with one of our friendly operators.

Sincerely,

(Richard Brown)
President

CLAIM OR COMPLAINT LETTERS

Business organizations are usually careful while responding to orders or sending goods. But there is always the probability of things going wrong as the element of human error and natural forces can't be ignored. Since people in an organization work as a team, it becomes a collective responsibility and propriety to own the faults when complaints pour in. The tendency should not be to blame the charge to someone else. Moreover, people keep changing organizations but organizations can't stop listening to complaints.

Organizations often receive complaints of delayed and dilapidated consignments and at times of wrong goods sent. Such situations arise not because of any ill intention but because of the huge orders or heavy demands to be supplied at a short notice. But as a customer you have the right to bring complaints to the notice of the organizations. Reliable and reputed organizations take due care of their customers' grievances. No organization would like to lose its valued customers. In fact, most of these organizations have a complaint cell where people are deputed to entertain customers' complaints.

It is a fact that you often get infuriated when you receive the wrong packet or a delayed consignment. You may at times write an angry letter. But remember that this will not serve your purpose. Instead, if you draft a polite complaint letter, there is always the hope that you will be heard and be sent the right consignment.

A claim or complaint letter, much like a sales letter, should be able to persuade but the approach will be different. As your main aim is to get the worth of what you have paid for, you need to act tactfully. Make a clear explanation of the problem mentioning the make, model, type, price, and all other specifications of the product. The language used should be polite and the tone formal. Avoid alleging the organization with charges, such as irresponsible behaviour and unfair practices. You should impress on the fact that your claim is genuine. Your aim should be to motivate the reader to take immediate action by referring to the integrity and reputation of the organization or company. Moreover, you can also state the sort of compensation or adjustment you expect.

Sample Complaint Letter-I

Alpha Electronics
Daryaganj, New Delhi

Your reference: MA/TO/312
Our reference: TC/TI/422

December 5, 2022

Sales Manager
HCL, Mumbai

Dear Sir

Subject: Regarding defects in computers

Please refer to our Order no. 256/10/Com for 25 Lenovo computers. We received the consignment from your company on November 1, 2021. But on arrival of the consignment, it was found that at least 12 out of the 25 computers have low speed and hardware problems. The order was placed following the immediate demand of computers from the secretariat and the chief minister's office.

We have been a regular supplier of electronic equipment and enjoy a good reputation for our good quality products with lifetime guarantee. We had been motivated by our peers who have been satisfied with the quality of computers bought from your company for the last 15 years. Before dispatching the consignment, our computer engineers tested the computers and found complaints in at least 12 of them. It was found that while 7 of them had ineffective keyboards, at least 5 of them had software problems. The computers took too much time to boot and the systems often got hanged. The keys became inoperative and the computers needed to be restart. This would result in loss of important data that might be unsaved at that moment. In an age of heavy workload, it is speed and efficiency that matters. We wish to keep both your and our reputation in order. I request you to immediately supply us 25 new computers having Pentium IV processor supported by other hardware components.

I am returning the consignment in due hope of your cooperation in this regard. In view of our past reliable business relationship, I request you to send the new computers at the earliest.

I look forward to your early response.

Yours faithfully

Manjari Mishra
Purchase Manager.

Encl: Letter of Order & Copy of receipt.

Sample Complaint Letter-II

November 15, 2022

The Chairman
Guinnea Motors Inc.
Kapilavastu Marg
Govindpuri, Mumbai

Dear Sir

Sub: Complaint regarding malfunctioning of Sprint 900

This is to bring to your notice that last week we bought 10 models of the newly launched Sprint 900 from your company. Unfortunately, almost all the models except two that we have sold have come up with complaints of malfunctioning.

The duel fuel engine of the car is not compatible with diesel and other such fuels as expected and assured by you. Moreover, the power steering system usually loses control and fails to respond to a full 360 degree turn. In addition to this, the built-in speaker added as a facility, too, does not work properly in many models. The service engineers in our workshop also could not identify the reasons behind these.

Consequently, we are returning 8 of these models for servicing to your company. As we have promised our customers to deliver the cars before Christmas, should we request you to send 8 new SPRINT 900 soon? Since you are an old associate, we hope that you won't let us down again.

We hope to hear from you soon.

Sincerely

(David Brown)
Chief Managing Director

Encl: Letter of Order and Copy of receipt.

ADJUSTMENT LETTER

Most of the business houses, as mentioned previously, have a complaint cell. The task of this cell is to listen to customers' grievances and act on their genuine complaints. The letter written for this purpose is termed as *adjustment letter*. Through an adjustment letter, an angry or a disgruntled customer is brought back in order to continue the goodwill between the customer and the organization.

While writing an adjustment letter, the writer has to be more polite than the receiver of the letter. A proper verification of the complaint is to be made. The writer should appreciate the reader for bringing the inconvenience to the notice of the organization. He should not only admit the mistake but also apologize on behalf of the company. In case the claim of the complainant is genuine, offer the adjustment. But if the customer's adjustment can't be met, the reasons for this may be stated reasonably.

Adjustment letter too has an opening, a body and a close. Such a letter should begin with appreciating the reader. It should then follow with the good news of adjustment that has been made. Further, the reasons for the inconvenience should be explained. The letter should end on a note of cordiality and consideration which can bridge the rift.

Since people or the company writing complaint letters and seeking adjustments are often in an enraged state of mind, the language used in response should be very mellow. There are occasions when you have to offer adjustments for the sake of business though reluctantly. In such cases, the use of some key phrases may help you tide over the situation. For example,

(a) I was very disappointed to read your letter of ... dealing with ...
(b) We extend an apology for the inconvenience caused to you.

(c) As someone who values your business, I have already ...

(d) Also, we will deduct another X per cent of the bill for the misunderstanding. Thank you for your patience.

Read the following sample adjustment letters:

Sample Adjustment Letter-I

Hindustan Computers Limited
Andheri Road, Mumbai
www.hclmum.net.in

Our reference: TC/TI/422
Your reference: MA/TO/312

December 25, 2022

Dear Sir

Sub: Regarding your complaint against the supply of 25 computers

Thank you for bringing to our notice the malfunctioning of some of our computers. We are sending brand new 25 computers with the specification as desired by you. The consignment will be delivered to you in a couple of days.

Since the order was placed just two days before the dispatch, we could not check for the quality of all the computers. It was rather very kind of you to have brought this fact to our notice. We would, henceforth, pay special attention to the hardware components as well.

We extend an apology for the inconvenience caused to you. We admit our lapse and hope such a thing will not be repeated in future. The quality control division has been strictly ordered to test the computers within 24 hours before dispatching the computers.

I admire your consideration for our reputation and hope to serve you in the future as well. Please keep writing to us about our services. We shall accept the payment only after you approve of the computers' quality.

Yours faithfully
Rohit Sharma

Sample Adjustment Letter-II

Document Makers
2398 Red Street
Salem, Mumbai 34588

August 27, 2022

Thomas M. Smith
403, Star Enclave
Mumbai-16
India

Dear Mr. Smith

I was very disappointed to read your letter of August 27, 2022 dealing with the issue of incorrectly produced publicity leaflets. As someone who values your business, I have already begun to find a solution to resolve this problem.

The problem occurred because of the excessive workload during this festival season. The heavy demand of production and satisfying everyone's order in time has led to this lapse. We are extremely sorry for this and hope that such a thing is not repeated in future.

My top photographer will call you to arrange an appointment at your earliest possible convenience to re-take photos in full colour. Also, as a policy we will deduct a small amount from the bill for the misunderstanding.

Thank you for your patience.

Sincerely

Reeta Menon
President

COLLECTION LETTERS

Business organizations believe that one of the most difficult tasks is to collect money from the customers they give credit to. While it is customary to grant credit, it is also mandatory to collect the amount in time. Timely clearance of credit leads to better and healthy business transactions and relations. The process of collecting money given on credit entails various apprehensions. While it is advisable to decide the nature and procedure of collection during the time of granting credit, one has to send intimations on a regular basis.

Though there are different ways of reminding customers to pay on time, yet the importance of sending written requests in the form of letters cannot be ignored. The collection letter has to be drafted cleverly keeping into consideration the inability of the customers to pay the amount in time because of some genuine reasons. The letters sent initially should be cordial and persuasive. The main objective is to get the money without losing the customers, so the language used should be indirect. But once the reminders don't bring any response, the language can be a little harsh using tough words and choosing sentences which are formal in nature. One can make the customers aware of their responsibilities in a subtle manner. Sometimes, negative words may be used too. While sending the last reminder, a symbolic hint of the next action can also be given.

The first letter should be sent as any other business letter. It should look like a formal information. Language used should be cordial and the tone pleasant.

Sample Collection Letter-I

Dear Sir

Please find the credit statement of 250 DVD players against your order no. 21/Gaya/207, dated 24 August, 2022.

We are in the process of collecting previous balances. This will help us invite orders for the next financial year. Please send the payment in the form of demand draft.

Yours truly
Vikas Sharma

When the first letter fails to bring any response, the second one should act as a reminder. The impression should be as if the receiver has forgotten to pay.

Sample Collection Letter-II

Dear Sir

We want to bring to your notice a balance of ₹ 75,000 against the credit purchase of 25 DVD players. A letter in this regard had been sent to you vide SP 252, dated 25 September 2021. We have not heard anything from you.

We hope that you will send the payment soon. Our business relationship in the past has been quite cordial. Please send the payment before we send our agent at your end.

Yours sincerely
Vikas Sharma

The third letter should show that the earlier intimations have been ignored or neglected. With reference to the past transaction, the aim should be to make the creditor pay the amount. The writer makes use of words, such as 'quite unfortunate' which points towards the creditor's carelessness.

Sample Collection Letter-III

Dear Shri Kumar

It seems quite unfortunate that there has been no response to two of our communications reminding you of a balance of ₹ 75,000 for the purchase of 25 DVDs.

We consider you as one of our bonafide customers. Your credit record in past has always been praiseworthy.

Please write to us soon and transfer the sum of ₹ 75,000 to the company's account number 756888432 of SBI, New Delhi branch.

Yours faithfully
Vikas Sharma

When all other communications fail to make the creditor pay the amount, a few negative and harsh words too can be used. There is no harm to indicate towards a legal action. Read the following letter which uses words, such as regret, suffer and also negatives ones such as *fail, terribly, no option left*. The salutation also changes and the tone becomes quite severe.

Sample Collection Letter-IV

Dear Mr. Rajesh Kumar

We regret to inform you that your firm has failed to pay the sum of ₹ 75,000 (Seventy five thousand) for the purchase of 25 DVD players. Three letters sent to your end did not bring any response. In the meantime, we have suffered terrible loss.

If the outstanding amount is not paid by 27th February, 2023, we will have no option left than to consult our legal advisor.

Yours faithfully
Vikas Sharma

Thus, we find that though business letters may be of different types but ample care and consideration is to be taken while drafting them. Since business letters are meant for people we are not acquainted personally with most of the time, care must be taken that the language used is polite. The role of letters is to bridge gap and clear misunderstandings, not to widen them. Though written by an individual, business letters reflect the identity and work culture of an organization. The better the business letters, the better the organization. The age we are living in is that of advertisement and nothing can be as good as to advertise one's company through the communications sent from it to the outside world.

• EXERCISES •

1. Describe the types of business letters. How are they different from each other?
2. Explain the important ingredients of a successful sales letter.
3. Why is it said to be more emphatic towards the close of a sales letter?
4. What do you understand by credit references?
5. How can you refuse a credit customer without losing them?
6. The purpose of every sales letter, as of every advertisement, is to convert a reader into a customer. Elucidate the statement in the light of AIDA technique.
7. Shivalik Company is going to launch three soft drinks in the market. As the sales manager of the company, you have been asked to draft a sales letter to promote these products. Write the sales letter.

8. Your firm had ordered for 50 water coolers for Alpha Electrical and Appliances Ltd., Preetampur. Out of 50, 15 water coolers were found in a damaged condition on their arrival. As the Manager of your firm, write a complaint letter to the supplier seeking replacement or adjustments.
9. Ramsung India Limited, Mumbai invites applications for Computer Analysts in their new branch offices throughout the country. The candidate should not be more than 22 years and should have two years' experience in addition to the required qualification in their area. Those with postgraduate degree in the relevant field will be preferred. Salary shall be commensurate with performance in the interview.
10. Read the following complaint letter and point out its weaknesses. Revise the letter and make it an effective complaint letter.

> Dear Mr. Browning
>
> We had ordered for 100 cartons of chocolates to distribute it amongst our students on the eve of children's day. But whatever you have supplied is outdated and seems quite pungent. We also found the majority of these cartons torn and broken. One should be responsible while taking orders. Why don't you send another consignment?
>
> Tell us what to do with those cartons? Can you make some adjustments so that we can sell it to local vendors at a low price? Should you ensure such things won't repeat we shall continue to do business with you?
>
> Sincerely,

11. Write a letter refusing credit to Bageria & Bros. who are seeking credit for 30 ceiling fans for supplying to a newly opened private bank.
12. **Shivram and Sons** are in search of a firm who could establish a computer lab with 20 booths in their school. As the manager of the school, write a letter to Lingua Com seeking the sort and quality of software and their price list available with them.

6

Techniques of Writing

Words—so innocent and powerless as they are, as standing in a dictionary, how potent for good and evil they become in the hands of one who knows how to combine them.

—NATHANIEL HAWTHORNE

In the tough competitive world of today, much of your success depends on your writing ability as a professional. In Chapters 4 and 5 we read that letters represent our existence even in our absence. The responsibilities of a professional being manifold today often necessitate him to be abreast of various patterns of writing in addition to handling business letters. Success at workplace does commensurate with effective techniques of various forms of writing. Organizations depend not only on business letters alone but also on other important documents, such as reports, proposals, instructions, notices, handbooks and manuals. Most of these documents play a key role in evaluating the progress, performance and market conditions of an organization. Moreover, these documents help the organization get an indication of the market demands and customer needs, besides understanding the internal atmosphere and employee's attitudes in order to mend and amend further planning.

It is an undeniable fact that preparation of documents requires some essential writing skills. As the texts are aimed at producing desired results, their framing has to be much in consonance with the readers' education and familiarity with the subject matter. Experience says that since most of the subjects are new and novel to the readers, they on most occasions tend to develop lack of interest in the content. Hence, it becomes the writer's responsibility to bring animation and spontaneity in the document. His writing may put life into the document, making it readable and understandable.

An effective writing technique alone can make a dull piece interesting. As information of most technical documents is often factual, the writer has to make it presentable without disrupting the flow. This is possible when he follows a technique which suits his readers. The ability to express one's ideas in the most convincing and logical way with consideration for readers can be studied under style of writing.

W. Somerset Maugham in his book *Summing Up* said "A good style should show no signs of effort. What is written should seem a happy accident". What Maugham meant is not that an effective writing comes even without efforts. But that an effective writing should look natural. Any writing that seems natural makes an easy reading for the readers. An effective style is one that ensures directness, simplicity and coherence. In much the same way as readers, we too, expect any piece of information to be straightforward and plain. A document which is garbled having complicated sentence structures that are very long often tire the reader's mind. As a rule, most of the business documents, even informative ones, have to adopt a persuasive style. But care has to be taken that they conform to the principles of unity, coherence and logic. Moreover, an effective style comprises selection of words and phrases, proper sentence arrangement, proper paragraph organization that help in smooth flow of ideas. At the same time, lengthy sentences, abstruse expressions, wordiness, jargons, clichés, redundant expressions, etc. appear as stumbling blocks in the effort of making a sense of a thought or an idea.

SELECTION OF WORDS AND PHRASES

The content of any text, whether technical or non-technical, achieves its effectiveness with the selection of words. Since the basic principle behind every message or written text is to ensure understanding; it can be facilitated with the use of simple and plain words. A good thought too can get choked if the words selected to describe it are not familiar and natural. Difficult words often impede the readers' flow of thoughts and compel them to consult a dictionary every now and then. As a reader, you too would not like to refer to a dictionary when reading an interesting write-up. When writing, people often use words according to their background, many a time failing to anticipate the background of their readers. Nathaniel Hawthorne, the famous 19th century American novelist states a very significant truth about the use of words. He rightly says, "Words—so innocent and powerless as they are, as standing in a dictionary, how potent for good and evil they become in the hands of one who knows how to combine them." See Figure 6.1.

As a writer you should show your concern for your readers by using familiar words in place of difficult ones. Difficult words are those which are not used commonly. Table 6.1 helps you find how words which you consider quite easy may be difficult for many readers.

Figure 6.1 Elements kept into consideration while writing a report.

Table 6.1 List of Difficult Words and their Corresponding Familiar Ones

Difficult words	Familiar words
Apogee	Orbit
Camaraderie	Friendship
Commute	Change
Configure	Arrange
Decipher	Find out
Dismember	Cut
Emanate	Issue
Entail	Cause
Euphoria	Happiness
Exiguous	Less
Expedite	Promote
Facsimile	Similar
Flair	Ability
Gamut	Complete range
Furore	Uproar
Germane	Relevant
Impasse	Obstacle
Influx	Rush
Initiate	Start
Kindred	Same
Obtuse	Dull
Propagate	Spread
Smorgasbord	Variety
Spur	Drive
Stigma	Shame
Synergy	Cooperation
Trenchant	Keen
Validitate	Prove
Veracity	Truth

We use words to convey our ideas. But at times to attract others' attention or to show our learning, we are unable to resist the temptation to use those words that are rarely used in day-to-day communication. As a careful writer, you must understand that familiar words facilitate the readers in understanding than the unfamiliar ones. Another factor that you should be aware of while using words is the context. Words are not confined to one meaning alone. The same word may have a different meaning if used in a different context. When a writer frames a message, he often supplies his intended meaning into it. But as people's background and experience vary, they tend to unearth their own meaning out of the word. The boss of a garment store advised his new salesman saying that "Customers these days pay as per their fashion without paying least attention to the shopkeeper's inconvenience. You have to be careful while dealing with them".

The salesman, a novice engaged a single customer for more than two hours showing him all sorts of designs available in the shop. Actually, what the manager was hinting at was the manner of payment and not the design of the dresses.

Moreover, the use of the same word as verbs, nouns and adjectives also brings about a change in the meaning. The examples given here are a case in point.

1. As summer *advanced*, people felt miserable.
2. You need to develop *advanced* communication skills.
3. He drew an *advance* against his remuneration.
4. She withdrew her steps as she saw a snake *advancing* towards her.

A careful writer uses words in such a manner as to bring home his point effectively. The felicity with which he uses words shows his concern for his readers. Difficult though to have a firm grasp over language, it can be done if practised regularly. You should remember that long-winded words not only look pompous, but also obscure ideas.

Examples

(a) The present report endeavours to propagate the government's policy matters regarding validation of masses and their configuration of bivouac in flood-affected areas.
Revised: The present report attempts to inform people about the government's policy to provide shelter to flood-affected masses.

(b) The need of the hour is to abandon all past hostilities and carve a niche of camaraderie to initiate peace process and ensure bilateral harmony.
Revised: We need to forget past enmity and start peace process in order to establish friendship between the two nations.

(c) The Planning Department utilized newspaper ads to disseminate further information concerning the General Plan update.
Revised: The Planning Department used newspaper ads to issue more information about the General Plan update.

(d) The property is located contiguous to the airport and comprises 30 acres.
Revised: The 30-acre property is located next to the airport.

ABSTRACT AND SPECIFIC WORDS

When writing documents, you should strive for plainness. Moreover, care ought to be taken that you do not use abstract words as they represent a state and fail to clarify the exactness of the situation. This may leave the readers in a quandary and compel them to interpret the implication of the words in their own way. The writer's purpose is to inform or to contribute to the existing knowledge of the readers and may receive a setback if the document is not written effectively. Generalized opinion tends to generate indifference among the readers. On the contrary, words which are specific evoke favourable responses from the readers. Specific words enable readers to understand and analyse the information in the same spirit that it has been written in. For example, when your boss comments that the report submitted yesterday was good, you are sceptic and uncertain. The statement does not mention which report or the degree of goodness. The use of good here denotes a generalized view. The boss could have been more specific by saying: *Mr. Khurana's report on new labour policy is excellent.* Table 6.2 gives a list of abstract words along with the specific ones having the same meaning.

Table 6.2 List of Abstract Words and their Equivalent Concrete Meaning

Abstract words	Specific words
Majority	Seventy per cent
Group	Twenty people
Near future	Next month
Later	In the afternoon at 3
Slump	Twenty per cent down
Engineering	Electrical engineering
Recently	Last week
Executive	Manager
Staff	Accountants
Meagre	Ten per cent
Substantial	Eighty per cent
A significant loss	Fifty seven per cent loss
The leading company	The first among 20 teams

Example

(a) A 'value orientation aspect' concerns, not the meaning of the expected state of affairs to the actor in terms of his gratification-deprivation balance, but the contents of the selective standards themselves.

Revised: The concept of value orientations in this sense is thus the logical device for formulating one central aspect of the articulation of cultural tradition into the action system.

(b) The room was big enough for the audience.
Revised: The room could accommodate hundred people.

MODIFIERS

Unskilled writers often make their writing cumbersome by loading sentences with too many modifiers. Such expressions sound pleasing in oral communication, such as speeches or lectures, but only burden the written messages. One should always remember that technical descriptions are not literary writings and, hence, one should control the excessive use of adjectives and adverbs. People often resort to such usage when they belabour to make their points clear but muddle the meaning instead. Moreover, the use of phrasal verbs should also be controlled to encourage effectiveness.

Examples

(a) A good report should be free from prejudices, preconceived notions and biases.
Revised: A good report should be bias-free.

(b) The construction department deserves all praises and credits for making such new and novel structures.
Revised: The construction department deserves praise for such new structures.

(c) The new proposal caught the manager's assumption fire.
Revised: The new proposal ignited the manager.

(d) Newly recruited junior managers failed to make out what the CEO said in his inaugural speech.
Revised: Newly recruited junior managers couldn't understand CEO's inaugural speech.

(e) Some files seem to be tampered with.
Revised: Some files seem corrupt.

You will also notice that sometimes modifiers are placed so remotely that they keep the readers dangling from one word or phrase to another in order to establish the connection. These are called *dangling modifiers* which obfuscate the meaning of the sentences. The way to tackle this dangle is to place the modifier close to the words they describe. The ignorance of the dangling modifiers may result in a cacophony.

(f) While interviewing the candidates, an urgent call came.
Revised: An urgent call came for the director while he was interviewing the candidates.

(g) Discussing the pros and cons, the report came across many hurdles.
Revised: The committee members came across many hurdles while they were discussing the report.

NOUNS AND VERBS

The use of nouns and noun clusters also affects the effectiveness of a sentence. Sometimes when you come across three or more nouns joined in a sequence, you feel taxed. It may tire the readers as well. You can overcome excessive use of nouns by breaking up the noun cluster. Another remedy to check this situation is to bring verbs in the beginning of a sentence. You will feel that abundance of nouns camouflages the verbs and makes the sentence complicated.

(a) Handling daily workers remuneration everyday caused inconvenience to accountants.
Revised: The accountants felt inconvenient to handle the wages of daily workers everyday.

(b) Online admission procedures in technical institutes have lessened the tortuous task of manual labour.
Revised: The procedure of online admissions in technical institutes has eased manual labour.

(c) Voters' identification procedure with the help of photo identity cards aims at elimination of fraudulent practices.
Revised: To identify voters on the basis of photo identity cards will check false procedures.

(d) Many people find withdrawing money at ATM counters free from the hassles of standing in a long queue.
Revised: Withdrawing money from ATM is not only easy but also hassle free.

(e) Plans are being prepared for identification and implementation of different livelihood enhancement activities using this renewable energy source which shall also increase the economic viability of these stations.
Revised: We are planning to identify and implement different livelihood activities and increase economic viability by using renewable source of energy.

JARGONS

While drafting technical documents, careful writers often try to minimize the use of esoteric words. But there are occasions when they fail to check themselves from the use of such words that are quite common in their trade and profession. Such technical words are known as *jargons*. Though it contributes new words to the language, it is inconvenient to the people of other professions who are totally ignorant of the meaning of such words. People of all trades and discipline have their own jargons which can be understood better when exchanged between individuals of the same profession. While one finds the use of 'debit' and 'credit' very popular among bankers, 'sensex' and 'slump' among shareholders, 'cognizance', 'summons' and 'writ' among lawyers, etc. these words may pose problems for those belonging to different professions. Likewise, the use of words, such as refraction, inventory, pedagogy, chauvinism, cerebellum, freeware, synthesis, hybridization, vegetative, etc. may ensure a smooth exchange of information among people for whom these words have clear meaning. But such words may confuse people working in other professions and can leave them high and dry as they find these usages as crippling the essence of the text. As considerate writers, you must save yourself from being a victim of jargons by discarding their use to the maximum. Table 6.3 gives some jargons with their meanings.

Table 6.3 Jargons and their Meaning

Jargons	**Meaning**
Canonical	Accepted
Generic	General
Bugbear	A thing that causes obsessive anxiety
Browser	An instrument to help in finding out something
Spam	Something unapproved
Blog	Online diary
Vegetative State	Alive but inactive
Roger	Term used to indicate reception of a message
Monitor	A device with a screen on which words or pictures can be shown
Kerogen	Solid bituminous material that yields petroleum when heated
Bugout	A hasty retreat
Goldbrick	Someone who habitually avoids work details
Golden Boys	A commander's favourite subordinates or subordinate unit

Jargons get used unconsciously in our writings. We have to be extra-conscious while using them.

Examples

(a) The spectrum of infection with the human immunodeficiency virus continues to evolve with the availability of new scientific information.
Revised: We are learning more each day about the range of infections in people with HIV.

(b) The recent announcement of a hike in DA has galvanized the aspirations of many employees.
Revised: Many employees feel encouraged by the announcement of increased DA.

(c) Grading activity required by new development would have associated short-term erosion impacts.
Revised: Grading would cause soil to erode.

CLICHÉ

Remember your school days when the use of a phrase caught your fancy and you would use it the moment you got a chance to write something. But in course of time you used that phrase so much that it lost its efficacy. This is an example of cliché. Any word becomes a cliché when it is overused and loses its significance in time. Good to listen though, it often conveys problems of meaning and makes our expression wordy. It mars the effectiveness and, hence, should be eliminated especially in technical writing. Though despite the care we take in eliminating the use of clichés, they often appear uninvited in our writings. You can always think of a substitute for a cliché and make your writing more precise and to the point.

Examples

(a) The new policy on education has thrown cold waters on students.
Revised: The new education policy has disappointed students.

(b) The manager smelt the rat in the deal and put it on the backburner.
Revised: The manager doubted the deal and put it aside.

You can guard yourself from the use of such clichés and substitute them by some other words. Table 6.4 gives a list of clichés with their meanings.

Table 6.4 List of Clichés and their Meaning

Cliché	Meaning
Acid test	A severe or crucial test
From the core of one's heart	Deeply
Head over heels	Heavily
Pay through one's nose	Pay unreasonable price
A long felt want	Urgent need
Bolt from blue	Unexpected
Breathless silence	Lull
By leaps and bounds	Rapidly
Conspicuous by absence	Remarkable absence
Goes without saying	Self-evident
Meets the eye	Look directly
Last but not the least	Finally
Nip in the bud	Stop something in the beginning
Axe to grind	Particular reason to argue
Motley crowd	Varied
An uphill battle	Challenge
Call the shots	Begin
Irony of fate	Unusual

(*Contd.*)

Cliché	Meaning
Iron hand of law	Firm
Spare no efforts	Whole hearted
Take by storm	Violently
Fall through the cracks	Fail to fit
Call it a day	Stop doing something
Writing on the wall	Prediction
Bottom line	Realistic
Below the belt	Unfair
Rough and tumble	Noisy and violent

FOREIGN WORDS AND PHRASES

The use of foreign words and phrases may also leave the readers exasperated. As the readers of a report, proposal, memo or technical description expect to understand the substance of the topic under discussion, they feel threatened when swamped with alien expressions. They somehow find such use unnecessary stumbling blocks in the flow of their reading and understanding. Moreover, the readers of your report are not necessarily people with exquisite vocabulary and exposure to foreign words; hence, you have to be quite careful while using such words and phrases.

Table 6.5 Foreign Words, Phrases and their Meaning

Foreign words and phrases	Meaning
Ab initio	From the beginning
Alcohol	Wine
Argus eyed	Vigilant
Avant garde	Pioneer
Bete noire	A person or thing you dislike
Blasé	Indifferent because of familiarity
De facto	In fact
Juggernaut	Excessively powerful
Laissez-faire	Non-interference
Obiter dictum	Incidental remark
Per diem	Daily
Modus operandi	Mode of operation
Prima facie	At first sight
Status quo ante	State of affairs existing before
Sine-qua-non	Essential, indispensable
Sine die	For an indefinite period
Sub-poena	Call by the court
Cortege	Retinue, funeral procession
Vide supra	See above
Vide ante	See before
Vide infra	See below
Exempli gratia	For example
Et cetera	Something similar
Et al	And others

Apart from foreign words and phrases, the use of abbreviations also should be checked. However, there are many abbreviations which are used these days as words and the use of their full forms may confuse people. You will find that people are familiar with many of the abbreviations, which pose no threat to their understanding. In many cases, the full forms of these abbreviations often irritate the readers. In case you use the abbreviations, it is better to ascertain their familiarity amongst the readers for whom you are using them.

Table 6.6 List of Common Abbreviation and their Full Forms

Abbreviation	Full form
CPU	Central Processing Unit
BBC	British Broadcasting Corporation
ATM	Automatic Teller Machine
AIR	All India Radio
DVD	Digital Versatile Disc
PMO	Prime Minister's Office
RAM	Random Access Memory
EC	Executive Council
PC	Personal Computer
ECG	Electro Cardiogram
DTP	Desktop Publishing
CNG	Compressed Natural Gas
PPT	Power Point Transparency
VAT	Value Added Tax
OHP	Over Head Projector
LPG	Liquefied Petroleum Gas
LCD	Laser Compact Disc
DNA	Deoxyribonucleic Acid
DA	Dearness Allowance
VCD	Versatile Compact Disc
PF	Provident Fund
MODEM	Modulator Demodulator
LASER	Light Amplification by Stimulated Emission of Radiation
HTTP	Hypertext Transfer Protocol

But the use of many abbreviations, may, at times, create confusion since people will interpret them according to their own understanding and preferences. Many of the abbreviations are still waiting to gain popularity among the masses. Following is a list of such abbreviations:

1. ABM (Anti-ballistic Missile)
2. ATR (Action Taken Report)
3. CAD (Computer Aided Design)
4. CVR (Cockpit Voice Recorder)
5. VDU (Visual Display Unit)
6. OCR (Optical Character Reader)

7. LSD (Lysergic Acid Di-ethyleamide)
8. TCP (Transmission Control Protocol)
9. TWA (Trans-World Airlines)
10. OTS (Officers' Training School)
11. FLAG (Fibre Optic Link Around the Globe)
12. SEZ (Special Economic Zone)
13. TAX (Trunk Automatic Exchange)
14. WLL (Wireless in Local Loop)
15. CTS Carpal Tunnel Syndrome

In many institutes, students often coin abbreviations which get very popular amongst themselves yet are little known outside the campus.

A few of them are as follows:

1. Rep-wri (Report Writing)
2. Techie (Technician)
3. Audie (Auditorium)
4. Langski (Language Skills)
5. Intro (Introduction)
6. Enthu (Enthusiasm)
7. Poly (Polythene)
8. Insti (Institute)
9. Bio (Biology)
10. Hi-tech (High technology)
11. Prof (Professor)
12. Prop (Proprietor)

Though these words may sound better to your ears but they still require authentication to be used in writing, especially any official document. Informal as they are, they are used according to convenience in casual communication. As careful professionals you should preclude the use of such abbreviations. In addition, you should also restrict the use of terms popularized by text message language, such as *becoz* for because, *b/w* for between, *4* implying for, *B* which stands for be, *C* for see, *K* for 2000, *m* for am, *n* for an, *r* for are, *t* for tea, *u* for you, *ur* for your, *urs* for yours, *asap* for as soon as possible, *affly* for affectionately, b^4 for before, *atb* for all the best, *nite* for night, *rite* for right or write, *mite* for might, *tmrw* for tomorrow, *Xitement* for excitement, *xellent* for excellent, CU for see you, etc. These new inventions may appear convenient to be used in sending messages through cell phones or electronic mails, yet their use in framing technical or any other document will make the user look ridiculous. Many of us even while deciphering the content of the text messages have often been found dwelling over such usage to understand the proper context. Those who use such acronyms in a way perhaps rely much on the intuitive powers of the receivers. And that often makes the context chaotic.

REDUNDANCY

Sometimes even careful writers while trying to make their writings more plain and free from ambiguous terms, make use of words which express the same idea. If you evaluate carefully, the sentence would read well even without the use of these words and there will be no loss of essential information. The words which are rather needless repetitions are called *redundant expressions*. They are also known as *pleonasms* and *tautologies*. They are appendages and don't add to the meaning of the sentence, rather make it clumsy. Read the following sentences to understand how they could mean well without the use of such unnecessary words:

Examples

(a) Most of the players assembled together to share their actual experiences of foreign tour.
Revised: Most of the players gathered to share their experiences of foreign tour.

(b) A detailed perusal of the report recommends an advance planning to avoid any casualty.
Revised: A study of the report recommends a plan to avoid injury.

Some of the common redundant expressions used in sentences are as follow:

- Actual experience
- Advance warning
- All alone
- Assemble together
- Basic fundamentals
- Detailed perusal
- Due to the fact that
- End result
- Final conclusion
- Final result
- Firm decision
- Free choice
- Integral part
- Last and final
- Narrow down
- Past history
- Personal opinion
- Refer back
- Repeat again
- Report back
- Retreat backwards
- True fact
- Unexpected surprise

CIRCUMLOCUTION

A technical writing is well received if it is free from circumlocution which means use of too many words where few would do. If any writing continues to use recondite figure of speech and doesn't specify the real implication, it will fail to create the desired impact. Any idea or statement expressed at once seems vivid and fresh than the one lost in the shrubbery of words.

Examples

(a) He that is down needs fear no fall.
Revised: A humble person doesn't fear any fall.

(b) Today's workplace offers a cushion of comforts consisting of cordial siblings striving for a process that does not divide them.
Revised: Today's workplace offers a friendly environment for people to work in harmony.

(c) The officials in the tax department undergo a harrowing time in the month of February and March when they work with lidless eyes to warrant rest and relief to the countrymen.
Revised: Tax department officials spend sleepless nights during February and March to provide relief to the countrymen.

SENTENCE STRUCTURE

You have already read that an effective writing style comprises simplicity, clarity and coherence. These qualities can be achieved not only by avoiding wordiness and eliminating the needless repetitions, but also by using clear and simple sentences. A sentence that is long and full of clauses is prone to be less effective than the one which is short and simple. Furthermore, the voice of the sentence also matters more. A sentence which uses active voice is more forceful and concise. A sentence in active voice not only appears vigorous, but also is easier for the readers to understand the implication. In a sentence which uses active voice, the relationship between the agent and the activity appears more natural. On the other hand, a sentence in passive voice denotes a sort of artificiality, indirectness and disassociation. But sentences in passive construction become significant when the need to state unpleasant information arises. Most of the time, negative messages and unfavourable responses to complaint letters are written in passive voice. As a passive construction focuses more on an activity, it lessens the intensity of the activity that is often disapproving. Moreover, it also lends a variety to the writing and makes it more interesting.

Examples

(a) Much of your research can be done from a computer that is connected to the Internet, which has enabled access to an increasing amount of information.

Revised: You can do most of your research from a computer with Internet connection enabling access to adequate information.

(b) The need to keep layouts simple, clean and attractive has been stressed by most desktop publishing and design guides.
Revised: Most desktop publishing and design guides stress the need to keep layouts simple, clean and attractive.

(c) Your proposal was discussed in the company's annual meeting and was found appropriate.
Revised: We discussed your proposal in the annual meeting and found it appropriate.

(d) We have not found your proposal cost-effective.
Revised: Your proposal has not been found cost-effective.

We have already discussed in Chapter 4 how while conveying a negative message, such as rejecting a claim or a proposal, passive constructions lend a helping hand to tide over a critical situation. Here are a few examples:

1. Your consignment was delivered to us in a damaged condition.
2. Clearance of past dues authorizes you for all credit applications in future.
3. All goods are checked before being packed and despatched.
4. The committee has not approved your credit request.

In all these sentences, we find that the writer doesn't express his involvement and, hence, offers neutrality. This also becomes an exigency at times to maintain business requirements.

Thus, while determining sentence structure, you should ensure that there should be a variety of both long and short sentences. So is the case with voice. Short sentences alone can make your messages lean. Even sentences in active voice can, at times, appear lopsided. On certain occasions, you as a writer will have to adopt the approach that will suit the purpose best. However, long sentences which are often of complex structure having phrases and clauses, can't be ignored of their importance since they reflect objectivity and detachment at times. But they often tire the readers. They can be placed in the midst of a report and not in the beginning of any subject under discussion. You can find how the examples given here can be made more compelling simply by bringing a little change in the sentence structure.

Examples

(a) Many of us understand that Nanotechnology, a very important branch of applied science, which deals with matters on atomic and molecular scale, has a considerable role to play in improvement of energy efficiency and we can reduce air pollution considerably with the help of nanotechnology.
Revised: Nanotechnology plays a vital role in improving energy efficiency. It can also help us reduce air pollution.

(b) The problem of order, and, thus, of the nature of *integration* of stable systems of interaction, that is, of social structure, thus focuses on the integration of the motivation of the actors with the normative culture standards which integrates the action system, in our context interpersonally.

Revised: People often share standards and expect one another to stick to them. Insofar as they do, their society may be orderly.

(c) That aspect of the theory of social systems which is concerned with the phenomena of the institutionalization of patterns of value orientation in the social system, with the conditions of that institutionalization; and of changes in the patterns, with conditions of conformity with and deviance from a set of such patterns, and with motivational processes insofar as they are involved in all of these is the moot point of our discussion.

Revised: Sociologists like me would like to study what people want and cherish. We would also like to find out why there is a variety of such values and why they change. When we do find a more or less unitary set of values, we would like to find out why some people do and others don't conform to them.

We find that the revised sentences not only look simple, but also are easier to comprehend. Care ought to be taken that the verb comes just after the subject, and readers don't face the ordeal of finding the verb which often is lost in the deluge of words. In case the sentence is too long, you can split it into two to make it more comprehensible.

In addition to sentence structure and tone, you should also save yourself from using gender sensitive words. As today's workplace consists of both the genders, one should use those words that are free from such biases. Words such as chairman, policeman, salesman should get restricted usage and words such as chairperson, police personnel, executive, sales representative should be used instead. Similarly, we should ensure the use of pronouns 'their' and 'them' in place of 'his', 'her', 'him', etc. Moreover, the pronoun referents should be used in such a manner that they don't create any ambiguity. The ignorance of the referent's position often may mislead the readers and may also obscure the meaning.

Examples

(a) Most of the CEOs are acquainted with the work culture of their subordinates and they find it easier to discover their lapses.

Revised: In every organization, the CEO knows his subordinates so well that he can easily point out their mistakes or lapses.

Effectiveness of a style can also be ensured by the proper arrangement of words in a sentence. The readers often attribute more attention to the words placed either in the beginning or towards the end of the sentence. There is a general tendency to ignore the words or phrases in the middle. Hence, you should try to transcribe your main idea in the beginning or at the end of the report.

Examples

(a) Some features of desktop publishing and top-end word processors as well as desktop publishing programs have powerful control over the appearance of printed words even in today's low cost word processors.
Revised: Today even a low-cost word processor can deliver features of desktop publishing programmes with a powerful control over the appearance of printed words.

(b) Simplicity, clarity and consistency, above all are the qualities that ensure effectiveness of style in writing.
Revised: Effectiveness of style depends on the qualities, namely simplicity, clarity and consistency.

The placement of words in their proper places ensures effectiveness and also helps in emphasizing a point. Hence, an attempt should be made to put the main idea first and prove its relative importance with the help of various structural devices. In case the need arises, variety can be exhibited by changing the order without obstructing the flow.

PARAGRAPH LENGTH AND STRUCTURE

While drafting a technical document, many of you would be wondering how long or short the paragraphs should be. This problem arises because of the deluge of information which you gathered so painstakingly and want to convey to your readers. But one has to show concern for the readers also. They would appreciate to get complete information but in a concise manner. Here all you require is the organization of ideas or statements in the most intelligible manner. Careful writers make serious efforts to write paragraphs that are arranged sequentially and they work assiduously to develop the ideas in the subtlest and coherent way.

Texts such as reports, proposals or descriptions are generally long and descriptive in nature. Most of these documents describe, analyse or propose a course of action and as such require so many paragraphs. As the readers are to be kept involved till they reach the conclusion or recommendation, the writer has to chalk out strategies as how to begin and develop the paragraph. We all agree that while a letter, memo or notice may comprise short paragraphs, the same can't be applied to a report, proposal or even technical description. The paragraphs in these technical documents are bound to be long.

A good paragraph is a group of sentences that are woven intimately. The guiding principles that can make a paragraph effective are unity, coherence and logic. Unity in a paragraph means that all the sentences in it are related to a singular whole. Moreover, it can be exemplified by the care that the sentences, which follow the main idea, don't appear as irrelevant or alien. The first sentence of the paragraph, which in most of the cases, is a topic sentence and acts like the family head to which the remaining sentences that are subsidiary.

The second step in making a paragraph effective is coherence. It helps in developing the main idea and ensuring a smooth flow of thoughts from one sentence to another. Coherence also helps in listing ideas from one level to another. If the topic sentence begins the paragraph on the foundations of unity, the other sentences bind themselves with the pillars of cohesion. You will often notice that transitional words and connectives, such as but, as, whosoever, after, later, first, secondly, thus, hence, also, further, etc. are used to bring coherence among the sentences. They not only connect the sentences and units of thoughts, but also help in making the transition from one idea to another smooth and continuous. These transitional words help in expanding and at times also in indicating the nature of information that is to follow.

Unity and coherence in a paragraph help in establishing logic. In the true sense it is logic that exhibits the thought processes and patterns of the writer, and convinces the readers with the conclusions or findings reached at. Moreover, logic also reflects the consistency of tone which the writer of the paragraph maintains. It is most important to make the readers subscribe to the view stated or the proposition projected in order to make one's stand viable, failing which the logic of the paragraph will be considered suffering from some fallacy or the other.

The paragraph that is logically arranged conforms to parallelism. You can employ parallel structure in your sentences to make them appear sequential. Moreover, this strategy helps you avoid verbosity. When you use parallel structure in a sentence, the main word ensures that the other words of the sentence are also relatively of the same family. If the first part of a sentence ends with a noun, the corresponding part also should be a noun and not a verb. Likewise, verbs, phrase or clause should also correspond accordingly as in the following:

Examples

(a) The job of a teacher is to inspire and not the instruction.
Revised: The job of a teacher is to inspire and not to instruct.

(b) This book aims at clarity, consistency and making it plain.
Revised: This book aims at clarity, consistency and plainness.

READABILITY

Despite the care you take in making your writing effective, its success can't be guaranteed lest it conforms to readability. The sentences may be long or short, the words used may be known or alien and the tone didactic or persuasive. But it is after all readability that adds quality to your writing. A book becomes readable only when it interests the readers. You often come across a book which has a beautiful cover and an attractive layout, yet it is not readable. You gloss over a few pages and soon feel like putting it aside. Readability is not confined to any single word rather it comprises all other qualities discussed above. One may select simple words and a straightforward approach yet may not ensure readability. The word 'readability' includes not only the purpose of the writer rather it also entails how the purpose has been fulfilled. You would agree that a text on purely technical subject can't be divorced of the terms which most often disapprove substitute. Yet an effective writer will belabour to bring readability by the structural arrangement and the flow that could sustain the readers' interest. One has to be simple without using non-standard words. Dexterity is required in the selection of the sentence structure. Consideration can be shown by the spelling, and tone used, while sympathy for the readers can be proved by selecting paragraphs that involve them instead of diverting their interest.

A good number of writers have suggested various ways to measure the readability of a document. Though such formats may not work in all situations, yet the very knowledge of understanding the difficulty level of text will facilitate in making your writing easy. Most of these writers agree that the number of difficult words and sentence lengths become the deciding factors for evaluation of the formulae given by Robert Gunning, considered authentic in this respect. Gunning employed fog index to measure the difficulty level and emphasized that any text or document having this index may be considered readable. In order to get fog index, first you have to find out the average sentence length. This can be done by dividing the number of words by the number of sentences. Average sentence length then should be added to the percentage of difficult words. The result derived should be multiplied by 0.4. Gunning believed that if the fog index of any text is below 12, then it is considered readable.

Fog Index = (Average Sentence Length + Percentage of difficult words) × 0.4

But the readability formula seems to have undergone a change. In the changing times people's background and their experiences have transformed drastically and, as a result, the difficulty level has also improved. The difficulty level of a particular group or section may be a facility for professionals of another group. The jargons of past have become more acceptable and easier to understand by readers even with poor and ordinary educational background. A writer's task, as of today is to maintain a balance between the dilemma of readers' varied life experiences and writers' endeavours to comply with the principles of effective writing. You should remember the suggestions of William Safire, an American journalist turned author, who won the 1978 Pulitzer Prize. The famous columnist in *Great Rules of Writing* says:

"Do not put statements in the negative form. And don't start sentences with a conjunction. If you re-read your work, you will find on re-reading that a great deal of repetition can be avoided by re-reading and editing. Never use a long word when a diminutive one will do. Unqualified superlatives are the worst of all. De-accession euphemisms. If any word is improper at the end of a sentence, a linking verb is. Avoid trendy locutions that sound flaky. Last, but not least, avoid clichés like the plague".

Safire's advice should act as the *summum bonum* of a good style and as prosperous professional you will pay the utmost attention to it while drafting your technical documents.

An effective writing should conform to the basics of clarity, conciseness and consistency. You can achieve this by selecting appropriate words that expresses the desired content. While selecting words, preference should be given to familiar than difficult, specific than abstract words. Moreover, your writing should be free from the use of jargons, clichés and redundancies. Care should be taken that noun clusters and dangling modifiers are used to the minimum. Moreover, adequate care is also required while constructing sentences and framing paragraphs. Long sentences and cumbersome paragraphs impair reading. As a careful writer, you should also ensure that your sentences have a positive tone depending on the intention of the subject under consideration. Notwithstanding the fact that your writing may appear quite simple, never give in to the use of long winded words, sentences and paragraphs in order to sound consummate.

• EXERCISES •

1. Rewrite the following sentences to make them simple, clear and effective.

(a) Put the pressure on the button so that the machine can be started.

(b) There is a necessity to satisfy customers for a business success to occur.

(c) All of them, with the exception of Ramesh and Prakash, will play tomorrow.

(d) The board of directors worked for the organization of the meeting and a new president was elected.

(e) She parked her car in front of the store, gets out, banging into the shop door and fell on the pavement.

(f) There is a need on our part to clarify the basic fundamentals.

(g) There is a cutter that cuts the plate from the coil, rolling it perfectly and completes the process.

(h) Special features of this machine are more durability, reduce noise and are efficient.

(i) The companies made a comparison of the two equipment and the deal was finalized.

(j) The concentration by the Training Division of its time, money, and other resources into a new program is not advisable from our point of view.

(k) Your survey on the annual export from our stock-house at the Kandla Harbor is no raison de' etre for increasing the staff here.

(l) Our lack of knowledge about local conditions precluded determination of committee action effectiveness in fund allocation to those areas in greatest need of assistance.

(m) Exert outward on the small, circular button that is red in colour.

(n) Enclosed herewith please find two copies containing identical information that must be completed, stamped and then returned in an envelop to Mendhak Enterprises.

(o) Personnel will take cognizance of high priority requisition of fifty pursuit planes. Immediate implementation of this policy directive is imperative.

(p) Subject to the above considerations, and while the larger classes at present in existence must necessarily lead to an undesirable formalization of contact between staff and students, the fixation of a quota is not at present desirable.

(q) They had met to discuss threadbare the strategies for combating poor sales newly introduced product but the sales manager was conspicuous by his absence.

(r) It is the privilege and birthright of every professional to handle reports without any cloud of despair.

(s) If doubt is entertained regarding an optimal solution to the problem of acquiring new equipment, may I suggest that we refer the problem to a newly appointed team.

(t) The members of the council were completely unanimous in their decision regarding the introduction of the new scale.

(u) As the temperature plummets the aspirants of education who have left their home and taken aegis of hostel bulwark should be cautious enough to keep their bodies warm. It is often found that the fairer sex flaunts in diaphanous diamante and complains of chilblains and edema. The doctor had no choice but suggests for detumescence by giving an incision.

2. Rewrite the following passages to make them simple, clear and effective.

(a) Exodus of employees from organizations these days is not a preternatural phenomenon. In spite of the fact that change in itself is natural the shifting roles and responsibilities in impending times often mark an unprecedented and abrupt suddenness. Those employers who are stuck with the paradigm that employees changing their jobs forsake their loyalties to the previous organizations often commit a faux pas and jump to a hasty conclusion ignoring the human part involved in the entire episode. As humans what one needs to explore is that there could be certain personal reasons grounded in such plights too. Who can however deny the true fact that an employee changing a company is a long-term investment for his erstwhile organization? Nothing that an employee carries with himself is as ponderous as his past experience. He as a matter of fact not only disseminates his past memory but also adumbrates what one should expedite as a present benediction. All organizational relations being entrenched in human decorum the oracles involved in maintaining the smooth running should arrange for a grand and magniloquent adieu to coronate the leaving employee not with a frown but with an optimistic approach that they always continue to exist as the goodwill ambassadors of their previous organizations. It is thus that a leaving employee's feedback can provide a fair feedback for all those living and joining the organizational structure with the best of their intentions.

(b) Organizations thrive today on work culture, which varies from one company to another and one individual to another. The people at plum posts in organizations often make high expectations about their underlings. The crux of the matter is that before enforcing any rule these panjandrums should ensure that they substantiate it themselves first. These seraphs most of the time like all other advisers labour under the impression that it is easy to instruct leisurely. On the other hand, the true fact is that in a world full of choices and working with equally qualified people it is generally assumed that each individual brings his own work culture with himself. Organizations world over have testified that excellence for an individual comes from within, his work habits and his sense of responsibility to the organization. The success of majoritarian organizations is a clear testimony to this fact. Employees in organizations don't resemble the small children who too can't be ruled by Damocles' sword. The maxims 'spare the rod and spoil the child' in their cases too have, barring a few cases become obsolete. A successful CEO of an organization influences his employees by his individual endeavour and excellence and without any instructions drives home the message that his colleagues follow the same examples. Those among you ready to shoulder the responsibility of young managers, exempli gratia, should ennoble and enrich from this short and roundabout message and hence should not ignore it as platitudinarian. Thus, the exegesis of this lecture stands crystal clear that the two factors responsible for organizational success is the abiding faith and cordiality between the boss and his employees that can facilitate individuals to prove work culture culminating in the overall growth of the organization he works for.

(c) A philosophic system is an integrated view of existence. As a human being, you have no choice about the fact that you need a philosophy. Your only choice is whether you define your philosophy by a conscious, rational, disciplined process of thought and scrupulously logical deliberation - or let your subconscious accumulate a junk heap of unwarranted conclusions, false generalizations, undefined contradictions, undigested slogans, unidentified wishes, doubts and fears, thrown together by chance, but integrated by your subconscious into a kind of mongrel philosophy and fused into a single, solid weight: self-doubt, like a bail and chain in the place where your mind's wings should have grown...

(d) Lead refining is a very significant and inevitable process. In this process we can easily obtain precious metals such as gold, silver, and platinum in the zinc crust of the Parkes process. We place this crust in a retort and then the next thing that we do is to distill off the zinc. We may find that the residue is an alloy, which contains gold, silver, and platinum in addition to lead. We cupell this alloy. That is we heat in an oxidizing atmosphere until the lead is oxidized, leaving an alloy of the precious metal.

(e) Motivation, the buzzword in the modern day organization, as many theorists propose is the willingness to exert high levels of efforts to reach organizational goals conditioned by the effort's ability to satisfy some individual need. Although general motivation refers to effort toward any goal, here it refers to organizational goals because our focus is on work related behaviour. The three key definitions of motivation then overboard is effort, organizational goals and needs. The malady of our times as regards motivation is that there can't be any definite definition of motivation since one definition of motivation gets de-motivated the moment there is another innovative experience waiting to motivate many and de-motivate some.

(f) The image on the retina is not permanent but in many cases it fades away after 1/20th of a second and overlaps the next succeeding image. This in a way gives the impression of frequency and continuity. There is of course no film in the eye that records the images permanently as a photo film usually does. More importantly and to the top of it all the focal length of the eye lens is changed when its attached cilial muscles change their tension. When they are after all relaxed, the lens is thin and distant objects expatiate clearly. While looking at near by objects, the muscles compress the lens so as to the brain through the optic nerves. The brain interprets these signals as the sense of light.

(g) I often wonder and feel envious of the way people with great stamp of education and licenses from top Alma Maters of the world evaluate the answer books of pupils spread in a labyrinthine web of colleges and universities. Knowing well the unalterable and true fact of life that their duty is to make the future generations in the dark, dingy classrooms no better than what they are; are yet not sure what they want to do with the treasure islands of their own nation. The majority of them appear replete with the firm rooted foundation that the modern day toddlers are far from the magical wand of wisdom and yet they never appear nervous or obsessed with the ennui of nights burning midnight oils before the grand finale of their destiny. Gone are the days when anyone noticed differences between a daytime creature and a nocturnal one. These makers of destiny belong to the Devil's party and are stuck with the proposition that how their own taught can never be so clever, so worldly wise and so full of knowledge that fainting seems to be a bliss in some other world. These messiahs can never alter their ways and award marks a far lesser than what they have always earmarked. It is like living in penury in the midst of plenty. Such orthodox believers are much above the far progressed wings of time and age.

(h) Modern life, like modern art is benevolently misleading and shrouded in mystery, which only quite a few of us are able to unravel. The doctrines dissipated by these demons of knowledge are good to listen but too bad to put into practice. They tell you all the basic fundamentals; right from your morning chores to your bedtime proscriptions and you seem buoyed up with their circumlocutory suggestions. They perforce make you parasites and put you under duress so that you want to chastise them for all their evil niceties. Their dogmas comprise daily rituals, everyday commitments, buying and selling strategies and also the golden ways to succeed or fail even at job interviews. And these knowledge mongers have solutions for every wrong and recipes for every right. They time and again repeat the little tit bits, which our forefathers often dodged or shied away from. The essence of all that they propagate is to make you a thing to be successful, an object showcased and more like a picture poised in order that nothing goes wrong. Their precaution during critical hours is to muffle a silvery silence on your lips and roar inside once you enter a professional world. Avoid speaking the truth but never forget to blow your own trumpet whether musical or unmusical. Bring ideas that sound high and mean less, create ads which few can understand yet feel delighted to be called creative for once they know what you are hitting at, they cease to be your valued customer.

(i) Men with pot bellies for whom wild life conservation insinuates as just another posting are a frequent detrimenting sight in many reserves. This needs amelioration on war footing. Seasoned wildlife biologists have realised the importance of this after years of their sweating in the field and are votaries of well equipped front line staff. The formation of a special tiger protection force has to be expedited with utmost circumspection. It should not become just another run of the mill paramilitary force. It has to be populated by younger breed driven by passion for conservation. The training invariably has to measure up the standards of NSG. I would recommend that the desire for protection should be multiplied keeping in view the insurgents' way of moulding their recruits who stick to the maxim that the sole aim in life should be out and out conservation.

7

Report Writing

Nothing succeeds like reports of success.

—SUE SANDERS

IMPORTANCE

You write reports for different purposes. You must have come across various types of reports. The teacher takes the attendance every day in the classroom, the nurse writes the report after investigation of the patient's disease is done; a journalist after witnessing the untoward activity writes a column in the newspaper, a child gets his report card which conveys his progress, etc. These are all examples of reports of different nature. As a student also you must have been bothered with more serious forms of reports that require proper investigation, thorough assimilation of data and logical ordering of information. These reports fall under the category of technical reports. Once you join an organization, you will be required to write reports of all sorts. Sometimes you have to write about the progress of a project, occasionally about the assessment of some of your employees, and at times about the implementation of a new policy or procedure.

When you work whole-heartedly on a project, you have the sole authority and right over it. No one has the right to interfere with your work. But when you make a report of your work, it passes from one desk to another. Your report communicates the results and accumulates the knowledge through the findings and conclusions. You may have received plaudits for getting your research published in journals but the preparation of good research report is not a trivial task. However good work you may have done, if the presentation is not coherent, then it mars the effectiveness of the report completely. You have to put your best efforts to communicate the information clearly and completely. Lee Iacocca, former President of Chrysler Corporation has said, "You can have brilliant ideas, but if you can't get them across, your brains will not get you anywhere".

The word 'report' comes from the Latin word *reportare* which is the combination of *re* and *portare*. It means to carry back the information to someone who was not present at the scene of the event. Like the teacher takes the attendance record to show it to the superior or nurse maintains the record in the form of prescription and test results to show it to the doctor. These reports are of great utility at the time of requirement as they are systematic, and have the information and facts without distortion. Reports are important tools of decision-making. Therefore, they should be written very objectively so that right decisions are made. Reports usually flow upwards as directed by the controlling officer or the superior. Remember, before you write a report the terms of reference are to be defined. The 'terms of reference' provide the writer the guidelines to cover certain identified topics, to investigate a particular product, say, or an event or proposal. The terms of reference dictate what kind of report you have to write. The objective and the extent of coverage are clearly delineated. No report is written without authorization, i.e. it is always asked for.

At times you feel whatever is communicated or described is a report. Can we then call every description a report? Even literary pieces, such as a play, a poem or a novel, can then be called reports. It is time we must understand the term 'report' clearly. To clarify the difference between technical report and literary work, you should know the distinction between the two. See Table 7.1.

Table 7.1 Difference between Technical Report and Literary Writing

Technical reports	Literary writings
Written on request	Written on own initiative
Audience identified	Audience not assured
Fixed structure	No fixed structure
Language: simple, precise, concise	Use of rhetorical language
Objective in approach	Subjective in approach
No aesthetic pleasure	Aesthetic pleasure derived
Matter of facts	Heightening of feelings
Written for a specific purpose	Not written for any specific purpose always

Definition

A report is a technical document which is the result of a thorough investigation, written for a specific audience in a well-defined format, in an easy-to-understand language, it interprets and analyses the data and derives conclusion and recommendations, if asked.

A report is an outcome of a problem which needs to be addressed. You never write a report because you felt like writing one. A report covers all that is needed to be covered of a problem, nothing more and nothing less. That is why it is said that a report presents the facts in an economical way. That is the economy of words.

Objective

The primary purpose of a report is to present facts in an organized, ready-to-use form so that the decision can be made based on it. It offers solution to different business problems. However, the broad objectives of the report are to:

- Update the progress of a company's plans and activities.
- Produce the results in written form which could be used for future reference.
- Guide the organization for the corrective path for action.
- Record the work done.
- Disseminate the information and new ideas.
- Avoid repetition of the work done.
- Provide platform for cross-fertilization of ideas.
- Enhance the decision-making process.
- Check the validity of the information.
- Evaluate and compare the efficiency of new machinery, product or services.
- Assess the progress of any project.
- Record findings and recommend action.

Features

1. A report is written not to impress but to express, and its importance has nothing to do with its bulk.
2. The language in which it is written is clear, straightforward, simple English. Rhetorical language has no place here.
3. The objective of the report should be borne in mind while writing one so that your analysis, conclusions and recommendation can be oriented towards the basic purpose of the report.
4. The report must present the data as objectively as possible, without any distortion. The facts presented should be audience oriented. Twisting of facts may lead to wrong decision-making.
5. The report should be highly relevant apart from being precise. Unnecessary details cloud the relevant information, and, therefore, should be avoided. Let the report be sans frills.
6. The success of the report lies in clarity and brevity. A report must be systematic and well-organized. The purpose and objective should be clearly defined, the sources of collection of data mentioned, and recommendation properly limned. The report must have proper division and subdivision. Equivocal sentences misguide the readers, and so they must be avoided completely. Above all, the language should be grammatically correct.

7. The report should be structured such that it has title page, table of contents, introduction, discussion, conclusions, recommendation, bibliography, etc. Minor changes may appear in the structure according to the requirement of the organization.
8. To make the report more effective, proper use of illustration must substantiate the discussion which includes tables, figures, graphs, photographs, charts, maps.
9. There must be unity in the text. One idea should be dealt with in a paragraph, and sentences should be properly connected using appropriate cohesive markers.
10. The report should be neatly bound and documented for further reference. The report number and letter of transmittal help a lot in locating a particular report.

TYPES OF REPORT

Reports are classified based on the degree of formality, length, frequency of appearance and design. A formal report follows the well-defined format and subscribes to the same for better communication. However, informal and short report format is flexible and can be changed according to need.

The broad categories on the basis of which report can be classified are:

- Short reports and long reports (length)
- Management reports and technical reports (purpose)
- Routine reports and special reports (frequency)
- Oral report and written reports (mode)

Short Reports

Short reports are helpful when the problem is well-defined and the scope is limited. Their length varies from five to eight pages. Since they are not elaborate, they may contain only a few elements, such as note on authorization, problems dealt with, conclusions and findings to support. It is sans section and subsection headings.

These reports are in the form of 'Letter Report' and 'Memo Report'. The letter report follows the format of business letters and the most popular these days is the complete block form. In this format, the matter is aligned to the left margin, and the matter till salutation is devoid of punctuation marks. Also the complimentary close doesn't have punctuation marks. The tone is very similar to that of letters and personal style is appreciated. The use of active voice helps the writer to be more direct and economical. Memo report is another variety, which is used to send the information within the organization. It is more informal than the letter report because of its limited circulation. Every organization prescribes their format but, in general, they have 'To', 'From', 'Subject' format. It is sans salutations and complimentary close.

A few suggestions given as follows may help you in writing effective short reports.

- Broach the report by telling the purpose of writing.
- If the memo is an answer to a query, a notification, reprimand, information that should be limpidly told to the reader by raising a point and then answering the same. If needed, follow it up.
- Write in expository style with conciseness, plainness and directness.
- Review the report written before dispatching it.
- Include the matter, which obstructs the flow of the report in the appendix.

Long Reports

Long reports are classified into two broad categories: *technical report* and *management report*. This classification is according to the audience for whom the reports are written. Technical report is written for specialized audience of researchers while management report is written for non-technical audience comprising managers or clients. It is a difficult task to write one report which can cater to both the audiences. Therefore, it is judicious to write reports specific to the audience concerned. The receivers of these reports have different background, training, and objectives.

Technical report

This kind of report includes full documentation and discussion in detail. All the sources, which were prime sources of documentation right from the inception of the report are included. The researchers need to refer to each minuscule detail, as the audience is interested to know what was done and how it was done.

The primary focus, though, is to complete the job but all the relevant materials required to replicate the study should be included. In contrast, one should discard the non-essential materials as in the labyrinth of details, the important materials get sidelined. The report should include sources of data collection, research procedures, sampling design, and data gathering instruments in addition to data analysis methods. The information, which breaks the flow of reading, should be included in the appendix.

The technical report should include the data analysis and the discussion elaborately. These should be divided into proper sections and subsections. Conclusions should follow the findings and recommendation should delineate the future course of action to those interested to pursue the same study. Abstain from the use of jargons and registers. But if they are necessary, explain the same in the footnote or glossary. Don't be stringent in giving references of other similar researches, theories and procedures. Even if the reader is familiar with some of the researches and theories, explain them again in footnotes.

Management Report

When the client is more interested in results than methodology, communication then takes place with the help of management report. Sometimes a management report is followed by a technical report. Since a management report is for non-technical audience and the readers have more interest in the finer points like the main findings, the important paragraphs should come first followed by less priority paragraphs. Just after the prefatory and introductory part, the conclusions and recommendations are presented. If the readers wish to read the findings, they may read further on. Management report should make liberal use of illustrations so that verbal part can be curtailed which will save time of the reader. Report of this form is written for an individual and therefore, can cater to the specific demand of that person.

The style of the report should make unctuous reading and lead to quick comprehension of the major findings. The tone of the report is journalistic but accurate. Underline the headlines to draw immediate attention. Sentences and paragraphs should have clarity. Liberal use of white space and margins helps in easy reading. Put one finding in one page with a graphic image to support it.

Routine Report

Routine report is written regularly in a set format. Most of the people in an organization receive reports at fixed intervals, such as daily, fortnightly, monthly or yearly. The report can be on matters related to production, labour, efficiency, sales performance or the inventory record. There is not much use of language in this type of report. The format is decided beforehand and the respondent has to put a tick mark against certain items mentioned in the pro forma. Sometimes, remarks are required to be written but should not be very long. The routine report includes progress report, inspection report, confidential report, laboratory report. Some of the routine reports may also include recommendation but not all. Routine reports written at regular interval of time are called periodic reports.

Special Report

The management depends a great deal on special report for vital decisions. Of course, this report, unlike, routine report doesn't have a standard format. This report is written on the request of the management on the spur of the moment. It is specified who has to report and to whom. Objectives, too, are clearly mentioned. This report is written when some aberrations are observed in routine matters. For example, cleaning of the complex was not found satisfactory despite hiring of four more employees for the job.

The report writer is clearly given the objectives while collecting the required data and deciding the procedures. The time limit is maintained and is vital. The report writer need not go beyond the demarcated objectives set by the management.

The writer of such report ought to be diligent, shrewd and judgmental. He should be efficient and must have a capacity to interpret the data effectively. Based on the interpretation, he should be able to suggest measures for controlling the problem. The language must be appropriate and grammatically correct.

Oral Report

When researchers present their findings orally, these presentations are called briefings. They are different from public speaking as they are meant for a small group. The presentation is mainly focused on statistics, as the audience is interested to hear the critical elements only. The presentation timing is usually for 20 minutes and rarely runs for an hour. There is also a session of questions and discussion after the end of the presentation for further clarification.

Preparation

Even when the report is bulky, it requires to be put across the audience succinctly. Remember a normal speed should be maintained while speaking, i.e. 120 to 150 words per minute. Therefore, at this rate in 20 minutes you have to communicate the information effectively. For this you require careful planning. Ask yourself questions, such as How long should you talk? If you get more than the planned time, what more will you communicate? Identify what is the purpose of the presentation? Is it to add to the knowledge of the audience? Is it to uncover obfuscating problem? Is it that you have to give the audience conclusions and recommendation for decision-making? By answering these questions, you will arrive at the objectives of the report. Then it is time to work out on the detailed outline. Your outline should contain the following elements:

- **Opening:** This is the most important part of the presentation, therefore the report should start with an attention catching statement. Devote 10% of the total time for the opening statement. It should be direct, catchy and introduce the nature of the discussion that follows. Explain the nature of the project, how it began and what do you attempt to do.
- **Findings:** These and conclusions come immediately after the opening remarks and each conclusion is strengthened by the findings.
- **Recommendations:** The third stage is to present recommendations; each recommendation may be followed by reference to the conclusion from which it is drawn. It is the onus on the presenter to invite questions from the audience.

When you are in your planning stage, you have to decide what type of audio-visual aids you are going to use since you have to coordinate your presentation with the aid. If you are planning for power point presentation, do have a backup of your slides. Do practise rigorously but along with the audio-visual aids. If you have practised well using the aids, your presentation will take place with facile ease.

In Chapter 12, we will discuss the types of presentation. Know about all the four types of presentation and decide which one you are going to adopt. Impromptu presentation is ruled out as it is done without prior preparation. Will the report be memorized, read from the manuscript or given extemporaneously? Memorization will take lot of effort and a slight mistake can turn your presentation into a fiasco. The presentation will sound stilted and unnatural since it precludes establishing rapport with the audience. The speaker is more self-centred than audience-centred. Therefore, this mode of presentation is not adopted generally. Reading from the manuscript also has disadvantages, as there is no eye contact with the audience. As a result, the delivery sounds droning and lifeless. The head down posture is completely ruled out in management presentation. The extempore presentation is audience-centred and you rely minimal on notes. You will be more natural, conversational and flexible. While preparing for the presentation, have the complete draft along with the main points noted in cards. As all the points remain fixed in your mind, therefore you can elaborate when you refer to the cards. These cards should be of 5 by 8 inches and numbered serially. The final stage of preparation is rehearsal, a prerequisite of effective briefing. Work hard on the problematic areas, especially the parts that are awkwardly developed. There should be full-scale practice under simulate presentation condition. A videotape recorder is one of the best diagnostic tools.

Delivery

The way you present the report is as important as what you present. A well-structured presentation puts the audience in a receptive mood. The audience is highly interested in the presentation and that is why they have assembled. A word of caution is added here, you have to give presentation for information dissemination and not for entertainment. Demeanour, posture, dress and overall appearance should be apposite for the occasion. Control your volume, voice pitch, tone quality and inflection for proper communication. Since you have limited time, you have to get hold of the audience without anecdotes and other rapport building techniques.

Audio-visual aids

Though you have variety of aids available but choose the appropriate for the occasion. The help of audio-visual aids makes your presentation task quite easy. The following are the aids, which help you for better presentation:

- Chalkboards and whiteboards
- Handout material
- Flipcharts

- Overhead transparencies
- Slides
- Power point program

The choice of these aids will depend on the size of the audience and the time constraints. Do clarify before making the presentation. Remember that audio-visual aids should complement your presentation, and not dominate it. If there is some kind of failure, review quickly what you had said and continue with the rest of the presentation confidently.

Written Report

Written report is a permanent record, therefore we need to be more careful while writing it. It can be referred to at any point of time, and is more authentic. This report requires more time from the writer's side, however, the reader can quickly glance through the complete report. The writer should possess good writing skills along with comprehending abilities.

PRELIMINARY STRATEGIES

Before you undertake the herculean task of writing the report, various steps called preliminary strategies need to be identified. If these steps are followed effectively, then it is most likely that you will be able to produce a good report. A lot of time should be spent mulling over the miniscule details, such as collecting data, coherently relating them and the extent of coverage. Report planning is one of the most important stages of report writing. If this stage is seriously taken care of, it is rare a chance that your report will have errors in it. You must identify these following five steps clearly:

- Identifying the purpose and scope
- Knowing your audience
- Choosing the right methods and sources of data collection
- Organizing the data
- Highlighting the outline

Identifying the Purpose and Scope

If the purpose of the report has been identified, then the objective of the report will also be clear and the scope will guide you for the application of findings as well as the extent of coverage. ***Example:*** You, as the mess secretary of your hostel, have been asked by the Dean, Student Welfare Division to study the level of students' dissatisfaction with the mess food. You are also asked to give recommendation to improve the deteriorating standards of the functioning of the messes. If your objectives are obfuscating, you will not be able to produce an effective report. So in the above example, your purpose is (i) to identify the reasons for the dissatisfaction among students and (ii) to suggest measures to remove the dissatisfaction. The purpose will enable you to choose the right method of data collection, what information to be included, how to analyse the data and derive conclusions.

While writing a report, it is important to understand what type of report you are required to write. If your report is informative, then you will present the facts as they are at that point of time and if analytical, then you will analyse the data and draw conclusions out of it. Based on the conclusions, you will provide the recommendations.

Since reports are produced on specific demands, the objectives appear in the form of instructions called terms of reference. They act as guideline for the writer. So the thumb rule is to seek complete clarification if the objectives are not understood. False assumption will lead to waste of time and energy. Terms of reference can be compared with the foundation of a building on which the report will be erected.

Knowing Your Audience

"The customer is the king" is an old adage. Before you start writing the report, ask yourself the real purpose of writing it. If you are able to answer the question, you have crystallized the problem. Identify the readers, so that you can cater to their needs and temperament in the writing style. Remember not to distort the facts according to the audience. But while giving a presentation; if you bear in mind the background of your readers you can certainly come up with quality report. The length of the report is also based on the audience. The next consideration is technical background—the background knowledge about the subject. If the gap is large between the readers and the writer, the task of conveying meaningful information becomes more arduous.

You must also keep in mind your audience. Picturize who your readers will be? Whether they will comprise of directors of a company or the technicians? How extensively your report is to be read—a handful of senior managers or gamut of company's employees? If you can identify the audience, it will be easier for you to write a successful report.

The next concern is about the circumstances and limitations under which you are writing the report and also if there is a need for statistics in it. These can be decided according to the nature of the subject. Since the time available for the submission imposes limitations, therefore, you should know the deadline. The final concern is how the report is going to be used. Visualize the readers of the report and try to make the information convenient for them as much as possible. Know how many readers will be there, and get the production accordingly. Based on these facts go ahead with outline preparation.

The type of readership will determine:

- How to shape up the report—which places to be emphasized.
- What is to be included or deleted according to the readers' awareness.
- How to pitch the language, especially inclusion or omission of jargons?

Choosing the Right Method of Data Collection

After the first two steps, you come to the most critical step of data collection, i.e., getting adequate and authentic information. The credibility of the report is dependent on the nature of information collected. Therefore, you must know the various primary and secondary sources of data collection. You must know where you will be able to get the right kind of data. The major problem today is availability of a lot of information; you have to sift carefully to identify right information. Else, incorrect information will affect your report. The authenticity of the source should be checked thoroughly. Be sure there should not be any personal bias or preference. You must look at the source objectively. The two sources are as follow:

Secondary source

Secondary source can be searched by approaching the library. For the report of general nature, the books and magazines in the library may be quite useful. Don't restrict yourself only to one library but visit as many as possible. When writing a report on recent trends in advertising agencies or on pharmaceutical industries in India, library can provide enough information. These days online library catalogues are also available which help to quickly locate the relevant books, periodicals and journals.

The other secondary source of information is internal records. All the organizations keep their important activities documented in the files in the form of reports, memorandum, MOUs, notices, letters, etc. Depending on the type of organization, the activities are recorded. Even today when we are heading towards paperless offices, it is difficult to find an office without files. Internal records are useful for report on placement of the students of the institute in different firms or the impact of entrance exams on the admission trends in an institute.

The writers today completely rely on Internet search. It is easily approachable and one can get any amount of information with just a click of mouse. But you should know how to search information, otherwise you might waste lot of your time. Be aware of the several search engines available on the Internet. Don't stick to one search engine but search the matter on all the available search engines. Use appropriate key words and phrases with different permutation and combination. If you fail to get the results, try with synonyms. Avoid functional words. In computer terminology, these are called stop words. Keep refining your search till you are able to find the suitable information you are looking for.

Primary source

When the reporter directly interacts to get information from the source, it is known as primary source. Personal observation and investigation are used as source of data collection where you rely on sensory perceptions and memory. Remember when collecting information, you should not be under any psychological pressure but in a stable state of mind. You should have quick assimilation ability. Keep a pen and paper for recording the readings in the case of experiments in the laboratory. The following guidelines should be kept in mind:

- Ignore the obstructions
- Keep paper and pen handy unless caught unaware
- Don't be prejudiced
- Don't delay recording, you may forget them
- Look for what you want
- Neglect irrelevant information
- Double check the readings if required

Laboratory reports and journalist reports bank on this method of data collection.

INTERVIEWS

Interviewing is not everyone's cup of tea as it is an art. The interviewer needs to be shrewd, tactful and intelligent. An interview is a face-to-face or telephonic conversation between two parties with a specific purpose. It is the most suitable method of data collection where you need the opinion of the expert directly. Since you have the scope of going beyond the questions framed, it has an added advantage. When you are not able to understand the replies, you can always paraphrase the questions and seek the answers again. Information can also be gathered through the tone of the voice and non-verbal cues, such as appearance, gestures and expressions of the interviewee. You can ask the question to gauge the interviewee's frame of mind. These interviews are called *data collection interviews*. Sometimes you may distribute the handouts to the respondent while conducting the interviews; you opt out for the interviews as the method of data collection to:

- Support the information you have collected through other sources.
- Seek the opinion, attitude and preference about some subject.
- Seek clarification and find facts for making them public.

Strategies for Conducting Interviews

Interviewee sheet

You as an interviewer must be prepared with the interviewee sheet which includes set of questions to be asked. By doing this preparation, you will not waste time of the expert. Of course, this will also reflect your seriousness and clarity of purpose. Your interviewee sheet can have a few varieties of questions:

- **Subjective questions:** These are questions which seek the attitude and opinion of the respondent. It gives enough scope to the interviewee to provide reasons for crucial decision-making, etc. At the same time don't let him go endlessly on the topic as it will eat away time for other questions. The questions should be open-ended.
  Example: What do you think of selling Ranbaxy to Daiichi Sankyo?
- **Objective questions:** These include close-ended question which have dichotomous choices. It saves a lot of time and is easy for analysis. It doesn't give the interviewee the scope to place his opinion about the topic. These types of questions get very pointed and specific answers.
  Example: Do you feel entrance exam will select better quality of students?
- **Restatement questions:** These questions help the respondents to further elaborate if any aspect is left out. It is almost reconfirmation of facts.
  Example: You said that entrance exam helps in better quality of students to qualify. May I have further elaboration on that?

The following guidelines may help you to be better prepared for the interview:

- Put the respondent at ease.
- Prepare the questions beforehand.
- Switch over if the interviewee feels embarrassed or uncomfortable.
- Sequence your questions appropriately.
- Ask variety of questions to avoid monotony.
- Avoid unnecessary questions.

Planning and holding the interview

Always make an appointment from the person to be interviewed and tell him the duration of the interview. At the outset, clarify your purpose of conducting the interview. If he wants to be anonymous, respect his wish. Dress neatly and be ready with the interviewee sheet. Reach the place in time as decided when making the appointment. Take permission to enter the room. Greet the interviewee appropriately. Start the interview after giving your introduction and repeating the purpose of the interview. Be patient and a good listener. Don't unnecessarily interrupt, but if you feel the respondent is deviating from the topic, politely bring him back to track. Carry pen and paper, and take notes. If you want to record the interview, take permission. Don't linger on but if the interview has come to an end, thank the respondent for his time. Make him feel that his response will be valuable to your study.

Interviews are advantageous because so much information is gathered through non-verbal cues. There is always a chance of verifying the facts with the non-verbal cues of the respondent. You can clarify a point if you have doubt at any time and can adjust the questions to make the interviewee respond friendly. However, interviews have certain limitations also as a method of data collection. They take lot of time and patience to meet people located at different places. As the data collected is very subjective it is very difficult to analyse it.

Telephonic interview is the other option available if the respondents stay in distant places where it is difficult for the interviewer to go. In telephonic interview, you can ask only objective questions. If the duration of the interview is large, then it can prove to be expensive. Sometimes it lacks clarity because of the absence of visible cues. However, you need no time in planning and conducting the interview and the refusal rate is less. People today are easily accessible over telephones; therefore, you can cover wider range of people. The main disadvantage is that authenticity of information can't be confirmed as you are not in direct contact with the individual. He can't be held responsible for giving the answers. Privacy is another key issue.

Questionnaire

Surveys and questionnaires are very effective primary methods of data collection. When you have to cover large geographical area, questionnaires are most effective. You can distribute innumerable questionnaires at comparatively low cost. But you must be careful in planning and preparing the questionnaire. However, production of the questionnaire is not difficult because of technological advancements. The questionnaire is accompanied by a covering letter which specifies the objective of carrying out the survey.

While preparing the questionnaire, include the following variety of questions:

- **Personal information questions:** The questions that seek information on the personal traits of an individual, such as name, sex, date of birth.
- **Close-ended questions:** These are dichotomous questions which will have answers either in true/false, right/wrong, adequate/inadequate, sufficient/insufficient, good/bad, etc. form.
- **Rating scale questions:** These questions are framed to be rated on the scale of 10 or 100 where it is specified what is the highest and lowest scaling point.
- **Open-ended questions:** These questions draw the opinion from the respondents. For example, what exactly have you gained from the computer classes held in the evening?
- **Multiple choice questions:** They provide options to the respondents such that they have to select the best suitable answer available.

Compiling questionnaire is not an easy task. Here are some tips on wording and content:

- Phrase your questions as simply as possible. For example, "Will you retire by the month end?" rather than "Are you prepared to contemplate superannuated life by month end?"

- Phrase your question in a way which invites brief answers. For example, "Do you sleep early or late?" rather than "What do you think of the idea of sleeping early or late?"
- Arrange the questions in a logical order, revealing a clearly developed train of thoughts. It can be from most important to least or vice versa.
- Club all the related questions together, else respondents will be confused and irritated.
- Put the tricky questions at the right place if you want to check the respondents' consistency and sincerity.
- Keep the questionnaire as short as possible. The respondents get bored when answering long questionnaire.
- Don't reflect your prejudices in the questions. It might get biased answers.
- Don't ask leading questions. For example, "Do you smoke Wills cigarette?" is a leading question.
- Have a follow-up question to close-ended question. For example, "If the answer to the above question is no, then the reasons for dissatisfaction are…".
- Keep the layout simple and neat. Divide the questionnaire into section and subsection and, if needed, provide heading.
- If the respondent is supposed to write a few lines, provide enough space.
- Use an easily legible typeface for printing.
- Use good quality of paper as your questionnaire will pass through several hands.

Sampling

After you have framed the questionnaire, the next task is to decide the audience to whom it is to be sent. This can be done by sampling. For sampling, the first thing is to define the target population. You can rely on your judgement and logic for defining the target audience according to your objectives. If the population is small, distribute the questionnaire to all and that will be called *census study*. But most of the time the target audience is very large and, therefore, to distribute it to each member is impossible. Select the representative carefully so that the chosen sample reflects the characteristics of the complete population which it represents.

The two main methods of sampling are classified as **probability** and **non-probability**. In probability method, the chance of each member to be selected is non-zero. This method includes random sampling, systematic sampling and stratified sampling. However, non-probability method selects the members in non-random manner. It includes convenience sampling, quota sampling, judgement sampling and snowball sampling.

Random sampling is only sometimes opted out by the researchers. Each member of the population has equal chance of being selected. Always remember to define the population which you are going to select.

Systematic sampling is more often used than random sampling. It is also known as *Nth name selection technique*. After defining the population, nth record is selected from the list. It is more opted because of availability of the population list from the office records or computer file.

Stratified sampling is superior to both the previous sampling methods because it reduces sampling error. A stratum is selected from the population which shares at least one common characteristic. Each stratum may be student and teacher, male and female. The first job is to identify the stratum and the actual representation in the population. Then random sampling is opted when one or more of the strata in the population have a low incidence relative to the other stratum.

You might now be eager to know what type of question can be selected for a questionnaire. The sample questionnaire given here will make your task easier.

Dear respondent,

We are conducting a survey on sales promotions and their influence on purchase behaviour. We request you to fill this questionnaire. It will take approximately 10 minutes to complete, and all information will be kept anonymous and confidential. We hope you enjoy the experience and thank you for your precious time!

1. **Gender:** Male ☐ Female ☐

2. **Age:** ☐

3. **Occupation** (tick as appropriate):

Own business	
Service	
Student	
Housewife	
Unemployed	
Retired	

4. **Annual Income** (tick as appropriate):

Less than 1 lakh	
1–1.5 lakh	
1.51–2 lakh	
2.1–2.5 lakh	
2.6–5 lakh	
Above 5 lakh	

5. **Education** (tick as appropriate):

Below undergraduate	
Undergraduate	
Postgraduate	
Professional studies	

6. **Accommodation** (tick as appropriate):

Live alone (own house)	
Live alone (renting)	
Live with family (own house)	
Live with family (renting)	

7. **Do you buy goods for your own self?** (tick as appropriate)

Always ☐ Many times ☐ Sometimes ☐ Rarely ☐ Never ☐

8. **Do you buy goods for others in your family?** (tick as appropriate)

Always ☐ Many times ☐ Sometimes ☐ Rarely ☐ Never ☐

9. **Do you wait for 'Sales promotion' before purchasing branded goods?** (tick as appropriate)

Always ☐ Many times ☐ Sometimes ☐ Rarely ☐ Never ☐

10. What of the following brands would you wait for to buy from 'Sales promotion'? (Please tick one choice in each row)

Nima soap	Always		Many times		Sometimes		Rarely		Never	
Sony 42" plasma TV	Always		Many times		Sometimes		Rarely		Never	
Dove soap	Always		Many times		Sometimes		Rarely		Never	
Crown 14" colour TV	Always		Many times		Sometimes		Rarely		Never	

11. In a situation where you felt the need for the following brands, what is your likelihood of buying them if no sales promotion was available? (Most likely = 1; likely = 2; neither likely nor unlikely = 3; unlikely = 4; highly unlikely = 5)

Brand	**Nima soap**	**Sony 42"plasma TV**	**Dove soap**	**Crown 14" colour TV**
Likelihood				

12. How involved do you think you will be when buying the following brands? (Please tick one choice in each row)

	Highly involved	**Involved**	**Neither involved nor less involved**	**Less involved**	**Least involved**
Nima soap					
Sony 42" plasma TV					
Dove soap					
Crown 14" colour TV					

13. Of the following promotion techniques how much do you think they influence your purchase behaviour?
(Please tick one choice in each row)

Promotion technique	**Most influential**	**Very influential**	**Influential**	**Less influential**	**Least influential**
Price deal (discount – 10% off for this week)					
Price-pack deal (2 for the price of 1)					
Coupons (use this coupon to get 10% off your purchase)					
Rebates (bring proof of earlier purchase and get a free gift)					
Contests (solve puzzle inside pack and win holiday abroad)					
Free samples (try before you buy)					
Combo offer (related products for a low price)					

14. In the case of the following brands, according to you how influential each sales promotion technique will be in convincing you to purchase them? (Please put a relevant number in each box) (Most influential = 1; Very influential = 2; Influential = 3; Less influential = 4; Least influential = 5)

Promotion technique	**Nima soap**	**Sony 42" plasma TV**	**Dove soap**	**Crown 14" colour TV**
Price deal (discount – 10% off for this week)				
Price-pack deal (2 for the price of 1)				
Coupons (use this coupon to get 10% off your purchase)				
Rebates (bring proof of earlier purchase and get a free gift)				
Contests (solve puzzle inside pack and win holiday abroad)				
Free samples (try before you buy)				
Combo offer (related products for a low price)				

15. Following are some statements which describe benefits of sales promotion. Please rate the statements on how much you agree or disagree. (Please tick one choice in each row)

Using sales promotion...	**Definitely agree**	**Tend to agree**	**Neither agree nor disagree**	**Tend to disagree**	**Definitely disagree**
I really save money.					
I feel that I am getting a good deal.					
I really spend less.					
I can have a higher quality product at the same price.					
I can afford a better than usual product.					
I can update to a better brand.					
I can remember what I need.					
I feel good about myself.					
I can be proud of my purchase.					
I feel like I am a smart shopper.					
I feel like trying new brands.					
I can avoid always buying the same brands.					
I can get new ideas of things to buy.					
I feel promotions are fun.					
I feel promotions are entertaining.					
I feel promotions are enjoyable.					
I feel promotions remind me that I need the product.					
I believe promotions make my life easy.					

16. Following statements are regarding the promotion techniques. Please rate the statements on how much you agree or disagree. (Please put a relevant number in each box) (Definitely agree = 1; Tend to agree = 2; Neither agree nor disagree = 3; Tend to disagree = 4; Definitely disagree = 5)

This sales promotion...	Price deal	Price-pack deal	Coupons	Rebates	Contests	Free sample	Combo offers
Really save money.							
Gives me a good deal.							
Makes me spend less.							
Gives me a higher quality product at the same price.							
Gets me a better than usual product.							
Makes me update to a better brand.							
Makes me remember what I need.							
Makes me feel good about myself.							
Makes me feel proud of my purchase.							
Makes me feel like I am a smart shopper.							
Makes me feel like trying new brands.							
Helps me avoid always buying the same brands.							
Helps me get new ideas of things to buy.							
Is fun.							
Is entertaining.							
Is enjoyable.							
Reminds me that I need the product.							
Makes my life easy.							

Organizing the Data: the Outline

After you have made an analysis of the data, the first task is to draw a tentative outline. It is extremely important to develop an outline of the report prior to commencing work on it. The formatting of the report should be carried out only after completion of the outline. There are different methods of organizing the data. If your report is informative, you should arrange the material from most important to least important. In interpretive report you go from least important to most important. In some reports, it can be temporal as well, i.e. based on chronological order. It depends on the nature of the report to organize the data. Sometimes you can combine different methods to draw the outline.

Principles of outline

Remember your outline is the skeleton on which you will lay the flesh of your report. As a painter draws a sketch before making a painting, similarly, you too must draw an outline before writing the report. The outline is different from the table of contents as the outline is written before commencing work on the report while the table of contents is made after the report has been written. Moreover, the table of contents has page numbers whereas an outline doesn't have page numbers.

Take care of the following principles of outline:

- Indenting
- Proper numbering
- Coordination
- Subordination
- Parallel construction
- Logical ordering

An outline will look like the following:

1. Major Topic Heading
 1.1 Major subtopic heading
 1.1.1 Subtopic
 1.1.1.1 Minor subtopic
 1.1.1.1.1 Further detail

Software for developing outlines and visually connecting ideas simplifies this onerous task.

Sample outline

Advertising in India

1. Introduction
2. History
3. Types
    3.1 Print
    3.2 Electronic
        3.2.1 Radio
        3.2.2 Television
        3.2.3 Internet
    3.3 Outdoor
4. Current Trends
5. Major Agencies
6. Future
7. Conclusions

Indenting

The alignment of topics and subtopics should be proper. The subtopics get shifted to the right-hand side by one space. Look at the sample given here.

2. Advertising Types
   - 2.1 Print
     - 2.1.1 Magazine
     - 2.1.2 Newspaper
     - 2.1.3 Yellow pages
     - 2.1.4 Sales letter

You can observe that the subtopic and sub-subtopics get shifted to the right margin.

Numbering

With the appropriate numbering, the proper relationship between the topic and the subtopics can be set. Whatever numbering you use, consistency should be there throughout the outline. You can use either letters, numbers or numbers with decimal. In most of the situation, decimal numbering is preferred because of the convenience.

The sample of the type is given here:

I. Advertising Today
   - A. Indian scenario
   - B. World scenario
     - 1. History of advertisements in India
     - 2. History of advertisements in the world
       - (a) Internet advertising
         - (i) Interactive media
           - • Advantages

II. Future Trends
   - A. Ethical values
   - B. More interactive

The other method is the decimal numbering in which whole numbers are used to represent the sections and decimal numbers to show the subsections.

4. ADVERTISING TODAY
   - **4.1 Indian Scenario**
   - **4.2 World Scenario**
     - **4.2.1 History of Advertisements in India**
     - **4.2.2 History of Advertisements in the world**
       - *4.2.2.1 Internet advertising*
         - 4.2.2.1.1 Interactive media
           - 4.2.2.1.1.1 Advantages

5. FUTURE TRENDS
   - **5.1 Ethical Values**
   - **5.2 More Interactive**

Coordination

The topics of same rank should be put at the same level to give the topics equal importance. For example:

2. MODES OF PRESENTATION
2.1 Reading from the Manuscript
2.2 Impromptu
2.3 Memorization
2.4 Extemporaneous

Subordination

The subtopics get lesser importance than the main topic and should be differentiated. For example, in the above example impromptu is one of the modes of presentation and, therefore, is the subtopic and not the main topic.

Parallel grammatical construction

The construction of topic and subtopics should have parallel grammatical constructions. Either all the subtopics should be nouns or verbs in same tense. Observe these two examples.

2. Benefits of Advertising
2.1 Economic
2.2 Political
2.3 Moral
2.4 Religious
2.5 Cultural

The other example is as follows:

3. The Mutable Laws of Web Advertising
3.1 The law of dead-end street
3.2 The law of giving and selling

Report Anatomy

As machinery has got several parts which work in tandem to produce the desired output, similarly a report has various elements which are organized in a way to give it an elegant look. If you know these elements, your task of writing a report becomes simple. It is not necessary that your report has all the parts mentioned in this discussion, but it depends on the usefulness of the element for the report you are writing. You can also seek clarification when you are identifying the objectives in your terms of reference. Some organizations mention the element of the report according to their norms. If an organization for which you are writing the report mentions that you have to include a certificate, then you need not resist but include it as required.

Design Elements

The reports, irrespective of their types, have set elements in them. It is the headings and subheadings that will divide the sections. According to the type of the prospective audience, the parts can be elaborated or summarized. A short report has almost the same element as that of long report but in an abbreviated form. The methodology is part of introduction and succinctly takes a few paragraphs. The emphasis is on findings and conclusions and is incorporated in a letter or memo format.

The report, in general, is divided into three main divisions—*prefatory material*, *main elements* and *back matter*. The prefatory material has no direct bearing on the research, but it introduces the reader to the report. It tries to put the reader in receptive mood to read the report. Following elements are the part of prefatory items:

- Cover
- Frontispiece
- Title page
- Copyright notice
- Forwarding letter
- Preface
- Acknowledgements
- Table of contents
- List of illustrations
- Abstract (or summary or executive summary)

The main elements are as follow:

- Introduction
- Discussion/description
- Conclusions
- Recommendations

The back matter is as follows:

- Appendices
- List of references
- Bibliography
- Glossary
- Index

Prefatory Material

Cover

It may be white or neutral coloured, soft or hard paper which protects the manuscript from getting damaged. Just by looking at it, the reader can know who has written the report and what it is all about. It has title of the report, number if any, organization, and date. The information is spread well in the whole space and is not crowded. For the title, use the **bold** letters and compose the rubric well. If the report is too short, then the cover is not necessary.

Example

A Report RNC//812

On
Quality Management in Service Industries

By
Atit Jain
2006A3PS287

Birla Institute of Technology and Science, Pilani
July, 2022

Frontispiece

Frontispiece is usually found in bound reports. To create interest among the readers, artistic drawings, pictures or maps are superimposed on the cover. It serves as a window display of the whole report but is not used in technical reports. For example, the frontispiece for the above report can be a picture of Tourism sector.

Title page

The title page serves myriad purposes. As to dignify the report, it prefaces and helps the reader identify the matter and orients the reader to the reading task. It must be attractive by being well designed. The most important items are printed in bold and the lesser important items can be subordinated. The five items included in the reports are:

1. The title of the report
2. The date
3. For whom
4. By whom
5. The name of the organization

Pleonasm in the title doesn't serve any purpose but just adds to the length. Therefore, it should be avoided. Single-word titles should be avoided too as they add little to the value. Three popular ways to form the rubric of the report are as follows

(i) Descriptive study, e.g. the demand of four wheelers in Rajasthan over the last three years.

(ii) **Correlation study,** e.g. the need-based study of demand and supply of FMCG in rural sector.
(iii) **Causal study,** e.g. the effect of smoking on the youth of India.

Example

A REPORT
ON
Quality Management in Hospitals—A Case Study

Prepared
for
Director
Centre for Science
New Delhi

by

Shalini Ramachandran
2000A8PS182

BIRLA INSTITUTE OF TECHNOLOGY AND SCIENCE
28 November, 2022

Copyright notice

It is placed on the inside of the title page and can be stated either ways:

- @ Atit Jain, 2022
- All rights reserved. No part of this report may be reproduced in any form or by any means without written permission from the author (or publisher).

Forwarding letter

It is a record of transmission for the primary recipient of report. When the report has identified a group or single person as the audience, you include letter of transmittal. Usually, for internal circulation in an organization the letter of transmittal can be avoided. But when it is written for the audience outside a company, it should include the following details:

- Statement of submittal
- Statement of authorization
- Statement of subject, purpose, scope
- Limitations
- Statement of acknowledgement

This letter is also called letter of transmission, which can be both of covering type or of introductory type depending on the audience. The covering type of letter just has the information about who is submitting the report to whom and on which date. The sample of introductory type of forwarding letter is given here:

BIRLA SARVAJANIK HOSPITAL, PILANI, RAJASTHAN

23 June, 2022

Dr Anil Jain
Chief Medical Officer
Birla Sarvajanik Hospital
Pilani, 333031

Dear Sir

It is indeed a great privilege to submit the report on the effect of education and socio-economic status on maternal health care among the residents of Pilani.

I am grateful to my colleagues and friends for their support and encouragement during the course of my study. I am also thankful to my students who helped me a lot in data collection by contacting 150 people on campus.

Maternal and Child Health (MCH) refers to promotive, preventive, curative and rehabilitative health care for mothers and children. Maternal and infant mortality and morbidity are direct indicators of Maternal and Child health status of a country. India is among the countries that have a very high maternal mortality. It is estimated at 437 maternal deaths per 100,000 live births, which results primarily from infections, haemorrhage, obstructed labour, abortion, and anaemia. Lack of appropriate care during pregnancy and childbirth, and inadequacy of services for detecting and managing complications; explain most of the maternal deaths.

This study aims at examining the effect of education and socio-economic status on the Maternal Health care among the families of BITS and Seva Basti in Pilani. The Staff/families of BITS are provided with Medical care facilities including Maternal and Child Health care benefits as a part of employee benefits programme. It was of interest to see if education and socio-economic levels have an impact on a uniformly available health care system. Further, a community in Seva Basti in Pilani who hence low literacy rate and low socio-economic background were included in the study to compare their level of Maternal Health care with that of a similar group in BITS.

I sincerely hope this study will help in taking measures to improve the maternal health.

Warm Regards

Yours sincerely

Usha Manjunath

Health Care Officer

Preface

It introduces the report to the reader and has almost the same information as in introductory letter. Author writes the preface himself unlike foreword which is written by an authority in the subject area or an expert. The preface will include the following points:

- The background of the work
- Important points
- Significance of the study
- Section organization
- Acknowledgements

Preface is included in the report if you get it published.

Acknowledgements

You must give credit to all the people who have helped you in writing the report. You thank them for different reasons. Also acknowledge the sources which you have referred to and not mentioned anywhere. Seek permission if you are borrowing any text from the copyright work and acknowledge them. Keep the following guidelines in mind while writing the acknowledgements:

- Divide the people into different categories. Put them in hierarchical order in the paragraph. Don't put the secretarial assistance on the top.
- Make at least two or three paragraphs.
- Use varied expression to acknowledge the support. Always state the reason for acknowledgement. A few expressions are as follows:
  (a) I am deeply indebted to…
  (b) We owe a great deal to … for his unmitigated support…
  (c) My heartfelt thanks to…
  (d) I sincerely thank to…
  (e) I acknowledge a deep sense of gratitude
  (f) My profound thanks…
  (g) The work was possible with the support…
  (h) We acknowledge the great support…
  (i) With great pleasure, I thank…
- Avoid metaphorical language.
- Avoid clichés as they have lost impact because of overuse.

Example

Acknowledgements

My report on "Impact of Smoking on Youths of India" was possible because of the support of Prof L.K Maheshwari, our venerable Vice-Chancellor, BITS, Pilani. I have deep sense of gratitude for Prof G. Raghurama, Deputy Director, Academics for his constant encouragement. Special thanks to Prof Ashoke Sarkar, Dean, Instruction Division for his timely suggestions.

I acknowledge the help provided by my friend Usha Manjunath in providing the data for the report. My colleague Gajendra Singh Chauhan needs a special mention for being kind enough to clarify the doubts at some stages.

I am thankful to Mr Ishwar Bhatt, the Chief Librarian for making me access all books and journals. Special thanks to Mr Prem Mehta who word processed the report so meticulously.

However, the example of badly written acknowledgement is also given.

First of all I would like to thank Ms. Leena Garg for having done a commendable job in typing this report. Also, I take this opportunity to thank Mr. K.K Singh, Managing Director, Bharat Textiles Ltd., Mumbai for having permitted me to work on a project which was dear to my heart. Next, I must thank the binders M/s Verma Brothers who have given this report an elegant shape. It goes without saying that I am sincerely grateful to my PS I Instructor, Mr. Raghav. I also express my deep sense of gratitude to Mr. Triapati, Head, Quality Control Dept., Bharat Textiles Ltd., Mumbai, for having helped me in amassing the data for this report. Last, but not the least, I thank my friends for their constant encouragement.

Table of contents

The table of contents is the quick guide to find out the main topics and subtopics in the report. The most obvious function is to indicate the page on which the discussion of each major section begins; it serves the reader as a locating device. Before you start writing your report you draw the outline, which will act as the basis of report writing. It is very similar to the table of content except that the outline doesn't include prefatory elements, appendices and the page numbers. If a report is too short, then you need not have table of content. But if it is more than six or seven pages, you can include the table of content. Apart from the table of content if the report has too many illustrations, it is better to include the list of illustrations. The table of content.

- Usually included for reports of more than 10 pages.
- Provides an overall view, easy to locate information in report.

Example

Table of Contents

Preface *ii*
Acknowledgements *iii*
Abstract *iv*
1. Introduction 1
2. Causes of Smoking 2
3. Effects of Smoking 10
4. Techniques to Quit Smoking 20
5. Conclusions 34
6. Recommendations 37

Appendix A 38
Bibliography 40

Remember the table of contents should be exact and give the page number of topics and sub-topics correctly. The numbering for the prefatory part should be in roman numerals while the main body in Arabic numerals. There is no serial numbering for the prefatory and back matter.

List of illustrations

It is similar to the content page for the illustrations. If the illustrations are too large, then you need to list the illustrations. Tables and figures are classified separately. Tables can be dependent or independent while the graphs, maps, pictures, bar charts, all fall under the category of figures. Tables are preferred to be labelled in roman numerals on the top, and figures in arabic numerals below the figure. All the tables and figures should be numbered and labelled properly for easy location.

List of illustrations

Abstract

Abstract is a clear, concise, condensation of the main purpose and important results of the study. It is written by one specialist to another and, therefore, should be very specific. The abstract gives importance not how the study was carried out but on what was the focus of the study. Most of the reports, either have an abstract or a summary. It is also mentioned at the time of authorization. Abstract is briefer than summary, and is needed if a report is more than 15 pages. See the sample

In India, the health of mother and child revolves round three important factors of malnutrition, infection and consequences of unregulated fertility. This paper discusses the impact of education and social factor of conformity to social norms on maternal health. Implications of education as a crucial factor in development related to health are highlighted.

Summary

It is the entire report in the nutshell covering all its important aspects. In other words, it is the miniature form of the report. It is usually written after you have finished writing your report but is placed before introduction. Two pages are quite sufficient for this element. It should not include any new information but can take aid of illustrations to delineate conclusions. Summary might include the significant terms, which are used in the report since it is the representation of your entire report.

To write the summary, you can follow these steps:

- Pick out and state the central theme.
- Identify topic sentences indifferent paragraphs.
- Examine all topic sentences and see how they relate to the central or main theme.
- Verbalize the relationships.
- Write the first draft stating the central theme, and relate to the other topic ideas in the report.
- Expand or prune it.

The features of abstract and summary are as follow:

Abstract	Summary
Concise condensation of the purposes and most important results of the project. It is about the report and significance of achievement. Organized using rhetorical logic (impress). No equations, figures, tables. Emphasis on presentation of the idea not explanation. Qualitative description and independently circulated. Reader can decide on interest. Specialist to specialist (technical or research paper). Approximately 2% of the total report size.	Whole report in a nutshell. Beginning (why the project was done). Middle (highlighting most important features of the report). End (conclusions and recommendations). Presentation logic. May use table/data and equation. Self-contained, circulated independently; whole idea about the project is available. Approximately 5–10% the size of the whole report.

Main Body

Introduction

Introduction is the first element that is quite similar to a research proposal. A good introduction can delineate what is to follow in the report. This is the diving board for taking the plunge into the report. It includes the problem statement, objectives, and background material. Problem statement tells the real need of the research project. It is followed by a detailed set of objectives. The objectives address the purpose of the project. If your statement answers the question why you are writing the report, you have been able to put the purpose clearly. It also contains the significance of the report. The objectives may be research questions and associated investigative questions. It should include the variables of concern, the relationship among them, and the target group being studied. Jargons and operational definitions should be included to clarify the study. Background material contains the information about data collection. It can be secondary data from the literature review. The work starts from periphery and approaches towards the centre—the crux of the study. Sources securing information are incorporated in the appendix.

The literature should be cohesive and well-connected with the problem. The background includes definition, qualification, and assumption. It provides enough information to the reader to comprehend the research report. Background material can be placed either before the problem statement or after the objectives. The last part of the introduction mentions the various sections of the report and their layout. The sample introduction is placed at the end of this section. Report must have the following elements:

- Statement of authorization
- Background of the matter
- Statement of the problem (or hypothesis)
- Scope of the problem
- Limitations
- Sources and methods of data collection
- Definition of terms
- Report preview

Discussion

This is the longest section of the report with the objective to explain the data and not to draw in conclusions. The qualitative data should be presented through meticulously planned tables and graphs. The illustrations should be used to support the verbal material and not to replace them. Tables and graphs should be self-explanatory, or should be well explained in the study. Include the material which is important in the discussion, else organize and put it in the appendix. The sections and subsections should be properly numbered and divided. Use proper cohesive device to move from one section to another. Limit them to those that help the reader understand your data as they relate to the investigated problem.

Keep the following points in mind while writing the discussion:

- Discuss your data analysis.
- Data presentation—organized, clear; analysis should be clearly written.
- Findings should be explained in relation to the research problem solved.
- Describe topic/subtopics; analyse the data and organise the inferences.
- State the findings and then describe how such a thing happened.

Conclusions

In the introduction you promise to do certain things, in conclusions the readers check if you have done what you had promised. Match your introduction and conclusions. In *interpretive* reports, you draw conclusions from your analysis in the discussion, while in *informative* report, to give the reader the sense of completeness you draw aesthetic conclusions. In this part you tie up all the lose threads of the discussion. If you have summarized each section, you can just pick up the points and put them together. Else draw fresh conclusions. Nothing new is added at this juncture but should be completely based on findings. Sometimes your conclusions can be put in tabular form instead of narrative form.

Conclusion must:

- Answer the problem statements.
- Bring the discussion to a close.
- Draw the logical inferences and judgements based on the analysis.

Example

Group T (Teaching staff/families of BITS, Pilani)
Group NT (Non-teaching staff/families of BITS, Pilani)
Group SK (Safai-Karamcharis/families of BITS, Pilani)
Group B (Families from Seva Basti in Pilani)

The results of this study clearly indicate that maternal health care is related to education, especially female education and socio-economic level of the people. The number of children per couple increased as education and socio-economic levels decreased. The average number of children per couple among Group T is 1.53, Group NT is 2.53, Group SK is 3.13, and Group B is 2.73. Female sterilization to limit the family size is the most commonly used method of family planning. However, gap between two children is not rigorously practiced among Groups SK and B. Antenatal care is highest among Group T and lowest among Group SK in BITS. Marriageable is related to female education and societal norms. It is found to be above 20 years for all the Group T but less than 18 years for all in Groups SK and B. Some at least in Group NT have also early marriages. Infant mortality was found to be highest among this group.

Recommendation

These are the suggestions and ideas for the future course of corrective action which are based on your findings. They are based on the conclusions of your study. If your recommendation becomes the basis of the decision-making, then take extra care to write it. If recommendation is less than one page, you can club it with the conclusions. In research reports a recommendation suggests the further study that can broaden the horizon of knowledge in the same pale.

Write recommendation only if you are asked for. For example, if you give recommendation for the report on the functioning of the messes, it will help the authority to take a corrective action according to the recommendation provided by you.

There are three types of recommendation, *tentative* which give temporary solution, *conciliatory* which you feel is what the reader is wanting, and *aggressive* which are urgent and you want them to be put into practice immediately.

Back Matter

Appendix

All the documents that support the study are placed in the appendix. This part is not put in the discussion, because it may interfere with the discussion, and divert the focus of the study. These documents can be in the form of computer program, complex tables, statistical test, forms and questionnaire, description of methodology, instructions to field workers, etc. The appendix should be neatly organized and properly numbered as appendices A, B, C and labelled. It should not be cluttered. Though placed last, it should be given appropriate treatment.

Documenting Your Report

Once you have drafted your report, you need to acknowledge the resources you have utilized for the purpose. You will realize that various ideas and pieces of information in your report might have been taken from different sources. As these helped you in gathering information, it will do the same for others in future. This process is called *documenting* the resources and helps in disseminating knowledge. It saves you from plagiarising others' works.

Bibliography, footnotes and endnotes

The use of secondary data requires bibliography. Proper entries and formatting, style should be observed. Though there are different formats available, but the most popular are APA and MLA styles. Bibliography entries should be in alphabetical order and if required can be annotated. When you compile the report, you may refer to the published work or even directly take quotes from books. In such cases, you must give the complete details of the source. This can be done in three ways: (i) footnote which is at the foot of the page, (ii) end note which is placed at the end of the report, (iii) running text, which is immediately following the quotation. There are problems and inconveniences in both footnotes and endnotes. The endnotes are not at all distracting as they are put at the end but are inconvenient to find and check. Bracketed references within the text are distracting to the reader. Footnotes are the best option but are difficult for the one who types.

The entry in the footnote appears as:

- Sangeeta Sharma and Raghuvir Singh, *Advertising: Planning and Implementation*, 3/E, New Delhi: PHI Learning, 2021, p. 456.

The arrangement of entries is done according to the alphabetical order. Sometimes the bibliography may be annotated. There is the gist of the text provided after the bibliographical entries. If the work is cited within the text, you have to specify the author's name and the year of publication along with the page number of the source.

Example

"I heard him mutter a prayer under his breath—he always said a prayer when his son left the house" (Hosseini 2003, 53).

or

As Hosseini (2003, 53) observes, "I heard him mutter a prayer under his breath—he always said a prayer when his son left the house".

How do bibliography and a list of references differ?

Before you put yourself in a controversy between bibliography and list of references, you should keep the following into consideration:

1. A bibliography lists both textual references and other works which may have informed your thinking but which you didn't explicitly cite (meaning, 'refer to') in the text of your essay or report.
2. It is comprehensive as it lists all the reading you did, including background reading.
3. A list of references, on the other hand, contains only the works you have cited in the text of your essay/report.

Order of entries

The order of entries in the bibliography directs you to put the author's name followed by the title of the book and publication details. The author's name is put in reverse order, i.e. surname of the author first and then the first name separated by a comma, such as: Gibaldi, Joseph. The complete title of the book should be underlined. The details of the entry should follow the following order:

(a) Author's name
(b) Title of the book
(c) Name of the editor (if any)
(d) Edition, numbers of the volume
(e) Name of series
(f) Place of publication
(g) Name of publisher

(h) Date of publication
(i) Page numbers

In MLA style, an entry could be written as:

Gibaldi, Joseph. *MLA Handbook for Writers of Research Papers.* Sixth Edition. New Delhi: EWP. 2004.

In APA style, the same entry would be written as:

Gibaldi, J. (2004). *MLA handbook for writers of research papers.* Sixth Edition. New Delhi: EWP.

Though APA and MLA style sheets are two different terminologies, most of the guidelines to be followed in developing them are mostly same. Certain things that you should follow while developing a bibliography or 'works cited' list are the same.

1. The bibliography should be placed at the end of the report, research paper or any other document.
2. It should appear on a separate page.
3. It should appear in the centre and should be placed one inch from the top of the page.
4. It should maintain double space between the title and the first reference entry.
5. Double spacing is used within and between entries too.
6. All the entries should be listed in the alphabetical order.
7. Titles of books, magazines and journals should be underlined.
8. Title of a research article should be put under double inverted commas.

You can get detailed information of documentation in the sixth edition of Joseph Gibaldi's book *MLA Handbook for Writers of Research Papers.* However, some entries are given here as follow:

Book by a single author

(a) Kuralansky, Mark. *Salt: A World History.* New York: Walker, 2002.
(b) Guffy, Mary Ellen. *Business Communication.* Third Edition. Bangalore: Thomson South Western, 2002.

Book by two or more authors

(a) Rabkin, Eric S., Martin H. Greenberg, and Joseph D. Olander, Eds. *No Place Else: Explorations in Utopian and Dystopian Fiction.* Carbondale: Southern Illinois UP, 1983.
(b) Quirk, Randolph, et al. *A Comprehensive Grammar of the English Language.* London: Longman, 1985.
(c) Sharma, Sangeeta and Raghuvir Singh. *Advertising: Planning and Implementation.* New Delhi: Prentice Hall, 2006.

An edited anthology or a compilation

(a) Weisser, Susan Ostrov, ed. *Women and Romance: A Reader*. New York: New York UP, 2001.
(b) Mishra, Binod, ed. *Critical Responses to Feminism*. New Delhi: Sarup and Sons, 2006.

Two or more books by the same author

(a) Boroff, Marie. *Language and the Past: Verbal Artistry in Frost, Stevens, and Moore*. Chicago: University of Chicago Press, 1979.
(b) ———, ed. *Wallace Stevens*: *A Collection of Critical Essays*. Englewood Cliffs: Prentice, 1963.

An essay by two people

(a) Mishra, Binod and Sangeeta Sharma. "Significance of Silence and Pauses in Communication". *Communicating at Work: Shifting Paradigm and Emerging Trends.* (Eds.) M. Raman et al. New Delhi: Jain Brothers, 2005, 239–246.

Corporate author

(a) National Research Council. *Beyond Six Billion: Forecasting the World's Population.* Washington: Natl. Acad., 2000.

A work in an anthology

(a) More, Hannah. "The Black Slave Trade: A Poem". *British Women Poets of the Romantic Era*. Ed. Paula R. Feldman. Baltimore: John Hopkins UP, 1997. 477–82.
(b) Allende, Isabel. "Todds Mouth". Trans. Margaret Sayers Peden. *A Hammock beneath the Mangoes: Stories from Latin America.* Ed. Thomas Colchie. New York: Plume, 1992, 83–84.

An article in a newspaper

Guha, Ramchandra. "Recalling the liberation of Goa". *The Hindu,* 2 September 2007.

An article in a scholarly journal

White, Sabina, and Andrew Winzelbergy. "Laughter and Stress". *Humor* 5 (1992): 343–55.

An article in a magazine

Khushwant Singh. "Oh, That Other Hindu Riot Of Passage". *Outlook Magazine* 07 November, 2004.

An editorial

"Managing the Crisis." Editorial. *The Hindu* 11 July 2008.

A review

Mishra, Binod. Rev. of *Scripture on Stone. By Charusheel* Singh. Cyber Literature. 19 and 20 (2007): 89–91.

Introduction, preface, foreword, afterword

(a) Sears, Barry. Afterword. *The Jungle*. By Upton Sinclair. New York: Signet, 2002, 343–47.
(b) Singh, Charusheel. Foreword. *Inventing Ties & Bonds in English: Diasporic Literary Consciousness*. Ed. Binod Mishra & Paul Dhanasekaran. New Delhi: Authors Press, 2008. V–XII.

An abstract

Liberman, Serge. "Dispossession, Migration and Home Personalized". *International Conference on Commonwealth Literature*. 6–7. Abstract. IITR. 2005.

Internet citation

Gail Mortimer, *The William Faulkner Society Home Page*, 16 September 1999, <http://www.utep.edu/mortimer/faulkner/mainfaulkner.htm> (19 November 1997).

Online book

Peter J. Bryant, "The Age of Mammals," in *Biodiversity and Conservation* April 1999, *<http://darwin.bio.uci.edu/~sustain/bio65/index.html>* (11 May 1999).

E-mail entry

Danny Robinette, "Epiphany Project", 30 April 1999, Office communication (29 May 1999).

Glossary

It is the alphabetical list of technical or otherwise specialized terms you wish to define for your readers. If you have more than 10 terms, include it in the glossary. If there are less terms, then include in introduction or may be as footnotes.

Index

Index is included only in extremely long and detailed reports. It is easy for quick cross referencing by name, subject or both to the content of your report. Index serves as a detailed extension of table of contents, arranged in alphabetical, instead of page order. The index is arranged in alphabetical order and is the last element of the report.

Writing the Draft

After you have completed the outline, the inclusion of illustration should be decided. Each illustration should be matched to the particular section in the outline. The choice of illustration is discussed later, in the same chapter.

These days individuals use various methods to get their thoughts into written form. Some will write by hand and convert it into word-processed format. Others prefer to sit in front of the computer to word process. Whichever works for you, you can choose. Even when you have the spell check in the computer, you can't rely completely on it. The common confusing words, such as spacious/specious, affect/effect are not found by standard spelling checks. The software can't guarantee an error free report, but will greatly reduce your time in proof-reading. Ensure that report has the following

- Readability
- Comprehensibility
- Right tone

Readability

Readability can be achieved by considering the reading ability of the audience. Any text can be better piece of writing if you use simple, familiar and short words. It is said sesquipedalian words are more difficult to understand. Wherever possible, substitute the unfamiliar words by familiar ones. If the audience is not aware of the technicalities of the subject, avoid using jargons. As these terms are technical, they might-baffle the readers. To test writing for difficulty level, there are standard readability indexes. For example, the Fog Index was devised by an American, Robert Gunning to assess the readability of any text. In his view, the more a writer uses long sentences and words, the more the clarity of the text is 'fogged.' This simple method is calculated as follows.

1. Choose a sample text containing about 100 words.
2. Count the number of sentences and the number of words. Divide the number of words by the number of sentences to arrive at the Average Sentence Length (ASL).
3. Now count the number of long words (NLW—those with three or more syllables). You cannot count proper names, combination words like chairperson or firefighter or three-syllable verbs created by adding –es or –ed, such as united or arranges.
4. Perform this calculation

   Fog Index = (ASL + NLW) $\times$ 0.4

The figure you arrive at scores on the scale of readability:

(i) 5 to 10—easy
(ii) 11 to 15—difficult
(iii) 16 to 20—very difficult
(iv) Popular magazines score in the range of 8–12, while the average level for university students is 14–16.

Comprehensibility

The writing style varies with the writing objective. Research writing conveys the information with mathematical plainness and scientific objectivity. Therefore, it should be precise, concise and succinct in nature. Avoid structural and lexical ambiguity, multiple meanings and allusions. Use germane words to convey your thoughts accurately, efficiently and in a crystal-clear manner. While mentioning the concepts, define them operationally and descriptively.

The right choice of words, phrases and sentences makes the reading effective. It is also important to organize them carefully. The modifiers should be properly placed because if you are careless, the meaning of the sentences changes altogether. Subordinate ideas mixed with major ideas make the report confusing to the reader, forcing them to sort out what is most important and which is less important. It is your responsibility to place the information in the right order. Finally, it is the pace that is important. The pace should be properly maintained in the text. If the sentence has too much technical information, use few significant ideas. The pace of writing can be adjusted by following ways:

- Judicious use of white space for psychological effect.
- Use headings for the topics and break the larger units into smaller units.
- Corroborate the difficult text with usual aid.
- Underscore the important material and de-emphasize secondary material by proper use of italicizing, underlining, capitalization and parentheses.
- Choose the appropriate words, opting for concrete and familiar words than unfamiliar and long words. Avoid using jargons, pompous constructions, difficult and arcane words. When the report is written for audience of the same profession, you can use technical terms, else avoid them.
- Summarize the critical and difficult ideas so that readers have time to absorb.
- Connect the paragraphs properly by transitional words, such as 'however', 'in view of', 'despite the fact'.

Tone

Go through the writing to see if the tone is appropriate. The 'you' attitude makes the writing reader oriented. The message prepared for the reader conveys warmth, sincerity and personalization. Be positive in your tone than being negative.

Production

Once you have done the final editing, your report is ready for the process of production. These days it is most popular to get a computer printout. The presentation of the report conveys to the reader your professional approach. Use compatible fonts that don't stress the eyes of the reader. The paper quality should also be good.

When the reports are photocopied for more than one reader, make sure the copies are clean and have no black streaks or grey areas. Leave one-and-a-half-inch margin in the left and one-inch margin on the other three sides. Remember to label all the illustrations appearing in the report as they help the readers to return to the section they were reading in the report.

Illustrations

Illustrations are integral part of the discussion. All the technical reports, laboratory reports, interpretive reports, project reports include illustrations, such as, graphs, charts, tables, drawings, diagrams, photographs. The illustrations make the text livelier and explanation clearer. A lot of data can be comprehensively put in the form of well-organized illustrations. The writer should not be tempted to incorporate too many of illustration just for embellishment. But if you have a clear idea about each one of them, then you can judiciously use them to make your explanation better. The reports largely depend on these illustrations for better clarification and explanation. You must remember that the illustrations also draw and retain the attention for a longer time.

While using the illustrations, know what value addition is being done to the text. If the answer is negative, it is better not to use them. Put the illustrations along with the discussion and not in the beginning or end of the discussion. Illustrations if properly made generate lot of interest in the readers besides giving the report a professional look. The advantage of it is of occupying less space for explanation of complicated data. The readers can comprehend the details very fast as it represents the data in simple form.

A few guidelines for illustrations are as follow:

- Make the illustrations simple
- Put them vertical
- Place them close to the discussion
- Indicate the source, if borrowed
- See if the data is accurately depicted
- Keep decent margins above and below the graphics for clarity
- Choose the graphics which best depicts the data
- Do refer the illustration in the text
- Label each illustration as discussed in the chapter
- Use different shades to differentiate the segments

Types

Each illustration has different purpose. It depends on the type of explanation you want to support. Use your judgement to choose which one suits best to your report. Remember the objective and the audience, as that can make your task easy. You need not use colours for illustrations unless it is necessary. The illustrations are classified in two broad categories of *Tables* and *Figures,* which are further divided.

Table can be of following types:

1. Phrase table
2. Dependent table
3. Independent table

Figure can be classified as:

1. Graphs
    - 1.1 Rectilinear
    - 1.2 Bilinear
    - 1.3 Multilinear
    - 1.4 Bar
    - 1.5 Pie
    - 1.6 Pictorial
    - 1.7 Scatter
2. Maps
3. Drawings
4. Photographs
5. Charts

Table

You can use tables to represent the exact numbers used in your study in more logical and comprehensive way. You must understand what you want to represent through the tables. They enable you to make quick glance at the data and easy comparison of the information. Sometimes the tables also depict the trend if put in chronological order. But is not always the case and that is why graphs are used. The tables are divided into rows and columns, the vertical lines are called *rows* and the horizontal ones are called *columns*. The topmost horizontal section is called subhead, and the vertical column is called box head. You can make the boxes of equal size. As far as possible complete your table in one page. If it runs on the second page, mention it is continued on the next page, and repeat the information in the subhead.

Suppose you are showing the placements of the students in four major organizations in the last ten years, you can use table in that case also. Write the numerical values in the centre of the box and if any data is not available don't leave the box blank. Put a hyphen in that box. As discussed previously, the tables should be numbered in roman numerals and on the top.

Phrase table has no numerical values but only phrases.

Dependent table is the continuation of the text and can't be understood in isolation. You can use it when the data is very less.

Independent table stands on its own and is most commonly used. You can clearly understand the table without even reading the text. But there will be reference in the text of the table.

Example of phrase table is as follows:

Mobile model	Colour	Battery
Nokia 1600	Black	Normal
Reliance classic 632	Black	Poor

Example of dependent table is as follows:

The number of students, awarded merit-cum-scholarship for different disciplines.

Details of number of students awarded	
Mechanical Engineering	**55**
Chemical Engineering	**39**
Civil Engineering	**28**
Computer Science	**115**
Software Systems	**97**
Information Systems	**145**

Example of independent table is as follows:

Purchase of two-wheelers in Mumbai from (2000–2007)

Year	Cycle	Scooters	Bikes	Total	%
2001	3400	1900	1000	6300	10.2
2002	3300	2100	1300	6700	10.9
2003	2900	2300	1900	7100	11.5
2004	2200	2500	2800	7500	12.2
2005	2000	2700	4200	8900	14.5
2006	1500	2800	6700	11000	17.9
2007	900	3000	9900	13800	22.5
Total	16200	17300	27800	61300	100
Percentage	26.4%	28.2%	45.4%	100%	

Graphs

Another way to represent the data which can be presented in the tabular form is the graph. In the graph, the depiction becomes more interesting and arrests the reader's interest immediately. Sometimes the table has more clarity than the graphs. So you have to be clever in deciding which illustration will be better for the study. The graphs should be labelled on the x-axis and y-axis properly. The legend and key should also be provided. There should be cross reference of the graph in the text else, it will not serve much purpose. They are very good choice to indicate distribution, trends and comparison. The different types of graphs you may use in your report are rectilinear, bilinear, multilinear, pie, bar, semi-log, pictorial and scatter graph.

Rectilinear graph: It is used to show the changes or progress over a given period of time. You can observe the trend while reading it. Usually, for convenience you can plot independent variable on horizontal axis, i.e., x-axis, and dependent variables on the vertical axis, i.e., y-axis. This is because the magnitudes are represented through heights, the dependent variables are on the vertical axis.

The scales on both the sides have proper division. It might not start with zero and can take up the first reading, else long gap appears leaving the blank space.

Example

Line graph showing temperature of Jodhpur measured for four days in the month of May in Fahrenheit.

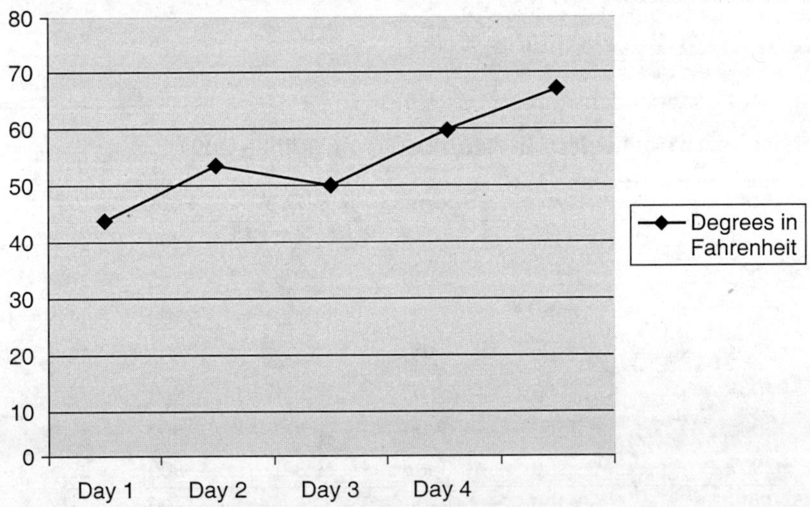

Bilinear graph: Rectilinear graph depicts the trend but if there is comparison made between the two variables, then you choose the bilinear graph. For example, if you have to show the temperature along with the humidity in air in four days you can show it with the help of a bilinear graph. Similarly, if variables increase in the number, you can use multilinear graph so there is comparison between more variables.

Example

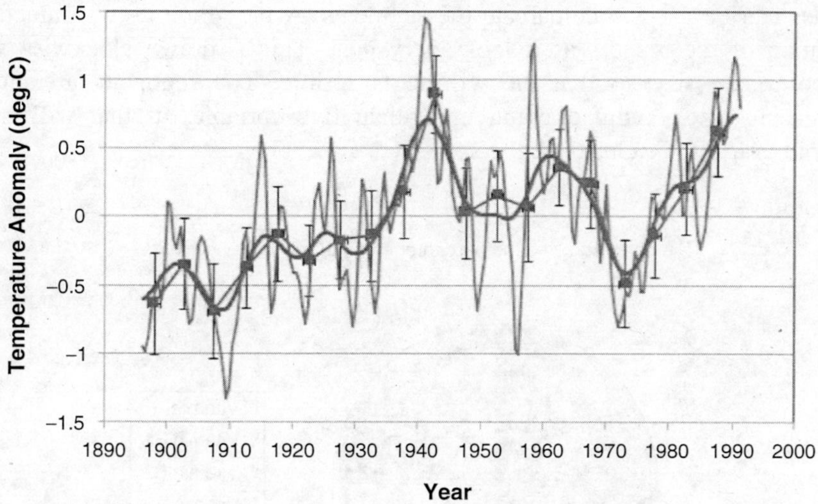

Bar graph: It is most commonly used in the reports as it compares several items in your data. The bar graph can show profit, cost, sales, and revenues in different month or year. You can quickly make comparison from a bar graph but must be careful in depicting the correct information. By a bar graph, you can depict the quantity over the same period or different period of time. The difference in the size of the bar will indicate difference. The different shades can be used for the bars to differentiate the variables. The bar can be placed horizontally or vertically. Try not to overcrowd the graph with too many variables, else the comprehension will be tough. Rather in such situation use two graphs.

Example

The purchase of two-wheelers in Mumbai from 2001–2007

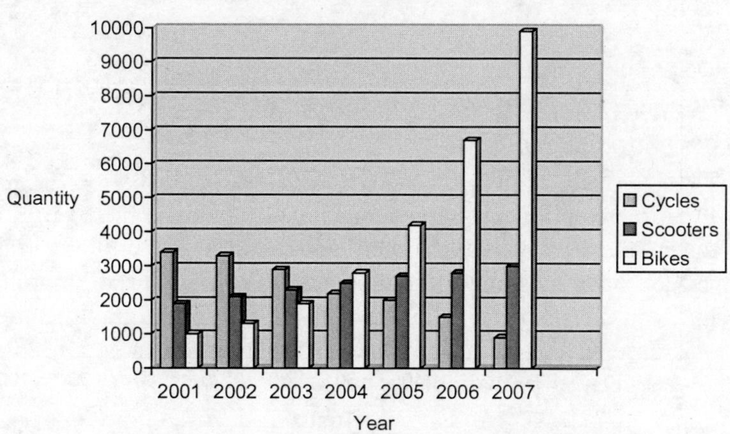

Pie graph: It is also called percentage graph. It is an effective way to represent the contribution of an individual segment to the whole. Different shades can be used to demarcate the segments. A pie graph draws immediate attention of the readers as it looks very neat. This is drawn clockwise with proportionate size so that the writing is visible. The segments are cut in decreasing size. Avoid drawing more than five variables as that will make the pie graph look cluttered.

Example

Pie chart showing the percentage of vitamin in orange fruit.

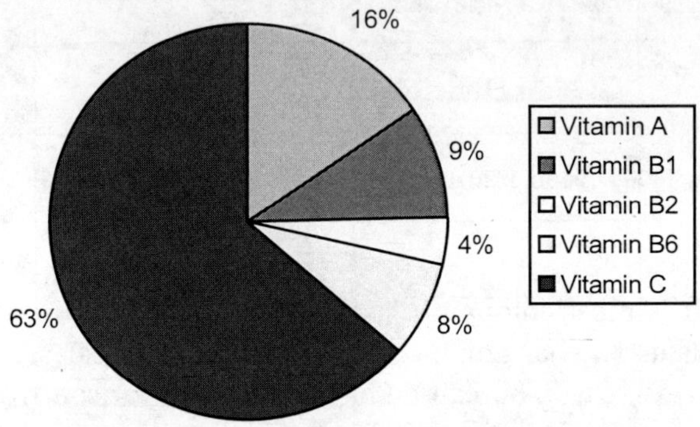

Scatter graph: It is used to show the correlation between the various variables used in the study. The variables are shown by dots or stars. The clutter shows the good correlation, but the absence shows that no correlation exists between the variables. This graph is used appropriately to do grading of the students.

Example

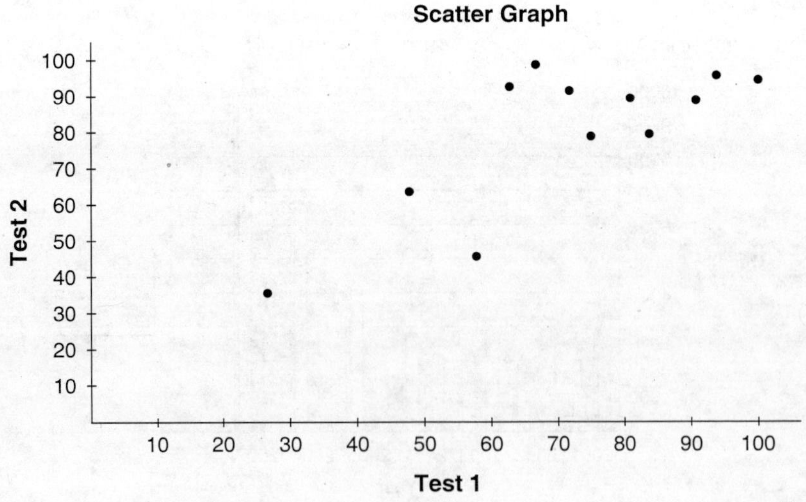

Pictorial graph: Small pictures are used to represent the real object in pictorial graph. This graph looks very lively as the clear picture emerges out of it. If you have to represent the population of the zoo, you can use the pictures of lion, peacock, crocodile, etc. One picture can represent 10 or 20 as per your assumption. It is very time consuming to use this graph and used less in technical reports.

Example

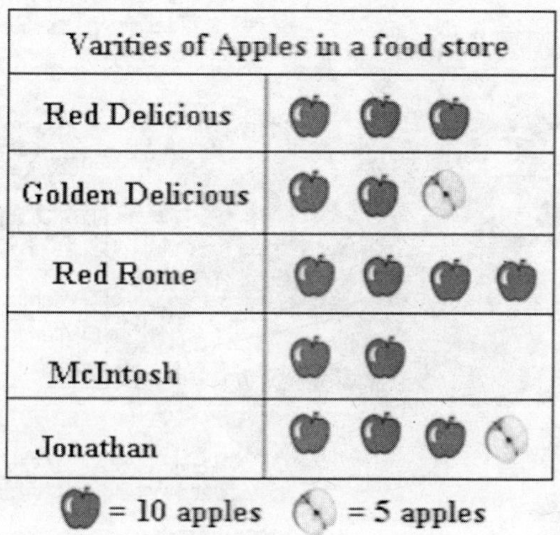

Maps

Depending on the purpose, maps representing area, route, historical places, market areas, etc. are chosen. Maps are mainly used to show to represent spatial relationship which is quite difficult to explain in words. Uses of colours exemplify the maps further. Scale is used as per the requirement, and the objective of the report. Try to be as exact in scaling as possible.

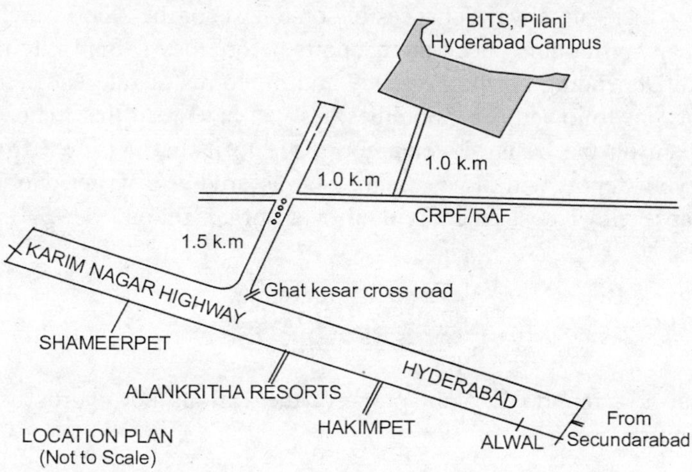

Photographs

They are rarely used in technical reports. You can use them when the exact description of the product or a person is needed. The representation of the photograph needs sharp accuracy else the whole purpose is lost. The reproduction cost is higher than other illustrations.

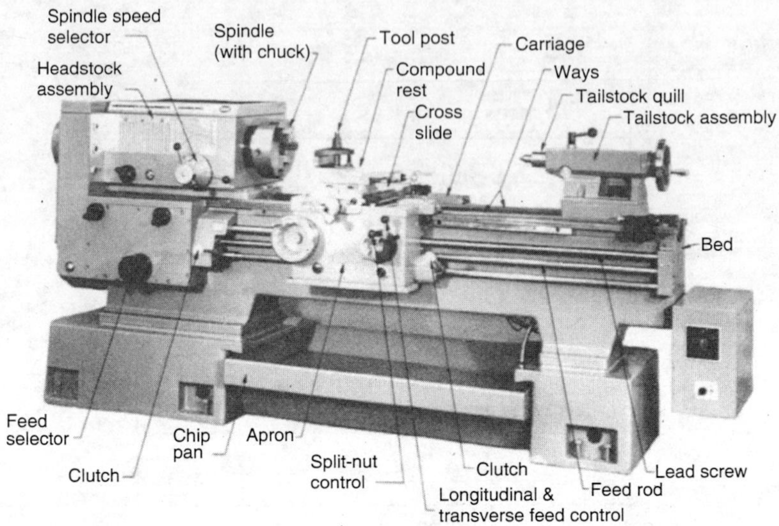

Drawings

Drawings represent line, area, cross-sectional views, etc. It is often difficult to use photographs in the entire situation, therefore drawings are better. For a building, you can use to view, side view, top view, cross-sectional, etc. The circuits can be best represented through drawings.

Once you have written your report, wisdom tells us to verify that all the required structural aspects have been taken into consideration. However hard we may try, there are always chances of some lapse or the other. Careful writers of reports always double check their reports before they submit it to the person concerned. Depending on the exigency and the terms of reference, ensure that your report has followed the guidelines. As you have read that major decisions can be taken on the basis of your report, see to it that it is free from errors. Revising your report will always make you assured as a writer. No one wants that his lapse either cost an individual or an organization.

• EXERCISES •

1. What is a report? Explain properly the various key words used in the definition.

2. What is the difference between oral and written reports? Give an example of each.

3. The Chairman, Energy Development and Conservation Council, New Delhi, has been concerned about the recurring mismatch between the demand for electricity and its supply all over the country. As the Secretary of this Council, you have been asked to study the sector-wise power consumption pattern and write a report to be submitted to the Chairman. The following table gives the data for three consecutive years.

Table showing sector-wise power distribution (in billion unit)

Sector	Year		
	2000–2001	2001–02	2002–2003
Agriculture	70.70	79.30	85.74
Commercial	34.91	39.52	41.30
Domestic	43.82	45.56	48.64

Now write only the following elements to be incorporated in the report:

Abstract
Introduction
Discussion

4. India Airways has been constantly incurring loss due to sharp decrease in the number of passengers travelling by this airway. The Civil Aviation Department, Government of India is serious about this problem and wants to know the real causes for the passengers' lack of interest in this airway. You being the Chief Commercial Manager have been asked to investigate this problem and suggest suitable measures to attract more passengers. Now write the **Discussion, Conclusion and Recommendation** (only) of your full-length report using the following data which have been collected by you from the passengers using mail questionnaire. Invent necessary details.

	Services	Very Poor	Poor	Fair	Good	Excellent	No response
1.	Response to telephone enquiry	18	32	34	14	1	1
2.	Response to personal enquiry	10	20	40	25	3	2
3.	Booking services	5	30	28	24	11	2
4.	Onward reservation system	15	26	33	12	6	8
5.	Cancellation of tickets	4	27	42	20	7	–
6.	Communication between booking offices	8	40	31	13	6	2
7.	Quality of announcements at airports	14	12	36	30	8	–
8.	Food	7	22	45	24	2	–
9.	Supply of reading materials	12	31	37	19	1	–
10.	Baggage clearance	21	27	34	12	3	3
11.	Facilities for transit passengers	9	33	41	15	1	1
12.	Coach services	4	18	43	26	6	3
13.	Coordination between city office and airport	10	35	36	18	1	–
14.	Punctuality	5	22	40	30	2	1

(The figure given are in percentage.)

5. In a recently conducted survey on "Shift in Students' Interest in Career Choices', it has been observed that students now prefer to study service-oriented courses rather than engineering-oriented courses. They prefer to take up electives in a wide variety of areas, such as financial services, management services, communication, behavioural sciences etc. This shift has resulted in a greater number of students being recruited in the services industry in recent years.

   Following is the student registration data for last four year in the four different career streams:

Year	Core engineering skills	Core management skills	Core IT skills	Core services skills	Total no. of students
2002	150	105	200	45	500
2003	120	115	185	80	500
2004	130	80	170	120	500
2005	120	70	180	130	500

   You, as the Placement Officer of Terra Academy of Science and Technology, have been asked by the Board of Directors to prepare a letter report giving adequate reasons for this shift, keeping into consideration the steps to be taken in the light of these changes. Now using the data given in Table write a **Letter Report**. Invent the necessary details.

6. As a life member of Red Cross Society, you have been assigned the responsibility to carry out a survey of local youths of your city reportedly involved in drug abuse. Before submitting a report to the President of Red Cross Society, you have decided to analyse *the reasons of youths' involvement, availability of drugs, and its impact on society and addicts' determination to quit.* Prepare a mail questionnaire that can invite objective and truthful answers. Your questionnaire should have 15 questions from the areas specified. Don't write personal detail questions and covering letter.

7. **Clearly bring out the differences between the following:**
   (a) Primary Data and Secondary Data
   (b) Pie Graph and Rectilinear Graph
   (c) Annual Confidential Report and Inventory Report
   (d) Terms of Reference and Letter of Transmittal
   (e) Personal Interview and Telephonic Interview

8. Coffee Day, a food chain that serves various coffee preparations, shakes and continental fast food, wishes to open an outlet on the BITS campus in Pilani. The Chief Executive Officer (CEO) of Coffee Day has asked the Sales department to judge the market for their products amongst the students of BITS, Pilani. As a senior market analyst in the sales department, you have conducted a survey on the preferences of the students through questionnaires and personal interviews. Samples of

50 students were selected from every year of study. The results of the survey are tabulated below. Write the **discussion and conclusion** of the full-length report to be submitted to the CEO analysing the feasibility of opening a franchise on campus. You can invent suitable details to augment the information provided, such as preferences for ambience, service, timings. The discussion should be complete with at least two levels of sub-headings and appropriate illustrations.

Preferences	**First year**	**Second year**	**Third year**	**Fourth year**
Coffee/Shakes	20	25	28	35
Health Drinks	25	25	20	15
Chinese cuisine	15	18	15	20
Fast food	18	25	27	32
North Indian	25	20	21	18
South Indian	23	15	12	12

Note: A student might have opted for more than one preference, i.e., a student may like Chinese as well as North Indian and so on.

9. Explain why objectivity is an essential feature of report writing?

10. What is the function of Annual–Confidential Report?

11. Brilliant Management Consultants, Delhi, is running a four-week training programme in Professional Communication for its junior executives. Since it is going to end on next Sunday, you as the Training Manager are planning to obtain the feedback and suggestions for the programme, with a view to improve the qualities of its training in future. Now prepare a questionnaire consisting of 15 questions for eliciting the required information. Don't write the covering letter and questions on personal details.

12. Eureka Advertising Corporation, Ghaziabad plans to promote its employees of marketing unit. The decision will primarily be based on the information collected through the Annual Assessment Report. Assuming yourself as Marketing Manager, prepare an **Annual Assessment Pro forma** to be submitted to the Unit Head PRU to evaluate the performance of the members of the unit.

13. As an Advisory Executive, you have been asked by the Director of the Board of Education, to inspect three newly established schools for affiliation to the Board of Education, Rajasthan. You have taken into consideration factors, such as number and qualification of teachers, infrastructure, education modules. After conducting your survey, you have to submit a letter report, justifying why you have recommended or rejected the schools. Invent the necessary details.

14. Feedback Communications, a leader in the world of advertising language is involved in various advertising assignments. The company of late wants to bring about certain changes in order to compete with rapid changing business scenario. Before taking the final decision, the company wants to make a market survey regarding the medium of advertising, its timing, target audience and effective messaging. Prepare a **Mail Questionnaire** comprising twenty specific questions from the areas specified.

15. The Ministry of Education, Government of India wishes to launch some new schemes for eradicating illiteracy among the schedule castes and schedule tribes of Bihar, MP, Rajasthan and Orissa. For this purpose, the Directorate of Adult Education, New Delhi has been asked to compare and analyse the following data collected from Census of India 2001 and submit a report on the same.

State	1981 SC	ST	Total	1991 SC	ST	Total	2001 SC	ST	Total
Bihar	6.53	11.65	19.94	10.40	16.99	32.05	19.49	26.78	38.48
MP	12.49	7.62	22.14	18.97	10.68	36.63	35.08	21.54	44.20
Orissa	15.61	9.46	26.18	22.41	13.96	40.97	36.78	22.31	49.09
Rajasthan	9.14	6.47	19.07	14.04	10.27	30.11	26.29	19.44	38.55

Your report should include title page, introduction, discussion, conclusion and recommendation.

16. The Centre for Social Research, Hyderabad is conducting an independent research on why Indian youths are adopting violent means to press for their demands and the findings of this research are likely to be published in national and international news magazines. As part of this research, views of people of different age groups from five metropolitan cities—Delhi, Chennai, Hyderabad, Mumbai and Kolkata—have been ascertained through mail questionnaire. The tabulated data are presented below:

Age group	Corruption	Unemployment	Faulty legal system	Easy access of arms	Cinema	Unitary family
10–20	10	15	07	13	32	23
20–30	23	32	20	10	04	11
30–40	20	35	16	11	10	08
40–50	27	11	24	09	12	17
50–60	20	07	33	08	10	22

(The given data are in percentage.)

Assuming yourself to be the chief investigator, prepare an analytical report to be submitted to the Director of the Centre, using the given data and inventing other necessary details. Your report should contain **title page, introduction, discussion, conclusion and recommendation** only.

17. The Indian Government is concerned about the exodus of Indian doctors, engineers and academicians to foreign countries like America, Britain, Germany and Gulf Countries and wishes to retain these professionals from the above cited fields to utilize their services for the motherland and fellow countrymen. In this connection the Chief Secretary, Ministry of Human Resource Development, New Delhi has asked for a report investigating the causes of this trend and suggesting measures to arrest the exodus. As a research analyst in the above Ministry, you have been asked to write the report to be sent to the Chief Secretary. The data you have obtained are given in the following table:

Profession	**Countries Immigrated to after obtaining degrees**			
	America	**Britain**	**Germany**	**Gulf countries**
Doctors	60	27	19	6
Engineers	06	24	08	7
Academicians	13	27	13	47

Note: The figures are in percentage

Your report should contain the following elements only:

- Introduction
- Discussion
- Conclusion

18. As the registrar of a residential university, you have been asked to study its existing communication system and to suggest measures for smooth flow of both vertical and horizontal communication within it. Write a short report in the form of letter, incorporating the results of your analysis and your recommendations for submission to the Vice-Chancellor.

19. You have just returned from an International Conference on Creativity and Innovation in Global Business to which you had been deputed by your company. Write **a memo** to your boss, reporting to him the various issues discussed in the conference. Emphasize the need of introducing some changes in your organization in the light of the steps suggested in the two-day gathering of eminent economists and technical experts.

20. Today's competitive business world has thrown challenges before the highest authority of any organization in how to retain the trained workers in the organization as well as how to motivate its employees for optimum performance. The chairman, Fundamental Research Laboratory, New Delhi is very much concerned about these issues. You being the Personnel Manager of the organization have been asked by the chairman to carry out a study in your organization in this regard and recommend some concrete steps to meet such challenges. Prepare an analytical report with suitable illustrations using the following data which have been collected by you from three different groups of employees using a questionnaire. The following table gives the frequency count for responses from each group.

Year	**Senior Scientists**	**Junior Scientists**	**Supervisors**
Money Rewards	80	60	90
Knowledge Training	85	30	15
Social Rewards	40	65	60
Free Lunches	20	55	65
Club Privilege	50	60	10
Flexible Hours	25	30	60
Total	300	300	300

Your report should include **Title page, Abstract, Content, Main Body (Introduction, Analysis, Findings, Conclusion) and Recommendations**. Invent necessary details wherever necessary.

21. The Indian Railways is considering major changes to improve the facilities currently available on its express trains. A committee has been set up to conduct a Customer Survey about various facilities travellers' need, their satisfaction level, and suggestions to make train travel enjoyable and comfortable.

You are required to prepare a questionnaire with about 12–15 questions that would elicit relevant information in the areas of study. Don't write covering letter and questions on personal details.

22. With a view to rescheduling its programmes, the Director of Delhi Doordarshan has asked its Publicity Manager to submit a report. Assuming yourself to be the publicity manager you plan to conduct a survey among one thousand families each in Mumbai, Delhi and Kolkata. Prepare a **Mail Questionnaire** to be sent to the viewers for this purpose. Your questionnaire should at least 10 questions to elicit the relevant information.

23. The recent earthquake in the Uri sector of Jammu and Kashmir has caused a large-scale damage to the government and the public properties. The state and the central governments want to assess the damage before they start the reconstruction work. Assuming you to be the Executive Engineer of the Public Works Department, Uri Sector, prepare the **outline** for the report to be submitted to the Chief Secretary, Jammu and Kashmir. Invent the necessary details.

24. Global Solutions Pvt. Ltd., Pune has achieved the highest rate of employee retention over the years. Micro Solutions, Gurgaon which is facing a huge problem in employee retention wants to implement certain schemes for retaining its employees. But before taking any decision, the top management of the company is interested in knowing how Global Solutions Pvt. Ltd could achieve it. You being the Executive Manager-HR of Global Solutions have been requested to send a report in this regard. Draft the **letter report** addressed to your counterpart in Micro Solutions inventing necessary details. Your report should include the following elements:

- Introduction
- Discussion
- Conclusion

25. Tourism is a rapidly growing industry in India. It attracts vast pool of foreign tourists from different parts of the world. Being India's premier traveling agency, Kings Travels conducted a survey of last three years' input of foreign tourists in India. The company wants to attract the larger chunk of tourists to avail its services and plans to know which group of tourists travel frequently, how much they earn and which class they represent. The company hires the services of your travel consultancy and asks you to submit the **letter report** to the CEO, Kings Travels explaining the results of the survey and its implications for the tourism sector. Your report should be in full block style. Invent necessary details.

26. In the present context, Educational Scenario has been deeply affected due to various external factors like introduction of quota system, reservation, curriculum design, etc. This has led to discontent among the educators as well as students. The Ministry of Education has formed a committee to enquire into this matter. You as the chairman of this committee must prepare a report to be submitted to the Head, Ministry of Education. Prepare an **Introduction** for this report.

27. The active participation of students in academic festivals, extra-curricular and co-curricular activities has helped them to get keyed up for their professional life. As the President, Students' Union, you have been asked by the Director to prepare a **Questionnaire** to be circulated among students to trace the benefits of these activities which are likely to help them in academic as well as professional career. Now prepare 15 questions besides the personal details for this questionnaire. You need not write the covering letter.

28. You, as a Human Personnel Director in All for Life Co., are asked to recommend to the executive committee a new provident fund plan, hospitalization plan and house allotment plan for the benefit of the employees. Prepare a Letter report for the same.

29. Ashtha Group of Education wants to establish a 100-bed hospital for the staff and students of Astha Institute of Engineering and Management (AIEM) at SHAMNAGAR. Before taking the final step, it wants to analyze the various requirements. You as the Chief Planning Officer of the group have been assigned the task of writing a report to understand the needs, requirements, facilities and manpower. Prepare a **Questionnaire** (containing twenty questions) to collect the data for this report.

30. You are the Public Relations Officer of Jindal group of Companies, Jamunanagar. Write a **memo** for circulation to all employees of your organization requesting them to contribute one day's salary to Prime Minister Relief Fund to help the victims of Tsunami.

31. Express Movers & Packers Jamnagar has got a tender of exporting goods to other nations. They find it difficult when it comes to communicating with foreign agencies and tourists. The director wants to train their employees in order to make them effective at workplace. You as the training manager of Lingua Plus have been asked to formulate a course in business communication for a fortnight. Write a *Letter Report* to be submitted to the director of Lingua Plus focusing on the different steps as well as ways to help the employees pick up certain business tricks and communicative skills.

32. Hungama Channels Private Ltd. has been recently sued for its inappropriate content. The Regulatory Board, in this regard, has asked the channel to come up with some TV instruction plan for teenagers, to be followed conspicuously by the channel. You as a Human Resource Manager have been asked to prepare the guidelines to be sent to the Board. Now prepare a memo report to be circulated to all the managers of the channel, asking for their suggestions and feedback on the guidelines prepared.

33. Manhattan Institute of Technology (MIT), Chirawa, well known for its innovative teaching ways, started in 2005 with good intake of students in different branches. The placement records added to its achievement and the institute attributed its success to introduction of new technology in teaching, modern labs, use of interactive media, friendly environment, etc. The Director of Benevolence Institute of Sciences, Bhagalpur, despite huge investments finds his institute lagging behind. Influenced by the success of MIT, he wishes to know its teaching pattern so that the same can be implemented in their institute also. Therefore, he has assigned the task to the Registrar to investigate the reasons of success of MIT and submit a report to him. Now you as the Registrar write an **Introduction** of the report.

34. T.V.R. Institute of Technology and Science is planning to open a souvenir shop to promote its brand. You as an In-charge of Purchase Department have been asked to prepare a report of the items to be sold in the shop. Your report should be the outcome of preferences made by the students and staff, reasons supporting the preferences and suggestions.

35. Annapoorna, a reputed group, which is a brand name in the supply of provisional items such as rice, pulses, cookies, toiletries and various goods of everyday use, wants to open its new branch in the newly established educational hub of Sharadanagar. You as the Area Sales Manager have been asked to collect a data on the need of buyers, their paying capacity, timings and other details. Based on your survey, write an analytical report to be submitted to the CEO. Your report should include Introduction, Discussion, Conclusion and Recommendation.

36. After two years of Pandemic, Marudhar Insitute of Technology, Shrirampur is going to start functioning in the offline mode. Yet because of the fears arising from time to time as heard from the media, the managing committee of the institution thinks of sensitizing its faculty, staff and students. As admissions and placement officer of the institute, you have been asked to write a report to be submitted to the Director. Think of the various pre-cautionary measures required to be taken before the institute starts functioning like in the past. Draft the said report. Invent necessary details.

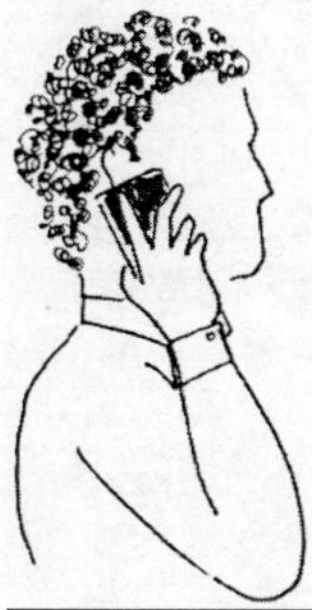

8

Sample Reports

One look is worth a thousand reports.

—CHINESE PROVERB

In Chapter 7 we discussed the principles, structures and various strategies of writing a report. You might have realized by now that writing a report is a cumbersome task, yet it can't be ignored. Professionals need to be trained to write reports. They need to write one at some point of time in their career. Reports, as you have read, can be long or short, informative or analytical, and routine too. Short reports include letter reports and memo reports. This chapter acquaints you with some sample reports, both short and long ones. It will help you understand how principles can be put into practice.

LETTER REPORT

Sample I

Country Arts Council, a non-profit group, raises funds and provides volunteers to support Radha Krishnan Library, a local library. Every February, the president of Radha Krishnan Library sends a report to this group as it allows for an annual grant of ₹ 5 lakhs. Now a letter report needs to be submitted to the Director of The Country Arts Council giving the details of the previous year's activities and informing the new activities that are being planned to be introduced in the coming year.

President
Radha Krishnan Library
New Delhi
Feb. 16, 2022

Director
Country Arts Council
New Delhi

Dear Sir

It is my pleasure to declare the annual report of the year 2020–2021. We have been able to close one fiscal year of accounting with accomplishments, benefits to the masses and the credibility and reputation of our group on a positive note.

We were successful in maintaining our books and observing the substantial increase of members from 60,000 (permanent) to 72,000, a growth of 20%. This is illustrated in Graph 1.

All our efforts were made possible due to a perfect tracking system of books, increased vigilance to avoid theft, maintaining the upkeeping of books, hygiene and good housekeeping. Further to our initiatives, we would like to implement and upgrade new software which maintains complete inventory of books, keeps track of new releases of books, (available online), and prompts us to buy when those books are available at a lower cost.

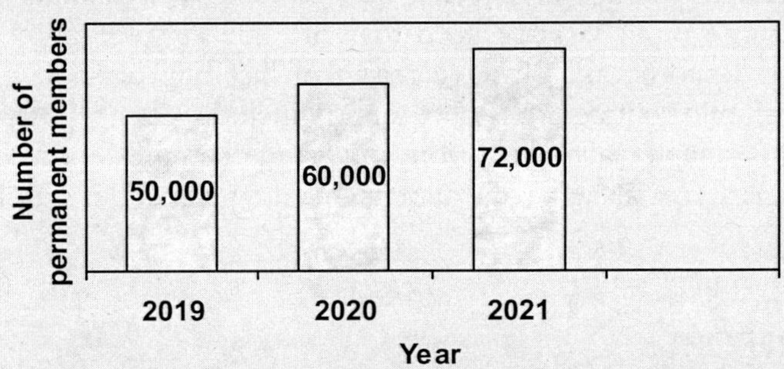

Graph 1

Expenditure	(All figures in lakh)
New book purchase	₹ 3.50
Salaries paid to staff	₹ 0.75
Furniture (book shelf)	₹ 0.1
Computers...............................	₹ 0.1
Security system	₹ 0.1
Fire protection system	₹ 0.05
Insurance	₹ 0.05
Total	₹ 4.65

Savings

Although ₹ 35,000 (thirty-five thousand) was the net saving, this amount has been reserved for the new recommendations and initiatives proposed.

Budget for the new initiative

Various proposals were evaluated to procure new software, and as per the vendor selection process, a company, "ABC", has been shortlisted with a quote of ₹ 2.50 lakh.

An additional ₹ 2.15 lakh would be required in order to enhance the objective of the group.

Therefore, I would request you to approve the aforesaid amount at the earliest.

Yours truly,

Lalit Kumar

Sample II

Tourism is a rapidly growing industry in India. It attracts a vast pool of foreign tourists from different parts of the world. As India's premier travelling agency, Kings Travels surveyed the last three years' input of foreign tourists in India. The company wants to attract a large number of tourists to avail of its services and plans to know which group of tourists travels frequently, how much they earn and which class they represent. The company hires the services of Nirupama travel consultancy and asks it to submit a letter report to the CEO of Kings Travels explaining the results of the survey and its implications for the tourism sector. The report is in full-block style.

Kings Travels
New Delhi, India

Ref. No.: 10023-B
10th May 2022

Chief Executive Officer
Kings Travels
New Delhi

Sub: Tourism Section

Sir,

This report is in reference to the survey conducted during April 2022 on the Tourism Sector by Nirupama Travel Consultancy, New Delhi, for the last three years.

The survey has been conducted according to the desired schedule, keeping the interests of the tourists in mind.

1. Introduction

Tourism is a rapidly growing industry in India. It attracts a vast pool of foreigners from different parts of the world. Over the past few years, our country has seen a boom in this sector and is looking forward to attracting a large number of tourists to avail of its services. Transportation and accommodation means have also increased tremendously over the years.

The methods of collecting data are as follows:

(i) Questionnaires circulated among certain tourists all over the country
(ii) Interviews with manager's of the tourist hotels
(iii) Personal experience

The report is limited since only the major tourist places could be considered for the survey.

2. Tourists

2.1 Tourist groups

The most frequently travelling groups are families, followed by friends. Business officials do not seem to be interested in the tourism aspect. The archaeological groups are restricted to only certain places within the country. The visiting groups are relatively low as compared to all the other groups. Figure 1 shall illustrate a bar diagram for the same.

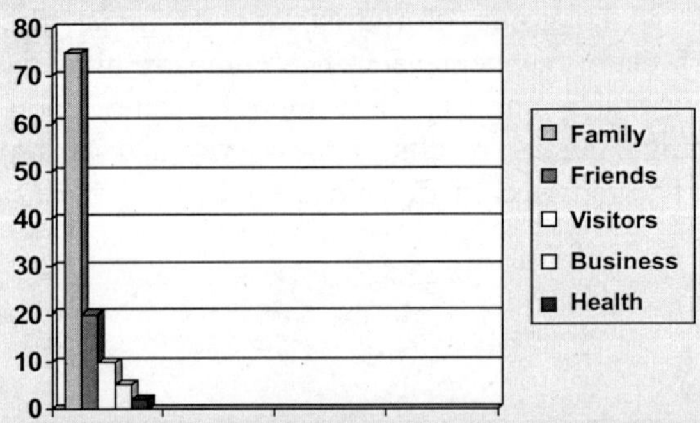

Figure 1 Y axis depicts the percentage and X axis the tourist group.

2.2 Income of tourists

From the statistics, we can conclude that the majority of the tourists comprise wealthy people. The rest of the tourists' segment includes only those that come for health purposes or business meetings and, thus, do not have the time or money for travelling within the country. The income of the tourists in 90 per cent of the cases is above ₹ 3 lakh per annum.

2.3 Class of the tourists

The tourists, based on income and accommodation, can be classified as 75 per cent belonging to the high class, 23 per cent belonging to the middle class, and 2 per cent belonging to poor sections. Thus, the majority of tourists choose to stay in high-class hotels.

3. Measures to be Taken to Increase Tourism

3.1 Improving accommodation facilities

The various hotels must investigate the environment and other facilities as most tourists belong to higher sections of society. This can be done either by talking to the hotel management or conducting workshops.

3.2 Transportation facilities

The number of international airports in the country is only 20, whereas the tourist places are around 20,000. For the comfort of the tourist, Air Indias service should be improved. The different modes of travel within the country must be made better, especially the railways, as most tourists complain about the trains being booked completely.

3.3 Food and service

Since Indian food is very spicy, foreigners have problems, which leads to their leaving the country early. This sector must be looked into as well.

3.4 Maintenance of tourist spots

The government must invest more in safeguarding tourist places and seeking a neat and healthy environment. This can be done by creating awareness among the local people and by conducting lectures, using posters, etc.

4. Conclusion

Although the tourism sector is growing rapidly in the country, many further measures need to be taken for development in the sector. The measures taken can be by individuals or by the government and can improve in transportation and accommodation.

I hope this report covered all the desired aspects.

Thank you

Yours sincerely

M Harini
Manager
Nirupama Travel Consultancy
New Delhi

MEMO REPORTS

Sample I

A memo report regarding the functioning of messes in BITS to install bakery ovens in them is given here.

BIRLA INSTITUTE OF TECHNOLOGY AND SCIENCE
PILANI, RAJASTHAN-333031

To: Dean, Students Welfare Division
BITS, Pilani

Date: 04 December 2018

From: Student Representative
Mess Committee

Ref: 2GHM/98

Subject: Installation of bakery ovens in bhavan messes.

With respect to your letter 2GHM/97 dated 28 October 2018, I surveyed the functioning of messes in BITS so as to have proper installation of bakery ovens in them. The result and analysis are put forth as follow:

Mess Strategy

There are twelve bhavans in BITS Pilani, comprising six messes, one each for two bhavans. There is a constant demand for bakery items from the students to supplement their appetite during other hours than mess timings. In early mornings and evenings, students go to messes for a cup of tea or coffee and want eatables along with it. Though there is a supply of bakery items produced locally, it does not fulfill the demand of the students. There is always a shortage, and many students have to return disappointed. Only one bakery outside the campus is there to supply edibles to the six messes. This is not sufficient. So according to the findings, installing bakery ovens in the messes is the right move. At least the mess workers can make the required quantity of bakery items at an appropriate time. However, there is not enough space in every mess to set an oven. So, to have proper orientation and size, different ovens must be examined. The available spaces in messes where ovens can be installed effectively are as follows:

Length = 2 feet
Breadth = 2.5 feet
Height = 3 feet

So, the ovens should meet the requirements and get fitted in the space available for proper functioning.

Oven Varieties and Strategies

To meet the deadline for the assessment of messes, I preferred to get a technician to help me with the size and fixtures. I contacted an authorized dealer of Crompton Greaves and studied the varieties and related utilities of different ovens. He handed me a catalogue consisting of the features, model numbers, sizes, costs, etc., of the ovens. The different strategies of the oven have been put in Table 1.1:

Table 1.1: Oven Features

Model no.	Width of machines front panel	Cost (₹)	Safety lock on panel	Timer on panel
VAC/1	1 ft 5 inches	5500	Yes – integrated	Present
VAC/2	1 ft 6 inches	6000	No – absent	Present
VAC/3	1 ft 7 inches	7500	Yes – integrated	Present
VAC/4	1 ft 8 inches	8900	Yes – automatic	Absent
VAC/5	1 ft 10 inches	10000	Yes – automatic	Present
VAC/6	2 feet	12000	Yes – automatic	Absent

Analysis and Recommendation

After having a detailed study and analysis of the features, cost, etc., of different model types, I have selected model number VAC/3 and VAC/5 for messes. As the breadth of the space available in messes is 2.5 feet, the ovens with these model numbers are of suitable size. Their front panel width are 1 ft 7 inches and 1 ft 10 inches, which is a suitable space. Moreover, their costs are also low as compared to ovens of other companies having similar make and features. As required, there are 'integrated safety' lock on the panel and timer in the first model and 'automatic' safety locks on the panel and timer on the second model too. As these ovens with model numbers VAC/3 and VAC/5 of Crompton Greaves Company are satisfying the requirements of the messes, I would recommend the installation of these in the bhavan messes.

Findings and Conclusions

Ovens with model number VAC/3 and VAC/5 of Crompton Greaves Company are matching the required statistics of ovens for messes. Their features and other details are forwarded in Table 1.1. Hope that this analysis will lead to the proper installation of ovens in messes in BITS, Pilani and their proper functioning, ensuring the safety of the mess workers.

Sourav Killa

Sample II

The director of Siemens Institute of Art and Sciences is concerned about the lack of enthusiasm among students for participating in academic activities.

He asks the Dean of Academics to study the cause and suggest measures to motivate the students to participating in all academic activities of the institute. The memo report highlighting the students' less participation in academic activities, the causes related to the problem and measures to overcome it is given here.

Siemens Institute of Art and Sciences
C-4, Dwarka, New Delhi - 110042

Inter Office Memorandum

To: Director — Ref: PN/4/1237
From: Dean of Academics — Date: 3 May 2021

Subject: Lack of participation in academic activities

Please refer to your Memo no. PN/4/1237, dated 26 April 2021, asking me to study the causes for lack of enthusiasm among students for participating in academic activities and to suggest remedial measures.

Findings

Based on responses from 64 students and 2 faculty members, the following causes for poor participation in academic festivals were determined:

Thirty-one per cent of students cited low participation of students other than the institute as the reason for their lack of enthusiasm for academic activities. It was found that insufficient advertising of the science festival *Positron* and less prize money for events in the festival *Expression* led to low participation from other colleges. This consequently led to low interest among the students of the institute.

Forty-eight per cent of the faculty expressed their inability to guide students in projects due to excessive administrative work. Hence, students were left without mentors for academic activities.

Thirty-two per cent of the students and forty one per cent of the faculty indicated that low participation was because of inconvenient timings. Both *Positron* and *Expression* were scheduled less than one month before the end-semester examinations, and, consequently, both students and faculties were not left with enough time to concentrate on the festivals.

Recommendation

The institute should ensure that banners and notices advertising academic activities are sent to all leading colleges in Delhi. For this purpose, the institute should hire the services of an advertising agency, which would also help in making the banners and notices more appealing.

Administrative work should be evenly distributed and not focused on only a handful of faculty members. This would allow faculty members more time to concentrate on academic activities and to guide students in projects. The science festival *Positron* and the arts festival *Expression* should be rescheduled so that they do not interfere with the students' preparations for exams.

Rajat Sharma

PROGRESS REPORT

Progress report
Construction of Jayanti Cinema Hall

S. No	
1	Total budget allocated
2	Date of start
3	Total cost incurred to date
4	Number of days left
5	Total number of workers on job site
6	Budget deficit
7	Percentage of inventory installed on work completed
8	Number of workers injured or accidents that occurred on jobsite
9	Expected time of finish of construction activity
10	Remarks:
	Signature
	Designation of reporting officer

INSPECTION REPORT

Sample I: Inspection Report on Car

Name: Date:
Brand name of the car: Model no:
Date of purchase:
Mileage:
Number of kilometre run by the car:

Visual inspection: (Put tick against appropriate one)

Exterior

1. Excellent ( ) 2. Good ( ) 3. Average ( ) 4. Poor ( )

Interior

1. Excellent ( ) 2. Good ( ) 3. Average ( ) 4. Poor ( )

Mechanical movements

	Excellent	Good	Average	Poor
Engine working condition				
Gear box				
Bearings				
Tyres				
Gadgets				

Accessories

	Excellent	Good	Average	Poor
Mirror				
Speedometer				
Fuel guage				
Deck				
Seat belt				

Suggested repairs:

Signature of inspection officer:

Sample II: Inspection Report on Mobile Phones

Gadget: Mobile Phone Date of Purchase:
Model no.:
Company's name:
Serial no.:
Checked by

Note: Please put a tick on relevant item.

Visual Inspection
Case: Broken/Scratched/Normal
Screen: Broken/Scratched/Normal
Keypad: Normal/Sticky/Dusty

Mobile Features
Battery: Poor/Normal
Battery backup: Good/Average/Poor
Bluetooth/IR: Distorted/Poor/Normal

Cables: Normal/Poor
Camera: Normal/Distorted
Voice recording: Dead/Noisy/Normal
Miscellaneous parts: Normal/Distorted

Suggested repairs and replacements:

General remarks:

Signature

Sample III: Annual Confidential Report

Annual Confidential Report for an employee working in HCL

Name of the employee:
Date of appointment:

Please assess each item by putting a tick in the appropriate column rate on a scale of 10.

	10	9	8	7	6	5	4	3	2	1
Productivity intelligence										
Drive/diligence										
Speed										
Consistency (regularity and punctuality)										
Initiative										
Creativity										
Technical expertise										
Communication:										
Written:										
Oral:										
Interpersonal character: Ability to work in a team										
Relation with subordinates										
Relations with superiors										
Relations with colleagues										
Character Cool head in an emergency										
Temper/stability										
Physical fitness/health										

Date:
Place:

Signature of the reporting officer:
Designation:

INTERPRETIVE REPORT

Sample I

A Report
on
Impact of BITS on the Local Economy

Submitted to

Dr. V S NIRBAN
(Instructor TAC312 Technical Report Writing)
BITS, Pilani

Prepared by

Pallavi Roy	2005BIA1816
Surbhi Agarwal	2005B3A4707
Saurabh Agarwal	2005B3A7805
Vipin Jain	2005B5A135

BIRLA INSTITUTE OF TECHNOLOGY AND SCIENCE, PILANI
12 April, 2007

Acknowledgements

We extend our sincere thanks to the instructor incharge of the course (Technical Report Writing) Dr. Sangeeta Sharma for providing us with an opportunity to undertake this study. We are deeply grateful to Dr. Virendra Singh Nirban for providing guidance during the course of this study, right from the preparation of the questionnaire to conducting the survey, and for constantly motivating us in the pursuit of our study.

We thank the shopkeepers, peddlers and local vendors who cooperated with us in our survey and provided the relevant information. We are thankful to Microsoft for providing the wonderful software MS Excel and the online assistance which came to the aid in analysing our data and preparing the graphs, etc.

TABLE OF CONTENTS

List of Illustrations

Abstract

The report discusses the various ways in which BITS, its students and faculty affect the local economy. It focuses on the interdependence of the various stakeholders, analyses their incomes at different times of the year and notes the trends.

The main purpose of the report is to provide statistics on the overall influence of BITS as an organization on the economy of Pilani. The study spreads awareness among the readers about how an institute like BITS provides employment to thousands of local people and avenues of income generation.

1. INTRODUCTION

Pilani has grown from the seed of a small desert hamlet into one of the finest centres of all-inclusive education in India. The population of Pilani is around 45,000. This transformation has been brought about through the munificence of the late Shri G.D. Birla. That is quite an achievement because Pilani has no natural advantages whatsoever.

It has boarding schools such as Birla Public School, Birla Senior Secondary School and Birla Balika Vidyapeeth. They also contribute a great deal to the local economy. The Central Electronics Engineering Research Institute (CEERI) of CSIR labs is also located here.

Our study '*The Impact of BITS on the Local Economy*' attempts to share how BITS, having a strength of around 4000 students and 500 faculty and staff with another 1000 comprising their family members, is the primary source of income for a large number of local people. This is quite a substantial number and requires the help of the local people for day-to-day needs. On average, a BITS student spends around ₹ 5,000 in one semester on things such as mobile phone recharges, clothes, food items, gift items, and cosmetics. These things they get from the shops in Pilani owned by the local people.

For our study, we created questionnaires for a sample population of stakeholders. The responses were noted down individually. The sample population included shopkeepers in Connaught and Nutan Market, beauty parlours, men's saloons, tailors, restaurants, the people in Akshay cooperative store, and *redi* owners.

We also tried to study the impact of competition from other sources such as the newly set up Student Activity Centre (SAC), Cafeteria, Skylab and Akshay Cooperative store. There were some constraints due to the fact that the shop-owners did not calculate the exact percentage of decrease or increase in their incomes. Moreover, a few of them were not willing to disclose their exact incomes.

In the report, we were unable to cover all shops due to time and staffing constraints. The sample population that we could interact with for the survey provides sufficient data to make a comprehensive analysis and present a clear picture. To get a broad spectrum of service providers, we have tried to cover shops providing different facilities.

The report contains the questions asked, the data collected, an analysis of the data and the conclusions drawn from them. In the ensuing paragraphs, the different stakeholders and their interests have been dealt with.

The report aims at showing how deeply the economy of Pilani is interlinked with BITS, which has led to the transformation of Pilani from a small desert hamlet into a prosperous town. Maybe the model can be implemented elsewhere in India too.

2. STAKEHOLDERS AND THEIR INTERESTS

2.1 Stakeholders

The stakeholders include the institute, faculty, students, and shop-owners.

2.1.1 Shopkeepers

Shopkeepers are the most important of all the stakeholders. They are the residents of Pilani who own shops in the Pilani market. As per the local sale and sales from nearby villages, Pilani is not a trade centre. Most shopkeepers are directly or indirectly related to the schools and colleges. The shopkeepers inside the campus depend on the BITS for their source of income. The shops at Connaught keep their facilities open, keeping in mind the convenience of the BITS population.

2.1.2 Students

With a number of 4000 in the aggregate, students are the ones who are the leading players of the game. The needs of the students determine the variety and quantity of the products sold in the market. As the students come from all over the country, their demands differ. New trends in the items sold are noticed when a new student population arrive at Pilani for the entrance exam.

2.1.3 Faculty

The faculty members in the institute are from different parts of the country. They belong to various cultures and backgrounds, so their demands differ, which determines the kinds of products sold.

2.1.4 Institute

The institute was founded by Shri Ghanshyam Das Birla in 1901 as a small school for the education of his children. During World War II, the Government of India established a technical training centre at Pilani for the supply of technicians for Defence Services and industry. At the end of the war, in 1946, it was converted into Birla Engineering College with degree programmes in electrical and mechanical engineering.

In 1964, the three Birla Colleges of (i) Engineering, (ii) Science & Pharmacy, and (iii) Arts were incorporated to form the Birla Institute of Technology and Science (BITS). In the initial period of inception (especially during 1964–70), BITS, Pilani received support from Ford Foundation and benefited from a collaboration with Massachusetts Institute Technology, USA. Now, with a student population of over 3500 and 1500 staff members, the institute acts as a major job provider to the local population.

2.2 The Stakeholders and their Interdependence

With over 4500 students and faculty members, BITS Pilani serves as a major source of livelihood for thousands of the local populations. It starts with the people with whom BITS students directly interact, like the shopkeepers and, *rediwalas*, Skylabs. These people earn their livelihoods mainly due to BITS students. The students buy goods from local retailers/dealers who in turn, interact with the distributors and the small industries in Pilani, like the bakeries. The chain continues to the families who own cattle and supply milk to all the shops and *redis* (Refer Fig. 2.1).

The suppliers to BITS' messes are also mainly dependent on BITS for their bread and butter. This does not end here, as the institute provides employment to about 500 non-teaching staff workers. Moreover, during vacation periods, renovations occur from which many labourers earn their livelihood.
The benefits do not end here as the non-teaching staff employed in BITS enjoy almost free schooling facilities for their children in the BET (Birla Education Trust). This helps in raising their economic and social standards.

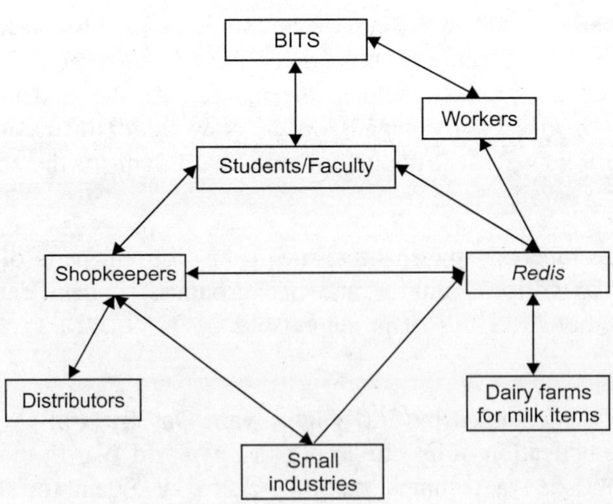

Figure 2.1 Stakeholders and relationships between them.

3. SURVEY RESULTS AND ANALYSIS

3.1 At Connaught

In our survey, we covered Connaught shops and beauty parlours, both inside and outside the campus.

Almost 70% of the shopkeepers of Connaught said that BITS was their major source of income (refer Figure 3.1). On the other hand, Volga and Kamal restaurant owners said that their major source of income was campus people (refer Figure 3.2).

Is BITS your main source of income?

Yes—70%, No—25%, Can't say—5%

Figure 3.1 Source of income (for Connaught).

According to the shop-owners of Connaught, they do not get any customers during the summer vacations. Hence, their income during that period is almost nil. The shop owners are forced to shut down their shops during vacation periods. Mittal's and Deluxe Tailors, though, get some local customers during vacations; still, the income is much less during this period (refer Figure 3.3).

Table 3.1 Data Collected at Connaught

Name of shop	Major source of income	Average monthly income during			Duration	Peak time of sales	Shop timings	Effect Cooperative	Main customers during	
		Semester	Vacation	Admission					Semester	Vacations
Arun stores	BITS	10k	Nil	12k	13 hrs	6-10 pm	10 am–11 pm	Decrease by 50%	Can't say	No
Mittals'	BITS	<10K	1K	Increase	13 hrs	5-11 pm	10 am–11 pm	Decrease by 50%	Not specific	No
Vijay's Restaurant	BITS	<10k	Nil	<10k	14 hrs	7-10 pm	8 am–10 pm	Can't say	BITS students	No
Kamal's Restaurant	Local	No idea	Nil	No idea	12 hrs	7-10 pm	10 am–10 pm	Decrease	Local	No
M.L. Barber Shop	BITS	5-7k	Nil	No change	13 hrs	5-8 pm	7 am–8 pm	NA	BITS students and staff	No
Blue Moons	BITS	10-15k	Nil	12-18k	13 hrs	5-11 pm	10 am–11 pm	No	BITS students	No
Volgas	Local	<10k	No effect	No effect	14 hrs	No specific timings	9 am–11 pm	No	Local	Local
Deluxe Tailors	BITS	4.5k	2.5k	No effect	12 hrs	No specific timings	9 am–9 pm	NA	BITS Girls	Local

Most of the shop owners said that their sales at the time of admission, i.e. during the months of July and August, increased by 20% approximately. But there were also others for whom there was no change (refer Figure 3.3).

What is your average monthly income during the semester?

< 10k – 65%

10–20k – 25%

20–40k – 10%

Figure 3.2 Pie graph showing the monthly income distribution.

Comparison of income at different times of the year

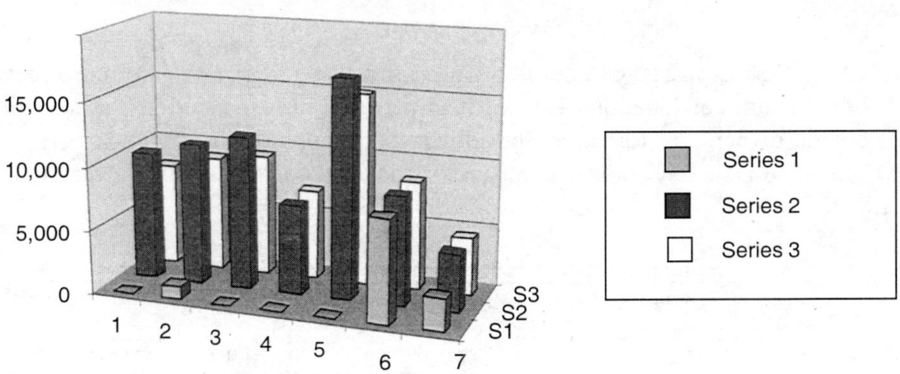

Figure 3.3 Income trends at connaught.

On average, the shops remain open for 13 hrs a day, from 10 am to 11 pm. The peak time of sale is between 5 and 11 pm for most of them (refer Table 3.1). The opening of the Akshay cooperative had an adverse effect on the sales of shopkeepers. Some held the opinion that sales were affected by up to 50%. (refer Table 3.1).

Major customers for most of the shop owners are BITS students, while for others, it is both BITS and local customers. Demand is the chief criterion for keeping the types of goods in the shops, along with affordability for the customers. The restaurants in Pilani have had the same menu for the past many years; they do not prefer to revise it often.

3.2 Beauty Parlours

Almost 55% of the local beauty parlour owners said that their major source of income is the BITS (refer to Figure 3.3).

In our survey, we learned about the existence of many beauty parlours which were yet to be discovered by female students of BITS. The parlours inside and nearby the campus are completely dependent on BITS as a major source of their income, while the parlours located in the city, near Sarvajanik hospital, get mostly local customers.

Is BITS your main source of income?

Yes: 55%

No: 40%

Can't say: 5%

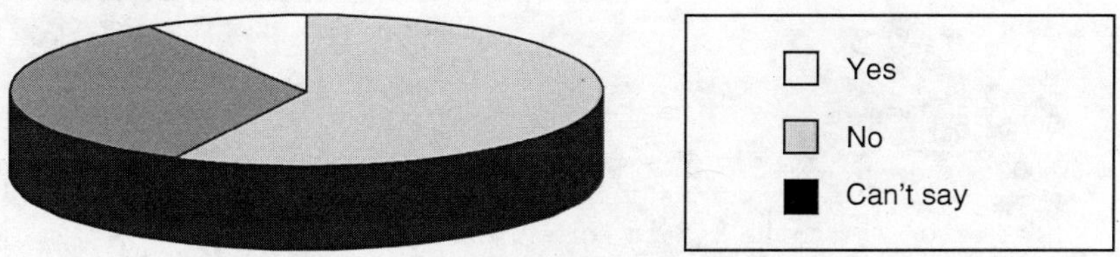

Figure 3.4 Source of income (for beauty parlours).

Table 3.2 Data Collected at Beauty Parlours

Name of beauty parlour	Major income-source	Average monthly income during			Duration	Timings of income (peak hours)	Timing of shop	Major customers during	
		Semester	Holidays	Admission				Semester	Vacations
Shehnaaz	BITS	30k	35k (Marriage)	No change	8 hrs	5-7 pm	10:30 am-7 pm	Campus girls and women	Local
Silky	BITS	No idea	Nil	No idea	Whole day	4-11 pm	8 am-11 pm	BITS girls	No customer
Cupid	BITS	No idea	Nil	No idea	7 hrs	5-11 pm	11 am-7 pm	Campus women	No customer
Cinossaur	BITS, Local	<1k	Nil	Lk	8 hrs	5-7 pm	10 am-7 pm	Campus women	No customer
Pooja	Local	<10k	Can't say	No change	8 hrs	5-7 pm	11 am-7 pm	Local	Local
Prachi	Local	No idea	No idea	No idea	9 hrs	4-7 pm	1:00 am-7 pm	Local	Local

The monthly income for Shehnaaz beauty parlour is highest at approxi-mately ₹ 30,000–40,000, while for others, it is less than ₹ 10,000 (refer Table 3.2).

For Cupid beauty parlour especially, it is low as its income is not even ₹ 1000. Summer vacation, on the one hand, is an off-season for most of them. However, for Shehnaaz beauty parlour, it is particularly a time when it earns the maximum, it being the marriage season (refer Figure 3.5). Parlours in the city also get some customers during this time. For most of them, the time of admission does not affect their income; it remains almost the same. The parlours remain open between 10 am–7 pm, i.e. for 8 hrs on average. Peak income timings is between 4–7 pm (refer Table 3.2). Major customers are BITS female students and staff, while some locals are also their major customers during the semester. Shehnaaz beauty parlour told that its major customers are wives of Deans and other influential people of the campus. Most of the parlours, when fixing rates of products, give over-emphasis on the affordability of customers, though, for some, demand is the major criterion. Shehnaaz beauty parlour has kept its rates fixed for the past 5–6 years, while Cynosure beauty parlour has its rates fixed according to the wishes of the customers. The prime goal here is customers' satisfaction.

Income of beauty parlours during different times of the year

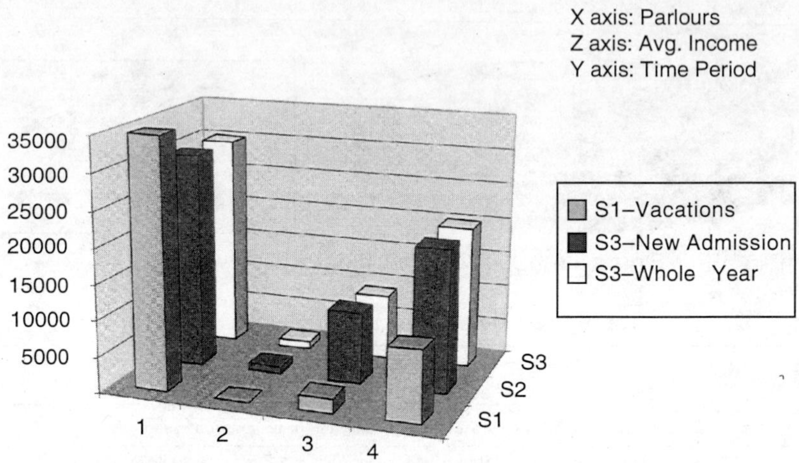

Figure 3.5 Average income trends for beauty parlours.

3.3 Nutan Market and Bus Stand

When surveying Nutan market and the adjoining bus stand market, we found that their sales did not depend much on BITS. Only 35% of them said that BITS had an impact on their sales (see Figure 3.3).

For Nutan market'

Is BITS your main source of income?

Yes—35%

No—65%

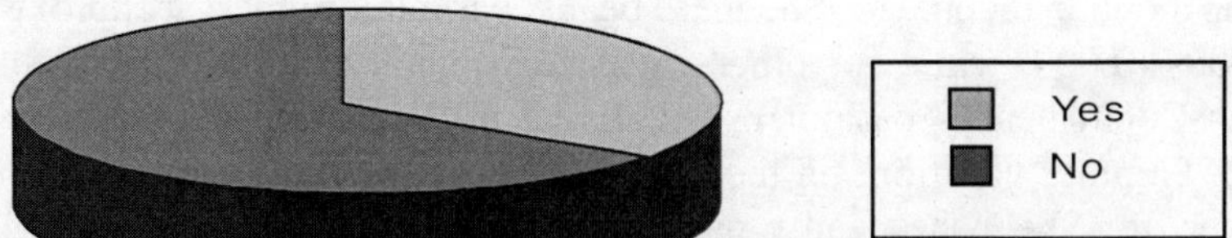

Figure 3.6 Source of income (for bus stand).

While looking at the data, we found that for most of these shops, the sales did not decline much during the BITS vacation (refer Figure 3.6). It declined only by 10%. There is an appreciable increase in sales for almost all the shops during—July and August, that is, during the time of new admissions. The shops which are most affected due to BITS are photocopy shops and shops dealing in mobiles (refer Table 3.3).

Table 3.3 Data Collected at Nutan Market and Bus Stand

S. No.	Name of shop	Sales			Main Customers	Products	Impact of C (I) on Sales
		Semester	Vacations	July/Aug			
1	Kapoor Novelty Store	A	0.85A	1.15A	BITS/CEERI/ eneral	Variety	Decreased S
2	Student Cycles	A	0.9A	1.1A	Local	NA	NA
3	Pragati Medicines	81,000	42,000	84,000	All	NA	NA
4	Khushi Clothes	57,000	57,000	57,000	Local	NA	NA
5	Amit Garments	150,000	60,000	180,000	Villages	NA	NA
6	Maheshwari Traders	1.8 lakh	1.4 lakh	2 lakh	Students/ Faculty	NA	NA
7	Metro Tailors	75,000	75,000	75,000	Villages	NA	NA
8	Vaidya Textiles	A	0.2A	1.7A	Bits students/ Local	NA	NA
9	BMB	2 lakh	2 lakh	2 lakh	Local	NA	NA
10	Avi Communication	5.5 lakh	4.25 lakh	8 lakh	Students and faculty	NA	NA
11	Colour Lab	60,000	30,000	75,000	All	NA	NA
12	Airtel	B	0.9B	1.1B		NA	NA
13	Sharma Enterprises	3.1 lakh	2 lakh	4 lakh	Students/ Faculty	NA	NA
14	Nishi Xerox	2.4 lakh	1.5 lakh	3.6 lakh	Students/ Faculty	NA	NA
15	BB computers	2.75 lakh	2 lakh	4 lakh	Students/ Faculty	NA	NA

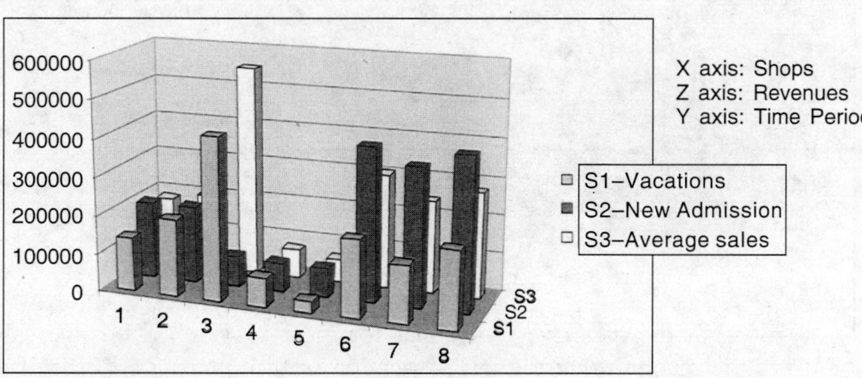

Figure 3.7 Average monthly revenue (Nutan Market and Bus Stand).

The impact of the Akshay cooperative is also very little visible on these shops. Only Kapoor Novelty Store had a significant impact because of the cooperative as they both relate to the same kind of business of cosmetics. After the BITS cooperative was opened for the local population (the rates are subsidized in the cooperative), the sales of Kapoor Novelty store decreased by almost 30% as more and more local people started going to the cooperative. For shops dealing with goods such as garments, cycles, etc., cooperatives had a negligible impact.

One major shock which came to us was the Student Cycle Centre. We always thought that BITS was their major revenue source, with an admission of more than a thousand students every year and almost 80% of them owning a cycle. However, we found that BITS is not their major revenue source but the local people who stay in Pilani and the people of the nearby villages. More interestingly their shop is the biggest in Chirawa Tehsil.

3.4 Skylab and Redis

Sky lab and *redis* are the lifelines for BITS students and staff during institute hours. While surveying we found that the BITS is the major source of income for these. They are entirely dependent on BITS for their bread and butter. Their sales decrease drastically during the vacations (refer Figure 3.7). Most of them do not open their shop during vacations (refer Table 3.4).

The *redi* owners and Skylab have the maximum revenue during the evening hours, i.e., after the institute gets closed. During this time, the major customers are the students.

During the vacations, the primary customers for these *redi* owners are the daily wage workers who work at the institute during this time to renovate bhavans and other activities. With the start of the BITSAT, the *redi* owners get some income during the exam times when outsiders come to write the tests.

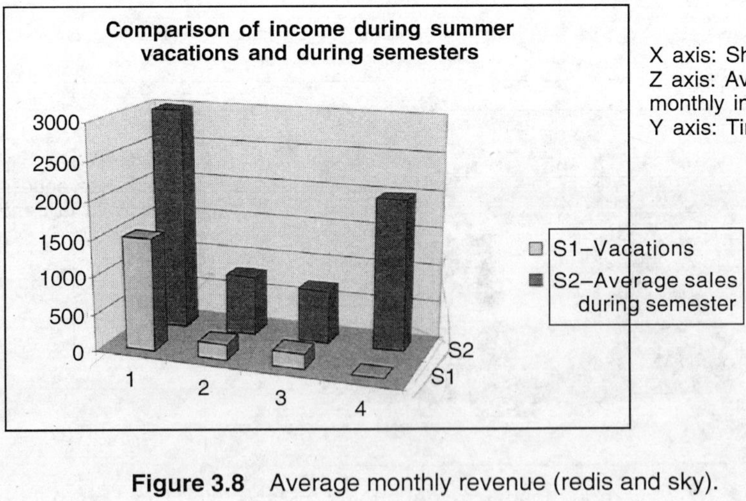

Figure 3.8 Average monthly revenue (redis and sky).

Table 3.4 Data Collected at Sky Lab and Redis

Name of Shop	Sales (per day) during			Shop Timings		Major Customers		No. of Employees during	
	Semester (₹)	Vacations (₹)	July–August	Semester	Vacations	Semester	Vacations	Semester	Vacations
Sky Labs	3000	1500	4000	8.30 am–7 pm	9.00 am–5.00 pm	Students/ Faculty	Visitors	6	2
Munna redi	800	200	850	9.00 am–7.30 pm	9.00 am–7.30 pm	Students	Local people	4	2
Krishna redi	700	200	750	9.00 am–7.30 pm	9.00 am–7.30 pm	Students	Local people	3	2
Nagar redi	2000	NA	2200	9.00 am–7.30 pm	Shop not open	Students/ Faculty	NA	5	NA

3.5 Comparison of Income Trends of Shops Inside and Outside the Campus

The shops outside the campus have both BITS students and local people as their customers. The shops inside the campus are dependent on the BITS faculty and students for their income.

As is indicative from the following graph, we observe a sharp dip in incomes for shops inside the campus during the vacations. For most of these shops the income is nil during vacations.

For shops outside the campus, there is a fall in income during vacations, but it is not as sharp as the drop seen in shops inside the campus. This is because they also have local people as their customers. Being solely dependent on BITS students and staff, the shops inside the campus also earn less as compared to the shops outside, as the latter has a wider clientele.

Series one: The Shops outside the campus. Series two: The Shops inside the campus

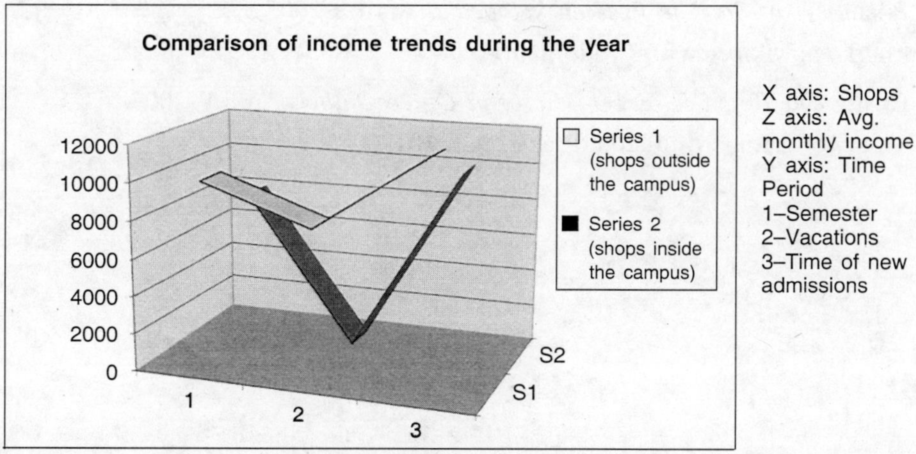

Figure 3.9 Comparison of Income Trends during the Year (2006–2007) for Shops Inside and Outside Campus.

4. CONCLUSION

BITS has upheld its motto of being one of the best technical institutions in the country. It provides quality education and, hence, has empowered many great minds. Another facet is the immense influence it exerts on the local economy of Pilani, a prosperous town now, and this transformation from a small hamlet is mainly due to BITS.

With nearly 4000 students and 1500 faculty members, BITS creates opportunities for the employment of local people for the fulfilment of their day-to-day needs. This has created job opportunities for the people living in and around Pilani. If one ventures out of this place, the conditions in the nearby villages are very different; hence, there is a mass migration from these places to Pilani. People come here from all around in search of jobs and better opportunities for livelihood.

During the preparation of our report, we observed that due to the heavy dependence on BITS for their living, the shop-owners income dropped heavily during the vacation months when there was no one on campus. Shopkeepers inside the campus suffer the heaviest blow, with their incomes practically becoming nil during this period.

Hence, we see that apart from imparting education to students, BITS also has an effect on the local economy.

Bibliography

Sharma, R.C and Krishna Mohan. *Business Correspondence and Report Writing*. 3rd Ed., New Delhi: Tata McGraw Hill Company Ltd., 2006.

Raman, Meenakshi and Sangeeta Sharma. *Technical Communication: Principles and Practices*. New Delhi: Oxford University Press, 2004.

Pilani, *Wikipedia The Free encyclopedia.* April 9 2007
<http://en.wikipedia.org/wiki/Pilani>

Charts and Graphics, *Excel–Microsoft Office Online*. April 9 2007,
<http://office.microsoft.com/enus/excel/CHO10003731033.aspx>

9

Advertising

Doing business without advertising is like winking at a girl in the dark. You know what you are doing, but nobody else does.

—**STEUART H. BRITT**

Advertising has become an integral part of your life. You can see different forms of advertisement on TV and radio, in newspapers and magazines, on billboards and even posters across the sides of the public buses. It is persistent and persuasive, but it would be too simplistic to believe that the power advertising has over us is just about how we spend our money. If an advertisement could really persuade us to buy a product, surely then it would have the power of influencing our thought process. The global market has expanded manifold in the past few decades. Innumerable products are getting launched almost everyday. Companies are engaged in cut-throat competition to highlight their products to the forefront, and herein enters the glamorous field of advertising. The more innovative the advertising, the better is the market. Advertising is actually brand building of a product or a company through effective communication. It is essentially a service industry and the media helps to reach more people to communicate brand effectiveness.

All forms of advertising serve three purposes: *to recruit new customers*, *to increase use of goods* or *services among existing customers*, and *to help potential customers choose among competing brands*. These basic principles hold true for all kinds of products and markets. These three purposes can be merged into a single purpose: market share, or to convince a customer to choose one brand over another, and retain him for life. So it basically deals with capturing human feelings and emotions, which makes it one of the most challenging jobs. Advertisers use various means to achieve their objective. Creativity leads the list. And the idea has to be unique.

Advertising has a great influence on our daily lives, whether you are aware or oblivious of it. Billboards, newspapers, television and magazines, all convey messages to the public about various products, companies, travel opportunities, etc. One cannot escape the constant invasion of such advertisements and, as a result, they have become a global phenomenon and we take part in it by being both consumers and observers. Advertisements have become an easily accessible persuasion tactic, and, as a result of commercials and other forms of advertisements, companies have been able to reach a wider range of potential buyers. Globalization of advertising has significantly increased consumerism and allowed certain companies to have the exposure needed to boost sales. Commercials for various multi-billion dollar companies can be seen all over the globe, enabling these large corporations to reach as many potential consumers as possible.

DEFINITION

The most standard definition of advertising is as follows, "Advertising is the nonpersonal communication of information usually paid for and usually persuasive in nature about products, services or ideas by identified sponsors through the various media". (Bovee, 1992, p. 7). Let us dissect the definition and explain the key terms used in it.

Non-personal

First, we find out what is non-personal. There are two basic ways to sell a thing, personally and non-personally. Personal selling requires the seller and the buyer to be together. There are advantages and disadvantages in this kind of advertisement. The *first* advantage is time; the seller has the time to discuss in detail everything about the product. The buyer has the time to ask questions, get answers, and examine evidence for or against the purchase.

The *second* advantage of personal selling is that the seller can see you, the person he is selling to. He can see your face, see how the sales message is getting across. If you yawn or don't retain eye contact with the seller, you are obviously bored. The seller can accordingly change the approach. The seller can also see if you are interested in the product, see what features or benefits have your attention, and emphasize them to close the sale. Finally, the seller can easily locate the potential buyers. If you enter a store, you probably have an interest in something that the store sells. Street vendors and door-to-door sellers simply shout at all possibilities. From there on they fit their message to the individual customer, utilizing all the time a customer is willing to give them.

Disadvantages of personal selling also do exist. Personal selling is expensive, since it is labour-intensive and concentrates only on one buyer at a time. Just imagine even when you try to sell chewing gum or chocolates, it would cost you large sum of money. In addition, in terms of time personal selling is time consuming. Selling a stereo or a car by this procedure can take days, while that of big computers and airplane years. In this fast moving world, no one has such large amount of time at their disposal to wait.

Hence, if personal selling results in more rejections than sales, then it can be nerve-racking, frustrating and ego destroying for the salesperson. In contrast, when the sales are good by this method, it is more directed and successful than advertising.

Thus, from the above discussion, it appears that personal selling is better than advertising, which is non-personal. This is true. Advertising has none of the advantages of personal selling; in a predecided time slot the advertiser has to present the sales message. There is no way to know just who the customer is or how he will respond to the message, and the message cannot be changed in mid-course in accordance with the customer's reaction.

Then the question arises why personal selling has been replaced by advertising. This is because advantages of advertising exactly replace personal selling's disadvantages, and at the same time emulate some of the advantages of the latter. Let us look at some advantages of advertising.

First, advertising is ubiquitous. It has been a part of us since the time immemorial. Unlike personal selling, the sales message and its presentation don't have to be created on the spot with the customer watching. It can be created in as many ways as the writer can conceive, rewrite, test, modify, and inject with every trick and appeal known to affect the consumer.

Second, although advertisers may not see the individual customer, nor be able to modify the sales message according to that individual's reactions at the time, it does have research data about the customers. Research identifies potential customers, finds what message elements might influence them, and figures out how best to get that message across to them. Although, research is meaningless when applied to any particular individual, it is effective when applied to large groups of customers.

Third, and perhaps the most important, advertising can be far cheaper per potential customer than personal selling. The latter is extremely labour-intensive, dealing with one customer at a time. Advertising deals with hundreds, thousands, or millions of customers at a time, thus reducing the cost per customer. In fact, advertising costs are determined in part using a formula to determine, not cost per potential customer, but cost per thousand potential customers.

Thus, advertising is an effective sales tool. For small items, such as chewing gum and chocolates, advertising is cost-effective as it does the entire selling job. Similarly, for large products, such as cars and computers, advertising can do a large part of the selling job, and personal selling is used to complete and close the sale.

Advertising is non-personal, but certainly effective.

Communication

Communication is a means by which one person passes information, ideas or feelings to another through speech or pictures. It uses all the senses: smell, touch, taste, sound and sight. Of the five senses, only two are really useful in advertising—sound and sight. The advertisement of Phoenix Mill in the 1940s, was done just through a picture. Sound and sight are the most effective and easily used channels of communication available to advertisers. For these reasons, virtually all forms of advertising rely on them.

Sound

Sound is extremely useful for advertising. It can be used in a variety of media, from radio and television to the new technology of binding micro-sound chips in magazines to present 20-second sales messages. It is also capable of presenting words and "theatre of the mind".

Words, the means by which humans communicate their ideas and feelings, are presented by sound—by speaking aloud. Through the use of words, it is possible to deliver logical arguments, discuss the pros and cons, and evoke emotions.

Moreover, through the use of sound it is possible to create what is called "the theatre of the mind". This means that sound can conjure in the listener's mind images and actions that don't necessarily exist. For example, if you wish to create before the mind's eye the image of a party, all you need is the sound effects of people talking and laughing, the tinkle of glasses and ice, and perhaps music in the backdrop. Even better, record a party and play it. To evoke the images of a soft spring day, the sounds of the breeze rustling leaves, the chirrup of insects, the soft tweeting of birds are sufficient. The listener's mind will take those sounds, combine them, make sense of them, and create an image suited to the individual taste. For example, a beer commercial may play the sounds of a bar in the background, and the listener may imagine himself in his own favourite bar, and perhaps ordering that particular brand of beer.

Thus, sound, in the form of word and effect, is quite useful to the advertiser in affecting a listener.

Sight

Sight is arguably the most useful of the communication channels available to the advertiser. Through sight, it is possible to use both words and images effectively.

You need not only speak words to convey meaning. They can be printed, as well. Although it is difficult to put in written words the emotional impact possible in the spoken words, with change in tone and subtle sound cues. Nevertheless written words are unsurpassed for getting across and explaining complex ideas or arguments.

There is an additional factor of visual representation that makes it excellent for advertising. The adage, "A picture is worth a thousand words", is correct. Think how long it takes to describe a thing as opposed to showing a picture of it. No matter how many words you use to describe a product, some details will be left out that are visible at a glance in a picture. Thus, a visual representation can quickly and concisely show a customer what the advertiser wants him to see, be it a product or how buying the product can benefit him. This is true especially in the case of products like cars, which have high value addition. See Figure 9.1. Automobile advertisements tend to depend a lot on the visual aspect.

Figure 9.1 TATA Indigo.

In addition, the mind doesn't have to consciously recognize what the eye sees for it to have an effect on the subconscious. An advertiser can put many inconspicuous details into a picture that will affect a customer at the subconscious level. For example, a drop of water on a rose petal may not consciously register (I see there is a drop of water on this rose), but will unconsciously leave an impression of freshness and vigour. A small child looking upwards into the camera, unsmiling and eyes wide, gives the impression of sadness and vulnerability, not shortness.

The five forms of human communication can be used to send any kind of message to the potential customers. However, not all the five senses are equal. Smell, touch and taste are of little use, but sound and sight are of great value and effectiveness in advestisement.

Information

Information is defined as knowledge, facts or news. However, you should bear in mind that one person's information is another person's scam, particularly when advertisers talk about their products.

Information comes in many forms. It can be complete or incomplete, biased or deceptive. Complete information is telling someone everything there is to know about a particular product, what it is, what it looks like, how it works, what its benefits and drawbacks are. However, to provide complete information about anything is time-consuming and difficult. For example, to tell all about a car would require its appearance, manufacture and manufacturer, what percentage of parts are made in which countries, cost of upkeep, mileage (both city and highway), cost (basic and with any and all combination of options), sales and excise taxes per state, preparation costs, insurance costs per state and locale, ride characteristics (noise by decibels interior and exterior, ergs required for steering and braking, relative comfort of seats, length of reach required to use controls, degrees of lean when cornering), acceleration, braking distance at many different speeds, etc. All these would require a documentary, not a commercial. It is impossible to provide complete information in an advertisement.

Thus in advertising, only that information is given which is necessary, it doesn't provide every detail that there is to know about the product. In advertising, the information provided is everything that the advertiser thinks the customer needs to know about the product in order to make a decision about it. That information will generally be about how the product can benefit the customer.

At times, the consumer is provided not with the information he wants, but only with the information the seller wants him to have. Sellers, for instance, are not inclined to advertise the negative aspects of their products even though they may be of primary concern to the consumer, particularly if they involve health or safety issues.

Bias is being partial towards a thing, a feeling that something is better or worse than another thing. One-sided information about a product is that which emphasizes only the good points and ignores the bad aspects. In advertising, this is not only normal, but also necessary. Of course, an advertiser is biased towards his own product and is against competition: selling his product is the way he makes his money, and when products in competition get sold, it affects his income. Thus, any advertising which uses words and images to show how good his product is and how poor the competition is, can be termed biased information. But recognized and accepted by the industry, regulators and consumers—it is called *puffery*, the legitimate exaggeration of advertising claims to overcome natural consumer scepticism.

Paid for

The meaning of 'paid for' is quite clear from the words. If an advertisement is created and placed in the media, the costs of creation and time or space in the media must be paid for. This is a major area in which advertising departs from public relations.

Public relations seek to place information about companies and/or products in the media without having to pay for the time or space. It creates news releases and sends them to news media in the hope that those will be printed or broadcast. Often public relations departments produce events that will be covered by news media and, thus, receive space or time. However, there is no guarantee that the media will print or broadcast any of the public relations material.

With advertising no such problem exists. If time or space is bought in the media, the advertisement then (as long as they follow the guidelines set down for good taste, legal products and services, etc.) will appear. The drawback is that advertisements are clearly designed to extol the virtues of the products and companies, and consumers perceive them as at least partly puffery. Public relations pieces are usually not so perceived.

Persuasive

Persuasive means to get the things done what you want the customers to do. The basic purpose of this form of advertising is to identify and differentiate one product from another in order to persuade the consumer to buy that particular product in preference to another.

Figure 9.2 Nike—powerful advertisement message.

Products, Services or Ideas

Products, services or ideas are things that the advertisers want consumers to buy (in the case of ideas, 'buy' means accept or agree with and lay out hard, cold cash). However, there is more involvement in products or services than simply items for purchase. (During the following discussion, 'products' will mean products, services and ideas unless otherwise noted.)

A product is tangible thing which is physically visible. It is a bundle of values, for the consumer. That bundle may contain not only the product's function, but also the social, psychological, economic or whatever other values are important to the consumer.

For example, let us look at a car. If the function of a car, i.e. transportation, is all that important, then manufacturers would need only to build motorized boxes on wheels, and consumers would be happy with them. Such is obviously not the case: the number of models and types of cars are huge and exist only because consumers didn't demand variety. Consumers must find factors other than mere transportation just as, if not more, important.

Perhaps the value is also related to social status. The type of car a person drives is often indicative of that person's social status. A Maruti car symbolizes lower status than Mercedes Benz. A sports car exemplifies that a person is (or wishes to be perceived as) more socially active, and fun loving than a person in a Sedan or Station Wagon. The type of car can even indicate which social grouping a person wants to be considered a part of: in the 1980s Volvos and BMWs were the cars for young urban professionals.

Economic value is also a factor. Some cars may be cheaper to run, give better mileage, carry more people or cargo, and cause less damage to the environment.

The above four values—function, social, psychological and economic, can stand alone. However, for most consumers, the values are grouped together in varying proportions. How closely a product approximates an individual's proportion of values will often determine whether he will buy that product or not.

Companies, through research, try to determine what values consumers want in their products, and then advertise to show how their product satisfies the customers' group of values better than competitors' products. To do this, the company must differentiate their products from that of competitors. There are three basic differentiations: *perceptible*, *imperceptible*, and *induced*.

Perceptible

Perceptible differences are those that actually exist and make one product obviously different from others of the same kind. The difference may be in colour, size, shape, brand name, etc. In any case, the consumer can easily see that this car, couch or camera is different from other cars, couches or cameras. Perceptible differences allow a person to make an instant identification of one product as opposed to another.

Imperceptible

Imperceptible differences are those that actually exist between products, but are not obvious. For example, there are imperceptible but profound differences between CP/M, MS-DOS and Apple Macintosh computers. You can't simply look at a computer and tell which it is; machines can and usually do look alike. And yet buying either precludes being able to use software designed for the other.

The same applies to Beta and Video Home System (VHS) format in Video Cassette Recorders (VCRs). Although both are designed to do the same thing, that is to record audio and video from a television broadcast so it can be played back later, there are differences between them that are imperceptible on the surface but preclude using one tape in the other. There are other differences besides the size of the cassette: the machines use totally different ways of recording and playing back tapes. Beta records and plays cassettes diagonally across the tape, VHS records vertically. Such a difference may seem small, but it means that anything recorded on Beta cannot be played back on VHS, and vice versa. Also, Beta's system used more tape per instant, and, thus, had an advantage in the amount of information per inch of tape, meaning a better sound and picture but less available time. However, VHS overcomes its deficit by improved electronics and better processing of what information it gets per inch of tape. In addition, VHS (read RCA) managed to corner the market on rental tapes of movies (a major use of VCRs) and VHS has virtually killed off Beta (read Sony). All the differences between Beta and VHS are imperceptible but they are crucial.

Induced

For many products, there is no actual substantive difference between one and the other. These are many brands of cigarettes, beer, cleansers and soaps, rice, over-the-counter health products, etc. Essentially there is no difference between one brand and another. These products are called *parity products*.

For these products, the only way to differentiate one from another is to induce that difference, to persuade people that there actually is some difference, and that too an important one. However, these differences are the creation of the advertisements, not actually inherent in the products, and often appeal to the customers. For example, take the advertisement of POLO, does the "mint with a hole" makes any difference to the inherent nature or quality of the mint. See Figure 9.3.

Figure 9.3 POLO, an ad with difference.

Another approach is to project an image on a parity product. Marlboro is rugged male, Virginia Slims is independent female, Benson & Hedges is intellectual, Camel is cool and sophisticated. That there is no real difference between these brands of cigarette is beside the point. The thing is, if you want to project a particular image, you must use that product which is associated with it. This image approach is so successful that a macho man would not be caught dead smoking Virginia Slims or Benson & Hedges—he would feel very feminine.

Parity products have the greatest difficulty in differentiating one from another. They must rely on creating a trivial or even non-existent difference in the bundle of values their target audience might find important to their purchase decision. However, if and once that difference is firmly established in the target audience's perception, a company can often rely on habit, brand loyalty and/or cognitive dissonance to get repeat business.

Identified Sponsors

Identified sponsors mean who is putting out the advertisement must be established to the audience. There are two reasons for this: *first*, it is a legal requirement, and *second*, it makes a good sense.

Legally, the sponsor of an advertisement must identify himself. This prevents the audience from getting a misleading idea about the advertisement or its contents. For example, many advertisements that appear in newspapers look like news articles: same typeface, appearance, use of columns, etc. If the advertisement is not identified as such, the reader could perceive it as news about a product, rather than an attempt to persuade the reader to buy it. Case in point: what looks like a news article discusses a weight-loss plan. In journalistic style, it talks about the safety, efficacy, and reasonable price of the product. The reader might perceive the article as having been written by a reporter who had investigated weight-loss programmes and decided to objectively discuss this particular one. Such a perception is misleading, and illegal. Since it is an advertisement, somewhere on it there must appear the word advertisement to ensure the reader doesn't think it is an objective reporting of news.

Second, it makes good sense for a sponsor to identify himself in the advertisement. If the sponsor doesn't establish himself, it is possible then for the audience to believe that the advertisement is for a competitor's product, thus wastage of time, creativity and money that went into making and placing that particular advertisement.

Various Media

The various forms of media are the non-personal channels of communication that people have invented, used and continue to use. The media include newspapers, magazines, radio, television, billboards, transit cards, sandwich boards, skywriting, posters, floating hoardings, balloons, anything that aids communicating in a non-personal way, ideas from one person or group to another person or group. They don't include people talking to each other: first, talking is personal and advertising is non-personal; and second, there is no way to use people talking to each other for advertising—word-of-mouth is not an advertising medium, since you can't control what is said.

CLASSIFICATION OF ADVERTISEMENTS

Advertisements have numerous objectives, sometimes other than just selling products. First, let us have a look at the basic outline of the development of an effective advertising campaign. The classification of advertisements is directly related to the advertising plan. By developing an effective advertising plan, the likelihood of a positive return on your advertising investment is increased, regardless of the amount spent. Following are the questions, which the advertiser is supposed to know the answers for before designing the advertisement.

- What do I want my advertising to accomplish?
- Whom should my advertising speak to?
- What should my advertising say?
- Where should I place my advertising?

There are different classifications possible depending on which of the above questions you have in mind when designing an advertisement. We will discuss each of the points separately.

What Do I Want My Advertising to Accomplish?

The first step in developing an advertising plan is to specify our advertising goals. One should be as precise as to why he is advertising and what is to be achieved. Everyone wants advertising to increase business, but for the advertising plan to work, it requires the advertiser to be more precise. What is important is the prioritization of goals. Advertising works best when it is developed to meet one specific goal at a time.

Whom Should My Advertising Speak To?

Once the advertising goals are determined, the next step is then to select the target audience for our message. Advertising that tries to reach, 'everyone' rarely succeeds. Successful advertising is written with a specific customer in mind. Target consumers should be described in each of the following:

1. **Demographics:** Such as gender, age, income, location of residence or business.

2. **Behaviours:** Such as current awareness of your business; the products, services or vendors they currently use; loyalty to you or your competitor's business.
3. **Needs or desires:** Such as what benefits consumers look for, the basis on which they will decide whether to use your product or service, and how your business can fulfil those needs.

What Should My Advertising Say?

Once the target audience is decided and what they are looking for in terms of the product or service offered is known, it is time to decide what the advertising will say. Advertising should always be written to communicate a message that will be seen as important by your target customer. The advertising should clearly and convincingly 'speak' to your target audience, explaining the important benefits your product or service offers.

In deciding how to discuss the major benefits of the product or service in the advertising, 'AIDA' should be kept in mind: attract Attention, hold Interest, arouse Desire and motivate Action.

Where Should I Place My Advertising?

Apart from the usual newspapers, magazines, TV, transit, we have today Internet also to advertise on. See Table 9.1.

Table 9.1

By target audience	By geographic area	By media used	By purpose
Consumer	International	Print	Product or
Business	National	Newspaper	non-product
Industrial	Regional	Magazine	Commercial or
Trade	Local	Electronic	non-commercial
Professional		Radio	Primary demand
Agricultural		Television	or selective demand
		Out-of-home	Direct action or
		Outdoor	indirect action
		Transit	
		Direct mail	
		Directories	
		Other media	

Purpose

Product or non-product

The answer to the first question gives rise to the fourth column. The reasons for advertising are numerous. It is not selling a product always. A company might advertise to build its reputation. A product is a goods or service for which customers will exchange something of value. The purpose of product advertising is to sell the advertiser's goods or services which are intangible in nature. They include financial, legal, medical and other recreational services.

Non-product advertising constitutes institutional or corporate advertising, in which the advertiser is trying to polish its image or influence public opinion about an issue. Here the aim is not to sell something but just to let the public know that such an organization exists.

Commercial or non-commercial

Commercial versus non-commercial advertising is pretty much easy to understand. If the idea is to make a profit, it is commercial. Otherwise it is non-commercial. Most of the advertisements you see are commercial.

Primary-demand and selective-demand advertising

The famous De Beers advertisement "Diamonds are forever" belongs to the primary-demand category. The advertisements stimulate the need for a particular category and the aim is not to sell one brand. The slogan was used to arouse the need for diamonds and not to sell 'De Beers' brand. Associations that represent many manufacturers usually do this type of advertising. Once the need for a particular category is established, selective demand advertising comes into picture. These advertisements concentrate on a particular brand of a product and try to promote it. De Beers, after it made diamond jewellery popular, went in for selective-demand advertisements.

Direct-action and indirect-action advertising

Sometimes, advertisements are designed to get the audience to respond immediately. These types of advertisements are called direct-action advertisements. Typically, these advertisements carry a toll-free number and sales-promotion incentives. Indirect-action advertising is done primarily to build awareness of the product.

Media Used

Now comes the answer to the second question. How to tell? In other words, which media to use? Popular forms of advertising include newspaper, magazine, radio, television, outdoor and transit. Television is considered to be the best medium for huge audiences across wide geographic regions. Today, we have Internet also. But its reach is still limited compared to television.

Geographic Area

This was the third question. Today advertisements are aimed at the whole world. With the inception of the concept 'global presence', no advertiser would waste money on reaching a small segment of the audience unless, of course, he is interested in being only a local player. In a way, the second and third questions are interrelated. Usually, media is decided based on the geographic coverage. Accordingly, you have international advertising, national advertising, regional advertising and local advertising. Retailers in their areas do local advertising and, thus, its scope is very narrow.

Target Audience

This is the most important criterion as there would not be a more foolish thing to do than advertising to the wrong audience. Target audience is the word used in the industry. The most common advertising in this category is consumer advertising. It is aimed at consumers of the products, and the message is very simple. The idea is to make the consumers buy goods and services. Business advertising is not for a single customer. The advertisement is aimed at business institutions, non-profit organizations and government agencies. Photocopiers belong to this category. Sometimes the media is common to both the consumer and the business advertising. Industrial advertising targets people who buy or use the materials and services needed to conduct business or to manufacture other products. Earth Moving equipment is a good example. Trade advertising targets intermediaries in the supply chain, such as wholesalers and retailers. The objective is effective distribution of goods in the supply chain. Professional advertising aims at professional practitioners, such as lawyers, accountants, doctors, dentists and engineers. This category of advertising may be used to persuade professionals to buy a particular product useful in their work. Recent advertisements about software, which would help doctors in efficient diagnosis, are an example of this category.

Advertising Functions

Advertisement is one tool that can help to achieve the goals. It is not the end but a means to reach the end. Advertising functions depend on the type of advertisement, with the objectives to:

- Make the product distinct from the other competitors. Maggie Noodles uses advertisement to promote its taste, and quality and how it is distinguished from other noodles.
- Communicate information. When Maggie noodles advertises, it informs how it is to be cooked. The procedure of cooking is narrated step by step.
- Goad the users. The Maggie noodles advertisement claims the product to be both healthy and tasty. By offering extra in the same amount and also telling you several recipes for making it, the advertisement gives the customer a further push to buy.

- Expand the distribution. The Maggie brand initially started with production of only noodles, later it expanded to soups, ketchups so as to go for wider distribution. It also made the packaging handy so as to expand the market.
- Encourage brand preference and loyalty. By offering a slogan of 'easy to cook and easy to eat', it gave the consumers a good reason to stick to the brand. Now it has given one more offer of providing *atta* noodles, as Indians have penchant for food items made of wheat flour.
- Reduce the sales cost. Different strategies for advertising were tried to achieve more sale which would automatically reduce the cost. Maggie noodles sold in small packet is an attempt to penetrate into the lower income group of the society.

Non-governmental organizations and other non-profit organizations use advertising for many other reasons than to sell the product. They build their image through advertising or do well to the society by taking up any social issue.

ADVERTISING PYRAMID

The basic aim of an advertising campaign is draw the attention of the viewers or prospective customers. The whole gamut of creative team is involved in the designing of the advertisement.

Figure 9.4 The advertising pyramid.

The five basic elements of the pyramid are as follows:

1. Attention
2. Interest
3. Desire
4. Action
5. Satisfaction

Attention

The first objective of advertising is to capture attention of the reader. This job is easy as even shouting or clapping can draw an individual's attention. For print advertisement this task is done by the headline, as it is the first element of the advertisement that catches one's attention. Therefore, the copywriter usually makes the headline very catchy by using bigger fonts. The other techniques are to use punch lines but in conversational language. If abstruse language is used, then the purpose will be defeated and the reader will not read further.

"Behind every great adventure lies a great spirit". The headline for Tucson, the four wheeler, is quite appealing as the reader's curiosity is raised. The second way by which the attention can be caught is by using the picture, which can be very appealing. Titan has been very successful by roping Aamir Khan to feature in their advertisements. Once the attention is caught, the next task is to retain it by creating interest in the reader.

Interest

The advertisement's next objective is to create interest in the reader about the product. As the headline was appealing, the reader wants to learn more about the product. His interest is retained by further giving elaborations about the key features of the product. This is usually incorporated in the body copy. The copywriter does it explicitly or implies them. There is less scope of exaggeration in this part as this is more factual. But certainly how the information is presented is important.

The copywriter stimulates the interest by narrating a dramatic situation, citing a story or sprinkling humour. The illustrators use cartoons and pictures to generate interest. In radio, the sound effects and catchy dialogues in nasal voice may capture the interest of the listeners.

Desire

In this step, the advertisement creates a situation for the prospective customer to either enjoy benefits of the product vicariously. The writer creates a situation where the reader feels that he is missing something if he doesn't use the product. In print advertisements, copywriters fuel up the visualization by using phrases as 'think yourself to be the most successful person', or 'imagine'. In the television, the strategy used is after using the product, the user is shown delighted and contented, while in radio, you will hear the announcer saying, "you at your best with your suiting".

The desire lays down the possibility and captivates the consumer's mind. This part is handled delicately as the copy writer may sometimes offend the reader's sensibilities. Certainly, it is one of the difficult parts to write and that is why some of the copywriters omit it.

Action

The purpose of this step is to motivate people to do something. No advertisement is successful if it cannot induce any action. Several phrase such as 'offer closes by 30 Jan', 'buy now', 'limited stock', 'buy two, one free' are mainly used.

This is not a difficult step. If the copy is clear, then surely the readers will act. Action demanded may be explicit like 'call on us to book, the stock is limited' or implicit 'fly the friendly sky'. Sometimes, a sample of a product is attached along with the advertisement which acts as an action inducing device.

Satisfaction

The tip of the pyramid is satisfaction. After the product is bought, the buyer should have a feeling of satisfaction. He should not feel that he spent his money without getting the returns. This parameter helps to make the customer brand loyal in the long run.

• EXERCISES •

1. Define advertising. Can a product survive with good advertising?
2. "The world cannot survive without advertising". Give your arguments to support this statement.
3. Classify the advertisement in different types. How do you differentiate the product from the non-product?
4. For any advertising to be successful, it must follow the AIDA technique. Take an advertisement and explain it.
5. How is the advertising on television different from the print advertising? Which do you think has more recall value? Why?
6. What is the role of persuasion in advertising? Do you achieve persuasion through language or picture?

Part B

10

Effective Presentation

Great is the art of beginning, but greater the art is of ending.

—HENRY WADSWORTH LONGFELLOW

Why should I know the art of presentation? I never wanted to be a compère or a political leader. This is what most of you think when confronted with the question related to effective presentation. Let us assume this. You are a scientist and after years of study have discovered that the earth is square and not oval as believed by everyone. You address a group of scholars, with the intention of informing them about your findings. Since you are a novice and ignorant in the art of effective presentation, you end up putting forth the facts in a disorganized manner which the audience is not able to comprehend. Members in the audience mock at you and show disbelief in your theory. You are labelled as a nincompoop.

Now consider another situation.

You work in Cognizant Technology Solution Limited. Your company is working on a project, which has come to a stage of impasse. You have an excellent solution to deal with the problem faced by your company. The management committee asks you to make a presentation to communicate and share the solution. Since you are unaware of the techniques and style of presentation, you end up giving an ineffective presentation. Your colleague, on the other hand, has a mediocre solution but presents the facts in a very persuasive and convincing manner. What is the outcome? He is appreciated and his proposal accepted, while yours is rejected out rightly. See Figure 10.1.

The above two situations can be experienced by anybody. It is not just leaders who give presentations. There are innumerable instances when each one of us has to give a presentation. Invariably, we face many instances in our daily lives where we have difficulty in putting across our ideas clearly and persuasively to others. The simple reason for such situation is that we don't know the art of giving an effective presentation.

Figure 10.1 An individual giving a confident presentation.

Learning the art of effective presentation is absolutely essential to be successful in one's respective field of work. Remember it is a misconception that good speakers are born. There are several examples in history where people could not utter a word initially in front of audience but by perseverance and practice transformed themselves into articulate speakers. Abraham Lincoln, Winston Churchill were such people who became consummate speakers after constant learning and practice. Robert Frost has rightly said that half the world is made of people who have so much to say but don't know how to say it, and the other half have nothing to say but keep on saying.

COMBATING STAGE FRIGHT

Have you ever given a thought to why you are ineffective in giving a presentation? If not, here are some of the reasons:

One problem which is quite common is fear of the stage or dais. There are employees who don't fear writing reports but when it comes to presentation, they seem troubled. Some people fear giving a presentation more than death. It is true that most of us have an innate fear of facing the audience. But this fear needs to be overcome to become a good speaker. This kind of trauma and anxiety is not restricted to speakers alone, even a musician before the musical concert and an athlete before a marathon faces the similar fears. So everyone has a fear before undertaking the work, which has importance in their life. Hence, we must learn how to control our nerves and handle anxiety, so that we can give a good presentation. "Butterfly in the stomach will never go but after practice they will fly in formation", says Christina Stuart in the book *Effective Speaking*.

The first way to combat fear of presentation is to start giving presentation in front of a small group of familiar audience or friends and then move to larger audience. See Figure 10.2.

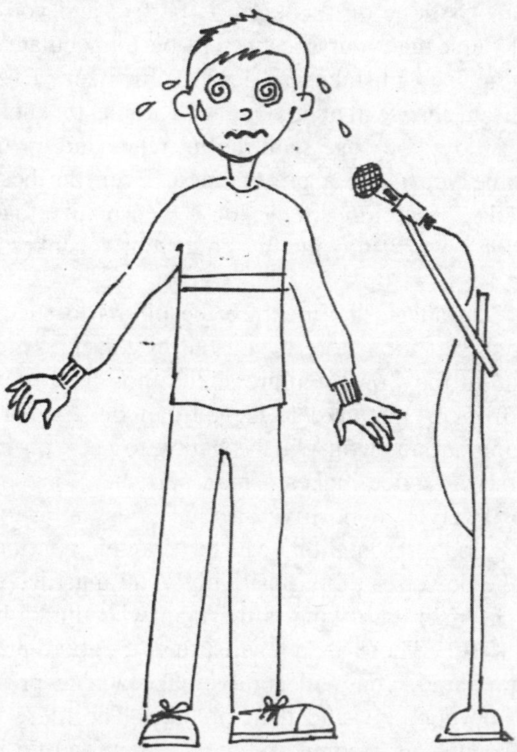

Figure 10.2 An individual getting nervous while giving a presentation.

In college, we had a friend named Ravindran. He was an average student and a taciturn. Not many would remember him speaking publicly in the college. When he was a sophomore he lost his father, who was a heavy smoker, and a victim of lung cancer. Father's death shattered Ravindran. He pledged to undertake a campaign against smoking and began giving presentations to small groups about the harmful effects of smoking. Ravindran encouraged people to give up smoking and join the anti-smoking campaign. Initially, Ravindran neither had the confidence nor the skill of giving a good presentation. But by exposure to the small group of trusted friends, he moved to larger audience. None would believe that this reticent boy could speak, leave alone addressing a large group of people. He learned and mastered the art of making good presentation and used it to bring a change for a noble cause.

The ways by which you can control your fear are as follows:

- **Friendly audience:** Always bear in mind that the people who have gathered to hear you, are your friends. The audience have assembled because they have interest in the topic and not because of any obligation or compulsion. They are keen to listen to your thoughts and ideas. Certainly they are not hostile to you, so why to worry for when they are eager to know what you are going to say.
- **Perfection:** No one on this earth is perfect and you are no exception too. Don't think that your speech will be immaculate and perfect. You should be open to mistake and learn from them. Even if you falter a bit, there is a chance that no one will come to know about it. More important is how you cope with the mistakes and try to overcome them the next time you make a presentation. Even the best of the speakers make mistakes; sometimes they don't even realize that they have made one. So, don't worry too much about your mistakes but learn to deal with them.
- **Failure:** The adage "failures are the pillars to success" is apt in the context of presentations too. If you fail in your presentation, don't think it is the end of the world. Failure should not dishearten you and neither stop you from trying harder. If you fail once, then practise and try again. People around you will be happy to see you making successful presentations. Practice makes a man perfect.
- **Think positively:** A positive attitude is essential to be successful in making a good presentation. Muster enough confidence as that will give you the power to think positively. You must have come across the saying: "The man who wins is the man who thinks he can".
- **Prepare well:** There is no substitute to good preparation. If you are well prepared, you will surely make a nice presentation. Choose the topic appropriately and then prepare. The more you rehearse, the more confident you become and, hence, you end up in making a great presentation.

PRE-PRESENTATION PREPARATION

Before making a presentation, you need to do a lot of homework, such as knowing your audience, choosing the right and interesting topic, assimilating material and collecting data etc.

Audience Awareness

To deliver an effective presentation, you need active audience participation. This is possible if you as the presenter know the interest and background of the audience. For example, suppose a doctor is invited to deliver a talk on *stress combating techniques* to a group of computer professionals. In the presentation, the doctor uses technical terms that explain the biological aspects of stress. The computer professionals will soon lose interest in the presentation as they are unable to understand what is being said and, secondly, they are keen to know the stress combating techniques which have not been mentioned.

This situation emphasizes that audience is of foremost importance. The style and the content of the presentation should be in accordance with the nature of the audience. An effective presenter understands the audience and adjusts according to their expectation. Gather information about your audience and while developing the presentation, try to analyse the impact of it on the audience at each stage. Therefore, when you prepare your presentation keep the audience in mind. This is called 'audience centred' presentation. This is very vital for the success of any presentation.

When concentrating on the audience, find some of their traits with which you can also identify. You have to find the audience's interest that will make them relate to the topic as much as possible. Find different ways to connect with the audience so that they also have more reasons to listen to you intently. If possible, obtain information about the audience and location where you will be making the presentation. If you are completely ignorant about your audience, spend some time to find out about them. Know the following facts:

- **Audience size:** If the size of the audience is restricted to 10–15 people, you can have an interactive and personal presentation. Questions can be put to the audience and the answers analysed. For example, when giving a presentation on creative thinking to the audience of small size, exercises of some kind can help to make it a good presentation. Since the audience can exercise their creative talent, they will find it an exhilarating experience. But for a large audience it has been found that if questions are posed to them, it is most likely that they will not be answered. Therefore, for such audience you should be more formal, less asking and more telling.
- **Age:** Always remember that audience in their twenties and thirties will have different motivations and interest than septuagenarian and octogenarian audience.
- **Education:** Try to know your audience's qualification or level of education. This will allow you to provide relevant examples according to their experience.
- **Occupation:** Get to know the audience's profession. Do they work in the same organization or company? Can you relate your topic to their work?
- **Gender:** We all accept that gender discrimination is wrong, but in some cases it helps to know the gender balance, of the audience. It would be inappropriate to give examples of topics which is of no interest to a particular group. For example, sports cars may be of no interest to an audience comprising women.

- **Marital status:** Is your audience single or married? Every group has varied interest and values. Some issues are more appropriate for parents than for those who are single. Sometimes, if we are ignorant of these facts, our presentation will not be well received.
- **Religion:** In some case, it is important to know the religious belief of the majority of the audience. If you know beforehand you can take pre-emptive measures. Quotations from the *Mahabharata* and the *Ramayana* are not appropriate for the audience who are mostly Christians.
- **Racial/cultural/ethnic background:** Apart from knowing the gender, religion, etc. of the audience, one should also be aware of their background. Try to find if the audience belongs to rural, suburban or urban class. Stereotyping can lead to myriad problems but it is helpful to know the audience's racial, cultural or ethnic similarities. Be very sensitive to empathize with the audience.
- **Hobbies/interests:** Does your audience have the same hobbies and interest? If so, then you can put them on the same platform. For example, if the audience share a passion for music, you can relate many instances of your presentation to the repertoire of musical notes, and that would make them more receptive.

CHOOSING THE APT TOPIC

Choose a topic with which you can also relate to. Be very careful and judicious in choosing the topic. For instance if you choose a topic to create your image, you are committing a blunder. Only if you feel that the topic is worth talking about, and helps you in making an effective presentation select it. Otherwise think of other options. Presentation is not the forum to make images, rather it is an opportunity to convey messages that you have gathered and researched.

No topic is good or bad. Always remember that people are uninteresting and not topics. It is important how you present a topic. A topic like 'Global Warming' can be made interesting by corroborating it with the right kind of statistics. 'How' is more important than 'what'. Always choose a topic which is close to your heart, and see yourself making a great presentation.

The next question that follows is where do you look for the ideas? They can be generated from newspaper articles or from events that happen around you. One can give a talk about, e.g. one's recent trip in the sand dunes of Jaisalmer. Students find topics, such as ambiguities in English language, mysteries of monuments in India, nanotechnology, schizophrenia interesting. A topic should be selected such that it is able to sustain the audience's interest.

ORGANIZING THE MATERIAL

After finalizing a topic, it is time to gather and sift information. Even when you know a lot about a topic; you have to add to the set of knowledge. Like any other thing in life, if you know more, you will have more choices when you apply this knowledge. In the case of presentation too, it is important to gather various types of information. Thus, you will have more choices when developing the actual presentation.

If the topic you have chosen is of your interest, then you will enjoy each step while developing the presentation. But some work needs to be done before preparing for the actual presentation.

SEARCH PLAN

- **Keep a file:** All the materials related to the topic should be kept at one place. It is important to cite all the sources of information in your presentation so that it will reduce your cumbersome task at a later stage. The day before your presentation is not the right time to waste in searching important information that have been misplaced.
- **Record all sources:** All the sources should be cited that didn't come from one's personal experience. If the sources are not cited adequately, it counts as plagiarism. When referring to any source, note down all the details—the author's name, the title of publication, the date and place of publication along with the year.
- **Strategy to gather material:** It is good to make adequate preparation. Plan ahead in a meticulous manner when collecting information. This includes searching the Internet, books and journals, and talking to concerned people. Don't surf the net for the appropriate material at the last minute.

GUIDANCE IN GATHERING MATERIALS

- **Begin at home:** Whatever information you have at home, make the best use of it. Chances are that you will find a lot of information in books, magazines and newspapers, which are available at your home.
- **Use the most valuable resource:** Always remember that people are the best resources. A university will have a number of experts in almost all subjects. If you take the initiative to search through the campus directory, you will find contact numbers of all the right people. Get in touch with them to gather information.
- **Use newspaper articles:** Newspapers contain the most contemporary information. It is the best source for collecting material on any topic. If you go through the newspapers carefully, you will find all the relevant information you are looking for. Always remember to write down the

details of the newspaper article for citation. If information is provided from a reliable source such as newspaper, it gives more weight and credit to your statements and people tend to be more interested in your references.

- **Use the Internet:** In today's world, Internet is the most accessible source of gathering information. You just have to type the topic in the search engine and you will get uncountable references for that topic at the click of the mouse. But care must be taken to use the material as reference and not as it is. The latter will count as plagiarism. Never forget to provide references of the resources from where you have gathered the information.

DEVELOPING A PRESENTATION

The presentation may not only be written, but also 'developed'. It is better not to write the complete presentation and then memorize it. Instead, the main points should be written which can then be developed. While making the presentation, adjust according to the response from the audience. Both the content and the delivery depend on the need of the audience. Any unexpected reaction from the audience could force you to shift to a new aspect. This requires adaptability. To sustain the interest of the audience, you have to be careful while developing the introduction, body and conclusion.

Introduction

Introduction is central to a good presentation. Your first impression on the audience is formed with the introduction. If you are able to impress your audience with the beginning, 60% of your job is done. Poor introduction can signal problems for the rest of the presentation. Give your best in the introduction which will help you in winning the heart of the audience. In general, an effective introduction should conform to the following:

- **Get the attention immediately:** Just getting the attention is not enough. Making the audience interested in the topic is more important. Standing in front of the audience, and making faces will get the audience attention. But for how long?
- **Reveal the topic:** By the end of your introduction, the audience should be clear about the theme and points that will be discussed in the presentation.
- **Establish credibility:** Try to gain the confidence of the audience. At the earliest you have to reassure the audience that you are sincere and not deceiving them. If credibility is not established fast, the audience might get suspicious. In contrast, if you have got the goodwill of the audience, they will overlook your mistakes.
- **Establish trust:** Make good impression on the audience through your appearance and words. Give the audience compelling reasons why they should listen to you and they will inevitably be attentive.

Tips for an effective introduction

- **Keep it brief:** If the introduction is too long, the audience will begin to lose attention. Don't straight away start with the actual presentation, only give the overview. The rule of thumb is that your introduction should be just 10–15% of your total presentation.
- **Attention getting devices:** Audience's attention can be drawn immediately by the following:
  - (i) *Stories*: If you narrate stories, then keep them brief. Talk about personal experiences with which the audience can relate the topic. Suppose you are giving a presentation on the effect of smoking on youth, then give instances if you have known anyone who had contracted the disease and died of it.
  - (ii) *Shocking statistics*: Always support your statistics with the study conducted or research done. You should not concoct statistics to shock the audience. For instance, by citing the latest statistics on the number of patients dying of AIDS, in the presentation 'AIDS: the enemy of mankind' will help create a lot of impact on the audience.
  - (iii) *Quotations*: If quotations are used at the right place, the audience's attention can be grabbed fast. But care must be taken in keeping them brief and to the point.
  - (iv) *Ask question*: A good tool to captivate the audience is to ask them questions, such as do you know who is the richest man of the world? Do you want to reduce weight in just ten days without dieting? These kinds of questions can really energize the audience and they will look forward to your presentation to get the answers.

The Main Body

A presentation should have four or five main points or categories that need to be discussed. The structure should be such as to enable you to share your ideas clearly and precisely. It should also be able to sustain the interest of the audience. The ideas should flow smoothly. The proper use of connectives can help in shifting from one topic to another. Without connectives, the presentation becomes very sloppy and fragmented, and will have less impact on the audience. A connective is a technique of using words and phrases to put the ideas together. Connectives give the overall presentation a natural and cohesive flow. They give the audience an initial framework of the presentation so they can see how your ideas fit in, as a unit. There are different kinds of connectives and which one you choose depends on where they are placed in the presentation. Some connectives are as follows:

- However
- In addition to
- Despite
- In spite of
- Because
- As
- Hence forth
- Hence
- Contrarily
- Since
- Moreover
- But

Conclusions

Conclusions are as important as the introduction. Just as an introduction creates the first impression, the conclusions are the last impression which the audience will carry back home. The conclusions give the audience a feeling that you have come towards the end of your presentation. Moreover, it is your last chance to state quickly the thesis to the audience. Your audience should be left with the feeling of satisfaction and completeness. Put an effort to remove all the fringes and loose ends.

Additional tips

- **Don't add new information:** Conclusion is not the place to introduce new information. If you have to put across some information, do it in the main body. By addition of new information in the conclusions, the audience will not feel a sense of closure.
- **Only review point:** Corroborate all the points in the main body. Any new information at this point will be only about the source to get additional information.
- **Refer to your introduction:** In the introduction you had promised what all you will talk about. Assure the audience that you have fulfilled what you had promised. You can do that by referring to your introduction. This brings a smooth closure in a natural way.
- **End with enthusiasm:** End your presentation with a bang and not with a whimper. A strong end leaves an indelible impression. Don't say 'This is all' as it doesn't make a lasting impression on the audience.

VISUAL AIDS

The use of visual aids adds quality to your presentation. The presentation gets lustre and becomes lively. In many instances, visuals can add clarity and make the talk impactful. Since more sensory perceptions are put to use, the audience will have greater retention of information. However, flashy visuals can't save an otherwise disorganized and poorly structured presentation. You have to plan out while developing the presentation how the visual aids can have an overall impact.

Types

The visual aids can be broadly classified as *static* and *dynamic*. Static visual aids don't change but remain the same. Examples are as follows:

- Flipcharts
- Overheads
- Posters
- Slides
- Non-animated computer graphics
- Blackboard drawings prepared beforehand

Dynamic visual aids are those which move and change as the presentation proceeds. Examples are:

- Animated computer graphics
- Video
- Actual objects
- Blackboard writings

Selecting the Aids

Once you know the types of visual aids available, select one which is most appropriate for your presentation. In general, dynamic visual aids are engrossing for the audience, but time-consuming for the presenter. Dynamic visual aids have greater chances for mechanical failure, e.g. power failure can disable any gadget at work. On the other hand, static visual aids may be not as exciting as dynamic ones. Yet they can be very effective. Static visual aids are easier to prepare and use.

Your choice mainly depends on your topic and the time available both for preparation and for presentation. You ought to have enough time to practise with the aid. Keep in mind that simple visuals are more effective than the complex and esoteric ones. You should consider the fact that the aids have to be transported to the location on your presentation.

Guidelines

Once you have selected the type of aid you are going to use, you should follow certain guidelines. Keeping in mind the guidelines will help in using appropriate and effective visual aids.

- **Visuals should enhance and not distract:** Make sure that the volume of the visuals doesn't exceed that of the text. If the audience remembers only the visuals, then your presentation has not been effective.
- **Visuals should be clear:** Even if you have put lot of effort in making the visuals, they will remain useless if every member in the audience is unable to see them. Use at least 18 font/point type for the text.
- **Use simple fonts:** Some of the fonts look overly ornamental and are difficult to read. Compare the following sentences.

  (a) *How easily can you read this?*
  (b) I can read this easily.

  Surely you can read the second sentence much easily. The time you are involved in reading the first sentence is the time where audience sans from listening.
- **Don't distribute handouts amidst a presentation:** You are always tempted to pass around the printed pages while speaking, or at the beginning of the presentation. It is indeed a bad practice as it distracts the audience and significantly reduces the effectiveness of the presentation. Try to distribute the written material at the end of the presentation. Avoid using visuals which are not visible to all the audience. Overhead projector can be used for photographs or small objects.
- **Practice in advance with visuals:** Your credibility will be ruined if you use the visual aids clumsily. It is always better to practice in advance with your visuals so that you can use them with facile ease.
- **Be prepared for a fiasco:** You should be ready with an alternate plan for your presentation so that in the case of failure of visual aids, you can continue with your presentation. For example, the overhead projector bulbs can get fused, posters may not stick or videotape may get jammed in the machine.
- **Speak to your audience:** While using visual aids, maintain eye contact with the audience and avoid looking continuously and reading from your visuals.
- **Keep video and audio clippings to the point:** Don't keep the audience waiting for very long if the aids are visible. Start the tape right in time and make sure the tape is of good quality.
- **Try to have one piece of information on the transparency:** Don't crowd the transparency with too much of information because then they become messy and difficult to comprehend. Just write the main and subpoints and elaborate them.
- **Present statistics on visuals:** Statistics when presented with visuals have greater impact. Your audience can see the relationship between the numbers instead of having to imagine how numbers relate.

PRESENTATION DELIVERY

After choosing the appropriate topic and collecting the materials for the presentation, the next step is to be careful about the delivery. You have to spend some time in improving the style and manner of delivery. Practice needs to be done. One can imagine standing in front of the audience making the presentation aloud. This gives a real feel of the presentation. Just imagining and keeping things in your head will not give you idea what is it like to actually put the ideas into words.

You must listen to your own voice. If possible, record it and listen so you can decide if you have to slow down, speak aloud to avoid nasalized and vocalized pauses, such as ur, um, ah. Since your delivery can make your presentation distinct, focus on proper pronunciation and clear articulation should be given. In order to be more confident, rehearse it twice or thrice and ask for honest feedback from your friends so that you may overcome any other lapse.

You also have to practise the use of non-verbal communication. It is important that the postures and gestures exude positive impression on the audience. Avoid excessive movement as it distracts the audience. Remember to follow through with actual physical practice to ensure that your efforts to give a well-developed presentation have not gone futile. By doing so, it will naturally boost your confidence.

The basic guidelines for practice and delivery are as follows:

- Know the content and how to say it.
- Keep the minimal writing on your index card.
- Be aware of distraction but strive for correction.
- Take a deep breath before starting the presentation.
- Let the audience settle down before you start.
- Preparation has no substitute.
- Run through the whole presentation in advance.
- Prepare well in advance and relax properly.

By going through these guidelines carefully, you will certainly be able to give an effective presentation. Since experience makes a man perfect, so grab the opportunity to make a presentation. Always mark your weaknesses by talking to reliable people in the audience, and improve that aspect in the next presentation. Following is a sample presentation that will help you in developing your own presentation also.

PRESENTATION ON INTELLIGENCE

Introduction

About one hundred and fifty years ago, a school teacher told the mother of an eight year old child, "I'm sorry ma'am, but I cannot teach your child anymore, he does not want to follow the conventions of school education at all". Thus ended the school education of the child. Should we now call this child unintelligent? Should we, on the other hand, refer to another child as intelligent who topped the class of that particular dropout child? Before answering, we should know that the school dropout was Thomas Alva Edison—deemed by many as the greatest inventor till now.

What is intelligence and who do we term intelligent? Can being the topper of a university or examination label a person intelligent? So, the topic of our presentation is INTELLIGENCE.

Intelligence is one of those concepts that is easier to recognize than to define. We often refer to other peoples' intelligence, describing them as sharp, bright and quick on the one hand or as slow, dull or even stupid on the other hand. What, precisely, is intelligence?

The term 'intelligence' refers to individuals' abilities to understand complex ideas, to adapt effectively to environment, to learn from experience, to engage in various forms of reasoning, and to overcome obstacles by careful thought.

Types of Intelligence

Is intelligence a single characteristic or does it involve several other components?

For example, let us take the example of a gymnasts performing in Olympics. Are we not amazed by their feats? Is their ability to perform complex manoeuvres simply the result of extensive training? Or do their performances show a special kind of intelligence? Yes, it surely does....

There are two theories which suggest that intelligence is multifaceted

1. Gardner's theory
2. Sternberg's triarchic theory

Gardner's theory suggests that there are several kinds of intelligence, such as verbal, mathematical, musical, bodily kinesthetic, personal intelligence.

A person may be intelligent in a particular field while he may be very poor in another field. So we cannot just refer to an individual as dull simply by considering his failures in a particular field. For example, Ramanujam failed in literature and social sciences but he was a genius in mathematics. Similarly, Beethoven and Mozart are epitomes of musical talent. So we cannot say that Mozart was dull just because he could not solve equations of physics.

A gymnast exhibits bodily kinesthetic intelligence. The ability to get along well with others explains personal intelligence.

Sternberg's theory suggests that there are three types of intelligence:

1. Componential or analytic
2. Experimental or creative
3. Contextual or practical

Componential intelligence involves the ability to think critically and analytically.

Practical intelligence is the ability that individuals use to find the best fit between themselves and the demands of the environment.

Experimental intelligence emphasizes insight and the ability to formulate ideas. For example: Johannes Gutenberg who invented the printing press, combined the mechanisms for producing playing cards, making wine and minting coins in his invention. Thus, he showed high level of creative intelligence.

Relation Between Genetics and Intelligence

Let us ask ourselves: Is intelligence inherited?
If yes, then it is evident that the more closely two people are related, the more is the similarity in their IQ level. Example:

(i) 90 → identical twins
(ii) 50 → brothers
(iii) 15 → cousins

Adopted Children

From the previous statement it is evident that adopted children should resemble their biological parents, because they should be similar to the persons from whom they got their genes and not those who raised them.

Colorado project: Identical twins reared apart

Two twins (identical) brought up in different environment, still found to have the same IQ level (similar to that of a pair of twins who were brought up in the same environment).

Hence, these three evidences very clearly show that genetics does play an important role in human intelligence and also a number of other psychological functions.

Environment's Impact on Intelligence

It has been found through a study that following factors increase the IQ level:

Sufficient nutrition, increased urbanization, exposure to society, good education, television and computer games.

Though we don't know the cause and effect of each of the above–mentioned factors, we know that they are related to our environment in some way or the other.

Environmental deprivation and Environmental enrichment

It has been found that a person's intelligence level may decrease in case he/she has not been exposed to environmental stimulation in earlier part of his/her life.

In terms of environmental enrichment, if a child is taken from a hostile environment to an environment which is friendlier to him, then the intellectual growth of the child was found to increase tremendously.

Extreme environment's impact

In the case of extreme environment the intellectual growth of a person may drastically increase or decrease. Both are harmful to the society because the child is going to grow up in the society, become an adult and play a number of róles.

Thus, environment also plays an important role in a human's intellectual development.

Diagram → self explanatory (a summary all of the above–mentioned points).

Gender Differences with Respect to Intelligence

Do you think gender differences exist?
Answer is YES.

There exists differences but they are small in size and subtle in nature.

Root cause

The root cause is ancestors. In olden days, men used to go out for hunting everyday and they had to remember their way back. Women whereas used to go out in search of food, and they had to remember the same place as they used to go to the same place every day to collect the fruits and vegetable for their survival as well as that of their family.

Creativity is the process of producing something original and valuable.
Well about 99% of the people would say that it is an alternating column of squares and circles. Well the genius would say that they are rows of alternating squares and circles.. that's some creative thinking ...!!

Coming back to the topic, creative people have various qualities. They are insightful, and they tend to do divergent thinking, thus developing a variety of unusual, new responses.

They have the ability to take intellectual risks and to be a non-conformist. There is a famous quotation by Shiv Khera which says "Winners don't do different things, they do things differently!"

Creative people have the willingness to criticize and to improve. They are self-disciplined and know how to motivate themselves. They are dedicated to their work and to high standards of excellence. They also have an in-depth knowledge about their area of expertise.

Creative people are flexible thinkers and seek novel solutions and imagine many possibilities.

Let me tell you a story on this point.

A physics teacher once held a quiz in his class. The question was "How would you measure the height of a building with the help of a barometer?" One student returned a blank answer sheet. On being asked, he said that he was unsure which answer to give as there were so many of them. A bit confused, the teacher asked him to explain. "Quite simple sir, just tie a rope around the barometer, go to the roof of the building and lower it to the ground. The length of the rope equals the building's height".

"Another way is to use the barometer as a scale and measure the height along the walls. You can also keep the barometer on the ground and measure the length of the shadow and that of the building by knowing the height of barometer, the building's height can be calculated using trigonometry. One more way is to drop the barometer from the roof of the building, measure the time it takes to hit the ground, and the height then becomes equal to $\frac{1}{2}gt^2$!!"

"But you still haven't made proper use of the barometer!" argued the teacher. "Ok that!" he said, "is quite simple and boring. You just measure the pressure on the roof and the ground and the difference in pressure equals pgh …".

Do you know who that young boy was? He was none other than the great scientist, Neils Bohr!!

So for the development of creativity, various factors are involved. This includes motivation, intelligence, knowledge, personality and environment. In the personality factors, there is the willingness to defy convention, and openness to new ways of seeing things, to take risks and to overcome obstacles. Creativity development flourishes from a supportive environment that encourages and recognizes creative endeavours. People who live in stimulating and exciting environment, where they get to choose there own interests and activities.

Now can creativity be measured?
It seems easier to assess levels of intelligence, through the use of IQ tests than it is to assess levels of creativity, as there is no such equivalent test. IQ tests usually select an activity or skill, and then design tests to measure individual performances in the specified activity. A high score will indicate a high level of performance and a low score will indicate a low level of performance.

However, it is difficult to measure creativity in such a way because the skills are harder to define, as they are usually unique and diverse. There is an apparent contradiction between the predictability of objective tests and the unpredictability of creativity. Confusion arises with the measurement of general and specific intellectual skills, as there is no clear idea about how they interact together in creativity. The Life Cycle affects measurements too as IQ-related skills, and knowledge improve with age until adulthood, whereas creativity seems to occur randomly at different ages. It seems impossible to measure creativity unless it depends on a non-creative, intellectual skill. On the other hand, intelligence is relatively easy to assess through IQ tests, which give clear indications of levels of performance.

However, in today's competitive world, creativity has taken a back seat.
Basically it is an inborn trait in any individual. The degree may vary from person to person. Everybody likes to be intelligent in one or the other way, but the question arises if intelligence can be substituted by systematic hard work or if heredity has a grip over it. Actually intelligence, in general, measures the sharpness of a person's thinking abilities, his capacity to learn fast and his analytical abilities. So if hard work with proper planning and

dedication can not replace intelligence, then people will stop working hard, they will stop striving for the best, for they will think that if we are not born intelligent then we cannot develop it in us through hard work.

Again there is another point to dwell upon: what if modern technology begins to produce genetically modified offspring whose IQ's are increased artificially. Then at some point in the future, all the individuals will have a high IQ so relatively there will be no difference. For example, if all the people of the world have an IQ of 300, then there's no difference in the world.

Besides, bookish knowledge does not always refer to intelligence.

Having a sharp intellectual ability is certainly advantageous but more important than that is how one achieves and what one achieves.
Success always favours the prepared mind. Without dedication to one's work, without hard work, nothing worthwhile can be achieved, even a genius like Einstein had to brood on his area of interest and concentrate deep on it which is but mental hard work…. If Newton would have sat idle he would not have discovered the plethora of laws he discovered.
Thank you!!!

Presentation slides

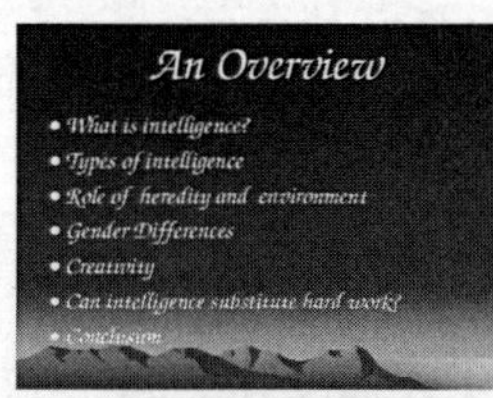

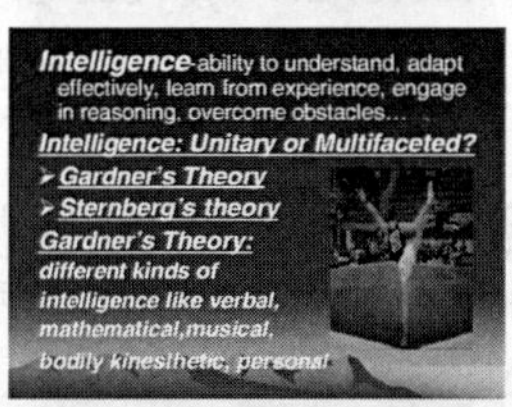

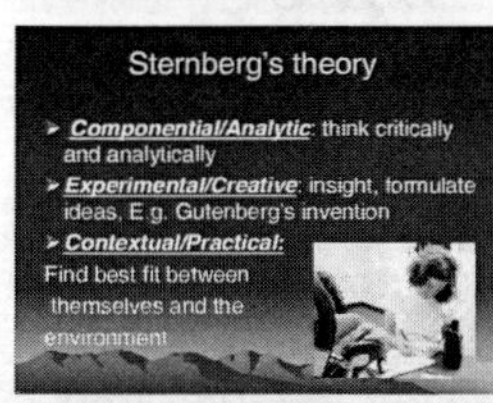

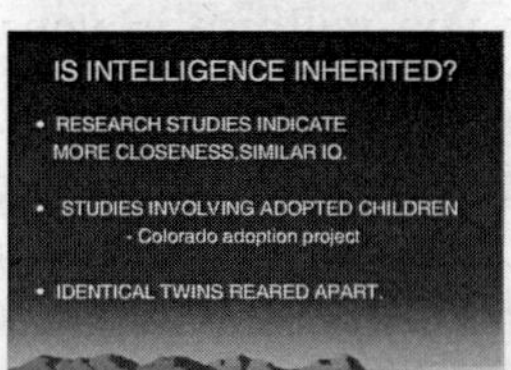

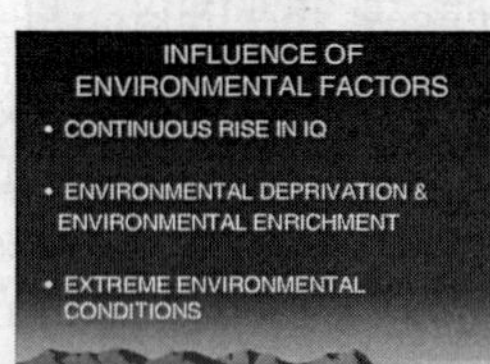

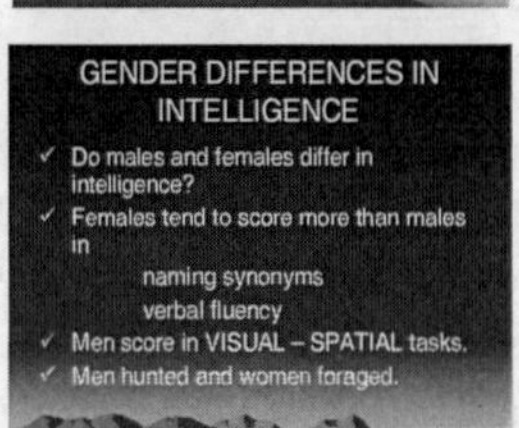

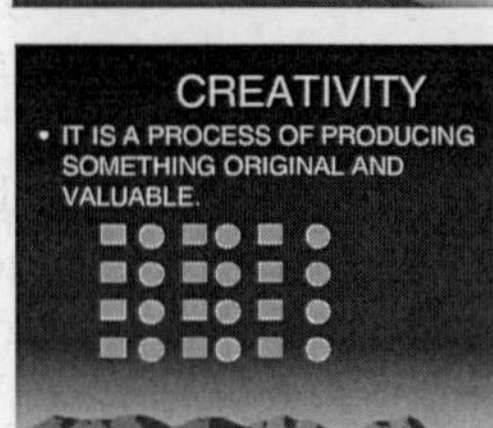

• EXERCISES •

1. Why do people fear when they have to give a presentation? What can you suggest to remove the stage fright?
2. Mention various common factors that frighten you before a presentation.
3. What are the different modes of presentation? Which is the best presentation mode during the seminars?
4. Assume that you are the HRD manager of your organization. You are deeply concerned over the recent stampede in Nehrunagar, Mumbai that took the lives of many. It was later discovered that the stampede was a result of rumour spread by a group of people saying that sea was on rise and there was an apprehension of Tsunami. Citing this as an example in your introduction, prepare a **ten-minute presentation** on '***The role of effective communication in an organization***'. You are to deliver this speech to the newly appointed junior executives of your organization, keeping in mind the essentials of a persuasive presentation.
5. Introduction of the presentation is said to be the tip of the iceberg. Why do you think introduction as the most important element of presentation? Prepare an introduction for your presentation on '**Appeal for eye donation**'.
6. Assume that you have been asked to make an oral presentation before a group of fresh graduates recently recruited by your organization. The topic of your presentation is '*The role of communication in human resource management*'.
   (a) Prepare a write-up giving detailed outline of your presentation.
   (b) Discuss the factors you would keep in mind in making your presentation effective.
   (c) Do suggest the linking devices you will use in your presentation.
7. Social scientists believe that water crisis the world over will be the cause for the next world war. Considering the seriousness of this problem, the Society for. Water Harvesting, Raipur, Chhattisgarh is holding an **International Conference on Water Management for the Sustenance of Humanity in 21st Century** on 6 August 2023. You being a renowned environmentalist have been requested to deliver the keynote address in the inaugural function of the conference. Prepare the full text of your presentation/speech in about 650 words. Your presentation/speech must contain a catchy introduction, a discussion containing at least four important points and a great conclusion.

8. As a man of experience you have been called to Oxford Management Institute, Jaipur to deliver a talk on "Soft Skills: An Empowerment Tool for Managers and Professionals". Now write the **full text of the presentation** in about 500 words and also **prepare four slides** to be shown to the audience. Your speech should be persuasive in tone and style.
9. What is the role of audio-visual aids in oral presentation? Write the advantages of blackboard over power point.
10. Assess the importance of voice in an effective presentation.

11

Communicating without Words

> *The most important thing in communication is to hear what isn't being said.*
>
> —PETER DRUCKER

Communication, the breath and soul of human existence, is dynamic but a complex process. When we communicate, we express our feelings and emotions, share information, seek advice and also give numerous pieces of advice to people who seek the same from us. All these are done with the help of words, as they are the representative of our ideas. But think for a while, do we always communicate with words alone? No. On numerous occasions we communicate without words. Just think of the other day when you went to meet your professor after being absent from his class for a week. The professor looked at you but didn't say a thing. Didn't you realize that his eyes were stern and he was very angry? He hardly said a thing, yet he communicated his anger. Sometimes you see a person who instead of speaking uses his hands, fingers, and tries to describe things by making certain gestures. He is speech impaired and it is difficult initially to understand what he is trying to communicate. Yet with time and long association you can understand what he is trying to say. The speech-impaired person you come across is also living his life though with certain hitches.

NON-VERBAL COMMUNICATION

You might have read in the history books that human beings, before the introduction of words, used to express their feelings with the help of gestures and postures. They used their bodies to communicate. They gritted their teeth to show anger, grinned to display their happiness and touched one another to exhibit affection. You have also read previously that communication can be both written and spoken. The history of language reveals that the written form of communication developed much later than the spoken form. Language became more refined with the passage of time when the notion of correctness, i.e. grammar came into being. The importance of words gained more prominence when the signs and symbols showed the speaker's moods and intentions.

Communication with the use of words (either written or spoken) is called **verbal communication**. Communication without the use of words or speech is called **non-verbal communication**. This chapter will deal with non-verbal communication. You have read in Chapters 1 and 2 that we can communicate without the use of words also. But one often wonders how communicating without words can be considered successful. Sigmund Freud had said,

> He that has eyes to see and ears to hear may convince that no mortal can keep a secret. If his lips are silent, he chats with his fingertips; betrayal oozes out of him at every pore.

Non-verbal communication occupies important place in human life. Since we keep communicating throughout the day, we don't use words always. Sometimes, we use body movements to strengthen or lessen the impact of our message. But on many occasions, we don't do so consciously. Since our body plays an important role in the framing of a message, the underlying emotions are easily stamped while conveying the information.

Non-verbal communication involves various features, and it appears through the signals given by the ambience. These signals are non-verbal cues, which on most of the occasions speak louder than words. Non-verbal communication differs from verbal communication as it:

- is less structured.
- has no vocabulary.
- is more spontaneous.
- is more reliable.

Non-verbal communication doesn't follow any fixed structure. The response to a piece of good news can be expressed by giving a small smile, whereas sometimes by evoking a whole-hearted laughter. No doubt, your reactions also depend on the audience with whom you are sharing such news. Non-verbal communication doesn't go by theories. The meaning of non-verbal cues can have different connotations in different communities, states or nations. The nod that means acquiescence in one culture, may mean denial in other. Also these cues are infinite in number. It may either overlap or contradict one another. While talking to a foreigner, avoid using any non-verbal cues whose specific meaning you are unaware of. Keeping cultural clashes apart, non-verbal cues are more spontaneous and reliable. The feelings of anger or irritation, expressions of delight or despair, despite our effort to control them appear clearly on our face.

Most of us, either at our workplaces or in our offices, pay more attention to non-verbal cues than we do to words. While asking for a make up test for the missed test, you look more at the face of the professor than on the piece of paper. The police officer while interrogating a criminal looks into the latter's eyes and the mother too concentrates at the child's mien when inquiring about his misbehaviour. We have more faith in the message conveyed by non-verbal cues sometimes, than we have in words.

Researchers also reveal that more messages are conveyed by non-verbal cues than by words. Ray Birdwhistell, an eminent scholar of body dynamics, is of the view that 35% of our messages are carried verbally and 65% non-verbally. Albert Mehrabian makes it more clear by considering 7% as verbal, 38% as vocal and 55% non-verbal. All these suggest that more messages are generally conveyed and interpreted non-verbally.

In written communication, punctuation marks convey the message left out by words. But in oral communication, body movements, gestures, postures, voice, environment, time, space and vocal characteristics convey more than words do. Various non-verbal cues can be studied under different categories. Studies suggest that there are 700,000 forms of non-verbal communication. It is difficult to interpret all of them. They can be grouped in the following categories:

1. Kinesics
2. Proxemics
3. Chronemics
4. Paralanguage
5. Haptics
6. Metacommunication

KINESICS

We have read that formulation of any message takes place in our mind. Any idea which becomes a message has to be approved by our willingness and attitude. While conveying or receiving a message, parts of our body also get activated. Sometimes readily and at other times unknowingly. Thus, the role of our bodily action in communication becomes essential. Remember the first time when you were asked to make a speech, the way your limbs trembled and voice shook. It was your principal who noticed and said, "Don't be nervous".

Our body keeps giving indications of emotions which we can feel and others can see. The movements of our body can be studied under *kinesics*. Ray Birdwhistell coined the term 'kinesic'. According to him, kinesics is the science that analyses the movements of our bodily organs. Birdwhistell observed: all movements of the body have meaning. None are accidental.

As body language reveals the innermost feelings of human beings, it is emitted from every part of our body. You can at times hide some of your emotions but this can't be possible in every situation. A careful observer rarely fails to detect the deception, cleverness or betrayal, however hard the other person tries to overcome or control it. Body language or kinesics consists of appearance, eyes, posture and gesture.

Appearance

There is a famous saying that "appearances are deceptive". Let us analyse this adage. Those who make use of their facial expressions often deceive their listeners for their own advantages. Since your face speaks even before your words, it can convey emotions of all sorts. Much of your sincerity or gratitude, love or dislike appear visible on your face. Imagine your first impression of the speaker who comes to deliver a speech. You often tend to judge the speaker on the basis of his dress, shoes, hair and even the colour of the suit. All these comprise his bearing and background. A look of weariness or anger on his face makes the listeners lose interest in what the speaker wants to convey.

Both as a speaker and a listener, your facial expression can affect communication. A speaker with a positive expression, such as smile on face, formal dress and other required accessories for the occasion can win the crowd and make a propitious impact on them. Likewise, a negative expression from the crowd may make the speaker realize that he has failed to create interest in them. Hence, careful speakers work hard to ensure that their facial expressions engage the attention of the crowd and pay rich dividends. In most formal situations, such as addressing a gathering, attending a meeting, job interviews and also in your daily life, appearance plays a vital role.

Eyes

Eyes are an essential ingredient of your appearance. Your eyes mirror your heart and conceal your mind. A favourable glance at someone may be enticing whereas an angry look may unnerve others. While making a conversation, delivering a speech or a presentation, an eye contact with the receivers makes you accountable or responsible to them. Nobody likes a speaker who buries himself in his notes or is lost behind the screen. Your eyes help in establishing a rapport with your listeners and ensuring credibility of their words. Another advantage of eye contact is to get the feedback of your lecture or speech. You should all remember that in many countries and cultures, you have to follow certain norms about eye contact. Studies reveal that in the USA, even a positive message tends to become negative if delivered with averted eyes. As eyes are meant to arouse attention, interest, influence and interaction, you should always make them a useful weapon to convey meaning. Avoid gazing unnecessarily and restrict aggressive facial expressions. Whether speaking formally or informally, you should look at your listeners to help them understand your message and change your stance in the case of any incomprehension.

Gesture

Gesture is another aspect of body language. Not only our face and eyes but the movement of other parts of our body, such as hands, arms, head and shoulders have a vital role to play in communication. Imagine a dancer who moves her arms and makes various corresponding movements to convey the intended meaning by nodding her head and patterning her shoulders. In verbal communication too, the movement of these body parts become obligatory. You can, at times, express voluntary and involuntary messages through the use of gestures. Although gestures are natural, careful professionals use it to get desired results. People practising martial arts and even theatre artists get special training to use specific gestures to symbolize specific effects. We use our hands to indicate or point to something, raise them to say hello, wave to say good bye, etc. You often stretch your hands outwards to express comfort but squeeze them to show discomfort and restlessness. An orator uses clenched fists to locate something and also to use numbers. There are many other gestures which at times can give negative meaning. You should make a conscious effort to use gestures to convey the appropriate meaning. At the same time, one should avoid displaying negative gestures. Table 11.1 will help you understand the implications of gestures, both positive and negative. See Figure 11.1.

Table 11.1 Gestures, their Meaning and Effects

Gestures	Meaning	Effects
Looking at the watch frequently	Restlessness	Negative
Looking at the roof	Unable to face the crowd	Negative
Playing with buttons of the shirt	Unease	Negative
Biting nails	Nervousness	Negative
Leaning towards the speaker/listener	Enthusiasm	Positive
Nodding head at times	Agreeing	Positive
Playing with keyrings	Too nervous	Negative
Wringing hands at times/cracking knuckles	Reluctance	Negative
Smiling at times	Friendliness	Positive
Walking briskly while speaking	Restlessness	Negative
Wiping forehead	Unease	Negative

Though gestures have nearly the same meaning in many countries, yet there are some which are culture and context specific. The meaning of one gesture in a particular country may be completely different in another country. Tapping one's head in Brazil indicates thinking process while it stands for 'crazy' in other places. Likewise, tapping the nose means 'keep it secret' in Britain whereas it is a warning signal in Italy. Britishers hiss to show extreme disapproval but hissing is symbolical of social deference among Japanese. You should take some time to learn the implications of particular gestures and then use them if you are in a foreign country.

Figure 11.1 Different gestures.

Posture

Like gesture, posture, too, has its importance in communication. Posture, basically, is the positioning of your legs while standing or sitting. For every occasion a particular posture is appropriate. While praying, one needs to stand carefully as in attention or sit with the back straight. When attending a meeting you ought to sit properly. Your nervousness or confidence can get displayed in an interview by the way you sit. Likewise, while participating in a group discussion you show your active or inert participation by your sitting or bending posture. A speaker often tends to lean forward with one foot positioned in front of the other while delivering a speech. But his reclining on the lectern or pulling away his back often reflects his lack of interest in the subject and his listeners. Being too close to the microphone and sagging your shoulder may symbolize your morbidity and distract the attention of the crowd. The ideal way is to walk sprightly to the dais when called, and ensuring a relaxed feeling by changing your posture only when the need becomes so imperative. The frequent change of postures may lead people to dig more meanings than conveyed and, hence, ought to be regulated.

You are often faced with the challenge of either standing straight or walking. In many cases we either walk too much or too less. Remember, this is obviously an indication of mental disposition. The ideal posture is to ensure a proper balance of your body weight in consonance with the impression you want to convey. When you stand straight and balance your weight on both the feet, you reflect control and poise. Such a position allows you to have a proper control over your audience, and also helps in establishing a rapport with them.

Walking during an oral presentation has its undeniable role. Both the speaker and the audience can benefit from walking. As a speaker, walking allows him to be natural. While the audience gets some relief as they concentrate on the speaker. They can move their eyes saving themselves from looking in a particular direction all the time. Walking may, to a great extent, help a speaker in hiding his anger, frustration or boredom. But care ought to be taken as to how much one should be walking while giving a presentation. Walking too much or a military march is also negative. Proper practice and handling audience of all kinds will help you regulate your postures with perfection. See Figure 11.2.

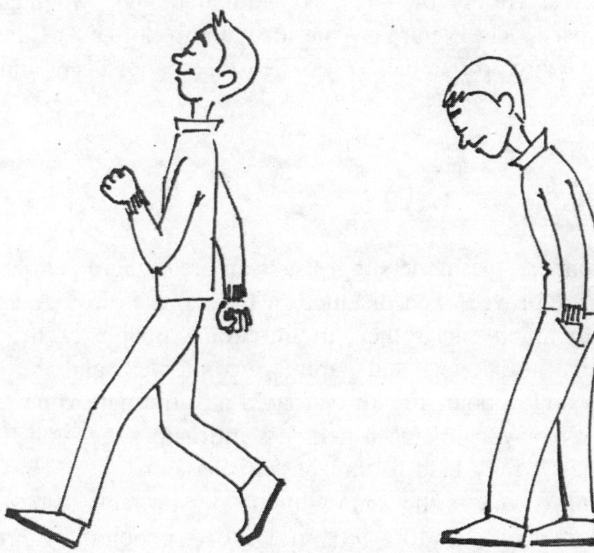

Figure 11.2 Different ways of walking.

PROXEMICS

Proxemics is the study of nearness or distance in a communication scenario. The word 'proxemics' has been derived from proximity which means the state of being near or distant. An important aspect of non-verbal communication, proxemics deals with the amount of space we usually occupy or demonstrate while communicating. Imagine yourself to be in a crowded place and you desire to feel free. Think of being in a crowded bus when a stranger slightly touching you seems to anger you. Do you know why it happens? All of us want some amount of space around ourselves. This space is our own. We consider it to be our treasure. But while communicating, the use of this space conveys some meaning. Careful communicators use 'space' with desired effect. But all of us are not aware of this space. As a result, we often violate the different space zones.

In communication, the use of space signifies relationships. When communicating with friends, parents or close relatives there is not much space between them and you. But you always leave more space while communicating with your teachers, elders and seniors. Also you usually maintain more space when communicating with strangers and outsiders. Imagine when you open your door to a stranger and simply ask "whom do you want?" You feel threatened and maintain a distance between the individual and you. But in the case of a familiar face, you not only open the door of your house but also allow him to enter. It is the kind of relationship that makes you decide the amount of space you should leave while communicating.

We usually violate spaces in crowded situations, such as in a bus, train, ticket counters and cinema houses. But in different contexts and cultures, space is interpreted in a variety of ways. As human beings, we ought to respect each other's space. The veteran American anthropologist, Edward T. Hall, who coined the word 'proxemics' classified the spatial needs into four zones:

1. Intimate zone
2. Personal zone
3. Social zone
4. Public zone

Intimate zone, as the name suggests, is an area where people having close relationships are allowed. The distance in this zone is less and may at times allow people to touch each other. In this zone, people of the inner family circle, close relatives, lovers and parents are allowed, and they are exposed to each other's body odour, breath or touch, etc. Intimate zone ranges from 6 to 18 inches. When you invade a person's intimate zone, you tend to offend him and at times it may lead to unnecessary hassles.

Personal space zone is the zone which a person feels to be his own. This zone ranges from 18 inches to 4 feet, and allows people to interact with each other not in a whisper but in a low tone of voice. People in this zone are friendly but not intimate, comfortable but not too close. Friends, colleagues, neighbours, etc. come under this zone. You can often find people during social functions, parties maintaining their personal space and keeping each other at arm's length.

Social zone is the area we usually maintain with people whom we don't know personally but know socially. This zone ranges from 4 to 10 feet. While interacting with postman, shopkeeper, milkman or your new colleague and with many people known to you formally, this zone is maintained. While interacting with people, you have to maintain some amount of formality without causing any inconvenience or discomfort to them. An executive while interacting with his clients or customers maintains this distance to ensure his superiority and preserve his privacy.

Public zone is the farthest and the widest gap maintained between the speaker and the listener. The speaker in this zone addresses a huge gathering from a raised platform and usually uses a microphone. Since the number of audience is unlimited, the speaker gets a better view of the public and feels more protected. The distance ranges from 10 to 15 feet between the speaker and the audience. This zone restricts the audience to raise doubts or queries, and protects the speaker from clarification. Communication in this zone is often one way and the speaker has less control over the crowd. The chances of violation in this zone are less. But at times violation of public zone has led to disastrous consequences.

CHRONEMICS

In communication, it is not only words and actions that communicate. Imagine how your professor behaved with you once when you had reached late to his class. Also consider telling somebody about his unkempt hair in the midst of a meeting. It is only later that you realize it was not the right time or place to tell your friend about his hair and dress style. Time is an important feature of communication. People judge you on the basis of how much importance you attach to time. Many people have succeeded because they have used time dexterously. Chronemics is the study that tells how human beings utilize time while communicating. Time reflects our sincerity and punctuality. It can hint at a person's devotion and dedication to his job or assignment. In many organizations, executives appreciate completion of a job within the stipulated period. While completing a task before the deadline may sometimes be considered lack of sincerity and also not serious towards one's work. But this is not true always. It may vary from individual to individual. A person determined to submit assignments only after several reminders may also give the hint of his being overburdened or feigned seriousness.

The importance of time has much to do in a professional world. The growth of an organization too depends largely on the importance given to time. Even if you verbally convey a positive message, if not properly planned, the result will be negative. It is only time that has made many of our old practices redundant and new ones significant. All you require in a professional world is timeliness. A right drive at a right time may bring laurels, whereas an untimely initiative may evoke harsh criticism. Think of talking about your raise in salary when your boss is having an important meeting. Such a gesture may be labelled ill-mannered. Instead raising the same matter after office hours when the boss is relaxed may give favourable results. In many cases, busy executives use time to assert authority. You can come across various situations where people are made to wait for long time outside an official's room. This gives the visitor some clue about the official's position and importance. Edward T. Hall has rightly said, "Time talks and space speaks".

Time language also differs from one country to another. In many countries, such as Scandinavia or Germany, punctuality brings admiration and delay shows less concerned. Latin American countries allow meetings to begin after appointed hours. Whatever the interpretation, in a country as ours, punctuality is not only admired but most often rewarded. As individuals, you ought to respect time and that will pay you rich dividends.

PARALANGUAGE

All forms of communication are language, whether spoken or written. When we speak sentences, we not only use words but also attach intended meaning to certain words. There goes a famous saying, *Words don't have meaning; we attach meaning to them.* No doubt, while sending intended meaning to a particular unit/part of a sentence, the shared assumption and common background can't be ignored. But the majority of people extract meaning on the basis of something other than words. It is more often than not that the delivery part of a spoken communication gets more prominence. When you speak a sentence, you attach specific meaning by the way you deliver it. The same sentence spoken differently may evoke different responses. The amount of pitch, the rate of delivery and the loudness help in imparting meaning to the sentence.

Paralanguage is how of language. It involves tone of voice, hesitations or speed of speech, and variations of language other than the actual words. A qualitative voice involves a proper blend of force, pitch, rate and quality. Force or volume signifies the energy or amplitude of the sound.

There is no such fixed rule about volume, but whatever you speak should be audible to your audience. You can always raise or lower your volume depending on the number of people attending the presentation and the acoustics of the room. Likewise, you should keep in mind the background of the listeners while determining the rate. Nobody would appreciate a speaker who either speaks too fast or too slow. The ideal way is to speak in a conversational tone, which allows you to pronounce words clearly and effectively.

Another important paralinguistic feature is the application of pitch while speaking. It can be understood by making an analogy with musical notes. Too high a scale usually becomes thin and tight. You can also experience people speaking in high pitch often during moments of anger and stress, and in low pitch being despaired. The role of electro-chemical reaction in the tightening of our muscles and affecting our vocal chords can't be ignored. We tend to mispronounce certain words when speaking rapidly. Fast delivery reflects our nervousness. Moreover, we also lose control over our audience. Instead, a proper synergy of rate, pitch and volume can work wonders.

The quality of voice is also important. But not all people have pleasant voices. Though a god-gifted attribute, the quality of voice can be improved by proper training. There are many instances where people who despite having shortcomings in relation to voice became successful speakers and orators by proper training. In addition to force, pitch, rate and quality of voice, careful speakers utilize proper timing of pauses in their speech. A timely pause is a meaningful investment. It helps the speaker in indicating what is to come next in the speech. The tone and tenor of our voice often become a victim of circumstances and we often become losers because of our excessive emotional outbursts. A careful speaker reaps the advantages of these paralinguistic features, which a casual speaker ignores. You should always remember that your language habits not only exhibit your background, it also affects the background of your audience.

To say that a speech is faulty or defective, we should keep in mind what a highly respected speech therapist, Charles Van Riper said:

> Speech is defective when it deviates so far from the speech of the other people that it calls attention to itself, interfere with communication or causes its possessor to be maladjusted.

Charles Van Riper, *Speech Correction*, 5th edition, Englewood cliffs, N.J.: Prentice Hall, 1972, p. 29.

But more often than not the fault in the speech is not only because of a defect in voice, but also due to a shortcoming in our personality. Quality of voice can be improved and our voice is affected because of our resistance to change or our morbid nature at times. Another expert in voice and diction training, Virgil A. Anderson makes quite a significant remark:

> Bluntly stated, one may have a dull, uninteresting, or unpleasant voice because his voice is defective or improperly used, but he may also have such a voice because he is dull, uninteresting or unpleasant person.

Virgil A. Anderson, *Training the Speaking Voice* (New York: OUP, 1942, p. xvii.)

HAPTICS

Haptics is the study of touch behaviour in communication. It is an important vehicle for expressing intimacy, warmth, comfort and discomfort. Imagine the impact of a mother's touch on her child. It obviously gives the child a reassurance and the mother a sense of possession. But while communicating you can't touch all and sundry. It may be like invading somebody's personal freedom and intruding on one's privacy. Even the most casual touch may generate positive feelings.

Touching may be misinterpreted in different contexts. You might have felt encouraged during your school days when patted on shoulder by your teacher. But as you grow in years you may not like people touching you. Though indicating warmth, it may invite wrath also at times. There are strict regulations about who can touch whom in organizational structures but you can always keep yourself away from the imbroglio by avoiding to touch your colleagues and subordinates. The norm of touching also varies from one culture to another. Cultural studies reveal different signals being sent while touching different parts of the body. You can notice how a common phenomenon in the West may become a debatable issue in a more orthodox country. Men and women in India don't walk publicly holding each other's hand as is done frequently in the West. Two males walking hand in hand in India may be attributed as normal while it may be viewed as a dubious relationship in West. You can still find a lady hesitant while shaking hands with a male in a traditional setup, whereas it is quite common in Western countries.

METACOMMUNICATION

We all know when communicating, at times, we are not able to say all that we had intended to. Sometimes a few things are left because of the structural pattern or due to unusual circumstances. You may often come across situations where you neither want to hurt somebody's sentiments nor want to applaud the other in high flying words. There are times when you want to say more or less than the words you use. All these can be studied under metacommunication which as the word itself implies 'beyond communication'. It entails implied meaning, which may be intentional or unintentional. Many literary devices come under this category. You can come across examples of metacommunication even in your day-to-day conversations. For example, if somebody says "you look well dressed today" may also mean that the person dresses shabbily on other days. Likewise, if someone says "his teacher was good", it may also imply that the teacher was not impressive but quite an average one.

People use metacommunication sometimes either to be on a safer side or hide what exactly they think. But while using words, you have to be quite careful. Scrupulous speakers often use neutral words to serve their purpose without belling the cat. To get the meaning in the metacommunication, both the speaker and the listeners have to pay due attention to the position of words in the sentences or expressions.

SILENCE AS COMMUNICATION

Many people treat silence also as a form of communication. As already stated, communication involves shared assumptions and unspoken agreements between individuals and teams. Not all words in a communication have equal effect. Some words are more important than others. And it depends wholly on the sender to choose the words according to the needs of the occasion. We have a number of methods at our disposal by which we can emphasize a word or a phrase. For example, italics in the printed page, bullets, indentations and so forth. Though the heavy usage of technical devices has eroded the value of punctuation marks in written communication where dashes, dots and hyphens chartered the surreptitious sentiments of the sender. The reflection of these then becomes vital through vocal nuances.

Vocal characteristics are inevitably important in an oral communication. Oral presentations comprise verbal and non-verbal messages. They differ widely from written communication. A successful oral presentation requires more of performance than of competence of the speaker. Albeit the content of the presentation is an asset, the way it is delivered gets an upper hand most often.

Sending verbal messages doesn't imply one should keep talking all the time. Strong messages and impressions are conveyed even without making any sound. Pauses and silence during presentations, conversations, interviews and speeches can be of great value. Most of us, whether we agree or not, show signs of nervousness while being interviewed for a new position or when giving a business presentation. If we take time to rehearse before we actually act, then we will appear confident and our interview or presentation will go well. More often than not nervousness propels us to talk faster than normal. Sometimes, inexperienced speakers tend to speak too softly.

A successful communication is one that tends to put forth the idea successfully to the majority of the audience. As Anne Morrow Lindbergh puts it, "Good communication is as stimulating as black coffee, and just as hard to sleep after". The comprehension of the audience depends on the vocal emphasis of the speaker. It is here that the beauty and blend of silence and pauses equate in an oral presentation. Silence and pauses give a respite to both the sender and the receiver.

When we speak too fast, we either tend to mispronounce or speak wrong. In such predicaments we tend to find ourselves using filler sounds such 'um', 'er', 'fine', 'you know', 'right'. We are also found making frequent use of question tags seeking confirmation either from ourselves or from our listeners. The more nervous we are, the faster we talk and the more fillers we use. There is always a way to come out of such critical moments. One should remember that it is not only the words, which convey the message rather it is also how we deliver the words to facilitate the understanding of our listeners.

Non-words

As we are careful when selecting words to speak, so we should be aware of our 'non-words'. They usually appear when we are not too sure of what we want to say. If we use too many of the non-words, our listeners start doubting our credibility.

In language, there is a provision for space. It always exists between words and phrases, between clauses and sentences sound clusters and threads of thoughts. It is not necessary to fill up these spaces with meaningless synapses. Further, if one is constantly making sounds, one deprives himself of the tranquil time to reflect about what one is trying to convey. This time can be utilized in putting brakes if the speaker gets off-track.

Silent time is thinking time. Silence provides a way to pace and punctuate our presentation. We all have the license to be quiet. The listeners don't find themselves in conformity with speakers who make too much noise. It becomes difficult for the audience to follow the train of thoughts. The use of a great many non-words creates a distraction or worse an annoyance. Going a little bit off the track but still showcasing the importance of silence, this quotation of Adrienne Rich is of great help; "Lying is done with words and also with silence".

The aim of a presentation or an interview is to convince the listeners and not to distract them. If at any time during the presentation, one is not sure of what he wants to say next, he should just be silent. A split second is usually all we need and our listeners will wait. The listeners are least aware of the fact that the speaker is buying thinking time. But, on the other hand, if the speaker fills up the space with non-words, he will be broadcasting the fact that he is not sure of what to say. This insinuates the belief that the speaker is either lost or confused. In turn, it can be misleading even when the speaker tries hard to be convincing.

Non-words are often interpreted as a lack of preparation and confidence. They are nothing but confused noises and are counter productive. No one has ever presented a convincing argument with non-words. Noise is a distraction but silence and selected pauses contribute greatly to our presentation.

Pauses during Presentation

We know that one should maintain eye contact while talking to a large group and delivering a presentation to an audience. This ensures a better involvement and a cordial rapport with the listeners. An effective way to do this is to give pauses that can help break our thoughts into units, thus making it more comprehensible for the audience. We can present an idea to a person, pause and then present the next idea to another person. This technique helps us in engaging everyone in the audience and also in promoting goodwill. The audience gleefully welcomes such pauses giving equal importance to all and sundry. Caution should be taken that a single person doesn't attract our attention for a longer period. The resulting silence indicates the comfort and preparedness of the speaker. The audience, too, is convinced that the speaker is talking to each and everyone of them.

Begin with silence. It takes 'guts' to stand in front of an audience after being introduced and not start talking immediately. But this can prove to be one of the strongest ways to get the audience attention and build rapport with them. Lee Glickstein, a well-known speaking coach and speaker from Mill Valley, California, suggests that we start our presentations by standing quietly, making eye contact with audience members, letting them also make eye contact with us, and then once everyone is comfortable and waiting with anticipation, start with a dynamic story. You will be amazed at the level of attention this method produces.

Pause to develop relationship between you and your listeners. During a pause, the speaker is more like a listener. This is a time when both are listening and the speaker can take note of the audience's quality of listening. We might realize that as the presenter we need to change course and tell a story or possibly ask for questions. If, however, we don't take a moment to evaluate reactions and interest, we might just forge ahead without maintaining the audience's attention.

Pause with Purpose

Many a time, throughout a presentation pauses can add emphasis and/or give the listeners a chance to ponder, or even laugh. When we have just made an important point, a startling or unusual statement, or a call for action, participants need a moment to take notes, think about what we just said, or catch up. Even though we hear words faster than we can speak, we do need time to think about what was said and then form our ideas. If, as presenters, we give participants enough time, they will be much more likely to buy into what we are presenting than if we just keep on moving with the information that is so familiar only to us. There are speakers who make a humorous statement and then don't let the audience members have time to 'get it' and laugh. People need time to laugh. And laughter is important because it bonds the audience and the speaker.

As a speaker with content, you have many different points to make. But if you jump too quickly from one point to another, you will leave your listeners behind or confused. When this happens, they will often times 'tune out' and you have lost them for the rest of your presentation. A well-placed pause will help you and the audience prepare for the next aspect of your presentation. We suggest picking transitional sentences as carefully as your openings and closings statements, and then taking a moment of silence for the ideas in these sentences to take hold before you launch into the new point.

Pause for a show of confidence. The confident pause is an earmark of the accomplished speaker. The courage to stop the flow of words is an act of trust in the power of your presence, your non-verbal communication, and your relationship to your listeners.

Pauses have their significance in communication in a variety of ways. An appropriate pause also helps in distributing proper accent at proper places. Most of us know that the effectiveness of the US President John F. Kennedy's famous line, "Ask not what your country can do for you; ask what you can do for your country", was not only because of its language but also because of its appropriate pause dividing the two thoughts.

Even when telling a story, a joke, a dramatic story, an anecdote or reciting poetry, the pauses enhance our effectiveness as a speaker. Famous actors, politicians, newsreaders, and orators convey meaning in their pauses by regulating them. Pauses also help in bringing variety in our presentation and saving the audience from monotony.

• EXERCISES •

1. Can you communicate without words? Give an instance when you communicated very effectively without language.

2. What is paralanguage? Does silence also fall under the umbrella of paralanguage?
3. Are kinesics and proxemics same? Distinguish clearly.
4. What is the difference between silence and pause? Explain the significance of pause in the presentations.
5. Explain all the four distances in proxemics. In which situation you maintain public distance from the audience?
6. Explain clearly what you understand by metacommunication.
7. What is haptics? Why do you pat someone when he/she has done a good job?
8. What is non-verbal communication? Underline the importance of body language in an oral presentation.
9. Silence and pause help the speaker buy time. Explain.
10. Underline the importance of eye contact in various forms of oral communication. Give suitable examples.
11. Explain the role of various factors responsible for effective presentation.
12. *Time talks and Space speaks.* Justify the statement with regard to a successful presentation.

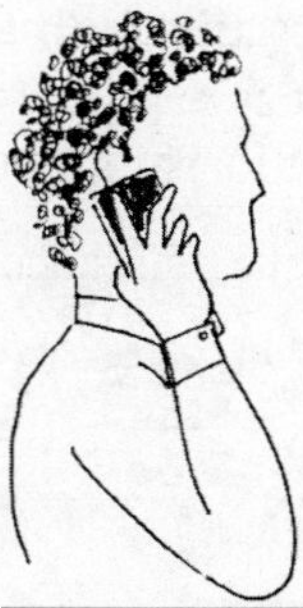

12

Interviews

An investigation may take six months. A quick interview, profile, a day.

—PAUL NURSE

A job interview plays a vital role when seeking employment in a company. It enables the employer to ascertain the suitability of the candidate for his organization. During the intense interactive process, which the interview involves, several personality traits of the candidate come to the fore and help the employer make the right decision. It also enables the candidate to get a glimpse of the organization's goals and opportunities that would offer an environment for professional growth if hired.

The fierce competition in the global market has resulted because of the growth of multinational companies; corollary interviews have become more crucial and are to be dealt with care. Individuals have to struggle very hard to prove their worth by taking the process of interview very seriously. Focus, enthusiasm, common sense, ambition, resourcefulness and analytical powers could get you a job, only if you can demonstrate to your interviewer that you actually possess the above-mentioned traits. You are tested in terms of alertness, preferences, interpersonal skills, oral communication, analytical ability, perseverance, special interest, etc. Be careful while answering questions, which can be of myriad nature. The types of questions you can face are: objective, subjective, closed ended or open ended.

JOB INTERVIEWS

You must get acquainted with the term 'interview'. It is a specific term, and has its origin from the word *intrevue,* which means 'sight between' two people. The word 'interview' can be defined as a planned conversation with a predetermined purpose that involves question sessions. Hence, it is a process of dyadic communication that not only fosters interpersonal relationship, but also proves the worth of the candidate. See Figure 12.1.

Figure 12.1 An individual being interviewed.

There are nine different types of interviews that are held for several purposes:

1. Job interview
2. Information interview
3. Persuasive interview
4. Exit interview
5. Evaluation interview
6. Counselling
7. Conflict-resolution
8. Disciplinary interview
9. Termination interview

All the above interviews are of varied nature. They require careful planning and specific strategies. In this chapter we will discuss job interviews. It has been observed that interviewers often avoid standard questions asked by many campus recruiters because such questions elicit over-rehearsed answers. Instead those questions, which probe into deep thinking, are put across to the interviewee. You are exposed to this nature of questions to find out what exactly you can do for the organization by exploiting the available resources.

An experienced interviewer knows when you are being genuine. Just spouting off some answer may be a memorized response. The best way to prepare for an interview is to think about the job. Think in retrospection and analyse what you have achieved in the related areas of the job. Although you may not face such questions directly but your understanding will be cleared through every statement you make. While evaluating candidates, it can be asked how they set priorities for various jobs or projects they are currently working on. That is where demonstrating your ability to juggle work with extra-curricular activities can help. The interviewer also looks at the interviewee's drive, ambition, resourcefulness and analytical ability. A student can show an edge over others by reflecting his creativity through the acts like using pen and paper or by going to a chalkboard and writing to elucidate an idea. Students should not be apprehensive to voice their opinions and views.

Stages in a Selection Process

1. Screening of application forms
2. Appraisal of CV (strong points and progression are checked)
3. Competency tasks (how good and qualified the candidate is)
4. Psychological tests
5. Group discussion
6. Stage-wire interviews
7. Negotiations
8. Medical test

Thus, interviews assume an important place in the selection process because decisions about who to employ is a very crucial question and interviews are a costly affair. The right person for the company is the one who is good enough for the company and repays the cost by staying long enough.

JOB APPLICATION

As prospective job seekers, your objective is not only to prepare for an interview, but also to find ways as to how to get an interview call. For this purpose you have to write job applications. A job application is a letter which is sent along with the resumé to prospective employers. Since a job application is attached to the resumé, it is short in length often about three paragraphs, and serves as a formality. It is also called a covering letter. The basic purpose of a covering letter is to prompt the employers to read your resumé.

Like all other letters, a job application or covering letter must have a beginning, a middle and an end. The first paragraph should be introductory in nature while the other two should act as body and concluding paragraph. A job application is meant to give a summary of the details mentioned in the resumé. However, all the three paragraphs have equal importance.

Introductory Paragraph

The first paragraph of your job application or covering letter, like any sales letter, should attract the reader's attention. It should stimulate the interest of the recruiter, and justify your suitability for the job that you have applied for. One needs to convince the recruiters that he can contribute to the company's goals. The opening line of the covering letter can start with a question, an unusual statement that captivates the attention of the reader. For example,

> One of the fastest growing publishing houses in the world, do you have an opening in your acquisitions department for a recent college graduate with a major in English, and publishing and editing experience?
>
> I believe that my knowledge of public relations and proven communication and leadership skills makes me a strong candidate for the position of Media Relations Coordinator that was posted by Delta Airlines Job Opportunities Program.

Moreover, you should mention briefly the qualifications in the letter. Be more specific by mentioning in the first paragraph where you learned of this job opening. For example,

> I would like to submit my candidature for the position of Media Relations Officer advertised in *The Employment News*, 7–14 February 2023 posted by BITS, Pilani Media Cell.

Body Paragraph

In the body of your covering letter, you have to highlight your strongest qualifications for the position you are applying for. Demonstrate how these qualifications will benefit the employer. If you have prior experience, refer the employers you have worked for in your enclosed resumé. One need not emphasize much about one's qualification in the covering letter as it serves as a ploy to persuade the employers to go through your resumé. In the example below you can find how the candidate gives a clue to his ability and shows his accomplishment.

> As a banking representative at Axis Bank, I provided quality customer service while promoting the sale of products to customers. I also handled upwards of ₹ 80,000 a day and was responsible for balancing the bank's ATM machine.

Concluding Paragraph

The concluding part of the covering letter should reflect your avidity to secure a face to face interaction with the recruiters. Seek a personal interview to discuss the various formalities. One needs to be flexible regarding the date and time for the interview. In case you have time constraints, mention clearly how, when and on which number you can be contacted.

Length and Style

One has to understand that no recruiter is interested in a lengthy covering letter. A job application or covering letter should not exceed one typed page. Since your resumé describes everything in detail, you can save yourself from repeating the same matter in your covering letter.

The style of the covering letter, like all other business documents, should be clear, precise and to the point. This can be achieved by using concrete words and not abstract ones. The sentences chosen should also be specific and strong instead of vague and lean. Expressions such as endeavoured, tried, hoped, should be substituted by initiated, undertook, handled, etc. You have already read in Chapter 6 about the different techniques of writing letters. Make use of them and begin each paragraph with a topic sentence. One also ought to be careful in the use of tenses. The right approach is to use present tense to discuss current activities and past tense for previous job duties or accomplishments.

SAMPLE JOB APPLICATION

The Manager (HR) — 2 January 2023
Yahoo India
MGM Road, New Delhi-110001

Dear Sir

The job requirements for application architect advertised by your company in *The Hindu*, dated 25 December 2022 tempts me to apply for this position. I feel confident as I fulfil the criterion mentioned in the advertisement.
During my first year B.E. in IIT Roorkee, I got highly fascinated by the real life application of computer programming techniques. Their implementation to provide ingenious cyber solution attracted me more. Pursuing my interest, I opted for three core-elective courses which specialized in application-based programming skills. It would really be a learning and working experience to apply my skills in your esteemed organization.
I hope to get an interview call so that I can prove my suitability for this post.

Yours faithfully
Shravani Dutta

RESUMÉ

You have already read about the different strategies that will help you succeed in getting interviews. But in order to get an interview call, your job application should be supported by an effective and informative resumé. As students, you are often struggling with words such as resumé, curriculum vitae and biodata. You should understand that all these are different names for the same document which describes your personal and educational achievements. Though its purpose varies as you grow in age and experience, it is most often aimed at attracting prospective recruiters in secure an interview for employment.

A resumé can be defined as a detailed document describing one's past achievements and future expectations for a coveted career. It includes information about one's career goals, education, work experience, activities, honours, and any special skills one might have. A neatly typed and properly formatted resumé, which is to the point and free from errors, is the one recruiters often prefer to those written in a casual manner having no care and concern for readers.

The purpose of a resumé is to generate the employer's interest and get an interview call. Be careful to arouse the employer's interest in your candidature. This can be done easily by briefly mentioning your skills. Resumés can have three different formats: chronological, functional and combination. While candidates at entry level should follow functional resumé, experienced ones can opt for chronological ones.

Analyze Yourself

Before you draft a resumé, you need to analyse your qualification, market trends and job preferences. One should properly evaluate oneself and assess whether he can suit the recruiters' expectations. It may, however, appear difficult to gauge yourself but a little bit of caution can always help. No one knows better than you about your own accomplishments, education, experience and personal traits. So, analyse yourself honestly.

Frame the Resumé Around Your Strengths

A candidate in the job market has to sell his abilities either for an entry level position or for a promotion. It is, therefore, imperative that one frames the resumé around one's strengths. Once you have analysed yourself, you will find that you possess a number of good qualities. Mention your best features and relate them to the job you are seeking. But at the same time, when you desire for a job change keep into consideration certain vital issues, such as gaps in your career, frequent job changes, continuing in one organization for a long time and at times job termination too. While you cannot hide these issues, you need not emphasize upon them too much.

Divide your resumé

While framing your resumé, divide into segments and put the concerned qualities or matter in the section to which they belong. For example, the section on education should include details of your school, college, projects, volunteer activities and related skills. Likewise, if you have prior job experience, put it in the experience section. On occasions, even an experience of six months also makes your case stronger than the candidate who doesn't have any experience. Moreover, one sounds more specific if the roles and responsibilities of the job are also mentioned. Many organizations attach much importance to references. Hence, you need to provide authentic references. Care ought to be taken that these referees are acquainted with your work, area of expertise and calibre. It is better to give the names of your professors, current or previous employers as referees. Decorum says that you seek their consent before mentioning their names in your resumé.

How to start

Every resumé begins with personal details, such as candidate's name, permanent and campus addresses, permanent and campus phone number and email address. There is a fixed formulae about the place where these pieces of information should be mentioned. They can either be placed at the top centre or top right of the resumé. Your name should be written in block letters to avoid any confusion. Remember to include your URL address or fax number if you have one.

Objective statement

Recruiters often look at the objective statement while perusing from the deluge of resumés that they receive. Hence, it should be restricted to one to two sentence summary of your area of expertise and career interest. Write complete sentences or descriptive phrases with minimal punctuation. Relate your existing skills directly to the job you are seeking. Demonstrate what you can do for the company rather than what they can do for you. Avoid generalized statements, such as

> A position allowing me to utilize my knowledge and expertise in different areas.

Instead one should be as specific as,

> Advertising assistance with print media emphasis requiring strong customer contact skills.
> To obtain a position as a software engineer allowing me to utilize my knowledge of Oracle and Linux.

Summary of qualification

Recruiters often look for some key words that could help them get an idea about the candidates' expertise and work experience.

> B.E. in Computer Science with specialization in networking. Worked as a part time analyst in IBM and introduced new software for pay roll.

Education

This section should begin with the highest educational qualification. Include information, such as university attended, degrees earned (major, minors), grade point average, date of programme completion, and so forth. In case you had opted for some extra courses other than your disciplinary ones, do mention them by their titles and not by course numbers. It is also mandatory to mention the duration of the course. The next important thing in this section is your accomplishments.

Accomplishments comprise achievements, honours and knowledge. Apart from your school, college and professional qualification, one also has some personal skills. Since all applicants for a particular job possess similar qualifications, mentioning certain extra attributes gives you an upperhand over other candidates. Special skills, such as computer proficiency, foreign language, effective writing, problem-solving and decision-making provide you an edge over other candidates. In addition, you should also describe personal attributes, such as enthusiasm, initiative, motivation, adaptability, and sense of humour.

Style

The language of your resumé should be short, simple and clear. You can achieve these qualities by using short instead of crisp phrases and figurative and vague ones. Sentences beginning with action verbs are more effective.

Example

(a) I was course in charge of Technical Communication for two years.
Revised: Handled Technical Communication course during 2020–2021.

(b) Responsible for streamlining a new filing system.
Revised: Streamlined a new filing system that reduced paper work by 50 per cent.

You can make use of the action verbs given as follows:

Accomplished	Eliminated
Administered	Expedited
Assembled	Generated
Assisted	Identified
Budgeted	Implemented
Campaigned	Initiated
Collaborated	Innovated
Consolidated	Interpreted
Coordinated	Investigated
Corresponded	Maintained
Delegated	Navigated

Demonstrated
Operated
Participated
Programmed
Recommended
Recruited
Represented

Negotiated
Researched Scheduled
Streamlined
Supervized
Synthesized
Systematized
Transformed

> The use of parallel phrasing also adds to one's style. In case you are using one particular pattern, follow the same throughout. If you choose to follow the verb pattern and particular tense, stick to it. Likewise if you use nouns or noun clusters, follow the same throughout.

Employment experience

This section is primarily for those who have prior job experience. But beginners can also mention any experience which they had during their vocational training or some short stint in any capacity. One should also focus at the relevance of such positions to the job applied for. Here again action phrases will come to your aid.

Teaching Assistant
(May 2021–August 2022)
SRM University, Chennai, India

References

In this section you should give the names of the people who are acquainted with your academic activities. In most of the cases, your professors can be the best choice, especially while applying for entry level jobs. Sometimes students write 'references available upon request'. This sounds ludicrous. Hence, the wise thing is to give the names of referees. Avoid giving only one reference. Provide at least three references. The names and addresses of the referees should be correct.

Prof. B.K. Khan
Director
BRCM College of Engineering & Technology
Bahal, Bhiwani
Ph. + 91 1255 265101-104,213
E-mail: bk_brcm@yahoo.co.in

Prof. Sangeeta Sharma
Department of Humanities and Social Sciences
BITS Pilani, Pilani-333031
Ph. +91-1596-234536
E-mail: 38.sangeeta@gmail.com

Prof. Monica Sharma
Department of Mechanical Engineering
MNIT, Jaipur

In addition to all the above-mentioned guidelines, you should also be careful about the type of paper on which the resumé is printed. Your resumé should be such that it can be scanned. One should also pay attention to punctuation, spelling and grammatical correctness before taking a print out of the resumé. Any lapse in your resumé can mar your chance of being called for an interview. Moreover, the resumé should be sent along with the job application. Following sample resumés will help you understand the nature and variety of them better.

SAMPLE I

Curriculum Vitae

Aakash Jain
Room No.-264, Ram Bhawan,
BITS Pilani, Rajasthan
Contact: Phone. No. 09983525962
E-mail: aakashgenius@gmail.com

Career Objective

To work in a professionally managed corporate environment where I will have the opportunity for learning and growth, and my competence will get the chance to change the productivity and effectiveness of the organization.

Academic Credentials

- ✓ B.E. (Hons.) Electrical and Electronics from BITS Pilani in 2023.
- ✓ Senior secondary examination (CBSE) in 2019 with an aggregate marks of 91.2%
- ✓ Higher secondary examination (CBSE) in 2017 with an aggregate marks of 94.4%

Achievements and Projects

- ✓ Represented the team to Techfest 2019 (technical festival of IIT Bombay) in a programming competition named 'Code maestros' and came seventh in the finals.
- ✓ Submitted a project titled 'Electro Vault' in Apogee 2019 (technical festival of BITS Pilani) involving microcontroller programming.
- ✓ Won first prize in a programming competition named 'Code Rash' in my first year during Apogee 2018.
- ✓ A regular beneficiary of MCN Scholarship provided by BITS Pilani.
- ✓ Obtained a score of 383 out of 450 in BITSAT (the entrance examination for BITS Pilani).
- ✓ Awarded Certificate of Merit from CBSE for being among the top 0.1% students in Mathematics.
- ✓ Awarded a Certificate of Merit for being placed in National Top 1% in Physics Olympiad in 2021.

✓ INDIRA AWARD for scoring highest marks in mathematics in the state board.
✓ Received merit certificate in Hindi in 10th standard from Hindi Academy, Delhi.
✓ Honoured with merit certificate in Sanskrit from Delhi Sanksrit Academy, Delhi for scoring 99% marks in the subject.

Computer Skills

✓ Six month diploma in **Computer Hardware** with first division in 2021.
✓ Being a computer savvy person I have working knowledge of many software, and am passionate about using and exploring new softwares.
✓ Operating Systems worked on: Windows (from Win-95 up to Vista), Linux.
✓ Computer Languages: C, C++, Java, Visual Basic, VB.Net 2005, Matlab, Assembly, Verilog

Personal Details

✓ FATHER'S NAME	Mr. N.C. Jain
✓ DATE of BIRTH	15 December 1998
✓ MARITAL STATUS	Single
✓ LANGUAGE	Hindi, English
✓ NATIONALITY	Indian
✓ HOBBIES	Playing football, computer games, listening to music, surfing and chatting
✓ PERSONALITY TRAITS	Analytical, hardworking with good learning power

(Aakash Jain)

SAMPLE II

Resumé

Ujjwal Kejriwal
Room No. 269, Ram Bhawan,
BITS Pilani, Rajasthan
Contact: Phone No. 09828622399
E-mail: ujjuforu@gmail.com

Academic Profile

➢ Completed B.E. (Hons.) Electronics and Instrumentation from BITS, Pilani, 2022.
➢ Senior secondary examination (CBSE) in 2017 with an aggregate marks of 85.6%
➢ Higher secondary examination (CBSE) in 2015 with an aggregate marks of 84.6%

Achievements

1) Presented paper on the topic 'To Increase the Revenue of Electricity Board' at IIT Delhi, got first prize in paper presentation.
2) Submitted a project 'electro vault' in Apogee, 2019 (technical festival of BITS Pilani) and presented a paper on the same. Got second prize in paper presentation.
3) Conducted a workshop on 'Hawk Eye' in Apogee 2018 (technical festival of BITS Pilani).
4) Secured 21st rank in level 1 of national talent search examination (NTSE).
5) Secured 10th rank in Rajasthan on state talent search examination (STSE).
6) Awarded merit certificate in social science in 10th standard from CBSE board.

Extra-curricular activities:

1) Event coordinator of instrumentation forum for the academic year 2019–20.
2) Coordinator of BOSM Hindi Press during BOSM 2019.
3) Core member of Hindi Press Club.

Personal Details

➢ Father's name	Mr. U.S. Kejriwal
➢ Date of birth	26 February 1987
➢ Marital status	Single
➢ Language	Hindi, English
➢ Nationality	Indian
➢ Hobbies	Playing basketball and guitar.

(Ujjwal Kejriwal)

SAMPLE III

Mr. Ankit Agarwal

Father: Sh. B.S. Agarwal
DoB: 29 January 2000
Category: General
Height: 5 ft 7 inches
Weight: 68 kg

Permanent Address
House No: 152
Chukhu Wala, Dehradun

Uttarakhand 248001
ankitbitspilani@gmail.com
Home Ph: (0135) 2650630
Mob: 09829776660

Education **BIRLA INSTITUTE OF TECHNOLOGY & SCIENCE, Pilani**
2015–2019 *Bachelor of Electronics and Instrumentation Engineering,*
Graduating: *June 2019*

- CGPA: **8.53/10.0** at the end of 6th Semester; Core Courses GPA: **8.25/10.0**
- Elective: Analog and Digital VLSI Design, Security Analysis and Portfolio Management, Image Processing, Fiber Optics and Optoelectronics, Financial Engineering and Management.
- Credited with transfer from Chemical Engineering to Electronics and Instrumentation Engineering for excellence in first year courses.

Projects completed:

- Implemented Blind and Non-Blind Image Watermarking Algorithm using MATLAB.
- Designed the Schematic and Layout of a 4-bit Flash ADC using CADENCE.
- Conceptualized Automated Tracing Device during APOGEE 2018, Technical Festival, BITS-PILANI.

Leadership, Sports and Extracurricular activities:

- 2017–2018 Student Coordinator (2nd National Convention on 'Energising Entrepreneurship through Innovation') EDIPR Unit, BITS, Pilani
- Project Leader (Stimulus—The Business Game) Center for Entrepreneurial Leadership
- Nucleus Member (Conquest 2017—The International B-Plan Competition) CEL
- Nucleus Member Center for Entrepreneurial Leadership

2012–2013 **ST. JOSEPH'S ACADEMY, Dehradun**
Indian School Certificate Examination, March 2013

- Marks Obtained: 90.8%
- Adjudged the best football player during Intra-School Football Championship.
- Won consolation prize in National Science Quiz organized by IRDE, Dehradun.
- Was the Treasurer of SJA Social Welfare Club.

2011–2012 **ST. JOSEPH'S ACADEMY, Dehradun**
Indian Certificate of Secondary Education Examination, March 2011

- Marks Obtained: 91.4%
- Scored twice 100% marks in NAM Test, District level Exam, organized by TSEVM.
- Directed an English Play which was declared first during the Annual Cultural Week, SJA Dehradun.

Experience
Summer 2018 **CBRI ROORKEE and IIP DEHRADUN, Dehradun**

Student Co-Instructor (PS I)

- Guided 21 students in their projects and monitored their progress reports.
- Was actively involved in the project allotment and development of evaluation components for students.
- Won appreciation from Dr. M.O. Garg, Director, IIP and CBRI as well as PSD BITS, Pilani for successful completion of PS I Program.

Summer 2017 **INDIAN INSTITUTE OF REMOTE SENSING, Dehradun**

Summer Trainee (PS I)

- Project: Developed LU/LC Class Extraction and Change Detection Tool using MATLAB.
- Won appreciation from Dean Dr. V.K. Dadhwal of IIRS for successful completion of project.
- Professional Assistant in Computer Programming I (2016–2017).
- Was actively involved in conducting Tutorials and Lab sessions for students registered in the course.

Additional Information

- C, C++
- Excellent in giving and preparing presentations.
- Software: Matlab, Labview, Spectre, Eldo, Xelga, PSPICE, Leonardo Spectrum, ModelSim
- Fluent in English and Hindi
- Play football and sudoku, read and track stocks and have passion for driving.

The Interview Process

Various types of organizations approach recruiting processes in different ways, so adjust your job search accordingly. Most employers conduct several interviews before deciding whom to offer a job. The first type, generally held on campus, is preliminary screening interview, which helps employers eliminate unqualified applicants from the recruitment process. This screening interview is structured, so applicants are often asked roughly the same questions. Many companies use standardized evaluation sheets to grade the applicant so that each candidate is measured against the same criteria. The best approach to a screening interview is to follow the interviewer's lead. Keep your responses short and pointed. There are some candidates who are glib talkers. They don't stop and, therefore, are able to answer only one question in the stipulated time. Given an opportunity, emphasize the theme used in developing the resumé and give the interviewer a way to distinguish you from the other candidates. At the same time, this will demonstrate your forte and qualification.

Interviews usually take various forms, depending on what aspect the recruiter is attempting to discover about the applicant. You might face a panel interview, i.e. meeting with several interviewers who ask you questions during a single session. They will determine from your answers, actions and attitudes whether you are a right candidate for the job. Your best approach during this round is to show zeal by relating your skills and experiences to the organization's needs.

In contrast to structured interview mentioned previously, unstructured interview is more relaxed in the format and constitutes of open-ended questions. To determine managerial skills, the recruiter might ask what motivators and disciplinary actions would you use to improve employees performance? To test your ability to get along with the colleagues, the questions might be on how to handle a particular argument or disagreement that came up amongst the people you worked with in your last job!

Another approach to evaluate interpersonal skills is to interview several candidates simultaneously to see how they interact. Do they smile? Are they supportive of one another's comments? Do they try to score at each other's expense? The candidates also face series of simulated exercises either individually or in group, which determine how they face challenges in an organization.

Perhaps the most unnerving type of interview is the stress interview, an interview designed to see how well a candidate handles a stressful situation. In this type of interview, the candidate might be asked pointed questions designed to irk or unsettle him or her. The candidate might be subjected to long periods of silence, criticisms on appearance, deliberate interceptions and abrupt or even hostile reactions by the interviewer.

Traits Employers Look For

In general, employers are looking for two things: proof that a candidate can handle a specific job and evidence that the person will fit in the organization.

Following are the attributes an employer looks for in his employees:

1. Integrity: Your answers must reflect the total character.
2. Intelligence: It includes basic common sense as well as presence of mind.
3. Endurance: Reflect endurance through your statements. Even the slightest sign of laziness will lay you out of the queue.
4. Team players: Project the ability to work in team. Top executives are team builders.
5. Self-confidence: Answers like 'maybe' etc. depict lack of commitments and self-confidence. At the same time, over-confidence and over-smartness should be avoided.
6. Sense of humour: Project grace even under difficult conditions. Occasionally, laugh at yourself and cultivate a readiness to accept the mistakes.
7. A 'can-do' attitude: This can be done by showing enthusiasm to take responsibilities.
8. Accomplishments: It is important to show what you have achieved. This contributes to meet the targets.
9. An ability to think quickly: Your answers should be spontaneous.
10. Logical professions: If there is a gap in the progression, then there is always a chance that one will be asked. Be honest about your failures.
11. Performance: Ensure to reflect that your performance is either industry specific or function specific.
12. Relevant experience: Talk of experience which will make value addition to the current jobs.
13. Motivation: What has led you to this 'position'

Employers are usually concerned with the candidate's experience, intelligence, communication skills, enthusiasm, creativity and motivation.

Qualifications for the Job

Each job requires specific qualification. When you are invited to an interview for a position, the interviewer may already have some idea whether you have apposite qualification based on the review of your resumé. In many cases, the interviewer will be seeking someone with the flexibility to apply diverse skills in several areas. Another consideration is whether a candidate has the right personality traits for the job.

A Good Fit for the Organization

What the interviewers try to determine most is whether the applicant has the right professional qualifications and personality for a particular job. They also gauge whether the candidate will be compatible with other people in the organization. Appearance creates the first impression. If you are smartly dressed and perfectly groomed, it will reveal a positive quality of your personality and you can nurture an aura of professionalism around you.

Apart from noticing your clothes, interviewers also consider other physical features, such as posture, eye contact, facial expressions and voice. Interviewers believe that personal background can also indicate how the candidate will fit in the organization. Hence, you might be asked about your interests, hobbies, etc. Expand your potential along these lines by avidly reading, mixing with people, participating in discussions and seminars. An employer may also consider a candidate's attitude and personal style. Frankness, enthusiasm and interest are likely to impress an interviewer. So are courtesy, sincerity, willingness to learn and a positive self-confident style—all of which help a new employee adapt to a new workplace and new responsibilities.

What Applicants Need to Find Out

You should be inquisitive to know about the prospective job and employer. This can be done by some ground work and advance research. Introspect on the following questions:

- Are these my kind of people?
- Can I do this work?
- Will I enjoy the work?
- Is this the job I want?
- Does the job pay what I am worth?
- What kind of a person would I be working for?
- What kind of future can I expect in the organization?

Keep track of your minimum requirements and don't apply for all and sundry jobs. You must know whether you are looking for the 'organization' or 'job', i.e. be a nobody in somebody's organization or be a somebody in a nobody's organization!

How to Prepare for a Job Interview

It is perfectly normal to feel apprehensive before an interview. You will be anxious as your future depends on it and you are not sure what to expect. But don't worry too much, preparation will help you perform well.

- **Do some basic research:** By learning about the organization and the job applied for, will enable you to review your resumé from the employer's point of view.
- **Think ahead about questions:** Most job interviews are essentially question-answer sessions. You answer the interviewer's questions about your background, and you ask questions to determine whether the job and the organization are right for you. By planning for the interview, you can handle these exchanges intelligently. The questions you ask in an interview are just as important as the answers you provide. Before the interview, prepare a list of questions, eliciting various types of information. Having a list of questions should impress the interviewer with your organization and thoroughness.
- **Bolster your confidence:** By overcoming your tendencies to feel self-conscious or jittery during an interview, you can build your confidence and create a better impression. Bear in mind, however, that you are more conscious of your limitations than other people are. Instead of dwelling on your weaknesses, focus on your strengths so that you can emphasize on them before the interviewer. The weaknesses should also be projected as positive points. But while doing so, you have to be tactful.
- **Polish your interview style:** Confidence and élan help you to walk in an interview but you will walk out without a job if you don't also give the interviewer an impression of poise, good manners and good judgement. If you maintain eye contact, smile, sit in an attentive position and use hand gestures adroitly, it will certainly create a favourable impression. The non-verbal signals convince the interviewer that you are alert, assertive, dependable, confident, responsible and energetic.

  The sound of your voice can also have a major impact on the success of the interview. Speak in your natural tone; try to vary the pitch, rate, volume of your voice to express enthusiasm and eagerness.
- **Dress to look good:** You can impress the interviewer just by the way you look. The best policy is to dress conservatively. Wear the best quality formal clothing, in solid colours. Avoid flamboyant styles, colours and prints.

Good grooming makes any style of clothing look better. Make sure your clothes are clean and well ironed. Your shoes are cleaned and well polished. Your hair neatly combed. Fingernails clean and the breath fresh. Remember that one of the best ways to look good is to smile at appropriate moments.

- **Be ready when you arrive:** Things that should be carried for an interview are a small notebook, a pen, a list of questions you want to ask, two copies of your resumé kept in a folder, an outline of what you have learned about the organization, and any past correspondence about the position. Tangible evidence of your job-related accomplishments, such as reports, performance, reviews, and certificates of achievement impresses the recruiter. Be sure you know when and where the interview will be held. Plan to arrive early, allow a little extra time just in case you run into a problem on the way. Anything you do or say while you wait may well get back to the interviewer. So make sure your best qualities become visible from the moment you enter the premises.

Success in Interviews

Presenting a bright and enthusiastic image, knowing the personal and professional qualification are vital for an ideal candidate. Some of the attributes sought by interviewers are integrity, intelligence, endurance, self-confidence, sense of humour, a 'can-do' attitude, motivation, logical progressions, performance, accomplishments and relevant experience. The qualities that should be reflected in your responses are clarity of thought and purpose, a structured way of thinking, a balanced point of view, sincerity, presence of mind, maturity, open-mindedness, a good understanding of fundamentals, capacity to conceptualize a given problem.

Interview–before, during and after

- Make a natural entry—enter as if you are part of the company.
- Don't forget the dress code.
- The voice should be clear, steady and animated. Don't grunt or groan.
- Carry your folder—it should contain certificates, testimonials, project papers.
- Arrive on time.
- Don't experiment on the mode of transport.
- Eat sensibly.
- Scan the newspapers' headlines of the day.
- Read the earlier two issues of the paper.
- Sit alert slightly leaning forward.
- Maintain eye contact—be honest and straightforward.
- Make eye contact with the interviewer while answering questions.
- Take time to think.

- Don't express emotions—never look at the watch.
- Say 'I don't know' when unable to answer any question—a frank admission will not go against you.
- Smile at times.
- Be confident.
- Accept cup of coffee or tea, if offered.
- Send a thank you note.
- Send maximum of two follow-ups.

Sharpening your skills

Questions on the following areas can be asked:

1. Academic knowledge
2. Hobbies and interests
3. Achievements—academic/extra-curricular
4. Strengths and weaknesses
5. Career plans and alternatives
6. Environmental sensitivity (geography, history, policies, economy, etc.)
7. Your current organization and your role if you have work experience.

Some typical questions are listed as follows:

- Tell me a joke.
- Do you have siblings? What are they into?
- If given a choice, which place in India would you prefer to live in?
- What are your views about marriage?
- What are your hobbies?
- Why this company?
- Why software when you are an electronics engineer?
- How do you see yourself—five years from now?
- What are your short-term and long-term career goals?
- Narrate an experience when you as a leader successfully accomplished an arduous task.
- What leadership qualities do you possess?
- Briefly summarize your strengths and weaknesses.
- What is the population of your town?
- Do you prefer to lead or to follow?
- What is the major international event taking place at present?
- How often do you lie?
- What makes you different from others who have applied?
- Convince me that you are suitable for the job.
- Narrate an incident, when you as a leader, or otherwise, used an innovative method for solving a problem.
- What if you are not selected?

Sample interview

Given below is the interview for the trainee position of Infosys on HR. The expected answers from the interviewee are also written to give you the idea to handle these kinds of questions.

1. Why should we hire you?

   I am definite that I am one of the best candidates for the job. Even when there are other students who might have the potentials, I am no less. My attitude for excellence lets me have the edge over others. I have perseverance that makes me go on and I strive for the best….

2. What do you want to be 10 or 15 years from now?

   It is not easy to say about future but I am very clear about my path of progress. In the next five years I will surely prove my mettle and be the best in your organization. In fact, the mission of the organization will be my mission, and I will work arduously to achieve the goals. I am mentally prepared for the additional responsibilities that might be given to me in times to come.

3. What qualities do you feel a successful manager should have?

   To work as a team is the key quality of the manager. He should be a visionary and people should enjoy working in his aegis. He should give the suggestions to put others on right path. His positive approach, dedication and honesty can make him the role model for others.

4. If you had to live your life again, what would you change?

   When I analyse the past, I realize that many moves could have been avoided and other steps could have been taken for better results. One has no control over the past but I have learned a lot from the past to take pre-emptive measures to avoid the pitfalls. That is why I strive to become a better individual every day. I always aspire to be the best in the organization I work. I learn from the past and look ahead to the future.

5. How much salary do you want?

   Salary is not a constraint for a prestigious institution like yours. For me, getting placed in your concern is an important thing.

6. Do you prefer to work in a group?

   Yes definitely, Sir. Basically I am a good team player so I am able to tackle people in groups easily.

7. What do you think of your boss?

   We must feel very comfortable in his presence. He should lead us amicably and support for the growth of the company and myself.

8. Who has inspired you in your life and why?

   My source of inspiration is our former president Dr. APJ Abdul Kalam. His words, “DREAM, DREAM, DREAM!” inspire me a lot. If we dream about our goal, then it will remain in our entire thoughts.

9. Can you work under pressure?

   I think working under pressure is an art. Every person can’t work under pressure. I can work under tremendous pressure...my past experience has given me a lot of courage and experience to work under pressure.

10. How do you feel about working nights and weekends?

    I always want to finish off everything within the stipulated time. Hence, if situation demands me to work at nights and weekends I will never mind and I will work.

11. How do you define success and how do you measure up to your own definition?

    In my opinion I feel that success is not something that can be achieved by putting few efforts.

The Close

Like the opening, the end of the interview is equally important than its duration would indicate. In the last few minutes, you need to evaluate how well you have done and rectify any misconception the interviewer might have held. Thus, to develop the right attitude, is of utmost importance than to be just an intelligent candidate. Remember every man can’t be a tree. Be a bush and be the best of it. Therefore, do the best during the interview.

Sample technical interview questions for HCL

1. What is the difference between a primary key and a unique key?

   Both primary key and unique key enforce uniqueness of the column on which they are defined. But by default primary key creates a clustered index on the column whereas unique key creates a non-clustered index by default. Another major difference is that primary key doesn’t allow NULLs’ but unique key allows one NULL only.

2. What is the output of SIGN function?

   1 for positive value
   0 for Zero
   –1 for Negative value.

3. How do you retrieve the first 5 characters of FIRSTNAME column of table EMP?

   SELECT SUBSTR(FIRSTNAME‘1’5) FROM EMP.

4. How do you concatenate the FIRSTNAME and LASTNAME from EMP table to give a complete name?
   SELECT FIRSTNAME || ' ' || LASTNAME FROM EMP.
5. How is memory management done in Win95?
   Through paging and segmentation.
6. In the transport layer, TCP is what type of protocol?
   Connection oriented.
7. What does the protocol FTP do?
   Transfer a file between stations with user authentication.
8. What are user defined datatypes and when you should go for them?
   User defined datatypes let you extend the base SQL Server datatypes by providing a descriptive name and format to the database. Take, for example, in your database there is a column called Flight_Num which appears in many tables. In all these tables, it should be varchar(8). In this case you could create a user defined datatype called Flight_num_type of varchar(8) and use it across all your tables.
9. How do you implement one-to-one, one-to-many and many-to-many relationships while designing tables?
   One-to-one relationship can be implemented as a single table and rarely as two tables with primary and foreign key relationships.
   One-to-many relationships are implemented by splitting the data into two tables with primary key and foreign key relationships.
   Many-to-many relationships are implemented using a junction table with the keys from both the tables forming the composite primary key of the junction table.

Another example of an interview with three members.

Interviewer 1: You have written about your involvement in organizing national level events, what were those?

Candidate: I was Organizing Secretary for Cognizance 2020, Annual National level Techfest of IIT Roorkee, before that in various positions in Cognizance 2019, 2018.

Interviewer 1: Which were the participating institutes?

Candidate: Mostly institutes from north and most of the IITs.

Interviewer 1: I specifically asked which institutes?

Candidate: IIT, MNIT, SRCC; DCE, NSIT, Colleges from Haryana, Uttrakhand and UP.

Interviewer 1: Your hobby is star gazing, what is that?

Candidate: It is a hobbies club section at IIT Roorkee besides I have been involved in such activities since my school days.

Interviewer 1: You also have written you like reading good literature. What have you read?

Candidate: I have read *War and Peace, The Great Expectations, The Fountainhead, The Alchemist, The Monk who sold his Ferrari, The Selfish Gene,* so on.

Interviewer 1: How do you define good literature?

Candidate: Literature which carries good reviews and recommendations.

Interviewer 1: Many people say *Playboy* is a good literature …

Candidate: Well that is true but for me reviews of trustworthy sources such as my relatives, teachers and friends matter most.

Interviewer 1: You have written you have learned some new languages?

Candidate: I have learned French, Punjabi besides Hindi and English.

Interviewer 1: People sitting over here know more languages than you.

Candidate: Sure, Sir.

Interviewer 1: How could you say it as a part of hobby or extra curricular activity?

Candidate: I took initiative on my own. It was not part of my regular studies in college.

Interviewer 1: Do you know the script of Punjabi?

Candidate: Gurumukhi.

Interviewer 1: Which script is it closest to?

Candidate: *Devanagari.*

Interviewer 1: Which is the oldest script?

Candidate: Devanagari, I think.

Interviewer 3: Then what is Sanskrit?

Candidate: Sanskrit is the mother language.

Interviewer 2: You are mistaken. Why are you trying to win over us?

Candidate: I am saying what I can recall from my high school, I am not trying to win over.

Interviewer 1: Why you want to do MBA?

Candidate: MBA is a stepping stone towards development of individual for versatile applicability in the industry.

Interviewer 3: Don't go round about, tell him clearly. You want money or position?

Candidate: Well that are the perks of the things but more importantly MBA creates avenues to higher responsibility positions in the hierarchy.

Interviewer 1: Why do you want to shoulder responsibility. Why can't you stay at one level?

Candidate: I have been inspired since my childhood and had been motivated to have a progressive outlook and be the one to effect the change rather than being one implementing it.

Interviewer 1: You are not giving answers. Do you not understand? {*leaves the room*}.

Interviewer 2: OK, a simpler thing. Do you understand difference between CGPA and SGPA, you have mentioned CGPA in year-wise column in this form of yours, why?

Candidate: Sir I have mentioned it to be my CGPA, besides a year-comprises two semesters.

Interviewer 2: Don't try to win over me. You could have calculated using calculator. A good analytical ability student would have done like that or you could have started it from the end.

Interviewer 3: We are here to help you out, give precise answers. Don't try to win arguments. Ok I would ask some simpler questions regarding electrical engineering.

(*There were questions pertaining to transmission losses, sources of electrical energy, how to minimize, losses etc. and a small case on how to reduce electrical bills in a normal mechanical shop employing 20–30 machines. Whole interview process took about 40 minutes.*)

• EXERCISES •

1. What is an interview? State all the different types of interviews.
2. What all qualities of an individual are evaluated during an interview?
3. What preparation do you need to face the interview? Is it necessary to read the newspaper before facing the interview?
4. What dress will you select for the interview? Why?
5. What do you understand by stress interview? How do you remain composed when the interviewer tries to unnerve you?
6. What all documents will you keep in file which you may carry in the interview? Does the organization of the documents also reflect something about you?
7. If the interviewer offers you tea during the interview, will you accept it? Why or why not?
8. How will you conduct yourself before and during the interview? Give four tips to create good impression on the interviewer.
9. Do you ask the interviewer about the salary he would offer? Support your answer.
10. Give some examples of how you will present your weakness as merit.

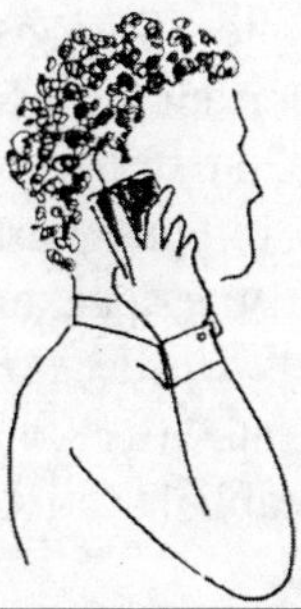

13

Speeches

All the great speakers were bad speakers at first.

—RALPH WALDO EMERSON

There is a famous saying, "speech is silver but silence is golden". But in the present-day world and in professional settings, the opposite of this saying is true. This may surprise you since you might not have ever thought that you would have to deliver speeches. You would have preferred to observe silence than to speak. Many people like you are under the impression that your professional requirements don't expect you to speak in a hall filled with people. But in today's scenario, as you have studied in Chapters 1–12, that apart from technical skills, our communicative skills also carry equal importance. A majority of people often confuse speech with presentation skills and give less importance to the former. But in reality the two are different. This chapter will focus on the differences between speech and presentation, and also elaborate on how to deliver speeches without hesitation.

HOW ARE SPEECHES DIFFERENT FROM PRESENTATIONS?

You have read in Chapter 10 that most presentations are technical in nature. Hence, the tone and tenor of presentations are very much objective. Moreover, they are made for specific audience and at times the choice of words too is technical. Formality is the hallmark of presentation, and time factor a compulsion. Speeches, on the other hand, are informal, subjective and personal. Since the audience for whom the speech is being delivered is varied, the words used are often familiar. In speeches the language is often figurative and various literary devices are strewn in and between the lines. At times, the speaker appeals to the emotions of the audience. Seldom is the length and span of a speech within the time limit. The speakers cite references and allusions in order to make their speeches more effective. The most important aspect that differentiates speeches from presentations is the speaker's recourse to his voice and experience. The use of audio-visual aids, which is an integral part of presentations, has very little role to play in speeches. Moreover, the speaker resorts to creation of visuals by words. Listening to the speaker's words, the audience frames an image in their mind. They seem to concentrate more on the words of the speaker and, hence, both the parties strive to establish active listening. See Figure 13.1.

Figure 13.1 An individual giving a speech.

SELECTION OF TOPIC

It is a fact that though you keep chatting with your friends and kinsmen, face-to-face or over the phone on innumerable topics of the world, you often find your foot in your mouth once you are called to speak in front of a crowd. This is not because you lack in confidence or don't know the content. This is the result of being unsure about the topic. Once you decide the topic on which you will be speaking, you will be able to organize your ideas and weave them into a speech. If given a choice to select a topic, most of you will decide the topic that not only interests you, but also the one you are well-acquainted with. Most of the times you will realize that the reasons for your worry are rooted in your lack of experience. If a certain topic is of your interest, you will find many points on it. For example, for students sports or movies are favourite topics to speak if given a chance. Similarly, topics that are either uninteresting or beyond you, will not give you sufficient points to write a good speech.

Every individual has some expertise in his or her related fields. This is the reason you find experienced cricketers becoming commentators, umpires and match referees. Likewise, most of the eloquent speakers also become speech trainers and analysts. However, there are exceptions when people without any experience of a field also emerge as excellent speakers. But they are exceptions and can't become rules.

A field in which you are experienced helps you to generate ideas. But that doesn't mean that you can't speak on an unfamiliar topic. In fact, an unfamiliar topic gives you more scope of research and provides you with understanding in that area. Think of some unfamiliar topics and ruminate the points that could be a part of the topic. Explore all aspects of the topic and this will provide you with an outline for your speech. Repeated efforts will arouse your thinking process and make you logical and analytical in the course of time. You can use certain methods such as recollecting, brainstorming and imagination to select a topic for your speech. While recollecting helps you choose topics from your experience, brainstorming provides you with a wide variety of subjects. Moreover, in an age of computers and Internet you can make an online search to find not only the topic, but also related information. Once the difficulty of selecting your topic is overcome, you have another task waiting. Mere selection of the topic is not enough. The topic requires to be explored, explained, elaborated and exemplified. Since speech-making is an art, you need to understand the various ways to make it artistic.

DETERMINING THE PURPOSE

After you have selected a topic, ask yourself about its purpose. Speeches are occasioned by time and, hence, purposes vary. Most of the speeches are either informative or persuasive. The speaker needs to know how he can best meet both the purposes. The various factors that help a speaker fulfil his purpose are time, language, style, and pattern.

Time

Time plays a crucial role in a speech. It helps a speaker lengthen and shorten the content of a speech. Moreover, time helps the speaker understand the occasion and, thus, in selecting the words and the tempo. Time also enables the speaker to regulate his voice. Careful speakers utilize time to enhance the efficacy of their speech. The time gaps while giving pause or inviting silence between the words, phrases and units of thoughts exhibit speaker's confidence. This is the reason many speakers often ask the time allotted for their speech in order to divide and accommodate their ideas dexterously and to drive home their points of view without browbeating their audience. Edward T. Hall in his book *The Silent Language* rightly says, "Time talks and space speaks".

Language

Speech is heard, thus it requires a language that is easy to comprehend and pleasing to ears. For different occasions and audience, the language may vary at times. Language in a speech refers to the words, phrases and sentences, and, as such, enough care is required to enhance the effect. In speech, the language may be ornate at times but the words used for this purpose ought to be simple and familiar. Audience neither expects the speaker to use difficult words nor lengthy sentences.

Style

A speech becomes effective not merely on how beautifully the words have been woven or the type of sentences preferred, but also by the style of the speaker. The style includes the speaker's bearing and behaviour, his vocal characteristics and also his rapport with the audience. A trained speaker dresses according to the occasion and at times uses his body to convey the desired message. He not only breaks the monotony or ennui by dividing his units of thoughts, but also plays upon words to bring efficacy. All this may not be planned but intelligence and wit, which is a part of style, helps him do so. The references to instances of our everyday life are very much a part of speaker's style. A beginner may have problems to bring such animations, but with time and experience it becomes an integral part of the speech. Excellent speakers tend to make various linguistic devices to ensure an effective style whereas there are others who feel comfortable in using slangs and jargons when delivering a speech.

Pattern

It is the way a speaker organizes his ideas. A speech is an abundance of points and sub-points. Providing a pattern to these points helps the speaker to ensure relationship of one point with another. In addition, the pattern helps the listeners to connect with the ideas. Since listeners consider the speaker to be a well-informed and enriched entity, their expectation of coherence is justified. Random scrambling of ideas distracts the audience and makes them impatient. You will read about various patterns while discussing the organization of speech.

PREPARING SPEECHES

The lexical meaning of speech is the "manner a person adopts to communicate his ideas or thoughts to a group of audience". The focus is more on spoken words. But in reality a speech becomes impressive depending on the way it is prepared. Here preparation stands for writing of speeches. As you have read previously that the first step in speech writing is the selection of the topic, the second and, of course, more important is gathering of materials. You might have often heard that most of the influential personalities and celebrities have speech writers. Much goes into the writing of a speech. Even before a speech is written, one has to be familiar with the topic. Since our interests are varied and tastes different, we don't be a know-it-all. At the same time, we do not have professional speech writers at our disposal. Hence, there are certain initiatives that can keep us abreast of the developments that are taking place around us.

Audience

As in presentation, so in speech too we ought to be aware of the audience that we are to face. Once we know the age, sex, background, tastes, facets of the audience, the task becomes easier. A little amount of imagination may also help us predict about the interest of our crowd. The background of the audience allows and restricts us to use words, quotations, experiences and references that may suit them. Reference to Harry Potter may be as tiring to adults as Buddha's renunciation of the world to children. Effective speakers are mostly audience centred.

Source

Once you know your audience and their preference, you can find yourself in a better position to gather materials for your speech. In case you have to address children, you should search for books/materials that are of their interest. Since the audience rely more on your credibility, you need to make your material authentic. When targeting young people, many newspapers often have supplements of their interest and this makes your task easier and saves you from the harrowing experience of making exhaustive search from the sea of information. Newspapers and journals are the most reliable source of information. They often provide you with updated information and, hence, you can rely on them for authenticity. Moreover, nowadays you have Internet too, which can be utilized for all practical purposes.

Quotes and Humour

Audience can often get bored with facts and figures. It may also lead to restlessness. Hence, at times some relaxation from the speaker is expected. You can introduce some funny stories in your speeches. But while doing so, the relevance of the stories should also be taken into consideration. Moreover, you should also know when to introduce the joke. A wrongly timed joke will become worthless and ineffective. One can't have ready-made jokes all the time. So is the case with quotes. It is, therefore, advisable to have a separate note book with proper categories of jokes and quotes ready for all occasions. One should update the note book at regular intervals. This will not only boost your confidence, but also broaden your knowledge.

Once you have gathered information, make a brief outline of the speech. Write the first draft of your speech keeping into consideration the fact and fiction, data and diction, shift and curve in addition to the use of signposts and subtle suggestions of how and in which aspect of the speech you are in.

DYNAMICS OF SPEECH

Most of the speeches can be structurally divided into three parts—the beginning, the middle and the end. All these three have their due significance in a speech. Despite the care you take in selecting the topic and then gathering materials and supporting materials, the speech loses its efficacy without a proper beginning. We are all aware of the proverb' "Well begun is half done". Hence, extreme care should be taken to give your speech a captivating beginning.

How to Begin?

Most of us remember Antony's speech in William Shakespeare's famous drama *Julius Caesar.* Remember Brutus the closest friend of Caesar had turned against him and had stabbed him. The mob was not only against Caesar, but also had validated his killing. But it was Antony's gift of the gab that had turned the tide and the mob's opinion. And do you know what was so wonderful about Antony's speech? It was a beautiful blend of fact and fiction.

> Friends, Romans, countrymen, lend me your ears; I come to bury Caesar, not to praise him. The evil that men do lives after them; The good is oft interred with their bones; So let it be with Caesar. The noble Brutus hath told you Caesar was ambitious: If it were so, it was a grievous fault, And grievously hath Caesar answer'd it. Here, under leave of Brutus and the rest—For Brutus is an honourable man; So are they all, all honourable men—Come I to speak in Caesar's funeral. He was my friend, faithful and just to me: But Brutus says he was ambitious; And Brutus is an honourable man.

In the above lines, you can find how impressive was the first line. Likewise, Swami Vivekananda too had captivated the attention of the audience in Chicago, and won the hearts of Americans in the following way:

> Sisters and Brothers of America,
> It fills my heart with joy unspeakable to rise in response to the warm and cordial welcome which you have given us. I thank you in the name of the most ancient order of monks in the world; I thank you in the name of the mother of religions; and I thank you in the name of the millions and millions of Hindu people of all classes and sects.

The first thing then that we should keep in our mind is how to address the crowd. The audience seems to generate a sort of intimacy in the way they are addressed. The speaker by addressing the listeners may also get to familiarize himself with them and make his task easy. It also gives him the initial confidence then to reveal his topic and expand it further. The forms of address also vary according to the occasion. The speaker is the best person to understand how he should address the audience. But in most of the cases the audience should be denominated in short, simple and specific manner. The following denominations will help you decide:

(a) Sisters and Brothers
(b) Respected Chairperson, dear colleagues and my dear students
(c) Honourable Vice Chancellor, Respected Director, Deputy Directors, Venerated Deans, and fellow friends
(d) Esteemed Chancellor Sir, Respected Vice Chancellor, Venerated Director, Deans and Participants from India and abroad
(e) Respected Principal, distinguished guests, faculty friends and dear students
(f) Ladies and Gentlemen
(g) Your Highness
(h) Mr. Chairman, Ladies and Gentlemen

The beginning of a speech undeniably plays a vital role in mesmerizing the minds of the audience. For the first timers, it is the lack of a suitable beginning that chokes their voice. An impressive beginning generates self-confidence and also helps in establishing credibility with the crowd. Moreover, there is no denying the fact that a proper posture and perceptive eye contact also add to secure confidence. Thus, the first step in speech-making is to attract your audience and this can be done in the beginning of the speech only. It is just at the start that the audience can be startled. The manner in which the speaker stands, looks at and addresses the audience helps him grab their attention. You can choose any of the devices given here according to the exigencies of the situation to begin your speech.

Introduce/relate the topic to your audience

It is human nature to listen to something that interests one. Likewise audiences don't pay any attention to a topic if they are unacquainted with it. Hence, it becomes essential to relate the topic to your audience. You can do so either by giving a personal touch or creating the impression that you are taking interest in the audience. Remember that if you reveal your topic in the first sentence, the audience will lose interest. A little amount of suspense can work wonders. If you adopt a 'you' approach it pays provided the sentences should be woven in such a manner that the audience is bound to enjoy the revelation a little later. Look at the following:

> It's Saturday morning and you are helping clean out your grandmother's attic. After working or while you stumble upon a trunk, open it and discover inside hundreds of old postcards. Thinking about getting to the football game on time, you start tossing the cards into the trash can. Congrats! You have just thrown away a year's tuition.

(Cited in Stephen E Lucas, *The Art of Public Speaking*, Singapore: McGraw Hill Book Company, 1989, p. 169)

State the importance of your topic

One way to attract the audience is to state the importance of your topic to them. While discussing a topic whose importance may not be clear to the audience, you should think about ways to demonstrate its significance in the introduction. Since the idea is to grab the audience's attention in the beginning, you have to do it cleverly as in the following:

> It is difficult to train the trainers. Trainers, a category who preach everyday things they rarely practice. A set of instruction, bookish most often, being loaded on immature minds reluctantly sitting to grasp the mantras. But then it's all embedded in a ten-lettered word. Today I am going to talk about how motivation can work wonders in effective teaching.

Startle the audience

You can also begin your speech with some startling or intriguing statement. It often excites the audience to listen further.

> Last week a man whom you all have heard of beat an innocent human being senseless. Hundreds of people watched him do it, but no one tried to stop him. He didn't do it in self-defence, or out of hate or revenge. He did it for money. The man is a professional boxer.

(Cited in Stephen E Lucas, *The Art of Public Speaking*, Singapore: McGraw Hill Book Company, 1989, p. 171)

Suppose you are to speak on the importance of ATM card, you also startle your audience with such a beginning:

> All of a sudden you get a mail to appear for an interview at Mumbai a day after tomorrow. There is no other way than to go by air. And you run short of money. The banks are on strike and none of your friends are around. You could have braved the crisis just with a small card—the ATM card.

Arouse the curiosity of the audience

One way to draw the audience into your speech is to raise their curiosity with a series of statements, which make them curious. For example, a speaker in his speech on 'The Silent Killer' (Hypertension) started like this.

> It is the most common chronic disease in the United States. Controllable but incurable; It is a symptom less disease; you can have it for years and never know until it kills you. Some 40 million Americans have this disease and 3,00,000 will die from it before the year is out. Odds are that five of us in a group have it. What am I talking about? Not cancer, not AIDS, not heart disease. I am talking about hypertensions or high blood pressure.

(Cited in Stephen E Lucas, *The Art of Public Speaking*, Singapore: McGraw Hill Book Company, 1989, p. 172)

Question the audience

We can also start our speech with a question so as to make the listeners think about the topic. For example:

(a) Have you ever wished you could see into the future?
(b) Have you ever thought what impedes us from speaking in public?
(c) Have you ever thought why you are still waiting for your dream job? Do you think it is because of your low percentile? Or is it because of your unattractive physical features? If so, you are wrong. What you lack in is effective communication skills.

Begin with a quotation

Every individual has an ear for a good sentence or quotation. One way to attract the audience attention is to begin with a quotation of a great poet, scholar or philosopher. For example, while giving a speech on 'Individual Freedom' we can begin as, Rousseau once said "Man is born free but everywhere he is in chains." There are many more quotes which can help you begin your speech. Some of them are as follows:

(a) Some men are born great, some attain greatness and some have greatness thrust upon them. (William Shakespeare)
(b) Eat to please thyself but dress to please others. (Franklin)
(c) Heard melodies are sweet but those unheard are sweeter. (John Keats)
(d) A thing of beauty is a joy forever. (John Keats)
(e) It is possible to fail in many ways...while to succeed is possible only in one way. (Aristotle)
(f) A man is wise with the wisdom of his time only and ignorant with its ignorance. (H.D. Thoreau)

Tell a story

Speeches can also, begin with a story which amuses and provokes the audience. In many situations, when the topic is a bit difficult or technical, the reference of a story will make it easier.

It was another beautiful day with the yellow tint of the sun spreading its warmth on the moist earth. People were readying themselves for their offices, parents to their workplaces and children to their schools. The vehicles on the earth ferrying commuters to their commercial centres and the planes in the sky carrying passengers flying from one country to another, flying from one territory to another. And who knew that all of them would reach their destination? Suddenly the elevator of WTC took an abrupt commotion and everything was brought to pieces. Men, machine and missions all perished under the heavy debris of a great structure. This accident on September 11 in New York was just the fault of a handful of miscreants who brought the life of majority to a halt.

How to Develop the Body of the Speech?

The introductory part of your speech is like the ignition key. Like the key, the introductory part starts the speech. But then you have to drive your audience to their destination. The audience needs to enjoy a safe drive which is possible only when the driver has control over the steering and the brakes. Hence, after beginning your speech with an attractive introduction, you have to develop it. A well-organized speech will enhance your credibility and make it easier for the audience to understand your message.

An organized speech requires coherence. It facilitates the audience to follow the ideas in progression. Your speeches should be organized strategically. The ideas should be ordered logically in order to avoid confusion. To develop the body of the speech, we should determine the main points, choose them carefully, phrase them precisely and organize them strategically. Adequate care should be taken when developing the points. Too many points often tire the listeners. It affects their attempt to connect with the ideas.

Experts refer to five orders for organizing and developing the main points of the speech. The choice of the topic alone will help you decide which order will suit your audience and your purpose the best. You can organize your main points in any of these orders depending on the topic, purpose and audience.

1. **Chronological order:** This order helps in following the time pattern. You can go for this order while speaking on a topic which requires the speaker to talk about time and event sequence. Informative speeches, such as development of human civilization, the success story of mobile phones, radar technology, etc. may follow this order.
2. **Spatial order:** This order follows a directional pattern. Suppose you have to deliver a speech on a topic which requires structural description mainly of space followed by spatial order. The focus of this pattern is on direction. In such a pattern, the main points move from top to bottom, left to right, front to back, inside to outside, East to West or some other direction. Speeches describing the design of some structure, building, organization chain, etc. follow such pattern.
3. **Causal order:** It shows cause-effect relationship. You can follow this order when you are to speak on a subject that requires cause and effect relationship. In such a pattern either you follow the cause-effect or effect-cause movement. Common among speakers, in this pattern there are two main points—one dealing with the cause and the other with the effect. Careful speakers sometimes reverse the order just to create a psychological effect. Speeches on subjects, such as deforestation, global warming, student unrest, pollution, may use this pattern.

4. **Problem-solution order:** This order is very much like causal order. For problem-solution order you break the body of your speech into two main parts—the first showing a problem, the second giving a solution. While causal order shows only the relationship, problem-solution provides remedies. Since this pattern gives solution to a problem, it is most appropriate for persuasive speeches on topics, such as cross border terrorism, infiltration, train accidents etc.
5. **Topical order:** When a speech doesn't follow any of the orders mentioned above, it falls into a topical order. In such a pattern, there is a main point followed by divisions and sub-divisions. One often talks in a topical order since it is easier and the speaker simply informs the listeners in such a pattern. Topical order helps you divide your main topics into sub-topics.

   Once you have organized your main points, you give supporting materials to ensure their relevance to the main points.

How to Connect Your Speech?

After you have gathered and developed materials for your speech, you need to connect them. Most of the time, the major chunk of information in the speech happens to be factual. Sometimes, it is data and on other occasion the description of a problem and its solution. The audience finds it hard to assimilate all facts and figures. Hence, you need to divide and unite them with the help of connectives. They not only show the movement from one unit of thought to another, but also bridge the different threads.

The body of the speech consists of thoughts or messages. While giving speeches, we have the impression that we are telling/narrating our ideas to others. In order to maintain the continuity of our thoughts and relate our messages; we use connectives which tie our speech together. Connectives are words or phrases that join one thought to another, and indicate the relationship between them. The four major types of connectives are transitions, internal previews, internal summaries, and sign points. Labelled under different terms, these connectives can be put together to make your speeches much more unified and coherent. Some common connectives are as follows:

- **Transitions:** End of one thought and indication of the beginning of another, such as; after having said that, it is time now; in addition to, also, again, as well as, besides, coupled with, furthermore, in addition, likewise, moreover, similarly.
- **Internal previews:** Indicating what the speaker takes up next, such as, after, now, yet, still etc.
- **Internal summary:** Recalling what has been said so far, e.g. in short, thus, hence certainly, in brief etc.

- **Signposts:** Indicating where the presenter is in the presentation, e.g. the first feature, the second, furthermore, therefore, similarly, in contrast to, on the other hand, more importantly, above all, etc.

Look at the use of these devices in the following expressions:

(a) Now that we have underlined the advantages of technology, let us turn to its other side that is disadvantageous.
(b) So much for today what about tomorrow?
(c) Remember to concentrate on.
(d) Let me restate what I hinted at in the beginning.

How to Use Language?

Imagine a person with a perfect sound body having beautiful face and deep-set eyes but an ugly voice. The impression created by his outlook vanishes when we hear his voice. And so is the case with speech. A speech with a good introduction and good body often loses charm if the selection of words is not good. The language of a speech is its voice. And an impressive speech requires impressive language. It is through language that we share experiences, formulate values, exchange ideas, transmit knowledge and sustain culture. Good speakers have a respect for language. Hence, while using language, we should be accurate. The selection of words should be intelligible and to the point. It can be made clearer by keeping in mind the average audience. Clarity can also be brought in by the use of imagery; the use of various figures of speech, such as simile and metaphor that beautify our language and add glory to our content. However, we can make preferences of one device or the other according to the occasion, audience and topic. You can learn the use of bringing variety in your speech by studying a few of the popular speeches of some celebrated speakers.

How to Make Use of Your Voice?

Speeches are heard and, hence, the speaker should have a pleasant voice. Despite your endless efforts, a pleasant voice is often out of your reach. Good voice is god-gifted and we can neither buy nor borrow it from anyone. Of course, with certain precautions we can ameliorate the quality of our voices and make ourselves presentable.

A good voice is one which lets you express your ideas with proper pronunciation, required pause at times and a control over the rate of delivery. You need to concentrate that your voice is clear, audible and with a little restraint you can create desired effect with the nuances of articulation. Effective speakers often use of their voice to create the effect of suspense and also of belief.

People nowadays can have adequate training of improving their diction but care should be taken that you don't sacrifice your natural ability for superfluous and artificial aping. Remember that God has provided everyone with a unique voice and one's regional and native influences add beauty to the expressions. Though in course of time your own experiences will tell you how you can ensure acceptable pronunciation with the help of an authentic dictionary.

How to Close Your Speech?

At times you come across such over-enthusiastic speakers who want to convey all that they had prepared. But from the listener's perspective, you will feel the speaker should indicate the end of his speech. No one wants to listen to a harangue though people are considerate enough not to interfere with the speaker when he is delivering the speech. It is, thus, the speaker's responsibility to signal the end of his speech. But have you ever thought how one can do it?

If you have a good beginning, half of your job is done. But we should not end the speech abruptly. Even a good speech loses its charm if it doesn't have a good conclusion. In order to continue the efficacy of a good speech, the conclusion should be cleverly situated. The audience should know that the speaker is going to end his speech. It is their seal of approval that makes the speaker qualify for success of his speech. The great English poet H.W. Longfellow has said: "Great is the art of beginning but greater the art is of ending".

There are certain ways of driving your audience towards the end of your speech. The significant way to indicate the end of your speech is by the use of vocal characteristics, namely the pitch, tone and intonation. Excellent speakers, as you have read earlier, aptly change the tone of their voice while ending the speeches. However, there can be many other words/expressions which can be used to signify the end, such as the following:

(a) In conclusion
(b) One last thought
(c) In closing
(d) Thus we can take the pledge
(e) Let me end by saying
(f) So once again let me assure
(g) And so before I wind up
(h) Last but not the least
(i) Let me remind

Since it is the conclusion of a speech that the audience finally remembers, the conclusion should be packaged in such a manner that the speech is not defeated. This can be done by reiterating the central idea of your speech. There is no harm if certain statements are repeated. However, there are other ways to reinforce the crux of your speech.

Conclude with a quotation

Speeches can also be concluded with quotations. This is the most common and effective way of ending one's speech. But you should ensure that your quotation is appropriate to the occasion. While giving a speech, e.g. to graduating students, one can always end with the following:

> I congratulate you again on becoming a graduate from an esteemed institution. But you should always remember that this is not the end but the beginning of your mission. All of you should make the famous lines of Robert Frost the mantras whenever you feel tired and lost in your life;
>
> The woods are lovely, dark, and deep,
> But I have promises to keep,
> And miles to go before I sleep,
> And miles to go before I sleep.

Summarize your speech

One way of ending the speech is to summarize the main points of the content. This helps the audience understand the key points again and preserve it with them. For example, the speech on terrorism in America can be summarized this way:

> Thus, we cannot sit with our fingers crossed. The accident that shocked America has opened the eyes of the entire world. Terrorism has become a worldwide phenomenon. Miscreants are only a handful; hence we must unanimously declare the end of such forces. Let us hope that we surely will come out of this darkness. The sun of unity will make a breakthrough piercing all the clouds of despair, and soon there will shine forth the rays of faith, fraternity and hence radiate delight.

End with a dramatic statement

Speeches can also be ended with dramatic statements. Some speeches have become memorable because of their closing lines. We can refer to Patrick Henry's speech on "Liberty or Death". Henry ended his speech with the following lines while exhorting his listeners to resist British tyranny:

> Is life so dear, or peace so sweet, as to be purchased at the price of chains and slavery. Forbid it, Almighty God! I know not what course others may take: but as for me give me liberty or give me death.

(Stephen E Lucas, *The Art of Public Speaking*, Singapore: McGraw Hill Book Company, 1989, p. 183)

Refer to the introduction

You can also end your speech on the same point from where you began. It makes a cycle and provides psychological unit. If you state a problem in the introduction, provide solution to the same in your concluding paragraph, e.g. Martin Luther King junior in his speech "I Have a dream" started in the following manner:

> I am happy to join with you today in what will go down in history as the greatest demonstration for freedom in the history of our nation.
>
> *He ended his speech on the following lines:*
> And when this happens, when we allow freedom ring—when we let it ring from every village and every hamlet, from every state and every city, we will be able to speed up that day when all the god's children, black men and white men, Jews and gentiles, Protestants and Catholics will be able to join hands and sing in the old negro spiritual, "Free at last! Free at last! Thank god almighty, we are free at last!"

Such ending not only unifies the entire speech but also reinforces the central idea and ends the speech on a strong note.

SPEECHES FOR SPECIAL OCCASIONS

Though in professional life, you get less time for speech-making, yet that doesn't annihilate the possibility of writing and preparing speeches.

At times you come across situations when you have to satisfy the expectations of your organization. Such a situation may come at very short notices and you don't have adequate time to prepare. Thus, it is always better to arm yourself for such occasions than to wait for them to knock your doors. Such occasions are always special and the speeches different from the informative or persuasive ones. We shall look at some of the situations in which such speeches are made.

Welcome Speeches

At times when a host organization invites some speaker from outside to speak on a particular occasion, it becomes mandatory on the part of the former to welcome the speaker. Such a speech comes under the category of welcome speech. Most often it is made to welcome the chief guest and the members of the audience at a function. A speech of this type is brief and factual. It sets the ball rolling by creating an atmosphere appropriate to the occasion. For example, as a Secretary of All India Conference of English Teachers, you may make the following welcome remarks:

> Mr. Chairman, delegates and guests, it is my proud privilege to welcome Shri Lekhraj Sharma, Hon. Minister for education to the conference. It is very kind of him to have consented to spend some of his valuable time with us and to be the chief guest at the inaugural function of this conference. I am sure his wise counsel will give a proper direction to our deliberations. I also extend a warm welcome to the guests who have responded to our invitation and to the delegates who have come from different parts of the country to participate in the conference….

Introduction Speeches

There are occasions, which require speeches of introduction. Very often you will be required to introduce the main speaker at a seminar, conference, meeting or function. A speech of this kind is also very brief, usually two or three minutes long. If the main speaker is known to the audience, the speech may be even shorter. When you are called upon to give an introduction speech, gather basic facts about the speaker you are going to introduce. You should collect information about his qualifications, experience, and fields of activity, interest and specialization well in advance. Above all, get his name right and learn the correct pronunciation. When you speak about the speaker's qualification and experience, try to establish his credibility in the eyes of the audience to show in what way he is qualified to speak on the subject at hand. Never try to give any information which may embarrass or cause discomfort to the speaker. Don't make an attempt to steal the thunder by discussing the topic in detail and expressing your own views about it.

A good speech of introduction is pleasing to ears and makes the task of the main speaker easier. A speech of introduction acts as a facilitator between the speaker and the listeners. Hence, it should arouse and satisfy the curiosity of the listeners about the speaker in addition to creating a friendly ambience. The person deputed to give the introduction speech has to say something relevant about the speaker and then make a few remarks about the topic on which the speaker will be speaking.

Let us assume that Dr. Ashotosh K. Verma, Civil Engineering, Jaypee Institute of Technology, Ahmedabad was to deliver a keynote address at the conference on 'Rural Transport' and you were asked to introduce him. In this situation you could begin as follows:

> It is a pleasure to introduce to you Dr. Ashotosh K. Verma, Professor of Civil Engineering, Jaypee Institute of Technology, Ahmedabad. As you know, he is going to give the keynote address on Challenges of Rural Transport in India and ways to combat them. Dr. Verma has successfully completed several research projects in this area and published the results of his study in various national and international journals. He has also authored more than a dozen books on rural transport, each touching upon multiple aspects of the problem in depth. In addition to his academic attainments, he is also working as an advisor to Road & Transport Minister. I believe the seminal thoughts of his address will inspire us and provide fruitful material for meaningful discussions.

Felicitation Speeches

These speeches are given to honour or praise a person for his significant achievement. This is done by giving a brief account of his contribution, eulogizing his services to the public. The purpose is to show respect and heighten the audience's appreciation of, or admiration for, the person. Here is an example of felicitation speech is given.

> Sir, it is a very rewarding occasion for us that we have you in our midst today. We offer you our heartiest greetings and felicitation on your election to the Legislative Assembly and wish to express our feelings of joy on your thumping victory. We are proud of your achievement and the services that you have rendered to bring about a qualitative change in the life of community.
>
> Sir, yours is a multifaceted personality and on this occasion it is a pleasure to recall the contribution made by you for the social welfare and community development. You have been in the forefront of all our efforts directed to the amelioration and upgradation of the weaker sections of the society and waged a relentless struggle for social justice and material well being. Your devotion to high ideals, indomitable courage and sense of sacrifice has been, and will always be a source of inspiration for us all.

Commemorative Speeches

A commemorative speech is given to honour the memory of a great person. In it, the speaker refers to the significant contributions and cherished ideals of the person concerned. It contains expressions of feelings and sentiments rather than a narration of the work accomplished by the person being commemorated. This speech captures the mood of the moment and reminds the audience of the services rendered by the concerned individual. A very good example of this kind of speech is the one given by Jawaharlal Nehru soon after the death of Mahatma Gandhi.

The following speech was delivered by the first Prime Minister of India, Pandit Jawaharlal Nehru on 30 January, 1948.

> **The Light has Gone Out**
>
> Friends and comrades, the light has gone out of our lives and there is darkness everywhere. I don't know what to tell you and how to say it. Our beloved leader, Bapu as we called him, the father of the nation, is no more. Perhaps I am wrong to say that. Nevertheless, we will not see him again as we have seen him for these many years. We will not run to him for advice and seek solace from him and that is a terrible blow not to me only but to millions and millions in this country, and it is a little difficult to soften the blow by any other advice that I or anyone else can give you.
>
> The light has gone out, I said, and yet I was wrong. For the light that was shone in this country was no ordinary light. The light that has illuminated this country for these many years will illuminate this country for many more years and a thousand years later that light will still be seen in this country and the world will see it and it will give solace to innumerable hearts. For that light represented something more than the immediate present; it represented

the living truth... the eternal truth, reminding us of the light path, drawing us from error, taking this ancient country to freedom.

All this has happened when there was so much more of him to do. We could never think that he was unnecessary or that he had done his task. But now, particularly, when we are faced with so many difficulties, his not being with us is a blow most terrible to bear.

A mad man has put an end to his life, for I can only call him mad who did it, and yet there has been enough of prison spread in this country during the past years and months and this poison, has effect on people's minds. We must face this poison, we must root out this poison and we must face all the perils that encompass us and face them not madly or badly but rather in the way that our beloved teacher taught us to face them. The first thing to remember is that no one of us dare misbehave because we are angry. We have to behave like strong and determined people, determined to face all the perils that surround us, determined to carry out the mandate that our great teacher and our great leader has given us, remembering always that if, as I believe, his spirit looks upon us and sees us, nothing would displease his soul so much as to see that we have indulged in any small behaviour or any violence.

So we must not do that. But that does not mean we should be weak but rather than we should in strength and in unity face all the troubles that are in front of us. We must hold together and all our petty troubles and difficulties and conflicts must be ended in the face of this great disaster. A great disaster is a symbol to us to remember all the big things of life and forget the small things, of which we have thought too much.

Farewell Speeches

In organizations and in our everyday lives, we come across situations when we have to take leave from some of our colleagues or friends or from some public figures. Speeches given on such occasions are called farewell speeches. There are two types of farewell speeches. The *first* is when we bid farewell to somebody, and the *second* when the person given farewell responds to the farewell address. It is customary in the former to refer to the achievements and qualities of the concerned person, and in the latter to state the pleasant association with the members of the association. The speech usually ends with courteous leave taking. Here is an example of the former in which the speaker bids farewell to the Managing Director of a company.

Ladies and Gentlemen, as you know, we have gathered here today to bid a farewell to Dr. Deepak Ahuja, our Chief Medical Officer. Like you, I have mixed feelings. On the one hand we are happy that he is going to head an international organization and on the other hand, we are sorry to lose him. First, let as congratulate him on his being invited for the new assignment. We wish him glorious success in the tasks ahead. However, we shall no longer have the benefit of his advice and guidance in our day-to-day work. I hardly need to remind you of the many innovative measures that he introduced to modernize the system of hospital management and administration. We should long remember the human touch in his dealings with us all.

The following is another farewell speech on the occasion of a Vice Chancellor getting retired from a reputed university.

Dear Faculty Colleagues, students and distinguished guests

We have gathered here to offer our profound regard, admiration and appreciation to Prof. K.K. Sabbarbal, our Vice Chancellor. It is a moment of great honour to express our esteem gratitude and affection in felicitating a genius on the eve of his superannuation after a memorable and insurmountable innings played at the pitch of the place called RIETS, Jodhpur despite the vagaries and odds of weather trying to interfere with the smooth functioning of activities. Sir, you have always been a driving force to steer the boat against the troubled waters from time to time. Your innovative efforts are not only commendable but worth cherishing. Your administrative acumen came to the limelight when you joined as the Director of the Institute in 1989, the time when the Institute was faced with innumerable challenges.

In the tenure of your leadership for a period of 17 years, RIETS has grown rapidly. Today it has sprawled like a banyan tree spreading its branches at Dehradun, Ahmedabad and now Pune on the anvil. And the credit for all this undeniably goes to you, Sir. Your able leadership has played a pivotal role in bringing many significant milestones, which the history of the institute can never erase. It is really difficult to reckon all significant contributions but we can't satiate ourselves if we don't name a few. The first and the most remarkable gesture shown by you was a judicious promotion policy and a benign care for the lifestyle of your employees. The education, health and shopping facilities provided in the campus to faculty and staff members really deserve applause. In addition to all this, the grant of extension to the retired faculty willing to serve the institute itself speaks of your prime concern and recognition of their services. Sir, this concern of yours has brought you close to our hearts. Your sojourn here has been like a book whose chapters are not only written with human concern, proximity to simple and jejune joys but also full of instructions and morals for the future generations to follow.

Sir, your foresightedness to get a new library with all the modern amenities that pep the readers' interest is an example of your being a bibliophile. The construction of a new lecture theatre complex with state of art facilities reflects your creativity and your interest in architecture despite your mathematical expertise.

Your due cares for the renovation of all buildings including staff quarters exhibits your humanness and sense of belongingness to one and all. Your rational thinking, logical reasoning and meticulous planning coruscated in all your decisions. The introduction of entrance tests is a burning illustration of your unconquerable will power and indefatigable nature. You have made RIETS system of admission and education an example to be emulated by many private and autonomous institutes. Sir, we are cognizant of the stark truth that your policy decisions have always been accommodating, transparent and self-sustaining. One wonders at the ratio of girl students in RIETS when one compares it with other Institutes and you qualify for plaudits of all sorts.

One often would envy your unassuming nature, your magnanimity to help and oblige the needy; one would also imitate your benevolent attitude and your profound humility. No one ever saw you losing your calm even in most adverse situations. And that perhaps helped you touch the pinnacles of a perfect human being.

Everyone knows that a healthy mind dwells in a healthy body and you have exemplified the same by getting constructed Student Activity Centre in a very short span. This is also a demonstration of your keen interest in sports apart from academics.

Sir, to quote in your own words "The world is a global village" lies the beautiful blend of a nation's pride and prosperity starting from a small hamlet sprouting to touch the horizon. The dreams have been translated to reality by your venture of CAMPUS-CONNECT, which enables us all to reach every nook and corner of the world just with the press of a button.

Sir, we all are well aware that after such an industrious and illustrious career of hectic schedule, you need moment of relief and relaxation. But, we really admire and envy your courage and gesture to act as Professor Emeritus as well as Advisor who would always play a significant role in guiding the ship to the right direction.

In the end as a matter of realization we wish you a salubrious superannuation, a happy, healthy and blissful life to you and all the members of your family. Though retiring from active service life we shall never let you retire from our hearts. Let us wish you again a happy retired life and dedicate the lines of the great English dramatist:

Fear no more the heat o' th' sun,
Nor the furious winter's rages.
Thou thy worldly task hast done,
Home art gone and ta'en thy wages.

Response to a farewell speech

Mr. Chairperson, faculty friends, distinguished guests, their family members and dear students,

Today when the time for me to take your leave has come I feel like reminiscing all my experiences since I came here. It has been a good time over all and I shall carry your love wherever I go. And I am really thankful to you for whatever you have done for me, for the bond that I feel. We are in a commercial age where investment in any bond pays rich dividends and I hope you too will get rich dividends for all sorts of co-operation. I know at this time of hour, my words will be given much importance but I know most of you whether you express or not share the same experience as me. People would love to hate me and hate to love me for many good reasons but truth is truth after all.

All of us remember the poem the world is too much with us but nowadays it is really not too much with us. My experience says that if you have done good to some, you are rewarded with the same return. But nothing to worry, you will reap good harvest. Our experience says that we see clouds somewhere but they rain somewhere else. This is the go of the world.

I have mixed reactions of the past since I have always been a lover of human beings. Being in the institute I not only taught but also learned quite a lot. I have played my part well here and tried my best to contribute positively keeping my self-esteem always above other things. During my tenure, I tried to discharge my responsibilities to the best of my knowledge and ability. People may criticize me for my way of life since one's professional compulsions often interfere with one's personal responsibilities. I have always preferred integrity to other things. For me words have always meant what they stand for. I don't attribute hidden meaning to them and restrict myself to their real ones because of the depth they come from.

I shall really miss many good people and especially some of my friends. Earlier most of my friends left me and today I am myself leaving this place with a hope of a better tomorrow for everyone. Academic life is longer and all of us are to meet somewhere or the other. I shall always carry RIETS and its rhythms within me for all the good reasons.

In the end I wish you all a good life ahead and wish the institute to burgeon forth as a junction of camaraderie, cordiality, co-existence and coherence where everyone has a role to play in the future and where there is respect for academic adventures and mutual love and respect. With these words, I take your leave. Thank you very much one and all.

What we have here are the samples of different kinds of speeches made on special occasions. There are, of course, many other kinds of speeches, such as inaugural speeches, presentation speeches, acceptance speeches, entertainment speeches.

However, if you master the techniques of speaking on the occasions mentioned above, you would not find it difficult to speak on any special occasion. You should remember that apart from the preparation of speeches, the way you deliver it is also important. Moreover, some other non-verbal characteristics, such as dress, voice, facial expressions and combating nervousness also add to your performance. As beginners, you may experience stage fright but with time and experience you will have control over it.

In the following pages, we give two most famous speeches made by two towering personalities of the world. You can also draft your speeches by taking cues of language, emotion, spontaneity and flow from these two speeches.

Two world famous speeches

This speech is by Martin Luther King, Jr. delivered on 28 August 1963 to some 2 lakh people who had gathered in Washington for a peaceful demonstration to further the cause of equal rights for Afro Americans. The speech is widely regarded as a masterpiece. It is marked by the use of familiar, concrete words that create vivid images. The extensive use of repetition and parallelism reinforces the message, and adds to the momentum of the speech. The phrase, "I have a dream" lends it a lyrical quality and enhances its impact.

I have a dream

I say to you today, my friends so even though we face the difficulties of today and tomorrow. I still have a dream. It is a dream deeply rooted in the American dream.

I have a dream that one day this nation will rise up and live out the true meaning of its creed. We hold these truths to be self-evident, that all men are created equal.

I have a dream that one day on the red hills of Georgia the sons of former slaves and the sons of former slave owners will be able to sit down together at the table of brotherhood.

I have a dream that even the state of Mississippi, a state sweltering with the heat of injustice, sweltering with the heat of oppression; will be transformed into an oasis of freedom and justice.

I have a dream that my four little children will one day live in a nation where they will not be judged by the colour of the skin but by the content of the character. I have a dream today.

I have a dream that one day, down in Alabama, with its vicious racists, with its governor having his lips dripping with the words of interposition and nullification: one day right there in Alabama little black boys and black girls will be able to join hands with the little white boys and white girls as sisters and brothers. I have a dream today.

I have a dream today that every valley shall be exalted, every hill and mountain shall be made low, the rough places will be made plain and the crooked places will be made straight, and the glory of the god shall be revealed, and all flesh shall see it together.

This is our hope. This is a faith that I go back to the South with. With this faith we will be able to hew out of the mountain of despair a stone of hope. With this faith we will be able to transform the jangling discords of our nation into a beautiful symphony of brotherhood. With this faith we will be able to work together, to pray together, to struggle together, to go to jail together, to stand up for freedom together knowing that we will be free one day.

This will be the day-This will be the day when god's children will be able to sing with new meaning, "My country 'tis of thee, sweet land of liberty, of thee I sing. Land where my fathers died, land of the pilgrims pride, from every mountainside, let freedom ring" And if America is to be a great nation this must become true.

So let freedom ring from the prodigious hill tops of New Hampshire. Let freedom ring from the mighty mountains of New York. Let freedom ring from the heightening Alleghenies of Pennsylvania!

Let freedom ring from the snow-capped Rockies of Colorado! Let freedom ring from the curvaceous slopes of California!

Let freedom ring from Stone Mountain of Georgia!
Let freedom ring from Lookout Mountain of Tennessee!

Let freedom ring from every hill and molehill of Mississippi. From every mountainside, let freedom ring.

And when this happen, when we allow freedom ring-when we let it ring from every village and every hamlet, from every state and every city-we will be able to speed up that day when all of god's children, black men and white men, Jews and gentiles, protestants and Catholics, will be able to join hands and sign in the words of the old negro spiritual, "Free at last! Free at last! Thank God almighty, we are free at last!"

(Cited in Stephen E Lucas, *The Art of Public Speaking*, Singapore: McGraw Hill Book Company, 1989, pp. 400–403.)

The next speech "India's Tryst with Destiny" was delivered by the first prime minister of India, Pt. Jawaharlal Nehru on the eve of India's independence, towards the midnight on August 14, 1947.

India's Tryst with Destiny

Long years ago we made a tryst with destiny, and now the time comes when we shall redeem our pledge, not wholly or in full measure, but very substantially. At the stroke of the midnight hour, when the world sleeps, India will awake to life and freedom. A moment comes, which comes but rarely in history, when we step out from the old to the new, when an age ends, and when the soul of a nation, long suppressed, finds utterance. It is fitting that at this solemn moment we take the pledge of dedication to the service of India and her people and to the still larger cause of humanity.

At the dawn of history India started on her unending quest, and trackless centuries are filled with her striving and the grandeur of her success and her failures. Through good and ill fortune alike she has never lost sight of that quest or forgotten the ideals which gave her strength. We end today a period of ill fortune and India discovers herself again. The achievement we celebrate today is but a step, an opening of opportunity, to the greater triumphs and achievements that await us. Are we brave enough and wise enough to grasp this opportunity and accept the challenge of the future?

Freedom and power bring responsibility. The responsibility rests upon this Assembly, a sovereign body representing the sovereign people of India. Before the birth of freedom, we have endured all the pains of labour and our hearts are heavy with the memory of this sorrow. Some of those pains continue even now. Nevertheless, the past is over and it is the future that beckons to us now.

That future is not one of ease or resting but of incessant striving so that we may fulfil the pledges we have so often taken and the one we shall take today. The service of India means the service of the millions who suffer. It means the ending of poverty and ignorance and disease and inequality of opportunity. The ambition of the greatest man of our generation has been to wipe every tear from every eye. That may be beyond us, but as long as there are tears and suffering, so long our work will not be over.

And so we have to labour and to work, and work hard, to give reality to our dreams. Those dreams are for India, but they are also for the world, for all the nations and peoples are too closely knit together today for any one of them to imagine that it can live apart. Peace has been said to be indivisible; so is freedom, so is prosperity now, and so also is disaster in this One World that can no longer be split into isolated fragments.

To the people of India, whose representatives we are, we make an appeal to join us with faith and confidence in this great adventure. This is no time for petty and destructive criticism, no time for ill-will or blaming others.

We have to build the noble mansion of free India where all her children may dwell. The appointed day has come-the day appointed by destiny-and India stands forth again, after long slumber and struggle, awake, vital, free and independent. The past clings on to us still in some measure and we have to do much before we redeem the pledges we have so often taken. Yet the turning-point is past, and history begins anew for us, the history which we shall live and act and others will write about.

It is a fateful moment for us in India, for all Asia and for the world. A new star rises, the star of freedom in the East, a new hope comes into being, a vision long cherished materializes. May the star never set and that hope never be betrayed! We rejoice in that freedom, even though clouds surround us, and many of our people are sorrow stricken and difficult problems encompass us. But freedom brings responsibilities and burdens and we have to face them in the spirit of a free and disciplined people.

On this day our first thoughts go to the architect of this freedom, the Father of our Nation [Gandhi], who, embodying the old spirit of India, held aloft the torch of freedom and lighted up the darkness that surrounded us. We have often been unworthy followers of his and have strayed from his message, but not only we but succeeding generations will remember this message and bear the imprint in their hearts of this great son of India, magnificent in his faith and strength and courage and humility. We shall never allow that torch of freedom to be blown out, however high the wind or stormy the tempest.

Our next thoughts must be of the unknown volunteers and soldiers of freedom who, without praise or reward, have served India even unto death. We think also of our brothers and sisters who have been cut off from us by political boundaries and who unhappily cannot share at present in the freedom that has come. They are of us and will remain of us whatever may happen, and we shall be sharers in their good [or] ill fortune alike.

The future beckons to us. Whither do we go and what shall be our endeavour? To bring freedom and opportunity to the common man, to the peasants and workers of India; to fight and end poverty and ignorance and disease; to build up a prosperous, democratic and progressive nation, and to create social, economic and political institutions which will ensure justice and fullness of life to every man and woman.

We have hard work ahead. There is no resting for any one of us till we redeem our pledge in full, till we make all the people of India what destiny intended them to be. We are citizens of a great country on the verge of bold advance, and we have to live up to that high standard. All of us, to whatever religion we may belong, are equally the children of India with equal rights, privileges and obligations. We cannot encourage communalism or narrow-mindedness, for no nation can be great whose people are narrow in thought or in action.

To the nations and peoples of the world we send greetings and pledge ourselves to cooperate with them in furthering peace, freedom and democracy. And to India, our much-loved motherland, the ancient, the eternal and the ever-new, we pay our reverent homage and we bind ourselves afresh to her service. Jai Hind.

• EXERCISES •

1. How are speeches different from professional presentations? Give examples.
2. Mention the various factors that help you determine the purpose of your speech?
3. What should one do when one has to prepare a speech?
4. How should one begin a speech? Underline the importance of words and tone in a speech.
5. Assess the importance of anecdote or story in a speech.

6. You have been invited to welcome Mrs. Paula, the director of a social service group. Draft a welcome speech for her.
7. After your active service of 35 years in Ashoka Industries, Gwalior, you are retiring as deputy general manager. You have been requested to speak a few words on this occasion. Prepare this speech. Your listeners comprise people of all departments.
8. Assuming yourself as the Head of Bio-technology department, prepare a keynote address that you are to deliver in a symposium on "Man-made threats to environment and their remedies."
9. Draft a commemorative speech on occasion of Engineer's day. You must focus on the contribution made by *Mr. Vishweshwaraiah* in particular and all engineers in general.
10. The Director General of your organization has been nominated for the honour of Padma Shree. You have been asked to deliver a felicitation address on this occasion. Draft the speech. Invent necessary details.

14

Negotiation Skills

> *In business, you don't get what you deserve, you get what you negotiate.*
>
> —**CHESTER L. KARRASS**

Negotiation is one of the most crucial aspects of communication. Knowing the facts and process of negotiation is of paramount importance. In your daily life, you negotiate in different situations. Deciding for the film you have to see with your friends, the colour and make of the car your parents should buy, the cuisine you want to eat, all have to be negotiated. Of course, there are various types of negotiating styles, depending on the contexts and attitudes of the people involved. But if you are aware of the problems you may face during the act of negotiation, it will be easier for you to find solutions taking into account the cultural diversities.

NEGOTIATION: PROCESS AND DEFINITION

Negotiation is a process of convincing two parties, in which one wants to convince and the other has to be convinced. It is a sort of mutual agreement and accepted by both the parties involved. The ability to negotiate is something which every individual ought to acquire. To be successful in life negotiating skills are mandatory. Negotiation is an act in which you are involved even when doing mundane activities. On numerous occasions, you confuse negotiation with haggling but the former is just not that. Rather it takes place for various other reasons as well. You negotiate for not only price, but also the choice of car, extra features, terms, services, options, places, timings, schedules, etc. Almost everything in life is negotiable.

With the ever-increasing collaborations in the organization, the need of negotiating skills is on the rise. Your decisions are based on your skills of negotiating. Often you nurture these skills as part of the growing process without being aware of them. Sometimes you have to consciously learn them.

Concise Oxford Dictionary of Current English defines 'negotiation' as

(a) The act to confer with a view to compromise or agreement.
(b) To arrange the affair to bring about the desired result.

We can say that negotiation is a discussion where two parties are involved; the deal is struck with win-win situation. In simple words, it is a bargain for mutually agreed exchange by using discussion and persuasion. The objective of any negotiation is to reach to an agreement where both the parties move together to achieve a desirable outcome. The following definitions will help you understand this process better.

> Negotiation is any form of meeting or discussion in which you and the persons you are in contact with use argument and persuasion to achieve an agreed decision or action.
>
> Alan Flower
>
> A process of combining conflicting positions into a common position under a decision rule of unanimity, a phenomenon in which the outcome is determined by the process.
>
> William Zartman

THE FACTS ABOUT NEGOTIATION

It is important to know the following basic facts relating to negotiating situation:

- Negotiation occurs between two parties where both are equally interested in the final outcome.
- Negotiation is a voluntary act. Both the parties involved have the freedom to refuse to negotiate at any point of time.
- The outcome of negotiation depends on values, beliefs, social customs and emotions of the people involved.
- The moot point of negotiation is the dissatisfaction with the present situation. They want to make changes in the situation which is mutually agreed upon.
- A successful negotiation is a win-win situation in which both sides are satisfied with the results.
- Timing is a crucial factor in negotiation. The right chord struck at the right time can lead to successful negotiation.
- Negotiation reaches an agreement not through authority or instructions, but through cordial discussion.
- The objective of negotiation is agreement.

NEGOTIATION SITUATIONS

There are innumerable situations in which you need to negotiate.

- Suppose you are working as a Manager in a firm. You find that everyone's salary in your organization was hiked but yours was not considered for an increase. For this you go to your controlling officer to negotiate a deal.
- You need to negotiate in a situation where an issue involves more than one person. A problem, however, complicated can be resolved through negotiation. There may be different opinions and views, but all the issues once laid on the table can be weighed and compared. It is not only by authority that an agreement can be achieved but also by discussing, persuading and influencing.
- It is mandatory that both the parties decide to meet and talk about the issue. The non-verbal cues play a significant role while the discussion goes on.

Types of Negotiation: Formal and Informal

Negotiation can take place in formal and informal situations. The formal situations are as follows:

- The agenda is already known to both the parties.
- The meeting is announced and the role of the individuals is also defined.
- Negotiation involves more than two persons for the discussion.
- The observer in the act of negotiation plays a key role as he keeps track of the drift and direction of the discussion. If any important point is missed, he reminds you of that point.
- Since formal negotiations are predetermined, you have ample time to prepare. So know about the strengths and weaknesses of the opposite party. Prepare meticulously the bargaining steps to be followed.

The informal situations where negotiations take place are as follows:

- ♦ A meeting is called on the spur of the moment because of sudden disappearance of one of your colleagues.
- ♦ A meeting for negotiation is often unannounced and both the parties do not get time to orient each other.
- ♦ Informal negotiations depend on people's personal relationship.
- ♦ You are assigned with work even when your hands are full.

In these situations, you have to negotiate according to your previous experiences. Remember if the parties refuse to meet and discuss the issue, negotiation has no scope. Then the situation is that of a stalemate, and you have no choice but to accept whatever is put on your plate.

QUALITIES OF A NEGOTIATOR

A negotiator should possess the following qualities:

- **Confidence:** You might be nervous, but should exude confidence when entering the meeting room. Introduce yourself confidently to everyone, offer your hand for shaking, look directly in the eyes of the opponent and smilingly say "How do you do?". Get the names of other members instantly and address them whenever possible during the meeting. If you don't remember the names, ask again. Decent, straight and unaffected manners will bolster confidence further.
- **Appearance:** Be careful about the appearance. Your dress should match your personality and your professional attitude. Let it be in accordance with the job you do. Of course, you must maintain personal tidiness and neatness—hair, shoes, nails and makeup. Avoid wearing dazzling dresses, loud makeup and strong perfumes. Put the papers neatly on the table so that they can be referred to when the need arises. It looks unimpressive to rummage through the briefcase to look out for the papers. Keep the pen ready to take notes. If you are organized, your mind will be firm and you are ready to persuade.
- **Outlook:** Exhibit zeal and positive outlook. Whatever your idea is, believe in the benefits completely and also see how it fits in other person's needs. Never use negative language about your competitors, but at the same time show your product is superior. If you are negotiating for better salary, never bank on the injustice of other's being better paid. Present your case in a way to demonstrate that your contribution is special and deserves financial recognition. You can indulge in flattery, but without making it obvious. Let your superiors feel that you enjoy working under their aegis. Only show that you deserve more than your fellow beings.
- **Honesty and reliability:** For your product or idea to excel because of superiority, you have to prove the worth. Don't leave it for others to guess. If you just say your product is the best, they will not take your word, you have to prove. In case the product or idea has a drawback, highlight the positive claims so that the drawbacks get diminished.
- **Competence:** Present your case in such a way that it ratifies efficiency. Go slow to make it credible. Enumerate positive points one after the other. Ensure that other people fully understand the overall thrust of your argument. See to it that they agree that your product is superior to others. People will surely have questions to ask. Handle the questions dexterously depending on how many people you are dealing at a time. Deal with each individual one by one. If the group is large, make a presentation beforehand and then take-up questions.

- **Flexibility:** If you are stubborn, get rid of the attitude immediately. You have to be ready for compromise, especially on less important issues. If you are not able to achieve your objectives, withdraw gracefully and move to another point. Return to the stumbling block later. If you have met a number of firms, use the experience to your advantage. After a meeting gets over, try to analyse the responses you received and also judge why some approaches worked better than others.

NEGOTIATION STAGES

The four stages to a successful negotiation are preparation, meeting, negotiation phase and implementation. They are discussed here briefly:

Preparation

You have to prepare well for your negotiation just like you do for a presentation. Never with indifferent look. You must know your subject. Also know about the strengths and weaknesses of the people involved. The objectives should be properly delineated. Answer questions, such as what are the real issues and which parties should be involved. Half the battle is won if you have done your preparation thoroughly. Your persuasive power will be strong, when you have done a detailed comparison. Collect all the facts and figures and place them neatly on the table. Identify the upper and lower limits. In case you are not able to achieve your target, be prepared for your BATNA (Best Alternative To Negotiated Agreement). You can convert them into illustrations for easy reference. When you are selling something, know everything about your rival products, their price, reliability and services. You must consider other party's strengths and weaknesses. You have to investigate for hidden agenda and factual data.

When negotiating for a pay hike, collect sufficient data about company profits and expenditure, inflation and pay in companies from similar industry, and in your own organization. The groundwork takes time and effort, but without evidence it will be very difficult to convince anyone. Therefore, go through the documents and extract what is important and relevant for you.

Be aware of other person's subjects too. Put yourself in the opponent's shoes. Try to anticipate the counter arguments you might face and, accordingly, keep the replies ready. Practise aloud the answers you have to give. Develop and plan your strategies in advance. Find the logical reasons why agreeing with you can be beneficial for the other person. What precisely can your product or idea do for him or his company? In the course of the meeting, you have to be direct. Don't get lost in the meanderings. Get to the point, be precise and stay firm on it.

Write down the order in which you want to present your argument. But at the same time be flexible and react as the situation demands. There is always a possibility that you may have to change the order of your presentation as something else which seems to be more promising may come on the table.

Be very sure about what exactly you want as the outcome of the meeting and what realistically you think you are likely to get. Divide the demand categorically as: (a) the minimum demand, (b) the actual demand, and (c) the optimistic hopes.

The minimum demand should be used only in a fallback situation. So don't resort to it unless in need. The actual demand you hope are realistically what you get from the meeting. All your arguments should revolve around this demand. Your data must support that this demand is reasonable and feasible.

Even your optimistic hopes should be reasonable as otherwise you will be mocked at. Remember seldom do both parties get absolutely satisfied. So it is better to be prepared to give in. You should be practical and eager to compromise.

Meeting

You decide the meeting according to the place and time. The place of meeting does influence the level of confidence. Try to choose your own premise as the venue for the meeting as you are more accustomed to the place. The other advantage is that during the course of the meeting you can get whatever information or material needed. You can also extend the social courtesies as a token of goodwill, enabling the negotiation more towards the agreement. Similarly, time should be fixed according to mutual convenience. But always keep adequate time for smooth exchange of ideas. The time to prepare for negotiation and implementation should be cautiously fixed. Once you have decided the time, stick to it.

Begin the meeting with the following:

- Your introduction along with the team members.
- Emphasize the importance of reaching a mutual agreement.
- Give your general views and invite the comments of the other party.
- Reflect your interest in their response.
- Emphasize on long-term relationship.

1. **Speak simply:** Try to speak naturally as it will inspire confidence. Avoid jargons to sound intelligent and, therefore, look more convincing. Give proper pauses so that the other person can hear what you are saying. Cut down vocalized and nasalized pauses, such as ers and ums. Short sentences can help better, and if you get nonsensical comments from the opponent, be polite saying, "I didn't get you properly, can you explain please?" Don't shy from asking direct questions: "May I have the name of people this would apply to?", "Would you be able to give the delivery by next week?", etc.

2. **Keep cool:** Never let others feel that you are being pushy. If people feel pressurized, then arriving at favourable decision is difficult. Don't take responsibility to fill in the lull by rushing into conversation. Silence helps for better decision as it is indicative that you are listening properly.

   Don't interrupt as the other person is getting into a tangle. Don't help him out. Take this time to decide your next move. If you are interrupted, then politely say, "Excuse me, may I also make a point". Never lose your countenance even when arguments have turned sour. Be polite, it will pay.
3. **Conducive relations:** The atmosphere for the meeting should be polite and conducive. Let the opponent feel that you respect his position and understand his problem. Both the parties have to reflect zeal and enthusiasm about the issue. A little humour can relax the atmosphere. But never hurt the other person's sentiments. Take care of non-verbal cues. Keep your eyes on the person you are dealing with. Watch for favourable responses and exploit them. The positive non- verbal cues can help you to search for areas of agreement. Build on them. When disagreement arises, deal by raising your objection tactfully, "I am sorry, may you clarify", "I am afraid I don't agree with this point". And then explain your point with figures and facts.

   Be gracious in victory and always be courteous. Be gracious in defeat too and learn from experience.

The Negotiating Phase

This phase follows with a set of sequence. It begins with defining the issue followed by the scope of negotiation. Each party puts forward their case, one by one. Then each give their initial response and define their initial positions. Once the ice is broken, more open phase begins. The possible solutions are laid supported by arguments. The proposals in more specific terms are made, discussed and modified before the parties agree to the terms. In the final stage, the agreement is worded and concluded.

Implementation

Implementation is argued by some scholars as the step away from negotiation. But implementation is very necessary even when it is after the concluding discussion. The basic purpose of negotiation is to implement what has been agreed upon. If implementation part is neglected, then the negotiation process is a failure. Don't forget to get all the terms and conditions in writing. Do chalk out in detail the schedule with time. Define every detail. Ensure all the persons concerned should be intimated of the agreement, its implication and the action followed.

NEGOTIATION STYLE

No two individuals are alike; similarly no two negotiating situations are same. Therefore, depending on the context and type of people involved, you should adopt the style to achieve the optimum effect. A successful negotiation will judge the situation and then adopt the germane style.

(a) **Collaborate:** An approach where the stress is on win-win situation. Both the parties cooperate and have creative problem-solving qualities. This style is adopted when the issues are of paramount importance and involve long-term relationship. Both the parties involved should be committed if they want to be successful.
(b) **Accommodate:** In this, the priority is avoiding conflict. It is observed as lose-lose or lose-win approach which gives the opposing party the opportunity to win. In this style, you create a situation for more important issues to come up. You are in a weaker position and you want to abate the loss. Your focus is to achieve harmony and stability than victory.
(c) **Compromise:** In this both the parties have mindsets to accept some amount of win and loss. The main aim is to find a solution that both the parties can accept. Only one alternative is available in this situation. You look for short-term settlements as both the opponents are equal in status.
(d) **Control:** Personal goals are kept at priority and must be met, whatever be the consequences. The only aim is to win, whatever be the cost. The issue is important and you believe you are right. Quick action becomes vital.
(e) **Avoidance:** This style is more like cringing back from the issue in hand. You want to buy time as more important issues are pressurizing you. Since there are no solutions available at the moment, you just want time to resolve the issue.

HIATUS IN NEGOTIATION

Negotiation is a very subtle issue and once the situation slips from hand, it is a herculean task to set it right again. Therefore, it is more sensible to be alert in the beginning and do the proper groundwork before coming in forefront. The common mistakes which you are prone to make are discussed in the following sections:

Becoming rigid

In some situation you enter the negotiation with a predetermined outcome and, therefore, you become rigid and incapable of visualizing the other alternatives. This is likely to happen when you impose on the other party without understanding their perspective. This results in frustration and outright rejection of others' viewpoint. To overcome this situation do the following:

- Try to analyse the non-verbal cues of the other party. Encourage them to clarify their objective and be open to understand the problem from their perspective.
- Visualize your agenda as the framework. Let it be flexible to be changed according to the need of the time and demand.
- Summarizing in between helps to review the discussion. You will be able to place the discussion in right perspective then.
- Treat the information from both the sides as hypothesis than facts.

Accepting on win-lose situation

You can't always be a winner. Approaching the negotiation table with the mindset that you should be the winner will not allow you to appreciate others. You will take only your perspective as the correct one. This can lead to raising of voice and emotional outburst. To overcome this:

- Look for a common platform for discussion and see if some solutions can emanate from there.
- Do understand others perspective. Avoid verbal attack and defensive attitude.
- Have a long-term advantage and don't lose the string of the discussion by getting lost in the labyrinth of dispute.

Avoiding conflict

Problem is faced when the real issue is not addressed or is addressed only peripherally. Both the parties avoid the real agenda so as to be comfortable than to discuss the problem in hand. It might be due to lack of preparation or inability to collect the data needed for negotiation. In this situation, if the conflict is not serious, leave it. Time will solve the problem. Try to motivate the other party. Never compromise on preparation. Do identify the points when an agreement can be reached. Be open to discuss the issue with a serious mindset.

Despite the care you take to negotiate, on many occasions things don't go according to our expectations. In order to reach a successful negotiation, one should endeavour to accomplish the following:

- Plan discussion according to psychological needs and appropriate strategies.
- Set amicable tone.
- Highlight the brighter side.
- Be ready with alteration.
- Allow more time and space to other person.
- Allow concessions.

One should always remember what John F. Kennedy said about negotiation: "Let us never negotiate out of fear. But let us never fear to negotiate".

Since negotiation is a process of interaction between the two parties, the role of communication skills in it can't be undermined. You need to be positive even in case you have to make a little bit of sacrifice. That is possible only with the help of your communication skills. Things often do not go according to your expectations in negotiation. But your sacrifice will act as a dividend in future. If you consider this as investment, it will come to your aid in future negotiations. Someone has rightly said: "You must be fully prepared to lose a great deal in order to make a great deal".

• EXERCISES •

1. Explain the process of negotiation. How is negotiation different from haggling?
2. The negotiator must have a few qualities. What are they?
3. What are different situations of negotiation? Distinguish between formal and informal situation.
4. Explain different styles of negotiation. Give example of each style.
5. You are not able to achieve success in negotiation every time. What are the barriers in negotiation?
6. What is BATNA? Explain the preparation phase of the negotiation.

15

Group Discussions

Individual commitment to a group effort that is what makes a team work, a company work, a society work, a civilization work.

—VINCE LOMBARDI

When a group of people gather, they don't usually sit quiet. They start discussion on a topic which can be of frivolous or of serious nature, and related to social, economic or political issues. The discussion might be formal or informal. If a group of students sitting in a mess to have their meal indulge into a discussion, it will be informal. They will not pay attention to the language being used or the gestures made. Thus, discussions taking place in the train, bus stops, birthday parties, and canteen or at home will most likely be of informal nature. In contrast, the discussions which take place in offices, classrooms, conferences, interview centres are of formal nature. Group discussion (GD) is a form of group communication in which people give their opinion on the given issue, topic or problem. In a GD, various aspects of the issue emerge, enabling an individual to get a clear idea about the topic. It makes the problem easy to approach and decisions quick to make—the basic purpose of group discussion.

Group discussion provides a platform for the participants to resolve an issue, solve a problem or exchange information on a given topic. It is used to evaluate and assess a candidate for a specified job. Group discussion can also be used as an exercise for developing students' personality traits and communication skills. See Figure 15.1.

Figure 15.1 Group discussion.

DEFINITION

Group discussion can offer some of the richest and satisfying experiences where untapped spring of ideas and emotions begin to emerge. It brings out the originality and imagination of the individuals. Group discussion is a forum where there is a free exchange of ideas. There are legendary definitions that describe group discussions as, "They keep minutes and spend hours", "They sow but don't reap", or "A camel is a horse designed by a committee". However, discarding the cynical outlook, group discussion can be defined as a gathering where discourses occur with varied purposes encompassing almost all possible issues.

In today's competitive world, group discussion is used in addition to written test/interview during recruitment. However, from a student's point of view a GD holds meaning only in the context of getting jobs or admission in a reputed institute. Group discussion takes place in almost every organization at all fora. It is of utmost importance to hone our skills from the beginning. The GD can be as varied as the discussions among the jury before passing a verdict to the cabinet meetings held by the government.

In a GD, the number of persons involved may vary but, generally, on average seven to eleven members participate. The group may have people of equal or different standings; it may have a designated leader. The discussion may or may not even have a structured agenda. The participants should quickly adapt themselves according to the ambience.

FORMULATION

After a panelist announces the topic, the participants have to clearly understand the topic by analysing the key words used. If the topic is misunderstood, then there is a danger of the whole exercise becoming futile as people would always digress with their views rather than converge. So it is beneficial if the topic is clearly stated for everyone to analyse and the first few minutes are spent in understanding it. This job becomes much easier if the group has a designated leader. However, the leader of the group emerges as the discussion progresses. It is not necessary that the person who has initiated the discussion is the leader. There are different ways of mooting the discussion. Sometimes the topic is given before the discussion commences so that the participants get time for preparation. Otherwise it is given on the spur of the moment which helps the panelist to be evaluated on criteria, such as creativity, knowledge and adaptability.

PURPOSE

Participating in the discussion effectively with confidence is one of the important skills that an individual should possess. Whatever be your profession, you need to have good group communication skills. The purpose of a GD varies slightly according to your role as a student, an engineer, a doctor, a CEO or an administrator. As a student, you have to participate in GDs for academic evaluation, selection process, competitions, meetings, etc. If you are seeking a job, then also you have to participate in a GD as part of the evaluation before the final interview. As a professional your opinion and views presented in a GD can help a great deal in making the decision towards the company's goal.

No discussion is considered fruitful if there are no tangible outcomes from it. This is why the group involved in the discussion should be made aware of the purpose of this exercise and the members should set the goals themselves. There may be times when a group is just asked to analyse a given situation but more often they are asked to come out with concrete ideas or suggestions. The orientation of any group is in keeping with this ideal. Before concluding the discussion, the group should employ the philosophy of collective responsibility, as is expected of the union cabinet, and present their recommendations in an organized manner.

The importance of a GD has increased tremendously over the years as it has become a tool in solving problems, making decisions and assessing personalities. Whenever the organization faces a new challenge, GD acts as a tool for decision-making. Group discussion helps in exchanging different ideas, and approaches the problems with different perspective so that all the pros and cons are pondered over to make the right decision. This certainly converges to effective decision-making.

In the job selection process, many skills are tested with the help of a GD. The candidate should not only possess good communication skills, but also have comprehensive skills. Originality, creativity, leadership qualities, group behaviour are a few parameters that the candidates are tested on during the selection process. In the GD, the candidate with superior qualities emerges as the leader and is shortlisted for the interview.

GROUP DISCUSSION FOR DECISION-MAKING

Group discussion is used as the aid in decision-making in the organization. Each member of the group has the onus to explicitly give opinion and ideas to arrive at a consensus. The GD exercise is futile if it ends without a group consensus. While participating in a GD, one should forget about the hierarchy, else in order to maintain unity and loyalty, open enquiry will be inhibited. For smooth discussion and open exchange of viewpoints, the techniques, such as *brainstorming*, *nominal group* and *Delphi* are adopted. In brainstorming, one has to be least critical so that variety of ideas and perspectives can be generated. Six or seven people sit around the table, and the problem is clearly understood by all. All suggestions and alternatives are discussed threadbare with the help of visual aids, such as flip charts, blackboard and handouts. All the ideas are generated without any criticism and the points are discussed and analysed in detail. In nominal group technique, each member operates independently. The problem is announced and each member understands it and writes down the ideas independently without any kind of discussion. Later each member is aloud to speak his opinion which is recorded. No discussion starts until every individual gets the opportunity to speak over. After the recording, the discussion takes place for clarity. Each member ranks the ideas generated, and the one which is ranked highest is considered.

The Delphi technique, on the other hand, is a convoluted and time-consuming process. The main difference in Delphi technique from that of nominal group technique is that in the former physical presence of the group members for the discussion is not required. After the problem is identified, the solutions are collected through well-designed questionnaires. The questionnaires' results are compiled and reproduced to be distributed to each member. After this, the members are again asked for their solutions. New solutions emerge after this round, changing the original viewpoints. This procedure is repeated unless consensus is arrived at. In this technique, one is not directly influenced by others' opinion. Since physical presence is not needed, this technique is best suited when the members are scattered at different geographical places, saving the travelling cost. But certainly one can't use this technique when one has to make quick decisions as it is an extremely time- consuming process.

FEATURES OF SUCCESSFUL ORGANIZATIONAL GDS

Unless you know the norms of a successful GD, it will be difficult to arrive at the appropriate decision. And even when all the members have spent so much time, it will end without any decision being made. To avoid such situations let us know the features common to effective group discussion.

Focus on Group Goals

The purpose of the GD should be clearly understood by all the group members. Once they know the reason for the GD, they will do justice with their roles.

Agreement on the group goal will enable the participants to focus from general purpose to specific goal. This will bring more clarity and manoeuvre the group towards right direction.

Positive Interaction

After an agreement is achieved on the group goals, the interaction is also positive and goal oriented. An effective GD takes place when the discussion proceeds towards the goal with positive contribution in terms of views and opinions. The participants should forget their personal interest and contribute to group goal by promoting meaningful interaction which helps in executing the purpose of the discussion.

Disciplined Procedure Adoption

In a successful GD, each individual is given equal importance. So procedures on how to present and exchange the views are decided to achieve group consensus. For this norms are developed to attain goals in a disciplined way. Failing to this agreement, the discussion will become more of a din as more aggressive members are likely to dominate and push their points. Such a discussion will be completely meaningless.

Amicable Milieu

It is very important that for a successful GD, the environment be friendly, cordial and cooperative. Disparity in opinion may occur but that should not lead to conflicts. Members should be positive and open enough to the views of the others, so that each member's opinion is appreciated. This is how all the ideas can be accumulated in order to lead to group consensus. There may be varied but goal-oriented altercations where individuals' viewpoints are presented. But their different opinions, approaches and perspectives should enrich the process of discussion, and orient towards right decision.

EFFECTIVE COMMUNICATION SKILLS

No GD can be successful without good communication skills of the participants. Both verbal and non-verbal communication should be effectively used. Use of simple, concise words and sentences help in effective communication. Participants give special attention to proper articulation and correct pronunciation. They avoid the hindrances in group communication by being direct and specific. The members are cautious when using non-verbal communication by avoiding ungainly gestures. Communication is just not speaking, it is also giving equal importance to effective listening, encouraging the other speakers.

Equal Role of Participants

In a successful GD, it is ensured that all the participants get equal opportunity to share their views. Else vociferous speakers dominate and monopolize the discussion. Reticent participants are encouraged politely by others to give their opinion which leads to a balanced and effective GD.

Shared Leadership

There is no designated leader in a GD but they emerge. The leadership functions are shared at different stages. One participant can begin the GD, the other lets the ball rolling, someone can encourage the taciturn speaker to give his viewpoint and another can summarize. This gives different roles to the participants making them leader of the said task.

Selection Group Discussions

Group discussions, of late, have become very powerful and common in evaluating a candidate for personality testing in job selection or for admission to courses, such as MBA or PGDM. A few years back it was only part of the selection process in the army for NDA. But today it has become an important way of evaluating the candidates in all type of admission tests and interviews. The selection board is able to evaluate candidates' subject knowledge, communication skills, systematic approach, temperament, leadership qualities, comprehending abilities, etc.

Environment

In any form of oral communication, it is very important to gauge your audience, not only beforehand, but also during the course of the exercise continually re-evaluate their responses. However, in GD the importance is laid on the group of participants as audience is optional. Even if the audience is present, eye contact should be maintained between the group members. While it is important to note things like seating arrangements, it is more important to be aware of the background of the fellow members. Sometimes, such prior information may not be available and in that case one should make a quick assessment of the members early in the discussion. There may be times when one will discover that his analysis is wrong then he should immediately reorient himself. A rigid attitude is just not criminal but also suicidal in a GD. For example, one can state that one will not discuss the technicalities of a car with a group of economists but can go into deep technological discussions with a technocrat. Another important aspect to be kept in mind is the person or organization to which the final recommendations have to be submitted if the purpose dictates so.

FEATURES

Group discussion as part of a selection process has the following features:

Different from Debate

Many people have the misconception that GD and debate are similar. Group discussion is not a debate. Everyone gets the fair opportunity to express their opinions on a given topic. In a debate once you are in support for the topic you can't change your stance even if you are convinced by your opponent. This is not the case in GD. You can approve of the opinion of any participant if they can convince you. You are not conditioned as in a debate and can take your time to express your opinion freely. In a debate you are restricted to talk for an allotted time. In a GD if you are interested to spend more time in listening, you can do that as well.

Form of Conversation

Group discussion is a form of conversation with many sides. It is a spontaneous act as there is no prior preparation. Sometimes in informal situation it can start on any interesting topic and can go on endlessly.

Examiner is Observer

The participants are free to discuss the topic, oblivious of examiner's presence. The evaluator or examiner acts as a silent observer in the background. The participants sit in semicircle or in a circle facing each other. They make eye contact with each other, and not with the observer.

Cordial Ambience

The atmosphere is quite friendly as all the participants have almost the same background. There is no trace of fear as in the case of an interview; therefore the natural behaviour of an individual can also be easily assessed.

Traits for Evaluation

In a group discussion, the participant is evaluated for individual and group behaviour. The most important evaluation components are discussed in the ensuing sections.

Ideas and knowledge

If a solution to a problem had been readily available, the entire exercise of a GD would have been redundant. So it is important to think deeply and come up with innovative ideas that have relevance to the topic under discussion. While it is most impressive to come with ideas, there is no shame in supporting a good idea mooted by a fellow participant. A good member always tries to take the discussion ahead and prevents the discussion from becoming an exercise in just generating one idea after another without any of them reaching a logical conclusion. It should be remembered that once an idea has been presented it becomes the property of the group and everyone collectively holds the right to either accept it or reject it. One must not allow one's ego to have an effect on the discussion here. It is a universally accepted fact that very few of the ideas that are put forward as solutions to the problem are feasible. So it is important to select the right idea quickly and discard the rest. Furthermore, an idea by itself can't solve a problem and so the idea has to be discussed threadbare by the group to arrive at concrete set of steps towards the goal. Again here rigidity will serve no purpose and so one should always be ready to discard an idea for a better one.

The participants should possess in-depth knowledge of the subject which is given to them for discussion. This requires having extensive knowledge on varied range of topics. The members are expected to know all about national and international issues, social and economic topics, current burning problems, controversial topics, etc. One can't achieve this knowledge and awareness in a day but by perseverance over a time. For this one has to read magazines and newspapers to be abreast of the latest happenings and information. Unless the participants have thorough knowledge of the topic, they will not be able to do justice with their participation. People with more knowledge than others are sought by the panelist and the companies.

The topics of GDs are very tricky. If the participant is not aware of current issues, it might make him go astray in his ideas. For example, if a topic like "Euthanasia should be made legal in India" is given and the participant has no clue about what euthanasia is, it surely makes him inferior to others. Internet is also a rich source to gain knowledge about the latest happenings and ideas.

Articulation and listening

Knowledge without implementation is useless. It is, therefore, necessary to be able to deliver one's ideas in an effective manner. Exchange of views among the participants takes place with the help of language. Success depends how confidently and convincingly you put across your ideas. The members of the committee closely evaluate your oral communication skills. Communication skill competence includes clarity in articulation and pronunciation, listening skills and effective language.

Ideas by themselves gain momentum and newer ones are developed and refined when expressed, so verbal communication is of paramount importance. Incoherence leads to good ideas being rejected. Thus, one needs to be fluent and cogent when delivering the idea. Voice modulation is necessary to highlight the important points and keep the attention of the participants. Avoid using slang, jargons and hackneyed expressions as they are often misinterpreted.

Some people use an affected accent to impress but usually it ends up having the reverse effect.

A good speaker is essentially a good listener as well. So it is important that we listen to what everyone has to say. Appreciation of others' ideas can be done openly but condemning a bad idea has to be done very carefully so as not to offend the sensibilities of the fellow member. One ought to be a patient listener but should not remain taciturn throughout the discussion.

Body language and emotions

A person's body language is probably the subtlest aspect but majority members ignore it, which sends out very wrong signal at times. Since this aspect deals mainly with the subconscious, one needs to remind oneself from time to time to drill it into the system. It is not a crime to sit comfortably but care should be taken that the posture is not offensive. For example, even unconsciously pointing one's finger at another person is an almost open invitation to confrontation. Similarly, if a person slouches in his chair or leans too much on the table it may send out signals of ennui in the former case and over eagerness in the latter case. Both extremes should be avoided.

It is always a disadvantage to show one's emotions in public and in a GD it should be avoided at all cost. Even if you feel strongly about an issue, it is advisable to maintain proper demeanor without displaying anger. The latter should always be controlled and every idea scrutinized to the minutest detail and analysed properly. You should prove yourself to be a cool customer, analysing everything seriously and not as a headstrong individual ready to get into quarrels at the earliest opportunity.

Initiative and creativity

This is an aspect, which requires moderation. It is important that a person takes the initiative to broach the topic and manoeuvre the discussion to right direction in order to make it meaningful. While it is always impressive if you give a good start to the GD but it will work against you if you end up fighting from the start. Further, take the initiative to start the discussion only if you have deluge of ideas and have the confidence to give a good opening. This is not supposed to be a deterrent but only a requisite precaution. Even while the discussion is in progress, one should not be subdued by better speakers but express one's own ideas pellucidly. If there is no specific leader appointed, it is very important that you don't take on the role of the chairman by yourself. This brings us to the factor of leadership, which is connected to initiative.

Leadership

One of the most important managerial skills is leadership. The leader of a group should keep himself in check even if he happens to be appointed or designated one. He or she should try to influence the proceedings by constructive participation, rational arguments, convincing others, building support or in summarizing.

There are following three main types of participants in any group:

(a) **Driver:** Someone who thinks that he is always right, and tries to impose his own will on others as a driver. He refuses to accept the fact that everyone is entitled to hold their own opinion. The driver considers himself as the self-appointed evaluator of others. He passes unwanted judgements on others and creates a ruckus when the discussion is not proceeding in the manner he desires. The driver is a sort of an autocrat who may make not so vociferous members feel subdued, and reduces the discussion to a slinging match.

(b) **Amiable:** This person can be considered to be the weak link of the group who can easily be bullied by others. He seldom has any view of his own, and even if he has an opinion rarely expresses it. The amiable supports whatever others say and tries to conform to the majority point of view. This individual always tries to avoid conflicts of any kind and keeps everyone in good humour even if the ultimate goal of the discussion is to be sacrificed in the effort. He is typically indifferent towards other group members and puts all efforts to sweep every conflict under the carpet.

(c) **Democrat:** He is one who ensures that everyone in the group express his/her ideas without inhibitions of any kind. If there is anyone who he thinks is reticent due to any reason, he sees to it that the person feels comfortable. A democrat tries to resolve any imposing condition and ensures that the discussion proceeds in the right direction. When people get agitated, he foresees a conflict arising and nips the problem in the bud.

The leader of the group functions according to the third style and reins in the member who functions according to the first style and discourages practices of the second one.

GROUP BEHAVIOUR

Apart from the above discussed parameters, each individual should display proper group behaviour for a successful GD. The leader should be able to control the group in spite of the differences of ideas and bring the discussion to logical conclusions in the stipulated time.

Each of us is a unique individual with our own set of prejudices, notions and characteristic traits. While it is natural to come with the baggage of personal ideologies or interest for a discussion, one should be careful not to let that override the group goals. A point to be borne in mind is that there will be occasions when we will take part in meetings not as an individual but as a representative of an organization. At those times it is important to have subservient personal ideas to the objectives of the organization.

The panelist judges the participants who contribute to the group goals, and who are fighting for the individual ego. Therefore, the participants should display team management skills so that the team can work effectively. Positive thinking, adaptability, cooperation and coordination must be there in the participants. The team player must possess positive attitude as everyone detests the person with negative outlook. If one remains negative, it will quash all the fruitful ideas. Therefore, the participants should encourage each other to contribute positively to the group process. With positive attitude, aggressive, recalcitrant, rude participants can be molded tactfully. In fact, a team member with positive attitude can make other member look up to him for support and help.

No two individuals are alike but for proper discussion, adjust and adapt with other members. This is one of the leadership qualities which one needs to reflect for proper group behaviour. One should forget about personal likes and dislikes and think about the group objectives. Every individual will have different background, temperament, IQ, knowledge, opinion but a natural leader will put them on the same level by being flexible and adaptable.

Cooperation and coordination are two other parameters for proper team management in the group. The basic idea for group discussion is to nurture the concept of cooperation amongst the members. Each member should support the other members for the success of the discussions. If one has hostile approach, then it will result in fear and that will delay the articulation of ideas. Therefore, every member should encourage other members to contribute to the discussions. If someone is quiet for long, then politely ask him what his ideas are. With this proper coordination is also needed. Else the discussions will come to a standstill. The natural leader can act as a coordinator who can handle the difficult situations.

Steps in Group Discussion

Since the formal GD is conducted with a purpose, it should be handled in a systematic manner. Though there is enough liberty for an individual to express the ideas, opinion, and views but in a planned manner. The various steps are as follows:

Broaching the topic

It is quite clear that there is no nominated leader; therefore anyone in the group can take the initiative to begin the GD. The evaluator announces the topic clearly, usually twice so that everyone gets it correctly. The duration of the GD is also announced simultaneously. After 2–3 minutes of complete silence to contemplate about the topic, on the indication of the evaluator, the group is free to start the discussion. The evaluator doesn't interfere with the GD till the end.

The person who begins the GD has the responsibility of explaining the key words of the topic. It is very necessary to take the discussion in the right direction. For more explanation, other participants can get in. Unless one of the participants is confident and assertive, the task of starting the GD remains tough. Let us take an example—if the GD topic 'Cinema today is neither a source of entertainment nor a means of social change' is to be discussed, then the key terms 'cinema', 'entertainment', and 'social change' should be explained first and then the individual opinion about the topic should be communicated.

A few examples of opening statements in GD are as follows:

- Hello everybody! Today we are here to discuss an interesting topic. Now let us quickly begin since we have 30 minutes for discussion. So here we are…
- My dear friends! Can I have your attention please! This is much talked about issue which we have to discuss. Let us not waste time and get to the serious discussion on…
- 'Teacher should be completely substituted by computers for classroom teaching' is a topic which needs serious thinking. Well friends shall we begin?
- Hello friends! So here are we for the discussion on contemporary topic 'Advertising is nothing but bilge'. Let us first know what is advertising and bilge…

The success of a GD lies in its beginning. If it begins on the right note, then the proceedings will be smooth. All the participants should be conscious of the procedures which include adequate participation, time management and group contribution. The individual should be careful for not being overenthusiastic and brash, and not giving chance to others. On the other hand, an environment should be created such that everyone feels free to participate.

Contributing judiciously

The GD is successful if all the participants give voice to their views. The process of reflective thinking should be understood and practiced by each participant. This can be done by contributing at different stages where one finds scope of participation. While participating in a GD, keep the following points in mind:

- Listen carefully and catch the discussion from what is previously said.
- Relate your topic to the point.
- Deal with the subtopic under discussion.
- Move according to the requirement of that stage.
- Group goal should always be kept in mind.

As discussed previously, your knowledge and creativity must be reflected through what you say. Don't say just for the heck of saying. Analyse the topic from your perspective and relate it with your personal experiences to give it a novel interpretation. In the topic 'Euthanasia is completely justifiable', if you had an experience where you had seen someone in a pathetic condition where the patient wanted mercy killing but was denied as it is not legal in India, you can give that as an example.

Creating conducive environment

Creating friendly atmosphere makes participation fun, which is the responsibility of each member. Only cooperative and conducive environment encourages participation, freely contributing to right conclusion. Despite GD being formal, there is no need to make it monotonous and dull. Each member should be helpful in creating conducive and friendly atmosphere. To do this, following tips may be useful:

- Keep in mind to make the discussion vibrant and enjoyable.
- Treat each other as friends and not as competitor.
- Empathize with others before retorting to the ideas.
- Show interest in what others say by giving signals that you are listening actively.
- Make participants feel important by asking them to express their views.
- Don't scare the taciturn participant by posing direct questions.
- Don't embarrass the participants by quoting something from their personal life and contradicting them.
- Avoid being too formal by calling a participant no. 4.

Handling difficult situation

It is very important that every individual should know how to deal with difficult situations and avoid getting into conflict. Never think that it is not your responsibility to handle the conflict. When you find two participants getting into tussle, take the initiative to act as the mediator and pacify them. It is an art but any individual can resolve an altercation by knowing the following tips:

- Be clear with the discussion procedures in the beginning.
- Continue friendly attitude by respecting feelings of each individual.
- Difference in ideas should not bring out difference in individuals.
- Give positive signals by providing summaries in between.
- When two participants are in conflict listen patiently to both, and summarize what they have said. This gives boost to their egos.
- Look at the problem objectively.

Closing effectively

The evaluator gives an indication for winding up the discussion. At this juncture, one of the participants who has been actively listening to all should take a lead to sum up what had been discussed in the previous 30 minutes. No new idea should be added at this point. The summing up should be done in three to four sentences and concisely. Once conclusions are made, don't be tempted to add new perspective. The points of agreement are concluded.

APPROACH AND PREPARATION

There are two types of group discussion, topic GDs and case studies. Topic GDs are more difficult than case studies as the participant has to generate ideas, prioritize them, develop on the ideas, think ahead for subsequent ideas and present them effectively. Listening carefully will also trigger off fresh ideas and open new avenues to probe into. Pay careful attention to understand the announced topic and interpret it with the key words. For instance, if a topic 'State of modern India-British imperialism then and American hegemony now' is given for discussion, then the key words, such as 'imperialism', 'hegemony' should be elucidated properly before commencing with the discussion. Case studies on myriad of situation in business help developing line of strategy for future action. Virtually all cases call for both analysis and decision-making. Logical analysis and firm grasp of the facts of the situation are crucial.

To hone your analytical skills and other faculties of brain, read analysis of budget in newspaper. It is always wise to be thorough with the contemporary issues. Reading the newspaper to remain updated is mandatory. Therefore, gather a group of friends and regularly discuss current topics, editorials and issues with them.

Limitations of the group

The group should be aware to the extent of its authority and the members should ensure that they never overstep the mark. For instance, never be in a haste to start the discussion unless indicated by the panelist or instructor. It is futile to make suggestions when the group is not authorized to do so.

MODERN DEVELOPMENTS

In today's world, it is not necessary that all the members be physically present together to hold a discussion. Technologies such as teleconferencing and video conferencing have discounted distance as a factor and blurred the boundaries. Large organizations provide such facilities so that expert around the globe can discuss without having to travel long distances.

• EXERCISES •

1. Make the group of seven and discuss the following topics:

(i) Military retaliation is the best method to suppress and eradicate terrorism of any kind.

(ii) Indians talk of morality and value system to use it as a shroud against their inherent hypocrisy.

(iii) The *Pandavas* were justified in their unlawful killing of all *Kaurava* generals during the war.
(iv) The process of economic liberalization is the only path for the country to develop at a satisfying pace.
(v) The north is north and the south is south and never shall the twain meet.
(vi) Those who leave the country for greener pastures consider the self above the state and so we should ensure compulsory service in the country before being allowed to depart.
(vii) Hiding behind customs, logical or illogical in opposition to change is a cardinal sin.
(viii) Trying to secure the best for oneself even at the cost of others is a perverse act.
(ix) Global warming a challenge to mankind
(x) Specialists versus versatilists
(xi) TV channels and Indian value system
(xii) Playing cricket is spoilsport
(xiii) Women empowerment: a myth
(xiv) Women managers are better performers
(xv) Good politics makes bad economics
(xvi) Retailing: a booming sector
(xvii) Conventional education versus professional education
(xviii) Indian economy beyond 2020
(xix) Retailing and e-tailing
(xx) Knowledge economy versus manufacturing economy
(xxi) Parliamentary versus presidential form of government
(xxii) Jobless growth not sustainable
(xxiii) Investment in agriculture is prerequisite for development
(xxiv) Human rights in India
(xxv) Criminalization of Indian politics
(xxvi) Politics of religion and caste in India
(xxvii) Killer thriller: a fake encounter
(xxviii) Challenges for the brave new world
(xxix) Indian economy: job bonanza
(xxx) Cyber crimes are greater challenges
(xxxi) Technical revolution is ahead of cultural revolution
(xxxii) Great middle class: a trend setter
(xxxiii) Intellectuals often end up as failed leaders.
(xxxiv) Private coaching centres most often curb students' individual creativity and thinking.
(xxxv) Children born and brought up in rural areas tend to become better citizens than those born in urban areas.

2. What are the individual traits which one should reflect while participating in the group discussion?
3. What is role of creativity in group discussion?
4. There are different types of leaders which emerge during the group discussion. Explain each type with example.
5. Is listening also important in a group discussion? Why or why not?
6. What is the difference between a topic GD and case GD?

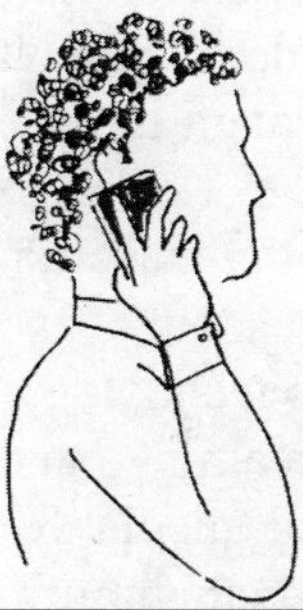

16

Technology in Communication

It has become appallingly obvious that our technology has exceeded our humanity.

—ALBERT EINSTEIN

INTRODUCTION

In the previous chapters, you have already read about different types of communication. And you might have realized that there is no time when we do not 'not communicate'. Moreover, while facing the onslaught of Covid-19, most of us could realize that because of humans' will power, no work can stop however hostile the conditions be. The immediacy of keeping mankind isolated from his fellows both at business and also at homes could help us innovate different ways to keep pace with our professional responsibilities. It was no wonder to find organizations, institutions and even homes buzzing with the movements be it on computers, tablets, laptops, and smartphones. People were home yet the work continued. It was technology that helped mankind come out of the crisis of pandemic. All of us could realize how technology had the key to all our problems and life did not come to a halt.

The crucial role of communication in the sociability of humans through mediums and methods of communication have progressed along an evolutionary trajectory at par with the advancement of human society. From the rudimentary use of symbols and gestures to the invention of language, literary script and printing press, human communication has made a breakthrough with each milestone. The present century has witnessed a revolutionary shift, with the Internet and technology becoming the most ubiquitous communication medium. The involvement of technology in human communication, thus, has assumed major significance in the 'new-normal' of the post-pandemic era. It has ushered in a culture of remote work and virtual meetings through the use of technological applications.

The advancement of technology has diversified the process of communication by offering a plethora of digital gadgets and platforms. The academic and business world has increasingly adopted and adapted themselves to technology-enabled communications through virtual conferencing, live streaming, and webinars. Furthermore, the use of digital platforms and social media for fostering personal and professional connections has witnessed an upturn. Of late, technological innovations in the form of smartwatches and other wearable gadgets, virtual and augmented reality, voice assistants, and Artificial Intelligence have led to a blurring of the boundaries between humans and machines in this new age. With the expansive outreach of such technological and digital devices, the use of technology in human communication has become indispensable.

Technology today has taken a new leap over certain tasks where the role of humans has just been secondary. While many of professionals showed reluctance during Covid-19 to keep pace with technology, it is no wonder that today most of them have become proficient in participating in various academic and organizational activities in hybrid mode. Discussions, seminars, conferences and workshops and even majority of competitive examinations have become possible with the help of technology which has helped in saving time, energy, distance, resulting in ensuring the required cordiality, co-operation and commitment.

But excessive dependence and reliance on technology are not without disadvantages. The use of technology in communication has gendered both positive as well as inevitable negative consequences. While mobile technology and the Internet have greatly improved the speed, accessibility, and efficiency of communicational transactions, on the other hand, the indiscreet use of technology has severely impacted the human touch of interpersonal communications. Digital interactivity, immediacy, responsiveness, and ubiquity have lately been hailed as some of the most crucial and distinct features of technological communication. They offer qualitatively different experiences compared to the face-to-face dialogue exchange as the presumed ideal mode of interpersonal communication. Nonetheless, the revolutionary impacts of technology on communication have led to serious concerns of breach of privacy and digital security and neglect of ethical issues of plagiarism and intellectual property rights. Technology-enabled learning employs informatics resources and digital interfaces to enhance the process of knowledge dissemination. This has brought the world populace together through cosmopolitan connectivity. However, inequitable availability, affordability and awareness of information and communication technology have concurrently deepened the rift between the haves (cyber citizens) and the digital have-nots (technologically marginalized) in the form of a digital divide. These concerns, although significant in themselves, cannot make one turn a blind eye to the benefits of online interactions, such as portability, reduced need for physical infrastructure, greater flexibility, and cost-effectiveness.

The momentous stride of technology has unplugged a new world of communication featuring infinite potential, improved ways to communicate and specific challenges as well. One of the most significant learnings that the Covid-19 pandemic generated is that connection and interaction are invaluable and indispensable to humanity. The Internet and digital technology are its chief onus-bearers in the contemporary cyber era. The coming decades hold the promise of technology-driven communication comprising Artificial Intelligence (AI), Natural Language Processing (NLP), Virtual and Augmented Reality, Internet of Things, automation, and robotics. The Internet of Things and VR/AR have already become game changers in the industrial and business world with their enhanced connectivity and virtual interfaces to improve the efficiency of manufacturing tools and production systems. The AI-enabled devices have taken over the redundant responsibilities and administrative tasks of the employees, freeing up time and resources for the companies to invest in building customer-focused relations and driving innovations.

If technology has spawned its wings in every field, why are we often interfaced with the phantoms of fear? Needless to say that the incorporation of technology in communication should be aimed at improving the quality of human communication experiences, enabling transparent and efficient communications through human beings rather than replacing them with fully automated robotic systems. Technology has branched communication out into three distinct fields: machine-to-machine communications, human-to-machine communications, and human-to-human communications. Machine-to-machine communications are wholly technology-enabled programs which employ Artificial Intelligence and Machine Learning to exchange information between a network of devices with zero human assistance. Human-to-machine interactions resort to the Artificial Intelligence of technological devices to improve customer experiences in businesses. A notable instance is the incorporation of automated chat messenger software as an integral component of their customer service program in various business websites. Wearable devices enabled with sensors, for example, smartwatches and Google glasses, are other examples of human-to-machine communication. Alongside the advancements in machine-to-machine and human-to-machine interactions, the extensive use of technology in communication has also substantially strengthened human-to-human communications. From e-mails, tele-messages, chats to video conferencing applications like Zoom Meetings and Microsoft Teams, digital resources and electronic gadgets have enabled human-to-human communication to overcome spatial-geographical barriers. The recent Covid-19 pandemic bears testimony to the pivotal role of technology as a collaborative tool in facilitating human-to-human interaction.

In the wake of these influential technological advancements of the digital age, our vision of the future is shaped by limitless possibilities and opportunities of technology-enabled communication, which tend to magically transform how we interact and communicate in the cybernetic age. This reminds us of the famous prophetic statement by the renowned entrepreneur Elon Musk: "Artificial intelligence and machine learning will create computers so sophisticated and godlike that humans will need to implant 'neural laces' in their brains to keep up". While this may seem daunting to humankind at present, our best course of action at the moment is to educate ourselves about the uses of technology in communication, its possibilities, challenges and limitations. This chapter explores the dynamic and evolving landscape of technology-enabled communication, acquainting readers with the latest innovative digital tools and technological platforms that are reshaping communication media. It emphasizes the advantages of using technology in communication while also drawing attention to the potential risks of misuse and its subsequent implications.

TYPES OF TECHNOLOGICAL TOOLS IN COMMUNICATION

Communication has gained greater significance than ever in today's fast-paced and over-competitive world. It has been made possible because technological tools have played an important role in making communication more efficient, accessible, timely and authentic. These tools have revolutionized communication, allowing us to connect with people worldwide in real time. One of the most widely used technological tools for communication is the **Internet.**

Internet

With the invention of the Internet, we can now send e-mails, instant messages, and video calls within seconds, making our communication even faster and more convenient. Social media platforms like LinkedIn, Instagram, Twitter, and Facebook have simplified our communication. We can now connect with friends, family, and colleagues, share information, and communicate with people worldwide.

Laptops and mobile gadgets such as smartphones and tablets have recently become vital communication tools. We can use these devices to make phone calls, send text messages, and communicate with others using several applications such as WhatsApp and Telegram. These platforms have improved our communication by allowing us to share our information with others even while travelling.

Furthermore, such technological tools have grown exponentially in the workplace as well. In this globalized set-up, we have to deal with local clients and those from abroad. In this regard, technological tools such as video conferencing software like Google Meet, Zoom, Microsoft Teams, Webex, and

Skype have enabled organizations to hold virtual meetings and conferences, making communication more efficient and cost-effective, saving time and money that would have been spent on travel otherwise.

Virtual Meetings

It is a type of communication in which people from different physical locations meet in the same virtual room through internet-connected devices, such as laptops, tablets, or smartphones. We use virtual meetings to contact our family, friends, clients and even our colleagues and employers, etc.

Virtual meetings have become increasingly popular in recent years due to their time and location flexibility convenience. With the rise of remote work, they have become necessary for businesses to communicate effectively with their teams and clients. It is no wonder nowadays to organise most crucial urgent meetings such as recruitment drives and interviews to help participants from different corners of the world. Such meetings are typically held when employees are spread out in different locations. However, colleagues in the same company may also choose one solely to avoid leaving their desks. While virtual meetings have grown in popularity for business, they have also become regular for family and friends and online classes. They can be held at anytime, anywhere.

What distinguishes such communication from other forms in the business world are its features of saving time and money by removing the need for travel and shortening the time required to prepare for the meeting. Furthermore, they offer a more accessible platform for attendees who may be unable to attend in-person sessions owing to physical disability, geographical location, or scheduling conflicts. Virtual meetings offer a valuable alternative to in-person meetings providing a convenient and inclusive platform for effective communication and collaboration.

However, virtual meetings may pose issues such as; technical difficulties, distractions and difficulties in understanding body language or facial expressions. It is critical to address these issues by establishing explicit norms and expectations, employing effective communication tactics, and ensuring that all attendees have access to the required technology and resources. Participants in a virtual meeting must check proper connectivity, clarity of their voices in addition to their visibility and audibility. It is advisable that they take adequate care to have a test run to avoid technical glitches that most often cause embarrassment.

Live Streaming

In recent times Live streaming has grown in popularity as a communication tool, giving individuals and groups an engaging and participatory platform to reach audiences in real-time. It has become a contemporary reality and it enables content creators to disseminate information, communicate with their audiences, and promote their businesses rapidly and cost-effectively.

One of the advantages of live streaming is the opportunity to reach a large and diverse audience. Live streams are accessible from anywhere in the world, allowing creators to engage with people who might not have been able to attend a physical event or presentation otherwise. Furthermore, live broadcasting enables real-time audience response and involvement, building a sense of community and engagement because of its wide coverage.

However, live streaming has several pitfalls, such as technological difficulties, audience involvement, and the necessity for adequate planning and preparation. To achieve a smooth and successful live stream, content creators must make a thorough research about their audience background and fully grasp their goals, as well as work on the required resources and technology. Overall, live streaming is an exciting and dynamic instrument for communication, providing individuals and organizations with a unique opportunity to connect with their audiences and promote their businesses.

Webinars

Webinars are online seminars that have become popular as a quick and effective way to exchange information, engage audiences, and raise brand awareness. They provide a more cost-effective and efficient alternative to in-person events, providing a greater reach and accessibility for attendees. Webinars help in educating the audience about new products, policies and tools especially in business.

One of the primary benefits of webinars is their capacity to deliver crucial instructional content to a global audience. They are conveniently accessible from any location with an internet connection, and participants can engage in real-time or watch recorded sessions at their leisure. Furthermore, webinars enable interactive audience interaction through tools such as live chat, polls, and Q&A sessions, building community and involvement. However, webinars have several drawbacks,.including technological issues, a lack of involvement, and the need for proper planning and preparation. To create a successful event, webinar hosts must properly grasp their audience, goals, and the necessary resources and technology.

In a nutshell, webinars are an excellent medium for communication and education, allowing individuals and organizations to share their knowledge and experience with a larger audience. Webinars are set to become an ever more critical component of our communication landscape as technology progresses and remote work becomes more popular.

Technological tools have played a crucial role in transforming communication. Technology has made it easier to connect and communicate with people across the globe, from social media platforms to virtual meetings and webinars. These tools have also provided new opportunities for businesses to market their products and services and for individuals to share their ideas and opinions with a broader audience. However, it is essential to recognise that technology is not a panacea to all communication challenges. It can also pose new obstacles, such as the potential for online harassment and the loss of face-to-face interaction. Therefore, it is essential to use technology responsibly and thoughtfully and to balance the benefits of these tools with the need for authentic and meaningful human connection.

Technology has increased communication options and opened new channels for creativity, cooperation, and connection. As technology advances, it will be critical to realise its full workplace potential while being aware of its limitations and potential disadvantages. Apart from business, webinars have also proved beneficial in education sector where experts from different fields shared their knowledge with the outside world.

Finally, technological advances have transformed communication, making it more accessible, efficient, and convenient. As technology advances, we may expect even more innovations in the field of communication that will make communication faster and more accessible to everyone.

ADVANTAGES OF TECHNOLOGY IN COMMUNICATION

Communication has been a vital part of civilization as it has helped individuals connect and communicate with each other by expressing their thoughts and ideas more efficiently. Technology has revolutionized communication, allowing people to share information via online mode. Individuals because of fast Internet and gadgets like smartphones and laptops connect faster now than in the past. After going wireless, people don't have to worry about carrying wires and cables to a different location as they can connect to the available Wi-Fi. Technology has come a long way, paving the way for better accessibility for long-distance communication. Today, anyone can communicate information online from around the world by using online platforms like Google Meet, Zoom, WhatsApp, Telegram, YouTube and Cisco WebEx, etc., while sitting in the comfort of their rooms. Not only can they listen to the other party, but individuals can also communicate face-to-face on video calls now, which was very difficult for the masses a decade ago. Sharing files on these platforms has helped cut unnecessary costs, and it has also helped in lowering paper wastage which is more environmentally friendly. Technology has dramatically benefited pedagogy, corporate and mass media sectors. Since it is cheaper and faster, people rely more on technology to communicate. People who aren't able to attend offline classes or conferences because of various issues can easily connect to these classes online. It has been a boon to society because of its inclusivity of the needs of individuals. Many students are no longer at a disadvantage because technology provides remote access to knowledge and classes. Students with disabilities have the opportunity to take courses from their homes since it is sometimes difficult for them to access certain institutions because of a lack of accessibility.

Information and Communications Technology, or ICT, has brought a change in the ways of teaching as well. Teachers have shifted from teaching the traditional way to a more modern way by promoting higher-order thinking skills. This is achieved by letting students make presentations online using tools like PowerPoint presentations and slideshows, which involve planning and reflecting on their material. This has enabled learning in an interesting and informative way. Students can discuss their work with their classmates, which leads to healthy communication and the exchange of ideas in different ways. It encourages them to work on the material provided by teachers instead of memorizing it. ICT is also helpful to students who work simultaneously or live in remote areas, as they have the flexibility to access educational material such as video lectures and PDFs on their own time. During and after the Covid lockdown, ICT helped students and teachers interact in an online mode since everyone was confined to their houses. Students could take classes online without worrying about going out during the Covid pandemic.

The impact of communication technology in the operation of businesses is undeniable and helps the functioning of a business. Consumer satisfaction and service have become more accessible and more efficient with the use of instant messaging services such as WhatsApp and E-mail. The use of bots also allows for customer service without the need for another person to be available. Communication amongst employees has become a lot more efficient. The lockdown imposed on account of the Covid-19 pandemic has proven how essential communication technology is to reach out to employees who may be unable to come in to work physically. There has been an increased trend towards "work from home", which has been made possible only because of communication technology. It has also become easier than ever for businesses to collaborate, work together and network by use of services such as Google Meet or Skype. It also allows companies to interact with and reach out to vendors, suppliers quickly, and all mediators in-between to streamline their back-end work. ICT has increased efficiency and instantaneous communication while maintaining a low cost of operation and ownership.

Technology has taken new strides and is constantly growing along with mass media communication. Media is an integral part of society. Be it cultural, social, economic or political; mass media spreads information to almost every household across the globe. With the advancement of technology, it has become easier and more accessible for people to contribute to the pool of knowledge. Online content creation has increased drastically after platforms like YouTube and Instagram started paying content creators for the work they post on their channels. Other platforms like Twitter and Facebook pay the creators to post ads on their channels in order to get more coverage. Mass digitization has also led to people running their independent blogs and news websites, slowly replacing physical forms such as newspapers and magazines. People prefer online sites to physical papers because they are faster than newspapers. News gets delivered within minutes of something that has happened. ICT is also useful for people who are outside of their houses. They get their news and entertainment on their smartphones when earlier they had to wait to go home and watch it on their televisions or hear it on the radio. This cut the costs of buying newspapers and magazines as well. Online content distribution has become more popular because it gets delivered more creatively and engagingly. ICT has become an inalienable part of daily life, running and operating businesses, schools, government bodies and other institutions. Technology has made it possible to have instant, efficient, accurate, and inclusive communication on demand at a low cost of operation. It is inconceivable to think of how quickly technology has changed, how people interact with each other and how pervasively it has been adopted in all facets of life. Online channels of education have helped people of all ages learn from experts mostly from highly reputed institutions sharing their latest researches which had been a distant dream for many. In India too, the ministry of Human Resources Development and university grants commission have played an instrumental role in providing access to all and sundry through MOOCs (Massive Open Online Courses) on platforms like NPTEL and SWAYAM (Study Webs of Active-Learning for Young Aspiring Minds). Such courses are free from the hassles of fees and have been prepared by the best teachers of the country.

DISADVANTAGES OF USING TECHNOLOGY IN COMMUNICATION

All of you might agree that every coin has two sides and technology too is not an exception. Though technology has revolutionized communication in a positive way, it certainly has some disadvantages which cannot be ignored. The excessive use and dependence on technology, of late, has lent mankind with numerous problems. The major problems with using technology in communication can be assumed to be the following:

Issues of Privacy

With the rapid progress of the Internet, communication has changed in a big way, be it virtual meetings, webinars or live-streaming lectures. Technology, in general, and the internet in particular, enables ease of access, cost-efficiency and even anonymity to its users, but it certainly comes at the cost of the invasion of privacy. The Internet-based platforms like Zoom, Webex, Skype, and many other apps and websites enable their users to connect remotely and easily, but these platforms always pose the risk of potential intrusion into the user's privacy. The technological glitches and goofs on the platforms like

Google Meet and Zoom during the Covid-19 pandemic can be taken as classic examples of this cause.

When Covid-19 hit the world, cutting off all forms of physical communication, people switched to different online platforms and apps like Zoom or Webex to conduct meetings, give lectures and even carry out interviews and PhD viva voces. These platforms gave people an alternative medium of communication with relative ease through the Internet. However, the problem began when cases of intrusion into the virtual meetings and conferences in these online platforms started to surface frequently. The popular case of "zoombombing" during the pandemic can be a classic example of the issue of privacy on the internet. In its definition, zoombombing is an act of disruptive intrusion into video-conferencing apps and platforms like Zoom where unwanted and uninvited internet users would gate-crash into the teleconferencing sessions and insert lewd, obscene, and other malicious materials. It posed a great concern at the global level and raised the questions of privacy of the users to the forefront. Despite the significant advantages of virtual communicative platforms, the concern of privacy always looms around in the case of such platforms.

Ethical Issues

Any medium or kind of communication calls for issues related to ethics. In such a scenario, the role of ethics in any communicative web or environment cannot be sidelined. The incoming of technology into communication increases the risks related to ethics involved in any interpersonal or group communicative process. One of the primary concerns related to ethics in communication remains the case of plagiarism and copyright issues. And with the significant progress of the internet and data sciences, the modes of plagiarism are changing to a very bad effect. The recent advances in the AI technologies like ChatGPT by OpenAI and Google Bard contentiously raise the question of intellectual property rights. Though these platforms facilitate information to its users and make them resourceful, the usage of such AI-based platforms to land a job or write a business report or write assignments (as has been reported of such incidents in the case of ChatGPT) calls into question the value of ethics in communication. Further, these platforms impinge on the value of communication ethics by being capable of writing phishing emails, generating cultural prejudices and creating other objectionable contents. The issue of ethics can also be called for in the case of virtual assistants like Siri by Apple, Alexa by Amazon and Google Assistant, as these platforms make humans mere proxy/shadow figures in the interpersonal level of communication. The value ethics of communication is entirely thwarted as it makes humans replaceable figures, the supposed primary actors of a communication process. The real process of interpersonal communication is totally lost in the case of such communications.

Technological Distractions

Modern-day communications, more often than not, rely on technology to deliver and receive messages. Technology has not only made communication fast-paced, remotely accessible and economically more viable but also converted it into a high-stressed and high-pressure process. At every minute of the hour, people are flooded with emails, social media messages and work-related notifications. People have to make themselves constantly vigilant to keep up with the whirlpool of communication channels. Indulging themselves in the barrage of communication channels, people may sometimes themselves get lost and burnt out in such circumstances. In addition, just to keep themselves updated and prompt people might commit mistakes of several types. Excessive use of technology may at times unknowingly though forward many unwanted messages to unwanted people and lend themselves in difficulty. Those who are inexperienced and unfamiliar with the nuances of technology use have often been victimized either because of over enthusiasm or curiosity. Newspaper reports and media most often keep sensitizing people about the discreet use of technology. A very serious offshoot of overuse of technology has been found with the distraction caused in terms of language use. While digital world may allow the use of signs, symbols and acronyms, the same may be considered a sort of interference with language, resulting in bad sentence constructions, bad spellings and use of cryptic codes which may unnecessarily creep in examination papers.

Health and Psychological Issues

The other side of technology, at times, frustrates people too much. Many researches find that while technology is facilitating, it is irritating too at times. Those in the prime of their lives are found obsessed with the use of technology to an extent that they grow impatient soon and develop reduced tolerance levels. According to psychologists, prolonged hours of engagement with virtual modes of communication on the screens of laptops, desktops, and mobile phones may lead to a lack of motivation, attention deficiency (the average attention span of an average human has dropped to six seconds) and sleep disturbances. Further, the constant need to respond to the multi-channel web of the technological communicative environment has created a dire need to stay connected at every hour of the day. This has far-fetching mental and physical implications for the actors in such a communicative process. It may lead to greater levels of stress and bad mental health. These ever-demanding technological channels of communication can further push people from real-life interactions. The rise of newer and fraudulent ways of crimes, means of harassing people in the shape of cheap, lucrative patterns have most often lent enthusiasts into unending depressions. While technology enables people to be innovative and creative, it has instead deprived them of real creativity as regards independent thinking.

Lack of Immediate Feedback

One of the main building blocks of a communication process is the prospect of getting appropriate feedback. Genuine feedback can make a communication channel strong and effective. But in the case of virtual communication, the prospect of getting immediate and appropriate feedback becomes more difficult as compared to the physical mode of communication. In the physical mode of communication, one can gauge the nuances of a message by keeping track of non-verbal forms of communication like body language, voice inflection and proxemics other than the content of the message. But when it comes to virtual modes of communication like Skype calls, Zoom meetings, and MS Team classes, the prospect of getting genuine feedback becomes very difficult since both the senders and receivers of the communication process do not have the efficacy of the full context of a constructed message. Further, the chances of miscommunication also get higher as one's words can be misconstrued sans access to non-verbal forms of communication and the immediate physical context. The physical mode of communication also allows one to instantly explain and clarify any miscommunication, which any virtual mode of communication lacks. Virtual mode of communication may, at times, become one way since the receiver may not exactly check their mails or their messages instantly. While this may vary according to the age and habit of communicators, not everyone keeps waiting for information every now and then. For example, if a virtual communication is sent under the impression of it being fast and urgent, the possibility of the receiver ever ready to receive the message cannot be ensured always. It has been found that information or communication even of urgent nature might fail to be responded because of the lack of proper ambience, connectivity and remoteness. Hence, one should always enquire the availability of the receiver before sending any urgent or important messages virtually.

Additional Features

The post-pandemic scenario has made us realize the propositions of 'new-normal' in various domains such as media, communication, education, politics, science and even society at large. The new era signals an interference into an innovative society where communication gets simplified; transmission gets quicker than ever; details of communication get richer through emojis, GIFs (Graphics Interchange Format) and JPEGs (Joint Photographic Experts Group) and other attachments sent in almost close to negligible charges—making communication possible and affordable to all. It is not an exaggeration to find tremendous leverage of various communicative platforms in the past decade. Communication industry has aptly capitalized on the information technology (IT) sector of Silicon Valley(s) networking from the U.S. to India in a globalized fashion. The gradual rise of generational shifts, as noticed in communication service industries, such as starting from 2G, 3G, and 4G, to the current induction of 5G, comes as revolutionary for a technologically-developing country like India. The latest intervention of the State in improvising the communication industry and ambience of the nation, at large, through initiatives like 'Digital India' has come very fruitful. The Pan-India movement initially sneaked its way by making many services available digitally for rural populations for whom it was previously a distant dream. The recent digital boom, moderated through the paradigm of the Digital India initiative, has helped in multi-directional ways catering to the plural demography of India. Starting from banking to health and claiming other government subsidies and scholarships, the arduous process of communicating, negotiating and discussing has become simplified through verbal and haptic modes of communication as mediated through smart gadgets. For instance, the digitization of the bank is one of the most 'relieving processes of the last decade', enabling the common mass to skip the queue and spare time. Finance apps like Google Pay, PayPal and PhonePe have completely transformed the monetization of the local economy—starting from micro, small and medium enterprises to multi-national corporate level exchanges. Technological intervention in many sectors has significant positive roles when empowered through other social welfare apps and organizations—directing towards networking of social outreach, communication of existing social issues, and even in certain cases might help in 'crowdfunding' and 'awareness' amongst the community members.

The keyword of 'community' and 'communication' becomes imperative in order to understand the essential negotiations to be processed. This would eventually lead towards larger goals of social stability and upliftment. Communication with and amongst communities is not an option but rather a first step towards achieving an overarching goal of humanity, that is, mutual understanding. The effort invested towards mutual understanding can be through multiple modalities, as communicated earlier in this chapter, as technology diversifies itself into various platforms such as messaging platforms, social media, chatbots and AI-mediated information. There are plethora of messaging apps like WhatsApp, Telegram, Signal and FB Messenger, which are instrumental in sending and receiving information and data instantly. It goes without saying that social media and content-streaming platforms such as Facebook, Twitter, Instagram and YouTube have all started using algorithmic content to connect individuals with their community interests, as filtered through variables depending on their geography and cultural demography. These applications and websites call for content that helps one not just to communicate their personal interests but also motivate the larger social, cultural and economic relations. Communication with Communities (CwC) has become a key area of concern in several humanitarian organizations where they try to meet response that helps to connect with the people affected by the crisis or in need of help. AI-based communication through the medium of chatbots also becomes increasingly effective, which caters to the common queries elicited by people whenever facing a problem. The government sector of many nations has also recently started incorporating such innovative chatbots, which alleviate the digital gap, i.e. also known as digital illiteracy.

Amazon's Alexa and Apple's Siri have marked themselves as the pioneer of the new era of technology, being state-of-the-art "conversational AI" themselves. These hi-tech gadgets respond to multiple human languages as well as have a speech recognition system that adds multi-purpose usage to them. The industrial revolution of phones, as marked by Nokia, which came with the tagline of "connecting people", has reinvented itself at present, where multiple communication devices are parallelly connected. A human being becomes a symbiotic cyborg within an entanglement of technology when one carries one's smartphone, which is connected to their Bluetooth earphones, and a smartwatch which constantly keeps one in the loop. This communication revolution that is taking over the world by its possibilities is noticed as the "third wave" of global revolution. The world has become small and compact, where it has become technically 'nano'. Distance is trespassed by the matter of speed and bytes, which makes it possible for us to understand the overarching goal of 'One Earth, One Family, One Future'. We have historically transgressed over a long age of history which started from the print age that manifested itself in the present as digital.

Transformation from analog to digital, however, has come with its own unprecedented disadvantage. The main agenda of communication technology was only to enhance human connectivity and global networking. However, recent studies suggest that the over-immersive experience provided by the saturation of devices leads to signs of loneliness, stress, and depression—mostly stemming from a lack of in-person communication in itself. Communication generated out of the digital realm remains virtual and often fails to become personal. Such forms of digital detachment from society may cause adverse impacts on the beneficiary group than what is expected. Thus, caution is required when it comes to the complexity of communication and technology in order to make better use of technology and communicate more efficiently. Digital awareness is also seen as a mandate when we introduce a large number of the population to use novel technology and resources to communicate through multiple means. The popular American journalist, Sydney J. Harris, rightly mentions the intricate detail between the two words 'information' and 'communication' as to be signifying different things where they mean "information is simply giving out while communication is getting through". Thus, it is not only the raw data and its transmission through technology that counts but also the human efficiency to communicate that matters. The use of technology for communication cannot be ruled out because of the humans' mandatory desire and requirement to keep pace with the developments yet care and caution have to be exercised discreetly while doing so.

• EXERCISES •

1. How does the use of technology in communication impact the pace of progress?
2. Mention the various fields of technology-enabled communication.
3. Enumerate the different technological tools of communication and their significance.
4. Give your impressions of virtual meetings. Can they substitute meetings in the physical form?
5. The use of technology in communication is more advantageous than disadvantageous. Explain.
6. Discuss the significance of various digital platforms in communication.
7. How has the use of technology transformed human lives?
8. "There is no time when we do not communicate"? Exemplify.
9. Write short notes on the following:
   (a) Webinars
   (b) Live streaming
   (c) Zoombombing
10. Define the following terms:
    (a) CwC
    (b) GIF
    (c) JPEG
    (d) MOOCs

17

Most Often Wrongly Spelt Words

The difference between the right word and the almost right word is like the difference between lightning and the lightning bug.

—MARK TWAIN

As you are living in a world dominated by technology, you often get confused with the spellings of words used by various people at different times. The frequent use of technical devices, such as telegram, fax, e-mails, text messages, chats have compelled people to prefer shorter ways of using words. They find it easier to spell words according to the requirements of time. But this shortcut method later becomes a habit and, hence, we are often tempted to spell words wrongly. Advertisements and celluloid too contribute to this menace to the world of spelling. But as professionals, you have to remember that your control over written words with correct spellings makes or mars your reputation. No doubt, people often get confused between British and American spellings. The role of computers in this is also elemental. But one has to maintain a consistency as regards the use of spellings. If we follow British English, then due care should be taken to follow British spelling.

This chapter gives you a list of more than 600 words which you as a professional will have to use quite often. Practice of these words, their spelling and their use will help you gain confidence and will enable you to learn their subtleties.

A

Aberration
Achievement
Acceleration
Accessible
Accessory
Acclimatize
Accommodate
Accumulate
Acknowledgement
Acquiesce
Addendum
Addiction
Aggravate
Allegation
Alleviation
Allocation
Allotment
Altercation
Aperture
Apparatus
Appraisal
Appreciation
Apprehensive
Approximate
Argument
Assimilation
Attenuate
Attribute
Attrition
Automobile

B

Ballot
Balance sheet
Beginning
Biannual
Bifurcate
Bilateral
Bimetallic
Binoculars
Biography
Bisect
Blitzkrieg
Blueprint
Bluetooth
Bogey
Breakdown
Breakthrough
Brochure
Bulldozer
Bureaucracy

C

Cafeteria
Caffeine
Callous
Camaraderie
Camouflage
Cantankerous
Capricious
Carburetor
Carcass
Caravan
Caribbean
Cartridge
Cartilage
Carton
Casualty
Cellular
Celluloid
Centenary
Cessation
Changeable
Chauffeur
Chivalry
Cipher
Circumlocution
Circumscribe
Collateral
Committee
Commodity
Communication
Complementary
Complimentary
Concatenation
Conceivable
Concurrence
Condenser
Congruence
Connoisseur
Conscience
Contour
Convocation
Convenient
Correlation
Criterion
Crystalline
Crystallization
Curriculum
Cylinder

D

Debenture
Defer
Degradation
Dematerialization
Demolish
Demolition
Deprecation
Depreciation
Depression
Dereliction
Destabilization
Deterioration
Diabolic
Diarrhea
Diatribe
Dilapidation
Dilemma
Disbursement
Discrepancy
Discriminate
Dissatisfaction
Disseminate
Dissemination
Dissertation
Dissipate
Dissociate
Dissuade
Distemper
Dodge
Dossier
Douse
Dyadic

E

Effervescence
Efficacy

Efficient
Elimination
Elliptical
Eloquent
Embarrassment
Emulate
Endorse
Engineering
Entrepreneur
Equilibrium
Equity
Eradication
Erroneous
Espionage
Etiquette
Eulogy
Evaluation
Evaporation
Exaggeration
Exchangeable
Exemplify
Exhaustible
Exigency
Extempore
Extenuate
Extra personal

F

Façade
Fastidious
Feasibility
Features
Fictitious
Flaccid
Flammable
Fluctuate
Foetus
Foolscap
Forcible
Forecast
Forego
Forfeiture
Forthright
Fraction
Fragile
Fragmentary
Fraternity
Fulfil
Furore
Fusillade

G

Gainsaying
Gangrene
Gargantuan
Gasoline
Genealogical
Genesis
Geophysics
Gigabyte
Glimmer
Grammar
Grandiloquent
Grapevine
Grievance
Grotesque
Guarantee
Guardian
Gullible
Gymnasium

H

Hackneyed
Hemoglobin
Hemorrhage
Hallucination
Harbinger
Hardware
Hassle
Heartening
Hegemony
Herculean
Heterogeneous
Hibernation
Homogeneous
Honorarium
Horizontal
Horrendous
Horticulture
Humorous
Hydropower
Hygienic
Hypothesis
Hysterical

I

Idiosyncrasy
Illegible
Imbroglio
Impeachment
Impenetrable
Impoverish
Impromptu
Inadequate
Inadvertent
Inadvertently
Inconvenience
Indispensable
Innocuous
Inoculate
Inseparable
Installation
Instantaneous
Interchangeable
Interference
Internecine
Interrogate
Intolerant
Intractable
Intuition
Irrational
Irretrievable
Irrevocable
Itinerary

J

Jaggery
Janitor
Jaundice
Jealousy
Jeopardize
Jigsaw
Journalist
Jubilant
Jubilee
Judgment
Judicious
Juggernaut
Juncture
Jurisdiction

K

Kaleidoscope
Kernel
Kerosene
Kettle
Kickback
Kilometre
Kindred
Kitchen
Kleptomania
Knack
Knave
Knead
Knight
Knock out
Know how
Knowledgeable

L

Laboratory
Labyrinth
Laconic
Lactose
Landscape
Landslide
Latent
Lattice
Legendary
Leisure
Lessen
Leucoplast
Leverage
Levitate
Liability
Liaison
License
Lieutenant
Lineament
Linear
Lingerie
Longevity
Longitudinal
Loophole
Ludicrous
Luggage
Lukewarm
Luxurious

M

Macabre
Machiavellian
Magazine
Magnanimity
Maintenance
Malfunction
Mammoth
Manageable
Manoeuvre
Marijuana
Massacre
Mattress
Measurement
Medieval
Memento
Memorandum
Merchandise
Microscopic
Mileage
Milieu
Millennium
Misappropriate
Miscellaneous
Misshapen
Missionary
Misspell
Monetary
Monologue
Monopolize
Monumental
Morass
Moratorium
Morgue
Mortgage
Mortuary
Mosaic
Museum
Myopia

N

Naïve
Narrate
Nauseous
Nautical
Negligible
Neighbourhood
Netiquette
Neutralize
Nickel
Nonchalance
Noncommittal
Nonessential
Noticeable
Notoriety
Noxious
Nozzle
Nullify

O

Obedient
Obituary
Objectionable
Oblique
Obliterate
Oblivion
Obnoxious
Obscene
Obsequious
Obsession
Obsolete
Obviate
Occasion
Occupation
Occurrence
Odorous
Officious
Omission
Onerous
Onus
Opportunist
Ordeal
Ordinance
Oscillate
Outrageous
Ovation
Overriding
Overrule
Overrun

P

Package
Pageant

Pamphlet
Panorama
Para military
Parallel
Parameter
Paramount
Paranoid
Paraphernalia
Pasteurize
Peddler
Peerless
Penchant
Permissible
Pernicious
Perseverance
Phenomenon
Photo chromatic
Plagiarize
Polarisation
Possessive
Post script
Posthumous
Practice
Practise
Preamble
Precedent
Precipitous
Premonition
Presupposition
Proprietor
Profiteer
Propagate
Psychiatrist
Psychological

Q

Quadrangle
Quandary
Quantum
Quarrelsome
Quash
Quasi
Query
Questionnaire
Queue
Quinine
Quintessence
Quixotic
Quota
Quorum
Quotation
Quotient

R

Rabble
Radiation
Reappearance
Rebuttal
Receipt
Receptacle
Reception
Receptor
Recess
Recession
Reciprocal
Reconcile
Rectilinear
Recuperation
Redemption
Refereed
Refraction
Refrigerator
Regression
Rehabilitate
Reimbursement
Reinstate
Reiterate
Relieve
Relinquish
Relive
Remainder
Reminiscence
Remittance
Renaissance
Rendezvous
Requisition
Reservoir
Resins
Retaliate
Retardation
Retrieve
Retrovirus
Rheumatism
Righteous

S

Sabotage
Sacrilegious
Sanatorium
Satellite
Satiate
Saturate
Scarcity
Schedule
Scintillate
Segregate
Sensation
Serviceable
Settlement
Simulate
Simultaneous
Siphon
Skirmish
Sovereignty
Spectrometer
Spectrum
Spurious
Statue
Statute
Stencil
Steroid
Stethoscope
Storey
Stubborn
Substantiate
Succour
Succumb
Superimpose
Superintendent
Supersede
Supple
Supplementary
Surreptitious
Suspension
Symmetrical
Symptom
Synchronize

T

Tableau
Tabloid

Tactics
Tamper
Tangential
Tangible
Tantamount
Tariff
Technique
Teleological
Telepathy
Terrestrial
Theoretical
Theory
Threadbare
Thrush
Tolerance
Torrent
Traceable
Transferable
Transferred
Transit
Transparency
Transversion
Trepidation
Triumphant
Trivial
Tuberculosis
Turmoil
Tyrosine

U

Ultra violet
Ultrasound
Unanimous
Unavailable
Unbelievable
Uncontrollable
Unbiased
Underneath
Unfavourable
Unicellular
Unilateral
Unique
Unstable
Until
Urbane
Urbanization
Utilization

V

Vaccination
Vaccine
Vacillate
Vacuole
Vacuum
Valedictory
Valency
Validate
Validation
Vaporization
Variation
Variegate
Vehemently
Veneer
Veracity
Veritable
Vertical
Veterinary
Viability
Viable
Vicinity
Vicissitudes
Vivacious
Voice mail
Volume
Voluminous
Vulnerability

W

Wagon
Waiver
Wane
Wardrobe
Warehouse
Warranty
Whereabouts
Whisper
Whistle
Wholesome
Wily
Withheld
Witness
Wizard
Worthwhile
Wrath
Wrought
Wry

X

Xavier
Xenophobic
Xerox
X-ray
Xylem

Y

Yardstick
Yarn
Yearning
Yeoman
Yielding
Yoke

Z

Zealot
Zenith
Zest
Zip
Zeitgeist
Zig-zag
Zoological

• EXERCISE •

The words given below may have some spelling problems. Right the correct spellings and frame meaningful sentences that can be used in organizational communication:

Noticable
Omision
Overriding
Maintenence
Measurment
Proffession
Momento
Lukewarm
Liability
Leaisure
Juggernaut
Knowledgeble
Impromptu
Irrevocable
Forfeature
Eqilibrium
Obituuary
Millennium
Interrogate
Haemmorrhage
Garagantuan

A

List of Frequently Misused Words

ACCEDE: The manager finally acceded to my request and granted me a three days' leave.
EXCEED: The submission of the project report should not exceed the word limit.

ACCEPT: They have accepted my project proposal.
EXCEPT: No one except Mr. X gets undue favour from the boss.

ACCESS: Access to people in power may sometimes cost heavily.
EXCESS: Excess of expectations have affected the quality of work.

ADVICE (N): A doctor's advice should never be ignored.
ADVICE (V): The manager advised the newly recruited representative to be punctual.

AFFECT: Computers have affected workplace in a variety of ways.
EFFECT: One finds the effect of technology on children more than that of adults.

AISLE: He stood in the aisle and joined his voice with the prayer.
ISLE: We often long for staying on an isle.

ASSENT: He gave his assent for the proposal.
ASCENT: You may find many temples on the ascent of mountains.

BIANNUAL: Did you get the second issue of our biannual newsletter?
BIENNIAL: The biennial function of the association released a souvenir also.

BOUGH: Though it was dark something glistened on the bough.
BOW: He bowed his head in agreement.

CAREER: Concentrate on your career first and then anything else.
CARRIER: No one noticed the small polythene kept on an abandoned bicycle carrier.

CONTINUAL: India has witnessed a series of continual invasions.
CONTINUOUS: The continuous ringing of the phone broke my sleep.

CHORD: Love is a chord that unites everyone.
CORD: The computer could not get connected because some cord was missing.

COMPLEMENT: Your non-verbal cues complement your verbal message.
COMPLIMENT: Some people never compliment you even on your excellent work.

COURSE: He ignored the advice of his friends and went following his own course.
COARSE: The labourers protested against the supply of coarse foodstuffs in the ration-shop.
COUNCIL: His access to the corridors of powers helped him to get him a berth in the council of ministers.

COUNSEL: No one can be a better counsel than your teacher.

CESSION: The cession of opposition forces should not be taken as defeat.
SESSION: The second semester always appears shorter than the first one.

DEFER: They have deferred the meeting till further orders.
DIFFER: The work culture in an MNC and a government organization differ in many ways.

DESERT: Finding people with integrity is like finding water in a desert.
DESSERT: They also had some desserts after the dinner.

DISBURSE:	The manager disbursed all the cash he had.
DISPERSE:	The police firing dispersed the crowd.
DISCREET:	A discreet speaker takes due care of his audience.
DISCRETE:	Though lying unconscious he could watch the discrete movement of the thief.
ELICIT:	The judge could elicit all pieces of information from the culprit in a very clever manner.
ILLICIT:	Ultimately his name figured in an illicit deal.
EMINENT:	Dr. Sharma, an eminent scholar keeps her promise.
IMMINENT:	One should always be prepared for imminent challenges.
FLAIR:	No one can stop your flair for writing.
FLARE:	The evidence of the eye-witness flared the case that had gone slow.
FARTHER:	They went farther and farther yet didn't get any trace of the thief.
FURTHER:	I am not interested in listening to your story any further.
HUMAN:	The human touch still makes workplace more cohesive.
HUMANE:	The judge showed his humane attitude by granting the convict some more time on health grounds.
WHOLE:	One should not jump to conclusion before he has heard the whole story.
HOLE:	The labourers left many holes unattended in the wall.
HALL:	The hall was packed to its capacity to hear the chairman's lecture.
SCENE:	The ghost scene in any movie frightens my friend.
SHEEN:	Rising prices have stolen the sheen of gold.
SEEN:	Those who have not seen the Taj, have missed a rare work of architecture.
SCENT:	Spraying scent before every party has become a ritual.
CENT:	Spending few cents more could enable them to buy a new branded car.
SAINT:	It has become a tradition of seeking the blessings of a saint before you undertake a new assignment.

SEER: A seer can predict what is to happen next.
SHEER: Success requires not only sheer luck, it also requires industry.

SIGHT: It was a pathetic sight to see both the father and the son killed in the accident.
CITE: The director cited many examples from the scriptures to inspire employees.
SITE: The contractor paid the wages to all the labourers on the construction site itself.

PIECE: A new piece of information is always welcome.
PEACE: Rural life offers more peace than that of an urban one.

SUSPEND: The classes have been suspended as the teacher is on leave.
CANCEL: Harish cancelled his Mussourie trip because of inclement weather.

LOTH: The animal resembled a giant like creature, a loth.
LOATHE: I loathe going to bed early.

MINER: Many miners are reported missing after the explosion.
MINOR: One ought to be careful of minor lapses too.

PRINCIPAL: Satisfaction is the principal force of happiness.
PRINCIPLE: One is bound to be at a disadvantage if one is a man of principles.

PERSECUTE: No one should be persecuted on the basis of colour, race or gender.
PROSECUTE: He was prosecuted in a false case.

RIGHT: One should be conscious of one's rights.
RITE: They performed the funeral rites of the dead stranger.
RIOT: The government is trying hard to placate communal riots.
WRITE: Do not write anything in hurry.

DYE: Have you started dyeing your hair?
DIE: All his fears died when he saw the police arriving towards him.

IGNORANT: To be ignorant is often to be blessed.
ILLITERATE: An illiterate is one who does not know the art of reading or writing.

PILGRIMAGE: Most of us go on a pilgrimage when we are old.
JOURNEY: Man is always on a journey sometimes physical, sometimes spiritual.

ERUDITE: Our politicians of past were all erudite scholars too.
CLEVER: One ought to be clever while judging a stranger.

ANCIENT: The historian talked of all ancient things.
OLD: Old age requires care and caution.

ROOT: The root cause of poverty is the lack of awareness.
ROUT: Because of the collective efforts of the countrymen, the enemies were routed.
ROUTE: The route to happiness is honesty and nothing else.

STATIONARY: Love is a stationary force in life.
STATIONERY: My boss provided me with the stationery the day I joined my office.

MORAL: Moral values often take back seat in real life.
MORALE: The team maintained its morale both in good and bad times.

PERSONAL: Personal appearance plays an important part in professional presentation.
PERSONNEL: Many police personnel visited the site of the blast.

STATUE: The sculptor put life in the statue.
STATUTE: The new statute of government organization has the provision of transport allowance for all employees.

PERPETRATE: A handful of misguided youths perpetrated atrocities on the stranger.
PERPETUATE: New bonus scheme will perpetuate the demands of the striking employees.

B

British Vs American Vocabulary

British	American
Angry	Mad
Articulated Lorry	Tractor Trailer
Autumn	Fall
Banger	Fatter, Thicker Version Of A Sausage
Bap	Hamburger Bun
Bicarbonate Of Soda	Baking Soda
Biscuits	Cookies
Bonnet (Car)	Hood
Boot (Car)	Trunk
Bottom/Bum/(Slang)/Posterior/Backside	Glutes
Braces	Suspenders
Cupcake	Muffin
Candyfloss	Cotton Candy
Caravan	Trailer Or Motor Home
Chemist	Pharmacist
Chips	Fries
Cinema	Movie-House
Class	Grade (Pre-College Schools)
Clingfilm	Plastic Wrap
Clothes Peg	Clothes Pin
Courgette	Zucchini

(*Contd.*)

British	American
Crisps	Potato Chips
CV (Curriculum Vitae)	Resume
Dummy	Pacifier
Dustbin	Garbage Can
Elastoplast	Band aid
Estate Agent	Realtor
Film	Movie
Flagpole	Flagstaff
Flat	Apartment
Football	Soccer
Garage	Gas Station
Garden	Yard
Ground Floor	First Floor
Headmaster/Headmistress	Principal
Holiday	Vacation
Ill	Sick
Jacket Potato	Baked Potato
Jam	Jelly
Jelly	Jello
Jumper	Sweater
Ladysfinger	Okra
Lead	Leash
Lift	Elevator
Lorry	Truck
Lounge	Living Room
Mad	Crazy
Marrow	Squash
Minced Beef	Ground Beef
Moulting	Shedding
Nappy	Diaper
Parcel	Package
Pavement	Sidewalk
Peckish	Hungry
Perambulator (Or Pram)	Carriage
Petrol	Gas
Pork Scratchings	Pork Rinds
Porridge	Oatmeal
Postal Cost/Post Code	Zip Code
Postman/Postwoman	Mailman/Mailwoman
Power Point/Plug/Socket	Electrical Outlet/Outlet
Pram	Baby Carriage
Pub	Bar

(*Contd.*)

British	American
Queue	Line
Refectory	Cafeteria
Ring (Telephone)	Call
Roll Or Bap	Bun
Roundabout	Rotary
Rubber	Eraser
Rucksack	Backpack
Sacked/Get Your P45	Get Fired, Get A Pink Slip Or Become Unemployed
Sellotape	Scotch Tape
Shoelace	Shoestring
Shop	Store
Sideboards	Sideburns
Silencer (On Motor Vehicle)	Muffler
Single Ticket	One-Way Ticket
Sitting In A Tailback	Stuck In A Traffic Jam
Sleeping Policeman	Speed Bump
Smalls	Underwear
Snooker	Billiards/Pool
Solicitor	Lawyer/Attorney
Spanner	Wrench
Sultanas	Raisins
Surgery	Doctors Office
Swede (Or Yellow Turnip)	Rutabaga
Tap	Faucet
Taxi	Cab
Tights	Pantyhose
Timetable	Schedule
Tin	Can
To Be Made Redundant	Laid Off, Lose Your Job
Toilet/Lavatory	Restroom
Tomato Sauce/Ketchup	Catsup/Ketchup
Torch	Flashlight
Trainers	Sneakers
Treacle	Molasses
Trousers	Pants
Underground	Subway
Vest	Undershirt
Waistcoat	Vest
Wardrobe	Closet
White Sauce	Gravy

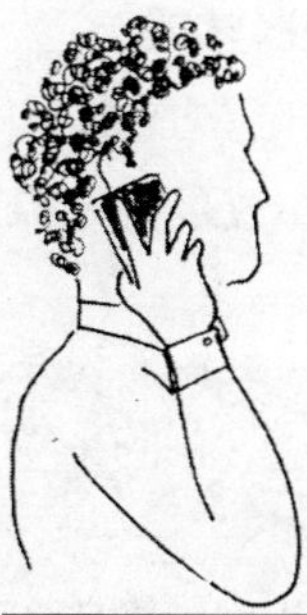

Bibliography

Adler, Ronald B. and George Roman, *Understanding Human Communication*, New Delhi: Oxford University Press, 2006.

Alverez, J.A., *The Elements of Technical Writing*, New York: Harcourt, Brace, Jovanovich, 1980.

Andreson, Paul V., *Technical Communication: A Reader Centered Approach*, USA: Thomson Wadsworth, 2007.

Andrews, D.C. (Ed.), *International Dimensions of Technical Communication*, Arlington, VA: Society for Technical Communication, 1996.

Andrews, D.C. and W.D. Andrews, *Business Communication*, New York: Macmillan, 1988.

Ashley, A., *Oxford Handbook of Commercial Correspondence*, New Delhi: Oxford University Press, 2003.

Axtell, Roger E., *Do's and Taboos of Using English Around the World*, New York: John Wiley, 1995.

Barrass, R., *Scientists Must Write*, New York: John Wiley, 1978.

Bates, J.D., *Writing with Precision*, Washington DC: Acropolis Books, 1980.

Blicq, R.S., *Technically Write! Communication for the Technical Man*, Englewood Cliffs, NJ: Prentice Hall, 1972.

Blumenthal, L., *Successful Business Writing*, New York: Grosset and Dunlap, 1976.

Bovee, Courtland L., John V. Thill and Barbara E. Schatzman, *Business Communication Today*, Singapore: Pearson Education, 2004.

Brogan, J.A., *Clear Technical Writing*, New York: McGraw-Hill, 1973.

Brown, H.M., *Business Report Writing*, New York: Van Nostrand Co., 1980.

Brusaw, C.T., G.J. Alred and W.E. Oliu, *The Business Writer's Handbook*, New York: St. Martin's Press, 1975.

———, *Handbook of Technical Writing*, New York: St. Martin's Press, 1976.

Castle, Dennis and John Wade, *Public Speaking*, Kent: Hodder & Stoughton, 1980.

Charrow, V., *What Is "Plain English" Anyway?*, Washington DC: American Institutes for Research, 1977.

Chaturvedi, P.D. and Mukesh Chaturvedi, *Business Communication: Concepts, Cases and Applications*, New Delhi: Pearson Education, 2004.

Classen, H.G., *Better Business English*, New York: Arco, 1966.

Colby, J. and J.A. Rice, *Writing To Express,* Minneapolis, MN: Burgess, 1977.

Coleman, P. and K. Brambleby, *The Technologist As Writer — An Introduction To Technical Writing,* New York: McGraw-Hill, 1969.

Connor, Ulla, *Contrastive Rhetoric: Cross-Cultural Aspects of Second-Language Writing*, New York: Cambridge University Press, 1997.

Crouch, G.W. and R.L. Zetler, *A Guide To Technical Writing*, New York: Roland Press, 1964.

Crystal, David, *The Cambridge Encyclopedia of Language*, New York: Cambridge University Press, 1997.

Day, R.A., *How To Write and Publish a Scientific Paper*, Philadelphia, PA: ISI Press, 1979.

De Vries, Mary, *Internationally Yours: Writing and Communicating Successfully in Today's Global Marketplace*, New York: Houghton Mifflin, 1994.

Ehrlich, E. and D. Murphy, *The Art of Technical Writing*, New York: Thomas Y. Crowell Co., 1964.

Elbow, P., *Writing Without Teachers*, New York: Oxford University Press, 1973.

Ellenbogen, A., *Letter Perfect*, New York: Macmillan, 1978.

Emberger, M.R. and M.R. Hall, *Scientific Writing*, New York: Harcourt, Brace and Co., 1955.

Ewing, D.W., *Writing For Results—In Business, Government, The Sciences, The Professions*, New York: John Wiley, 1979.

Fear, D.E., *Technical Communication*, Glenview, IL: Foresman and Co., 1977.

Gerson, Sharon J. and Steven M. Gerson, *Technical Writing: Process and Product*, New Delhi: Pearson Education Asia, 2000.

Gilbert, M.B., *Communicating By Letter — A Self-Teaching Guide*, New York: John Wiley, 1973.

Gilman, W., *The Language of Science: A Guide To Effective Writing*, New York: Harcourt, Brace and World, 1961.

Goeller, C., *Writing To Communicate*, New York: New American Library, 1974.

Graves, R. and A. Hodge, *The Reader Over Your Shoulder*, New York: Macmillan, 1944.

Gray, D.E., *So You Have To Write A Technical Report*, Washington DC: Information Resources Press, 1970.

Guffey, Mary Ellen, *Business Communication*, USA: Thomson/South-Western, 2002.

———, *Essentials of Business Communication*, USA: Thomson/South-Western, 2004.

Gunning, R., *More Effective Writing in Business and Industry*, Boston, MA: Industrial Education Institute, 1963.

———, *The Technique of Clear Writing*, New York: McGraw-Hill, 1968.

Hackos, Joann T., *Managing Your Documentation Projects*, New York: John Wiley, 1994.

Hartley, J., *Designing Instructional Text*, New York: Nichols, 1978.

Hicks, T.G., *Successful Technical Writing*, New York: McGraw-Hill, 1959.

———, *Writing for Engineering and Science*, New York: McGraw-Hill, 1961.

Hoft, Nancy L., *International Technical Communication: How to Export Information about High Technology*, New York: John Wiley, 1995.

Hoover, H., *Essentials for the Technical Writer*, New York: John Wiley, 1970.

Houp, K.W. and T.E. Pearsell, *Reporting Technical Information*, Encino, CA: Glencoe, 1977.

Houp, Kennith W., Thomas E. Pearsell, Elizabeth Tebeaux and Sam Dragga, *Reporting Technical Information*, New Delhi: Oxford University Press, 1998

Huckin, Thomas N. and Leslie A. Olsen, *Technical and Professional Communication for Nonnative Speakers of English*, 2nd ed., Boston: McGraw-Hill, 1991.

Janis, H. and H. Dressner, *Business Writing*, New York: Barnes & Noble, 1972.

Jones, W.P., *Writing Scientific and Technical Reports*, Dubuque, IA: Wm C. Brown, 1971.

Jordan, S. et al., *Handbook of Technical Writing Practices*, New York: Wiley Inter Science, 1971.

Kapp, R.O., *The Presentation of Technical Information*, New York: Macmillan, 1957.

Kirkman, John, *Good Style: Writing for Science and Technology*, New York: Spon Press, 1992.

Krizan, A.C. et al., *Business Communication*, USA: Thomson/Southwestern, 2008.

Krizan, A.C. 'Buddy', Patricia Merrier, and Earl Logan Jr., *Business Communication*, Florence, KY: South Western Educational Publishing, 2008

Lannon, J.M., *Technical Writing*, Boston, MA: Little, Brown and Co., 1979.

Lucas, Stephen E., *The Art of Public Speaking*, 3rd ed., Singapore: McGraw-Hill, 1983.

Lynch, B. and C. Chapman, *Writing for Communication in Science and Medicine*, New York: Van Nostrand Reinhold Co., 1980.

Mack, K. and E. Skjei, *Overcoming Writing Blocks*, Los Angeles, CA: J.P. Tarcher Inc., 1979.

Mandel, S., *Writing for Science and Technology*, New York: Dell Publishing, 1970.

Mathes, J.C. and D.W. Stevenson, *Designing Technical Reports—Writing for Audiences in Organizations*, Indianapolis: Bobbs-Merrill Co., 1976.

Menzel, D.H., H.M. Jones, and L.G. Bond, *Writing a Technical Paper*, New York: McGraw-Hill, 1961.

Mills, G.H. and J.A. Walter, *Technical Writing*, New York: Holt, Rinehart & Winston, 1978.

Mishra, Sunita and C. Murlikrishna, *Communication Skills for Engineers*, New Delhi: Pearson Education, 2004.

Mitchell, J.H., *Writing for Technical and Professional Journals*, New York: John Wiley, 1968.

Mitra, Barun K., *Effective Technical Communication*, New Delhi: Oxford University Press, 2006.

Monroe, J., *Effective Research & Report Writing in Government*, New York: McGraw-Hill, 1980.

Monroe, J., C. Meredith, and K. Fisher, *The Science of Scientific Writing*, Dubuque, IA: Kendall/Hunt Pub. Co., 1977.

Moore, R.H., *Handbook of Effective Writing*, New York: Holt, Rinehart & Winston, 1966.

Morris, J.E., *Principles of Scientific and Technical Writing*, New York: McGraw-Hill, 1966.

Murphy, Herta A., Herbert W. Hilderbrandt, and Jane P. Thomas, *Effective Business Communication*, New Delhi: Tata McGraw-Hill, 1997.

Murray, M.W., *Engineered Report Writing,* Tulsa, OK: Petroleum Publishing Co., 1969.

Nakanishi, Akira, *Writing Systems of the World,* Rutland: Charles E. Tuttle Company, 1994.

Newman, E., *Strictly Speaking*, New York: Warner Books, 1974.

———, *A Civil Tongue*, New York: Warner Books, 1977.

Niemeier, Susanne, Charles P. Campbell, and Rene Dirven (Eds.), *The Cultural Context in Business Communication*, Amsterdam: John Benjamins, 1998.

Norgaard, M., *A Technical Writer's Handbook*, New York: Harper & Row, 1959.

Pauley, S., *Technical Report Writing Today*, Boston: Houghton-Mifflin Co., 1973.

Paxson, W.C., *The Business Writing Handbook*, New York: Bantam Books, 1981.

Penrose, John M., Robert W. Raspberry, and Robert J. Myers, *Business Communication for Managers: An Advanced Approach*, USA: Thomson/ South-Western, 2004.

Perlmutter, J.H., *A Practical Guide to Effective Writing*, New York: Delta Books, Dell Pub. Co., 1965.

Provost, G., *Make Every Word Count*, New York: Writers' Digest Books, 1980.

Rathbone, R.R., *A Writer's Guide for Engineers and Scientists*, Englewood Cliffs, NJ: Prentice Hall, 1962.

———, *Communicating Technical Information*, New York: Addison-Wesley, 1966.

Redish, J., *Readability*, Washington DC: American Institutes for Research, 1979.

Redish, J.C., The Language of the Bureaucracy, *Technical Report No. 15, Document Design Project*, Washington DC: American Institutes for Research, 1981.

Renaissance Strategic Consultants, *Impact Series, Guide for Learners*, Pune: Renaissance Strategic Consultants, 2002.

Rizvi, Ashraf M., *Effective Technical Communication*, New Delhi: Tata McGraw-Hill, 2005.

Rogers, R.A., *How To Report Research and Development Findings To Management*, New York: Pilot Books, 1973.

Roirdon, Daniel G. and Steven E. Pauley, *Technical Report Writing Today*, New Delhi: Bizantra Dreamtech Press, 2004.

Roman, K. and J. Raphaelson, *Writing That Works*, New York: Harper and Row, 1981.

Ross, Raymond, *Speech Communication*, 4th ed., Englewood Cliffs, NJ: Prentice Hall, 1980.

Rutherford, Andrea J., *Basic Communication Skills for Technology*, New Delhi: Pearson Education Asia, 2001.

Ryan, C.W., *Writing: A Practical Guide for Business and Industry*, New York: John Wiley, 1974.

Sharma, R.C. and Krishna Mohan, *Business Correspondence & Report Writing*, 3rd ed., New Delhi: Tata McGraw-Hill, 2002.

Sherman, T.A. and S.S. Johnson, *Modern Technical Writing*, 3rd ed., Englewood Cliffs, NJ: Prentice Hall, 1975.

Smith, R.W., *Technical Writing*, New York: Barnes & Noble, 1963.

Souther, J.W. and M.L. White, *Technical Report Writing*, New York: John Wiley, 1977.

Sparrow, W.K. and D.H. Cunningham, *The Practical Craft—Readings for Business and Technical Writers*, Boston, MA: Houghton-Mifflin, 1978.

Strunk, W., Jr. and E.B. White, *The Elements of Style*, New York: Macmillan, 1972.

Thrush, Emily A., Bridging the Gaps: Technical Communication in an International and Multicultural Society, *Technical Communication Quarterly*, **2**, 1993.

Tichy, H.J., *Effective Writing for Engineers, Managers, Scientists*, New York: John Wiley, 1966.

Trelease, S.F., *How To Write Scientific and Technical Papers*, Cambridge, MA: MIT Press, 1958.

Turner, B.T., *Effective Technical Writing and Speaking*, London: Business Books, 1974.

Ulman, J.N., Jr. and J.R. Gould, *Technical Reporting*, New York: Holt, Rinehart & Winston, 1959.

U.S. Environmental Protection Agency, *Be A Better Writer—A Manual for EPA Employees*, U.S. Govt. Printing Office, 1980.

Van Hagan, C.E., *Report Writers' Handbook*, Englewood Cliffs, NJ: Prentice Hall, 1961.

Vardaman, G. and P.B. Vardaman, *Communication in Modern Organization*, New York: John Wiley, 1973.

Wallace, S.F., *Practically Painless English*, Englewood Cliffs, NJ: Prentice Hall, 1980.

Ward, R.R., *Practical Technical Writing*, New York: Alfred E. Knopf, 1968.

Weinberg, G.M., *An Introduction to General Systems Thinking*, New York: John Wiley, 1975.

Weisman, H.M., *Technical Report Writing*, Columbus, OH: Charles E. Merrill Books, 1966.

———, *Basic Technical Writing*, Columbus, OH: Charles E. Merrill Books, 1980.

Weiss, A., *Write What You Mean*, New York: Amacom, 1977.

Weiss, E.H., *The Writing System for Engineers and Scientists*, Englewood Cliffs, NJ: Prentice Hall, 1982.

Willis, H., *Structure, Style, Usage: A Guide to Expository Writing*, New York: Holt, Rinehart & Winston, 1964.

Woelfle, R.M. (Ed.), *A Guide for Better Technical Presentations,* New York: IEEE Press, 1975.

Woodford, F.P., *Scientific Writing for Graduate Students*, New York: Rockefeller University Press, 1968.

Wydick, R.C., *Plain English for Lawyers*, Durham, NC: Carolina Academic Press, 1979.

Index